AF574339

Emotions in American History

EUROPEAN STUDIES IN AMERICAN HISTORY
General Editor: Michael Wala

Celebrating Ethnicity and Nation
American Festive Culture from the Revolution to the Early Twentieth Century
Edited by Jürgen Heideking, Geniève Fabre, and Kai Dreisbach

The Society of the Cincinnati
Conspiracy and Distrust in Early America
Markus Hünemörder

Emotions in American History
Edited by Jessica C.E. Gienow-Hecht

Emotions in American History

An International Assessment

Edited by

Jessica C.E. Gienow-Hecht

Berghahn Books
New York • Oxford

To Joseph F. Kett
who inspires his students
to always keep a sense of wonder

First published in 2010 by

Berghahn Books

Library of Congress Cataloging-in-Publication Data

Emotions in American history / edited by Jessica C.E. Gienow-Hecht.
p. cm. — (European studies in American history ; v. 3)
Includes bibliographical references and index.
ISBN 978-1-84545-642-9 (hbk. : alk. paper)
1. United States—History. 2. United States—Social conditions. 3. United States—Politics and government. 4. United States—Intellectual life. 5. Emotions—Social aspects—United States—History. 6. Emotions—Political aspects—United States—History. 7. Social change—United States—History. 8. Emotions—Historiography. 9. Historiography—Psychological aspects. 10. Historiography—Social aspects. I. Gienow-Hecht, Jessica C. E., 1964–
E179.E55 2010
152.4--dc22

2010006548

British Library Cataloguing in Publication Data

A catalogue record for this book is available from the British Library

Printed in the United States on acid-free paper

ISBN 978-1-84545-642-9 Hardback

Contents

Illustrations

Acknowledgments

The publication of this manuscript has been one of the most emotional roller coasters the authors in this book may have endured in their professional lives. Many obstacles, scheduling conflicts, review delays, and communication lags seemed to hinder the editing process along the road. My foremost gratitude therefore goes to the contributors in this volume: You have been absolutely outstanding, patient, and tenacious, responding to several rows of stylistic and theoretical criticism, accepting delays, often sighing, rarely wavering, never giving up. *Vielen herzlichen Dank!*

This book grew out of a conference in Tutzing among German scholars whose work concentrates on the history of the United States. I wish to thank the Politische Akademie for hosting us on the shore of the beautiful Starnberg Lake and for sponsoring the conference. We are also gratefully to the German Association for American Studies as well as the US embassy for supporting our endeavor. Thank you also to Frank Schumacher for his initial ideas, his organizational skills before and during the conference, and his participation in the project.

I am grateful to Michael Wala for reading and inviting our manuscript into his series, "European Perspectives in American History," at Berghahn Books, to Kristin Hunt, a most dedicated and inquisitive copy editor, and to Marcel Will who helped putting the final touches on this manuscript. Many thanks to the anonymous outside reviewer who provided a stellar, insightful and encouraging report. Marion Berghahn has once again proved to be an astute judge, a wise adviser, and a good friend. Over the last fifteen years, her team and her press have seen a most dramatic development and rise in the publication industry, well deserved and eagerly welcomed by people fortunate enough to publish a book with "BB." It's been a pleasure working with you!

Jessica Gienow-Hecht, Gloucester, October 2008

Contributors

Andreas Etges is professor of North American history at the John F. Kennedy Institute for North American Studies of the Free University of Berlin and chair of its history department. Among his research interests are nationalism, the Vietnam War, the Kennedy presidency, and history and memory. He curated special exhibits on John F. Kennedy in Berlin and Vienna and is also the curator of the museum The Kennedys in Berlin. His publications include a comparative study of economic nationalism, *Wirtschaftsnationalismus. USA und Deutschland im Vergleich (1815–1914)*, (Frankfurt, 1999), and *John F. Kennedy*, (Munich, 2003). He is currently working on a study on "The Ugly American."

Bettina Friedl is professor emerita of American Literature and Culture at Hamburg University. She received her doctorate (English) from Heidelberg University and her habilitation (American Studies) from Tübingen University. She taught at the universities of Mainz-Germersheim, Mannheim, Tübingen, Stuttgart, and Greifswald. She was a postdoctoral fellow at Yale University in 1973–74, and as an American Studies Fellow of the American Council of Learned Societies, she was a fellow at the Mary Ingraham Bunting Institute of Harvard University 1983–84. In 1996 and again in 2002, she taught as a visiting professor at Smith College. As a visiting scholar at the Center for the History of American Civilization, she spent 2001–02 at Harvard University. Bettina Friedl's earlier presentations and publications focused on American literature of the nineteenth and twentieth centuries. In the past two decades, her research interest shifted towards documentary film, to aspects of visual culture, and particularly to dress and fashion art.

Jessica C. E. Gienow-Hecht is professor of international history at the University of Cologne. Before, she was a Heisenberg Fellow of the Deutsche

Forschungsgemeinschaft at Wolfgang Goethe-Universität Frankfurt am Main, and a John F. Kennedy Fellow at the Center for European Studies and a visiting fellow at the Charles Warren Center for American History, both at Harvard University. She has previously taught at the universities of Virginia, Bielefeld, Halle-Wittenberg, Harvard, Frankfurt, Heidelberg, and the Hertie School of Governance in Berlin. Her special field of interest is the interplay of culture and international relations since the eighteenth century. Her first book, *Transmission Impossible: American Journalism as Cultural Diplomacy in Postwar Germany, 1945–1955* (Baton Rouge: Louisiana State University Press, 1999), was coawarded the Stuart Bernath Prize and the Myrna Bernath Prize, both given by the Society for Historians of American Foreign Relations. Her second book, *Sound Diplomacy: Music and Emotions in Transatlantic Relations, 1850–1920* (University of Chicago Press) won the Choice Outstanding Academic Title Award 2009.

Horst U. K. Gundlach, born in Merseburg, Germany, in 1944, grew up in Hamburg, and studied psychology and philosophy in Heidelberg and Munich. He received his diploma in psychology in 1969 and his doctorate in 1973 in Heidelberg. After working in Heidelberg, he spent a year of research at Oxford; he then worked at the Max-Planck-Institut für Psychologie in Munich, before finally joining the Institute for the History of Psychology at Passau University in 1982, where he received his habilitation degree. Since 1990 he has directed the institute. His interests center on the history of psychology in nineteenth and twentieth century.

Fabian Hilfrich is a lecturer on American History at the University of Edinburgh. Previously, he was a researcher at the Foreign Office branch of the Institute for Contemporary History in Berlin and has taught at the Free University of Berlin and the Latvian Academy of Culture in Riga. He is currently completing a manuscript on the American imperialism debate in the wake of the Spanish-American War.

Michael Hochgeschwender, born in 1961, is professor for North American Cultural History and Cultural Anthropology at the Ludwig-Maximilian-University, Munich. He is the author of *Freiheit in der Offensive? Die Deutschen und der Kongreß für kulturelle Freiheit* (Munich: Oldenbourg, 1998); *Wahrheit, Einheit, Ordnung: Die Sklavenfrage und der amerikanische Katholizismus, 1835–1870* (Paderborn: Schöningh, 2006); and *Amerikanische Religion: Evangelikalismus, Pfingstlertum und Fundamentalismus* (Frankfurt am Main: Verlag der Weltreligionen, 2007).

Alf Lüdtke is honorary professor at the University of Erfurt and holds a Distinguished Visting Professorship at Hanyang University, Seoul/Korea.

His publications include: *Gemeinwohl, Polizei und Festungspraxis: Staatliche Gewaltsamkeit und innere Verwaltung in Preussen, 1815–1850* (1982; trans. English 1989); *Alltagsgeschichte. Zur Rekonstruktion historischer Erfahrungen und Lebensweisen* (1989, trans. into French 1993, English 1995, and Korean 2002); *Eigen-Sinn. Fabrikalltag, Arbeitererfahrungen und Politik vom Kaiserreich bis in den Faschismus* (1993); *The No Man's Land of Violence: Extreme Wars in the 20th Century* (as coeditor and contributor, 2006). He has founded and coedited the journal *Sozialwissenschaftliche Informationen* (SOWI), is one of the founders of the journals *Historische Anthropologie* and *WerkstattGeschichte,* and is a cofounder of the book series "Selbstzeugnisse der Neuzeit."

Juergen Martschukat, professor of North American History at Erfurt University, has published on the history of violence, gender, and race.

Jörg Nagler is professor of North American History at Friedrich Schiller University of Jena. He taught at the University of Kiel, where he received his PhD, and studied at Indiana University. From 1987 to 1992, Nagler was a research fellow at the German Historical Institute in Washington, DC. During this assignment, he also taught as a visiting professor at the University of Maryland at College Park. Upon his return to Germany, he became director of the John F. Kennedy House in Kiel, before he received tenure as a professor of North American History in Jena. He has written extensively on nineteenth- and twentieth-century US political, social, cultural, and ethnic history. His major focus is the subject of war and society in American history. His latest monograph, *Nationale Minoritäten im Krieg* (Hamburg: Hamburger Edition, 2000), investigates the role of national minorities and the American home front during the First World War. His latest work is a Lincoln biography (Munich: Beck Verlag, 2009).

Adelheid von Saldern was professor for Modern History at the University of Hanover before she retired in 2004. She was guest professor at Johns Hopkins University in 1989–90, at the University of Chicago in 1994, and at the Center for European History, Harvard University, in 1998. Her recent fields of interest have been the history of media, urban studies, and transatlantic perceptions during the 1920s. Her well-known books of the last decade are *Häuserleben* (Bonn, 1997, 2nd ed.) and *The Challenge of Modernity. German Social and Cultural Studies, 1890–1960* (Ann Arbor, MI, 2002). She edited *Inszenierte Einigkeit. Herrschaftsrepräsentationen in DDR-Städten* (Stuttgart, 2003); *Inszenierter Stolz. Stadtrepräsentationen in drei deutschen Gesellschaften (1935–1975)* (Stuttgart, 2005); and recently *Stadt und Kommunikation in bundesrepublikanischen Umbruchszeiten* (Stuttgart, 2006).

Stefanie Schneider completed her Erstes Staatsexamen and her MA in English and History at the Ruhr-University of Bochum in 2000 and was awarded the Prix d'Excellence de Québec for her MA thesis on a comparative sociohistorical analysis of wills in a nineteenth-century bilingual Canadian village. She completed her PhD on the symbolic representation of Anglo-American relations in nineteenth-century political cartoons at the Max Weber Research Centre for Social and Cultural Studies in 2004. Since 2005, she has been teaching English, History, and Bilingual History at Hittorf Grammar School, Recklinghausen. Her main fields of research are Anglo-American history, cultural history, Canadian history, and the teaching of history.

Peter N. Stearns is provost and professor of History at George Mason University. He has taught previously at Harvard, the University of Chicago, Rutgers, and Carnegie Mellon; he was trained at Harvard University. He has published widely in modern social history, including the history of emotions, and in world history. Representative works in social history include *Old Age in Preindustrial Society*; *Anger: The Struggle for Emotional Control in America's History* (with Carol Stearns); *Anxious Parents: A History of Modern American Childrearing; American Cool: Developing the Twentieth-Century Emotional Style;* and *American Fear: The Causes and Consequences of High Anxiety.* Since 1967 has served as editor-in-chief of the *Journal of Social History*. In most of his research and writing, Dr. Stearns has pursued three main goals. First, as a social historian he is eager to explore aspects of the human experience that are not always thought of in historical terms, and with attention to ordinary people as well as elites. Second, he seeks to use an understanding of historical change and continuity to explore current patterns of behavior and social issues. Finally, he is concerned with connecting new historical research with wider audiences, including, of course, classrooms.

Britta Waldschmidt-Nelson is associate professor of American History and Culture at the Amerika-Institute of the Ludwig-Maximilians-University, Munich. Her research focuses mainly on African American studies, gender, transatlantic relations, and American religious history. Among her publications are *From Protest to Politics: Schwarze Frauen in der Bürgerrechtsbewegung und im Kongress der Vereinigten Staaten* (1998), *Europe and America: Cultures in Translation* (2006), *Gegenspieler: Martin Luther King & Malcolm X* (2007), *Martin Luther King: Leben, Werk und Vermächtnis* (2008), and *Christian Science im Lande Luthers: Eine amerikanische Religionsgemeinschaft in Deutschland, 1894–2009* (2009).

Introduction

EMOTIONS IN AMERICAN HISTORY

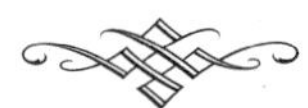

The View from Europe

Jessica C. E. Gienow-Hecht

EMOTIONS ARE HOT, in more than one way. Scholars of various branches have developed a passion for the study of emotions, and there is also a vibrant public debate on the constructive and destructive power of emotions in society as well as within each of us. In psychology, psychohistory, sociology, cognitive research, and the humanities, scholars have observed that modern research has focused too much on scientific and behaviorist models while there is little appreciation for culturally motivated reflection. The popular debate around emotional intelligence and emotional competence has challenged our belief in rationality and control as the pillars of human action; in today's popular and scientific understanding, emotions form the basis for actions, even or in particular when they are suppressed.

Most of the authors in this book are German historians or social scientists whose work concentrates on the history of the United States. Some of them labor in the vineyard of social history; others concentrate on US foreign relations. Some focus on colonial history while others address most recent political events. Some do not even regard themselves as historians but, instead, venture in neighboring fields, such as anthropology or psychology. Collectively, they have tested their respective findings with one question in mind: How do emotions play into the interactions, facts, and fictions pre-

Notes for this section begin on page 9.

sented in their respective stories and research fields? What is peculiar about emotions in America? How does the study of emotions change what we know about national and international history? And how do we as foreign scholars assess emotions in the United States?

* * *

Fifty years ago, in 1960, the psychologist Paul Ekman conducted several field studies, on the basis of which he argued that "when people are experiencing strong emotions, are not making any attempt to mask their expressions, the expression will be the same regardless of age, race culture, sex and education."[1] In other words, Ekman postulated, emotions are basic forms of human experience: they include anger, hatred, jealousy, happiness, fear, and sadness, which were developed during the course of genetic evolution. Their sensation is universal. But their expressions and their social meanings differ vastly according to cultural constructions and social practices.[2]

Since then, the field has been in turmoil. In the past decades, psychologists and anthropologists have passionately debated the question whether emotions are universal or culturally conditioned. A great deal of anthropological work, in particular, has directly challenged the claim that even the biological sensation of emotions is universal.[3] Adding to the confusion, scientists cannot agree on whether the principal variable in our assessment of emotions is the physiological existence or its cultural manifestation. A number of psychologists are convinced that cultural meanings do not have an impact on the development of emotional reactions. Many cultural anthropologists, in contrast, believe that emotions do not simply constitute part of the physiological system but attain their meaning through their expression and interpretation in social interactions. It is difficult to subscribe to either position completely. However, there is one place where the opinions of most psychologists and anthropologists concur: a study of the way in which emotions are being transmitted and communicated can possibly show us a tool to find out how to understand and define emotions proper.[4]

This is exactly what the historical study of emotions and emotional standards tries to do, and it is thus not surprising that it has come to constitute one of the most promising frontiers of social history. "Emotional history" rejects the notion that individual or collective human emotions represent static expressions independent of time and environment. Instead, it encourages scholars to interweave the analysis of emotions such as grief, anger, fear, hate, love, jealousy, and compassion in their specific historical and cultural contexts.

What does the history of emotions encompass? It traces emotional expressions throughout different periods of history; it examines the tension between impulses and socially accepted emotional standards; it analyzes the impact of feelings and emotional change in the history of nationalism, immigration, war, law, politics, or social and economic transformations; and it not only enriches the study of gender, race, and class but also fosters interdisciplinary work by connecting historical research to related inquiries in sociology, anthropology, and psychology.

In recent years, the analysis of emotions, their expression, and their control have moved to the core of American historiography. Pioneering studies by Peter and Carol Stearns, Jan Lewis, and Karen Lystra have demonstrated how certain emotions seemed particularly troubling in a given social context: for example, Puritan society regarded the expression of anger and aggression as a sin.[5] Likewise, other emotions have seemed increasingly desirable depending on the existing social norms, such as "coolness." Peter Stearns and others have emphasized the traditional tension between social, legal, and political attempts to define what constituted accepted emotional standards while also looking at the resulting efforts to suppress some emotions while releasing others.

A number of historians have focused on individuals and social groups by looking at topics such as the changing face of the family, the relationships between individual family members, the transformation of anger over the course of history, the evolution of jealousy, or boredom as an emotional experience.[6] Martina Kessel has shown how nineteenth-century German men and even more so women, by suppressing certain feelings like passion or anger in public, created a mask behind which they led a second (and often passionate) existence. As the century went by, however, both genders also increasingly feared to come across as "boring" if their emotionally reticent behavior went too far.[7] Some social studies have explored tendencies to resist or reshape dominant emotional standards. A number of diplomatic historians have begun to focus on threat perception, friction, fear, and, recently, gender as a force in international relations: Frank Costigliola, for example, has examined the impact of emotions on American foreign policy.[8] In a gesture to current debates in psychology and anthropology, some scholars have drawn intercultural and international comparisons, focusing on behavioral standards and interpretative differences. And again others have asked what exactly constitutes the language and expression of emotions.[9]

These studies transform our understanding of transitional periods in American history. They correlate the analysis of emotional change at the beginnings of the nineteenth and twentieth centuries to social, economic, and structural changes in the United States such as the emergence of a democratic form of government and an egalitarian social ethos, the market revolution, the creation of American middle class, the civil rights movement, the spread of urbanization and industrialization, and the development of a consumer economy with its attendant ethos.

In this book, a dozen scholars, most of whom come from Europe, combine their expertise to offer a transnational look on the study of emotions in the United States. The book analyzes the role of emotions in the study of American history between the eighteenth century and the present. The contributors look at emotions in war, emotions in the social and political discourse, and emotions in art and the media. They specifically seek to address the role of emotions in the context of imperialism, racism, patriotism, modern antiwar demonstrations; aesthetics, international relations, and public opinion; death sentences, sexual norms, and presidential election campaigns. Complementing nine case studies with three interdisciplinary essays, a social historian, an anthropologist and a psychologist critically review the approaches to the study of emotions in history, outline both promises and pitfalls in the field, and offer new insights regarding future research projects.

This book is thus designed as both an introduction to some of the most recent trends in the field and as an invitation to consider American history from an outside perspective. In this particular case, it is not merely the research or the sources as such, but the perspective of the researcher that seeks to shed transnational light on our understanding of emotional history. In this it merges seamlessly with some of the most dynamic and recent trends in the field, notably the effort to frame the history of the United States in an international perspective.[10]

* * *

Emotions in American History is subdivided into five parts, the first and last theoretical, the other three related to case studies: emotions in war, public opinion, and sociopolitical debates.

The first section looks at theoretical, historical, and psychological approaches to the study of emotions. In the first chapter, Peter Stearns calls attention to the emergence of the history of emotions in relation to social, cultural, and family history, but also to the growing array of research on emotion in several disciplines. Historians can focus on connections among emotional standards—themselves important in policy and behaviors; the ways people evaluate their own and others' emotions; and actual emotional experience. Key issues in advancing this field include appropriate interdisciplinary formulations, attention to social class variables, comparative analysis, and evaluation of the results of changes and continuities in emotional standards. Emotions history enriches our understanding of the past, but can also be used to provide vantage points on current issues and behaviors that result from recent trends such as "informalization" or the growing capacities of contemporary media to play on fears.

Alfred Lüdtke assesses the emotional approach from an anthropological point of view and asks how historians trace and interpret emotions in people's everyday lives. This chapter discusses approaches for reconstructing people's feelings in their daily practices. More concretely, the focus is on the emotional dimension of a pivotal figure of "modern times," the worker in the first half of the twentieth century. For example, the German case reveals industrial workers' disgust and tedium but also considerable joy at work and pride about producing "quality." The author gives special attention to feelings about work that directly contributed to warfare such as the German war effort after 1939. Lüdtke detects a seamless connection of production and destruction in peoples' feelings about their work: they stimulated acceptance of and cooperation with Nazi goals and policies.

The second section of this book focuses on the area that has recently emerged as one of the most prominent fields in this area: emotions and war. Fabian Hilfrich's essay focuses on the emotion of fear in anti-imperialist rhetoric after the Spanish-American War of 1898. More specifically, it analyzes the argument that imperialism would incite popular passions, thus undermining civic virtue and—by extension—democratic self-government in the United States. As insulting as the argument was to "the people," it is more adequately read as a representation of anti-imperialist emotions—the emotions of an elite group fearful of the "common people." The article demonstrates the potential of research into the role of emotions in foreign policy analysis, providing insights that would otherwise only be gained by sociological analysis and demonstrating how emotions themselves are not only time- but also class-bound.

Jörg Nagler looks at the role of emotions in the context of wartime mobilization during World War I. He is specifically interested in the campaign against German-Americans on the home front and the link between propaganda and emotions. In his essay, he argues that during the war the United States was in a "search for order" and identity, an identity that would entail the nation's new role in world politics. This dual task highlighted the highly emotional nationalist ardor and the inevitably disruptive social and psychological forces that always accompany nationalism supported by propaganda in times of war. To Nagler, all attempts to explain the eruption of violence on the home front must be placed in the context of the mobilization of emotions—with fear as its central component—of the government.

In the last essay of this section, Andreas Etges shows that despite a general sense of reconciliation regarding the Vietnam War on the national level, Jane Fonda remains a focus of hate for many American veterans. Exploring why Fonda ("Hanoi Jane") still triggers violent expressions of emotions among many veterans long after the war, the essay examines her political emergence in the late 1960s, her brief visit to North Vietnam in July 1972, and the ensuing public controversy as well as the changing veterans' relationship with Fonda until today. The actress became a central symbol of the veterans' general feeling of betrayal. For them Fonda betrayed not only America, but also her sex. Instead of playing the female role of nurse or healer, she sided with the enemy and figuratively killed some of her own countrymen. "She was the pinup who went AWOL," J. Hoberman wrote.

The third section turns to the link between emotions and public opinion. Bettina Friedl examines public reactions to artworks. She argues that in literature, emotions can be described. These descriptions can explain a character's emotional state of mind, illustrate the emotional impact of an event, or even portray a collective mood; they can, moreover, generate an emotional response in the reader. In the visual arts, emotions cannot easily be spelled out unless the theme or title of a work of art refers specifically to a narrative. They are, instead, suggested, either through a person's expression or through the evocation of an emotionally charged event or a mood prevalent at a certain time. Because emotions in painting are culturally determined, they are often difficult to trace. While many American painters of the nineteenth century rejected the anecdotal or the overtly narrative, they did refer to familiar narratives—such as the Bible or national history—or to a common iconography in order to elicit certain emotions. Despite their different approaches, painters such as Edward Hicks and Frederick Edwin Church could refer to cultural traditions that allowed viewers to participate in the emotions their paintings expressed. Towards the end of the nineteenth century, however, collective emotions were increasingly replaced by private emotions that are more difficult to decipher. Thomas Eakins's late portraits present such contemplative and introspective images that refuse any translation into a traditional language of emotions.

Stephanie Schneider's essay retraces the potential of political cartoons as historical sources for the analysis of emotions and emotional standards in international relations, in particular that of Anglo-American relations in the nineteenth century. It focuses on the way cartoons address emotions. Specifically, Schneider looks at the tools used in cartoons to appeal to the emotion of the viewer and the way in which representations of emotions in cartoons can be analyzed for the study of the symbolic representation of the nineteenth-century Anglo-American relationship.

Adelheid von Saldern considers the emotions involved in the comparisons between the United States and Europe through an analysis of American perceptions of European anti-Americanism published in US magazines during the 1920s. As the interpretation of other countries involves and demands reference to one's own country, the analysis also encompasses the reconstruction of debates over American identity in the 1920 and thus contributes to the growing historiography of interwar political culture in the United States. As shown, *qualitative magazines* interpreted European anti-Americanism as extremely emotional. American answers avoided anti-European emotions.

Instead, contributors drafted their articles as unemotional statements designed to reveal their nation's superiority based on evolution, history, wealth, and mission.

The fourth section considers the role of emotions in social and political debates. Jürgen Martschukat's essay traces the history of capital punishment in the New Republic as an history of emotions. It concentrates on the contemporary observation, description, and definition of the emotional spectator at executions. It indicates in its first part how the emotional spectator was shaped in discourses of medicine, philosophy, and law from the late seventeenth to the early nineteenth centuries. The second part analyzes how the figure of the emotional spectator contributed to the reevaluation of public punishments since the late eighteenth century. The final part specifies how the definition of emotions and their supposed effects significantly influenced the shaping of the political, social, and cultural landscape of the Early Republic.

Michael Hochgeschwender's essay turns to religion, raising some methodological issues about the usefulness of Foucault's discourse analysis in the context of the debate on sexuality, religion, and emotions: how is it possible to explain the hegemonic shift between rivaling discourses? The author proposes to try to solve this methodological and logical problem by generally reintroducing causal principles into discourse analysis in a twofold manner: according to him, it is necessary to combine discursive analysis with elements of a structural, socioeconomic analysis of modes of production that may serve as general principles of change. Moreover, he finds it also necessary to reintroduce the experiences of individual, free-willed actors who serve as agents of specific change since only personal agents can make a choice between rivaling discourses. This combination of a text-oriented, modified, structural interpretation and a history of individual agents and their specific experiences represent a dynamic concept for further research in the field of gender studies. The history of emotions and the history of experiences, he argues, enable a more synthetic interpretation of discursive shifts and rivaling discourses.

The section ends with an excursion into the contemporary political landscape. Britta Waldschmidt-Nelson argues that the history of emotions provides important clues to understanding human behavior and can provide a tool in our effort to understand wider political, social, and economic trends in American history. She believes that this applies in particular to the history of African Americans, racial conflicts in general, and the black struggle for freedom and equality in particular. In this context, emotions repeatedly stir(red) public emotions in the United States to a degree hardly ever reached by other domestic issues. Looking at race relations and election campaigns between 1865 and 2007, she argues that the question of whether black people have a right to full inclusion in American society touches fundamental issues of American self-identity and national purpose and has thus always polarized American society.

In line with the interdisciplinary approach, at the end of the volume we turn to a psychologist to ask for his judgment of our collective efforts to study the history of emotions in America. In response, Horst Gundlach examines the way the science of psychology has dealt with the topic of emotion since the introduction of experimental methods in psychological research. He relates some of the major points of dissent and elucidates why psychologists have not yet reached a consensus on how to define emotion. Following a look at the themes the history of emotions has dealt with, he suggests that social psychology might be a more promising partner for historians of emotions than the psychology of emotion, which is traditionally regarded as a branch of general psychology. Now the floor is open for discussion.

* * *

What, then, do emotions in American history look like when viewed from Europe? These essays cover a wide and diverse ground, as diverse as the history—and perhaps the minds—of the American people. Considering Peter Stearns' recommendation to remain aware of geographical and national differences, it is inviting to ponder the question whether emotions in the United States look different to foreigners (including foreign researchers) than to Americans and US researchers.

Traditionally, theories of emotions in Europe stressed physical expression such as laughing or crying as consequential expressions of emotions.[11] In the United States, the pragmatic perspective contrasts with this more essentialist European approach. The American philosopher and psychologist William James, for one, postulated that the soul followed the physical expression: people do not cry because they are sad; they are sad because they cry. Where James believed that we first react to a situation, before we experience the emotion, his German colleague, the much acclaimed Wilhelm Wundt, insisted that the emotion comes first, followed by physiological and behavioral consequences: people cry because they are sad.[12] We do not need to be concerned with the validity of either Wundt's or James's claim. Instead, their psychological research reminds us of the fundamental challenge posed by pragmatism to European scholarship and the competition between cause and effect: do emotions inspire expressions or do expressions inspire emotions?

To speak about a typically "American emotion" would therefore be overstretching the point. But as our case studies show, there is, indeed, a specific cultural way to express, accept, and standardize emotions, at certain moments in time, in the United States—and elsewhere. Collectively, the authors in this volume believe that emotions in American history are peculiar in that they have been inspired, shaped, digested, expressed, and analyzed through specific historical events and cycles unique in the history of the United States. Ekman may be right and emotions may be universal. But their expression and experience is not. We ask the reader to keep this differentiation well in mind when reading the ensuing essays.

Notes

Thank you, Heiko Hecht, for reading and commenting on this essay with the keen and critical eye of an experimental psychologist.

1. Cited in Antony S. R. Manstead and Agneta H. Fischer, "Beyond the Universality-Specificity Dichotomy," *Cognition and Emotion* 16, no. 1 (2002): 1; for a debate on the state of the art, see 1–9.
2. Paul Ekman, *The Face of Man: Expressions of Universal Emotions in a New Guinea Village* (New York: Garland STPM Press, 1980); Paul Ekman and Richard J. Davison, *The Nature of Emotions: Fundamental Questions* (New York: Oxford University Press, 1994); Paul Ekman and Klaus Scherrer, eds., *Approaches to Emotion* (Hillsdale, NJ: L. Erlbaum Associates, 1984); Amelie v. Griessenbeck, *Kulturfaktor Emotion: Zur Bedeutung von Emotion für das Verhältnis von Individuum, Gesellschaft und Kultur* (München: Akademischer Verlag, 1997); Horst Gundlach, *Reiz: Zur Verwendung eines Begriffes in der Psychologie* (Bern: H. Huber, 1976); Gary B. Palmer and Debra J. Occhi, eds., *Languages of Sentiment: Cultural Constructions of Emotional Substrates* (Amsterdam: J. Benjamins, 1999); Klaus Scherrer, *Psychologie der Emotion* (Göttingen: Verlag für Psychologie, 1990); Anna Wierzbicka, *Emotions across Languages and Cultures: Diversity and Universals* (Cambridge: Cambridge University Press; Paris: Editions de la Maison des Sciences de l'Homme, 1999); Heinz-Gunter Vester, *Emotion, Gesellschaft und Kultur: Grundzüge einer soziologischen Theorie der Emotionen* (Opladen: Westdeutscher Verlag, 1991).
3. Manstead and Fischer, "Beyond the Universality-Specificity Dichotomy," 1. See also the special issue of *Cognition and Emotion* 16, no. 1(2002).
4. Kenneth J. Gergen, *Realities and Relationships: Soundings in Social Construction,* 2nd ed. (Cambridge, MA: Harvard University Press, 1997).
5. Peter N. Stearns and Carol Z. Stearns, "Emotionology: Clarifying the History of Emotions and Emotional Standards," *American Historical Review* 90 (October 1985): 813–36; Fabian Hilfrich, "Manliness and 'Realism': The Use of Gendered Tropes in the Debates on the Philippine-American and on the Vietnam War," in *Culture and International History,* ed. Jessica C. E. Gienow-Hecht and Frank Schumacher (New York: Berghahn Books, 2003), 60–78.
6. For an excellent survey, see Peter Stearns and Jan Lewis, eds., *An Emotional History of the United States* (New York: New York University Press, 1998).
7. Martina Kessel, "Das Trauma der Affektkontrolle: Zur Sehnsucht nach Gefühlen im 19. Jahrhundert," in *Emotionalität: Zur Geschichte der Gefühle,* ed. Claudia Benthien, Anne Fleig, and Ingrid Kasten (Cologne: Böhlau, 2000), 156–77; see also Benthien et al., "Ein-

leitung," ibid, 7–20; Anne-Charlotte Trepp, "Emotion und bürgerliche Sinnstiftung oder die Metaphysik des Gefühls: Liebe am Beginn des bürgerlichen Zeitalters," *Der bürgerliche Wertehimmel: Innenansichten des 19. Jahrhunderts,* ed. Manfred Hettling and Stefan-Ludwig Hoffmann (Göttingen: Vandenhoeck & Ruprecht, 2000), 23–56.

8. Petra Goedde, *GIs and Germans: Culture, Gender, and Foreign Relations, 1945–1949* (New Haven, CT: Yale University Press, 2003); Frank Costigliola, "'Unceasing Pressure for Penetration': Gender, Pathology, and Emotion in George Kennan's Formation of the Cold War," *The Journal of American History* (March 1997): 1309–39; Emily Rosenberg, *Financial Missionaries to the World: The Politics and Culture of Dollar Diplomacy, 1900–1930* (Cambridge, MA: Harvard University Press, 2000).
9. Stearns and Lewis, *Emotional History;* Jessica C. E. Gienow-Hecht, "Trumpeting Down the Walls of Jericho: The Politics of Art, Music and Emotion in German-American Relations, 1870–1920," *Journal of Social History* 36, no. 3 (spring 2003): 585–613.
10. See, for example, the various contributions in the Berghahn Books series, "Explorations in Culture and International History."
11. Arthur L. Blumenthal, "A Wundt Primer: The Operating Characteristics of Consciousness," in *Wilhelm Wundt in History: The Making of a Scientific Psychology,* ed. Robert W. Rieber and David K. Robinson (New York: Academic Publishing, 2001).
12. William James, *The Principles of Psychology* (New York: H. Holt, 1890), see particularly the chapter "Emotion."

Bibliography

Blumenthal, Arthur L. "A Wundt Primer: The Operating Characteristics of Consciousness." In *Wilhelm Wundt in History: The Making of a Scientific Psychology,* edited by Robert W. Rieber and David K. Robinson. New York: Academic Publishing, 2001.

Cognition and Emotion 16, no. 1 (2002).

Costigliola, Frank. "'Unceasing Pressure for Penetration': Gender, Pathology, and Emotion in George Kennan's Formation of the Cold War." *The Journal of American History* (March 1997): 1309–39.

Ekman, Paul. *The Face of Man: Expressions of Universal Emotions in a New Guinea Village.* New York: Garland STPM Press, 1980.

Ekman, Paul, and Richard J. Davison. *The Nature of Emotions: Fundamental Questions.* New York: Oxford University Press, 1994.

Ekman, Paul, and Klaus Scherrer, eds. *Approaches to Emotion.* Hillsdale, NJ: L. Erlbaum Associates, 1984.

Gergen, Kenneth J. *Realities and Relationships: Soundings in Social Construction,* 2nd ed. Cambridge, MA: Harvard University Press, 1997.

Gienow-Hecht, Jessica C. E. "Trumpeting Down the Walls of Jericho: The Politics of Art, Music and Emotion in German-American Relations, 1870–1920." *Journal of Social History* 36, no. 3 (spring 2003): 585–613.

Goedde, Petra. *GIs and Germans: Culture, Gender, and Foreign Relations, 1945–1949.* New Haven, CT: Yale University Press, 2003.

Griffiths, Paul E. *What Emotions Really Are: The Problem of Psychological Categories.* Chicago: University of Chicago Press, 1997.

Griessenbeck, Amelie v. *Kulturfaktor Emotion: Zur Bedeutung von Emotion für das Verhältnis von Individuum, Gesellschaft und Kultur.* München: Akademischer Verlag, 1997.

Gundlach, Horst. *Reiz: Zur Verwendung eines Begriffes in der Psychologie.* Bern: H. Huber, 1976.

Hilfrich, Fabian. "Manliness and 'Realism': The Use of Gendered Tropes in the Debates on the Philippine-American and on the Vietnam War." In *Culture and International History,* edited by Jessica C. E. Gienow-Hecht and Frank Schumacher, 60–78. New York: Berghahn Books, 2003.

James, William. *The Principles of Psychology.* New York: H. Holt, 1890.

Kessel, Martina. "Das Trauma der Affektkontrolle: Zur Sehnsucht nach Gefühlen im 19. Jahrhundert." In *Emotionalität: Zur Geschichte der Gefühle,* edited by Claudia Benthien, Anne Fleig, and Ingrid Kasten, 156–77. Cologne: Böhlau, 2000.

Manstead, Antony S. R., and Agneta H. Fischer. "Beyond the Universality-Specificity Dichotomy." *Cognition and Emotion* 16, no. 1 (2002): 1.

Palmer, Gary B., and Debra J. Occhi, eds. *Languages of Sentiment: Cultural Constructions of Emotional Substrates.* Amsterdam and Philadelphia: J. Benjamins, 1999.

Rosenberg, Emily. *Financial Missionaries to the World: The Politics and Culture of Dollar Diplomacy, 1900–1930.* Cambridge: Harvard University Press, 2000.

Scherrer, Klaus. *Psychologie der Emotion.* Göttingen: Verlag für Psychologie, 1990.

Stearns, Peter N., and Carol Z. Stearns. "Emotionology: Clarifying the History of Emotions and Emotional Standards." *American Historical Review* 90 (October 1985): 813–36.

Stearns, Peter, and Jan Lewis, eds. *An Emotional History of the United States.* New York, London: New York University Press, 1998.

Trepp, Anne-Charlotte. "Emotion und bürgerliche Sinnstiftung oder die Metaphysik des Gefühls: Liebe am Beginn des bürgerlichen Zeitalters." In *Der bürgerliche Wertehimmel: Innenansichten des 19. Jahrhunderts.* Ed. Manfred Hettling and Stefan-Ludwig Hoffmann. Göttingen: Vandenhoeck & Ruprecht, 2000, pp. 23–56.

Wierzbicka, Anna. *Emotions across Languages and Cultures: Diversity and Universals.* Cambridge, U.K., New York, N.Y.: Cambridge University Press; Paris: Editions de la Maison des Sciences de l'Homme, 1999.

Vester, Heinz-Gunter. *Emotion, Gesellschaft und Kultur: Grundzüge einer soziologischen Theorie der Emotionen.* Opladen: Westdeutscher Verlag, 1991.

Approaches to the Study of Human Emotions

Chapter 1

EMOTIONS HISTORY IN THE UNITED STATES

Goals, Methods, and Promise

Peter N. Stearns

EMOTIONS HISTORY IS a relatively new field, filled with promise but also generating a variety of questions. These questions include: how can emotions history be done, and what's the point of doing it? This essay addresses these issues, while acknowledging the many gaps to be filled and the many unforeseen directions that the field may take in future. Enough research is being done now on emotions history to make it clear that scholars will interpret the category in various ways. I wish mainly to suggest some criteria to consider amid the variety.

I will argue that there are important signs of rising momentum for emotions history, both in Europe and the United States, despite its still-hesitant beginnings. I will argue, further, that not only can emotions history be done, with enlightening results, but that it serves as a fulcrum between individual experience on the one hand, and larger historical developments on the other. Understanding the history of emotions can assist in exploring emotions themselves, in figuring out how human beings function by exploring changes and continuities in emotional experience over time. But emotions history also explores factors that help explain larger developments, for example in law, or politics, or consumer behavior. Emotions and emotional standards

---

Notes for this section begin on page 25.

here serve as causes that need to be added to the more conventional factors historians use to explain some key changes in society at large.

The dominant focus of American work on emotion involves analysis of change, with the usual accompanying apparatus exploring concomitant continuities and relevant causation. Important examples of this approach include John Demos's evaluation of a crucial shift from shame to guilt in both private life and public punishment, between the eighteenth and mid-nineteenth centuries; or Susan Matt's treatment of the evolution of attitudes toward envy, from disapproval to approval, as part of the emergence of a new level of consumerism in the early twentieth century. Sensitive considerations recognize distinctions and relationships between shifts in emotional standards on the one hand, important in their own right, and the undoubtedly more complicated possibility of actual changes in emotional experience. In between are changes in public responses to emotion, which will show up, for example, in legal formulations or school regulations.[1]

While innovative historians called for research on emotions in the 1930s, with Lucien Febvre, the charge was explicitly taken up only in the 1980s. In the United States, emotions history responded in part to growing interest in sociology and anthropology, two other disciplines that examine the cultural components of emotional experience, but even more to findings in gender and family history. This differed to some extent from work in Europe that had a fuller theoretical base, often around Elias's idea of a civilizing process, and more connection to public and even political developments. My own work, in the American mode, was first spurred by findings in family history by Demos, Stone, and others, which argued for a great increase in family emotionality in the eighteenth century without, however, examining this strand very precisely.[2] It was also spurred by my work on masculinity, examining characteristic claims that men were held to "unemotional" standards when masculine norms clearly called for emotions like anger in certain circumstances. Explicit research on emotions seemed necessary to answer significant historical questions or provide greater clarity, particularly in exploring changes in gender standards and family life. Early focus thus involved particular attention to aspects of love, personal grief, and anger when enmeshed in private life.

It is vital to note that psychohistory, moderately popular in the United States and based primarily on Freudian models, has contributed to American emotions research only slightly. Dominant psychohistorical research focuses on individuals, not wider emotional patterns, and while efforts to extend to wider groups (for example, to generations) have been provocative, they have not been entirely persuasive. The marked decline of Freudian models in other disciplines involved in emotions research also complicates this approach.

Research in emotions history in the United States has already blossomed to include a variety of topics and periods. It is possible to explore change and continuity in such emotions as grief, anger, fear, guilt, shame, love of various sorts, jealousy, and envy—an incomplete list, to be sure, but a promising one. There have also been discussions of broader emotional style, cutting across specific emotions. This same growing body of work variously explains what causes change in emotional standards, with components ranging from new religious currents, new types of expertise (such as the rise of psychology), new economic arrangements such as corporate management structures that call for new emotional formulations, and even changes in health concerns. And of course the research looks to the consequences of emotional change, in areas extending from friendship to consumer behavior.[3]

A great deal of work has focused on two periods of significant change. One embraces the late eighteenth–early nineteenth centuries, when emotional redefinitions involved shifting gender norms, a rise in the approval and expectation of love in courtship, and (especially for women) a general increase in sensibility, along with (as John Demos has argued) an important shift from shame to guilt both in childrearing and in public punishments.

The second transition period involves the second quarter of the twentieth century, with a general movement to reduce emotional intensity, but also to make some of the nineteenth-century rules less formal. Gender prescriptions—for example, that respectable women not get angry, or that men and women strive for an intense but ethereal love—eased. Analysis of this period is complicated by a folk wisdom (replicated in some earlier sociology) that argued that the only trend was toward greater permissiveness, "letting it all hang out," which is very misleading. It is complicated also by the fact that in the same period, many media and sports performances highlighted more intense emotions—which meant that Americans began to combine considerable regulation of emotion in daily life with the capacity, as spectators, to watch displays of deep anger or fear. Discussions of American character, heating up in the late twentieth century, complete with claims of declining standards of self-control, increase the challenge for research on the actual evolution of twentieth-century emotional styles: what many Americans think is happening to emotion, on average, differs from recent historical reality. But, among relevant scholars, despite variations in specific formulations, the focus on increasing efforts to discipline emotional intensity provides a widely accepted framework.

Rather than further summarize a rich and available literature, I want to turn to five challenges to the ongoing effort that will further explain what emotions history is all about, and where it is heading, at least in the United States. Of course we must hope for an acceleration of the research effort overall and a commitment to cover a wider array of relevant topics, to uncover additional sources—the standard prerequisites for a successful historical subfield. But there are some guidelines peculiar to the emotions history field as well. The first three points in this category can be captured fairly quickly, while the final two deserve fuller comment in getting to the essence of how emotions history can be done and what purpose it serves in linking the private and public faces of past experience.

Issue #1: Interdisciplinary Connections

Historians of emotion can benefit greatly—indeed, have already benefited greatly—from contact with kindred disciplines. Work by sociologists and anthropologists sometimes has a historical dimension of its own, though the commitment to explore change is less systematic. Certainly there is a shared interest in exploring how particular cultural contexts shape emotions in various ways. Anthropological findings on emotional variance in different cultures are directly relevant to historical work.[4] With psychology, the dominant current discipline where emotions research is concerned, the relationship is more complex. A minority school of "constructivists" or discursive psychologists easily joins historians in exploring comparisons of emotional cultures in different places or different times. But mainstream psychology is interested in definitions of emotion that suggest less connection to history. Those aspects of emotion that are neural or chemical reflexes are not really open to historical inquiry—though they may have historical consequences in spurring individual behavior. Emotional responses like the startle reflex or flushing are differently valued by different cultures (blushing is far less popular now than it was for nineteenth-century women), and this does enter the historical arena, but the experiences may not change significantly. But emotions that have a larger cognitive or volitional element, like grief or love, obviously are affected by cultural valuations and expectations, and here is where a historian can link with psychologists in trying to figure out what emotions are all about.

Historians have every reason to participate in, profit from, and contribute to the growing interest in emotions research in several disciplines. Active connection with other disciplines will in turn help keep historical work on emotions honest, by avoiding unduly vague or loose references to what emotions are. References to "fear" in a particular time, for example, should be conditioned by some knowledge of what other disciplinary findings about fear are—how other disciplines define it in terms of individual and collective emotional experience. Historical work does not have to accept all the strictures of psychology, for some claims go too far toward the purely reflex end. Psychologists who seek to define emotion as a very brief process really miss the mark, given what we know about human capacity to anticipate, mull over, savor, and even recall emotions—which is where cultural conditioning particularly enters in. There is every reason, further, to keep working to make psychologists understand better the cultural component and the extent to which changes in emotion may help clarify actual human experience, including periodic requests for therapeutic help because of confusions over what this or that emotion is "supposed" to be. But historians do need to keep track of psychological work as well, as a spur to appropriate precision and as a reminder of the reflex component that emotions do contain.

We actually have some experience in the kind of oversimplification that contact with other relevant disciplines can help avoid. When family historians first started writing about emotional change, they frequently depicted a stark contrast between emotionless premodern families and their emotion-charged modern counterparts. This was simply wrong, in ignoring some standard or "natural" emotional propensities. Change did occur, and it was significant, but it involved the meaning, intensity, and acceptability of familial emotion, rather than the quantum leap that had first been claimed.

Issue #2: Diversity

Americans who work on emotions thus far have focused mainly on white, Protestant, middle-class formulations. This culture dominates the most widely sold sermons and childrearing tracts, and it has had wide influence. But there are other emotional subcultures operating in American history, and they deserve attention directly as well as in their relationship to the mainstream standards. We know that different ethnic groups maintain different standards of grief and mourning, for example. What happens to these standards when they interact with the growing hostility to grief in mainstream settings in the twentieth century? By the 1950s, African Americans were demanding increased emphasis on the importance of emotional assertiveness, as part of the civil rights movement. But this was precisely the time when mainstream culture stressed heightened control over anger, especially at work. Here, along with outright racism, is one reason for the employment difficulties of black males, especially in the service sector.

Attention to subcultures must involve religion as well as race and ethnicity. Philip Greven has shown the ongoing importance of the distinctive, tense emotional culture of the Evangelical tradition.[5] Recent work shows also how Catholics, while influenced by mainstream standards—for example, concerning invocations of fear—responded with their own formulations and with distinctive timing for change. Exploring the experiences and connections of key groups in American society will be enriched by attention to emotional expressions and behaviors.

Issue #3: Comparative Work

We have no good, careful comparative work in the history of emotion, and this constitutes an obvious invitation for the future. There are some trans-atlantic formulations, emanating particularly from several Dutch sociologists, which assume common twentieth-century patterns amid greater informality and a new democratization of standards.[6] But even if there is convergence in this direction, it at least occurs amid different timing; for key American developments began in the 1920s, as against the 1950s for Germany and the Netherlands. And probably there are other differences as well. The fact is, without explicit comparison, we do not know.

Social psychologists, looking at contemporary data alone, certainly suggest some contrasts. One study shows contemporary Americans as particularly eager to conceal their emotions, compared to other cultures. A project on jealousy argues that, with this composite emotion, Dutch people characteristically feel sad, French angry, while Americans race around checking with friends and acquaintances to see if they are behaving oddly.[7] Comparisons of this sort deserve to be enriched by historical analysis (as I think they can be, in the examples just cited; certainly the history of American jealousy backs up this segment of the findings in psychology).

Comparative issues have come to the fore with particular prominence in the case of contemporary fear. Several studies have explored the rise of fear and manipulation of the emotion in the Unites States, using a historical backdrop to explain change. But there are French studies that claim the importance of fear in contemporary France as well, and some relevant work on Islam and on Great Britain, again in current settings. The obvious question is whether fear is a constant across times and societies or (as most historians have argued) it has surged since the later nineteenth century, for reasons that can be historically explained; and within this framework, whether fear is as some argue the "dominant" modern emotion across boundaries (and if so, why) or whether it responds to more particular cultural and political settings. The opportunities for comparative work on this vital emotional, but also political, topic are truly urgent. Against the idea of some uniform social usage of fear, or some standard modern developments, several scholars have argued that, by the later twentieth century, Americans had accumulated a particular set of unreasoned anxieties, spurred by changes in media and by political exploitation, that continued to generate unusual national reactions in response to challenges in the first decade of the twenty-first century. This finding has broad significance, but it needs refinement and further exploration based on more precise and explicit comparative work.[8]

Issue #4: Examining Emotional Experience Directly

Emotions history has expanded, as Alf Lüdtke has put it, into looking at performative as well as normative features of emotions history, or how people behave and not just how they evaluate. Most emotions history begins, as we have seen, with an examination of emotional norms—what the culture says emotions should be. This approach mirrors earlier developments in social history, as in the field of women's history where examinations of feminine ideals and norms helped initiate serious research. Emotional standards are important in their own right. They do help shape emotional experience. And they have independent effects—for example, on law or institutional arrangements. And they change, which makes them grist for the historian's mill, a vital part in fact of any study of mentalities.

But research is now pushing beyond this, to seek emotional experience directly. This work uses letters, diaries, autobiographies (with caution), and, in the twentieth century, other inquiries: for example, surveys of parental anxieties or emotional problems at work or in marriage. A number of specific studies are now probing the ways people experienced emotion under the impact of changing standards around 1800. Authored mainly by younger scholars, and mainly in article or dissertation formats thus far, exemplary studies show how men and women presented love at a time when the emotion was gaining approval but when marriages were still formed as economic and political arrangements. Another study, based on a seven-hundred-page diary, shows how a young Rhode Island woman appropriated the new culture of sensibility but still carefully managed emotions in her family setting. The result was a need to use female friends as an outlet for fuller emotional expression, and a deep concern about sincerity. (The rise and evolution of the search for emotional sincerity is a looming topic for this period overall.) Similar work is proceeding for the second major transition period. One project, here using several diaries, shows how women found it difficult to adjust romantic expectations, based on books and movies but also a nineteenth-century cultural legacy, to their husbands' rather different emotional definitions at a time when more emotional energy was going into marital ties as opposed to childrearing or friendships.[9]

These studies suggest how one branch of emotions research can develop, exploring private and family experience and even the emotional sense of self. The studies allow emotions historians to join sociologists and psychologists in showing how emotions work, how culture shapes and interprets even "basic" emotions. They show how current emotional interactions have emerged from a complex past. And they demonstrate exactly the kind of maturation, from examination of standards alone to deeper inquiries into experience itself, that one would seek and expect.

A new challenge for contemporary historians, though in the same basic area, involves sorting out growing media impacts on emotional reactions, and actual experience of emotions like fear or grief. Excessive American fear about abductions of children—where studies demonstrate a huge gap between relatively modest actual incidence and vast overestimates by actual parents—provide a recent case in point in which media representations, actual emotion, and resultant behaviors combine to produce significant change.

Issue #5: What Emotions Cause

Many historians, whatever their reactions to explorations of emotional experience in the past, will want to see how emotions history relates to more conventional historical issues. The relationship exists, through treating emotions as either contributor or cause, and folding them into the complex task of historical explanation. At the same time, some work on emotions, particularly in psychology, treats them as ends in themselves, without much attention to larger social functions. Here too, historical analysis can add greatly to an understanding of emotions' larger impacts.

But, two cautions are appropriate here. Not everything warrants an explanation through emotions history, and while the field is rich, it is important not to overreach. As with other aspects of social-cultural history, it may be particularly difficult to connect with certain aspects of diplomatic activity. In addition, merely tacking on some references to emotion in a conventional project does not help much. Emotions should and can be a serious part of the analysis, and not just a throw-away line about Cold War fears or wartime jealousies.

I suggest two paths. The first involves emotions as concomitant, a serious part of a historical phenomenon though not necessarily a cause. Let me use consumerism as an example. We know that consumerism involves more than new shops, products, and advertising. It entails deeply emotional attachments to acquisition and goods. In the early twentieth century, sources allow us to see how people were deliberately building goods into their emotional lives—for example, in childrearing, as a means of distracting children from jealousy or fear. Whether emotions caused the new levels of consumerism is hard to say (though, for England, Colin Campbell argues precisely this sequence in the eighteenth century[10]). It is possible, and further analysis may show emotional preconditions. But emotional attachments were, regardless, a deep part of the emergence of modern consumerism, such that this important story is incomplete without the emotional element.

But emotions and emotional changes play an explicitly causal role as well. Several examples will demonstrate this. First, in law: Demos shows how shifting familial evaluations of shame led to the ending of primarily shame-based public punishments after 1800—as stocks and public executions shifted to imprisonment and private discipline—a huge connection based on emotional reassessment. The advent of no-fault divorce law in the 1970s was shaped by prior attacks, in familial emotional formulations, on guilt and jealousy. Divorce might in legal principle now be free from emotional intensity. Earlier condemnations of shame and jealousy also explain 1970s rules against displaying student grades in public, another big regulatory change. The connections are frequent and important: revision of emotions and emotional standards often lead, usually a few decades later, to reformulations in law.[11]

Another, more open-ended case, in a different field: since the late 1950s, the rate of strikes and unionization has greatly declined, save for a brief late 1960s upsurge. This important protest change is usually explained through the rise of the service sector, the relocation of industry to more union-hostile regions, and the expansion of female employment. And there is a tradition in protest research that ignores emotional factors in favor of purely structural determinants. But the decline of work-based protest also followed a decades-long campaign against workplace anger, through attempts to make this anger seem both disruptive and immature.[12] Many workers assimilated these standards, making it more difficult to be angry or at least to define and express anger collectively. Is this a necessary additional cause of protest decline? Or were emotions the channel through which structural change was translated to individual workers, effectively constraining protest? Either way, we need to consider emotions' causal, and changing, role in explaining protest history.

Americans have long been unusually eager to minimize deaths of their troops in wartime. But by the late twentieth century, this impulse was expanding, beginning to define military and diplomatic policy toward avoidance of significant ground engagements. The preference for air attacks obviously fit American cultural esteem for technology, but the hostility to ground action reflected not only specific experiences in the public reactions to Korea and Vietnam but a new level of emotional hostility to death and grief more generally. Policy analysis, here, must build in the growing aversion to grief and mourning that had been developing for several decades: careful efforts at minimizing the symbolic impact of American deaths in the war in Iraq are a fascinating outgrowth of a process that began in the 1950s.

One final case: emotional formulations clearly enter domestic political history. The excitement of elections and candidates, or the lack thereof, relates to emotional norms as well as to issues. From the 1960s onward, national political candidates began to be held to a reasonably clear emotional script: they must not be robot-like, but they must not express too much emotional zeal, for example, in public debates. They should not cry (one major candidate was done in by this), and above all they must not get angry. Debates revolved as much on restraint, despite provocative questions, as on policy issues. And another connection: at various points, emotional fervor shifts political sides, and this invites analysis. Between 1970 and 2000, for example, Republicans were far more likely to express (and apparently to feel) righteous indignation, to build on emotion, than were Democrats. Working-class and feminist issues lost fervor, in part because of some measurable gains. Post-1960s lifestyle issues like guns and abortion began to take center stage, emotions at the ready. In this process, further differential emotional bases began to separate the two parties and their styles. Republican aggressiveness fed on a disproportionately male clientele and on a regional concentration in the South and West, where the trends of anger control had made less headway and where fundamentalist Christian acceptance of righteous wrath was more firmly lodged. Emotional bases counted, in other words, in expressing and promoting shifts in political tactics and affiliations. Here again is a contribution to explanation that deserves serious attention, in this case and in other, earlier political shifts as well.

Exploring emotions and emotional standards as part of historical causation is innovative and challenging. The patterns suggested here need to be further explored, and of course there will be dispute and complexity. It's the invitation that counts at this point, the probability that emotions can help explain some significant and complex shifts in American public life.

* * *

Emotions history is establishing itself as a significant subfield in social and cultural history, with unusual interdisciplinary links in exploring the borders of "natural" and "learned" behaviors and experiences. It relates closely, in these respects, to historical work on the body, on disease, on the senses, and on sexuality. Pursuing this field involves an explicit commitment—hence the injunction not simply to paste in an emotional reference or two and assume that much has been accomplished.

The field involves three further, related tensions, all of which can be creatively employed. First, exploring "real" emotion involves more attention to biographical evidence than social historians are usually comfortable with. But the biographical examples must ultimately be combined toward establishing larger patterns, and they must be linked to what is known about emotional norms in the period involved and even to the psychology of emotion. Without the tension between biographical materials and larger patterns, we will either learn too little about real emotions in the past, or we will aimlessly drag out one biography or cache of letters after another.

Second, emotions history must deal both with private and personal experience and with public domains where emotion is involved—domains like work, leisure, and politics. Scholars interested mainly in one of these two targets must keep an eye on findings and implications in the other.

And third, historians must continue to look at emotions in themselves, broadening the number of emotions studied historically and the range of geographical and chronological cases. But they must also look to emotions as causes of broader, often more familiar historical phenomena, going beyond the self and even family relationships. Either channel, by itself, will shortchange the rich results we can expect from analysis of emotional change. Combined, they maintain real promise for the contributions of emotions history to emotions research and to historical research more generally.

Emotions history is genuine history—that is, it deals with a variety of periods in the past, for their own sake. Recent work, for example, on anger in the Middle Ages is a case in point. But emotions history also offers great potential for using history to help frame and explain contemporary emotional patterns and their consequences—an area that obviously invokes interdisciplinary linkages once again. Explorations of protest and its relationship to changing anger standards, or new public emotional displays associated with death (for example, the outpourings that followed the death of Princess Diana) are specific examples of how emotions history gains additional functions in addressing present-day behaviors—in terms of changes and continuities between past and present.[13]

Notes

1. John Demos, "Shame and Guilt in Early New England," in *Emotion and Social Change: Toward a New Psychohistory,* ed. Carol Zisowitz Stearns and Peter N. Stearns (New York: Holmes and Meier, 1989); Susan J. Matt, *Keeping Up with the Joneses: Envy in American Consumer Society 1890—1930* (Philadelphia: University of Pennsylvania Press, 2002).
2. Norbert Elias and Edmund Jephcott, *The Civilizing Process* (Oxford: Blackwell Publishers Limited, 1994); John Demos, *A Little Commonwealth: Family Life in Plymouth Colony* (New York: Oxford University Press, 2000); Carol Zisowitz Stearns and Peter N. Stearns, *Anger: The Struggle for Emotional Control in America's History* (Chicago: University of Chicago Press, 1986); Lawrence Stone, *Family, Sex and Marriage in England 1500–1800* (New York: Harper and Row, 1977).

3. Peter N. Stearns and Jan Lewis, *Emotional History of the United States* (New York: New York University Press, 1998).
4. J. R. Averill, *Anger and Aggression: An Essay on Emotion* (New York: Springer, 1982).
5. Philip Greven, *The Protestant Temperament: Patterns of Child-Rearing, Religious Experience, and the Self in Early America* (Chicago: University of Chicago Press, 1988).
6. Cas Wouters, *An Age of Informalization: Western Regimes of Manners and Emotions Since 1890: An International Comparison* (Thousand Oaks, CA: Sage, 2007). Cas Wouters, *Sex and Manners: Female Emancipation in the West 1890–2000* (London: Sage, 2004.)
7. Peter Salovy, *The Psychology of Jealousy and Envy* (New York: The Guilford Press, 1991).
8. Joanna Bourke, *Fear: A Cultural History* (Emeryville, CA: Shoemaker & Hoard, 2006); Frank Furedi, *Culture of Fear: Risk Taking and the Morality of Low Expectations,* rev. ed. (London: Continuum, 2002); Barry Glassner, *The Culture of Fear: Why Americans Are Afraid of the Wrong Things* (New York: Basic Books 1999); Christophe Lambert, *La Société de la peur* (Paris: Plon, 2005); Jackie Orr, *Panic Diaries: A Genealogy of Panic Disorder* (Durham, NC: Duke University Press, 2006); Peter N. Stearns, *American Fear: The Causes and Consequences of High Anxiety* (New York: Routledge, 2006).
9. Nicole Eustace, *Passion is the Gale: Emotion, Power, and the Coming of the American Revolution* (Chapel Hill: University of North Carolina Press, 2008); Beth L. Bailey, *From Front Porch to Back Seat: Courtship in Twentieth-Century America* (Baltimore: Johns Hopkins University Press, 1988).
10. Colin Campbell, *The Romantic Ethic and the Spirit of Modern Consumerism* (London: Blackwell, 2005).
11. Zisowitz Stearns and Stearns, *Emotion and Social Change.*
12. Peter N. Stearns, *Revolutions in Sorrow: The American Experience of Death in Global Perspective* (Boulder, CO: Paradigm Publishing, 2007).
13. Peter N. Stearns, *American Behavioral History: An Introduction* (New York: New York University Press, 2005).

Bibliography

Averill, J. R. *Anger and Aggression: An Essay on Emotion.* New York: Springer, 1982.

Bailey, Beth L. *From Front Porch to Back Seat: Courtship in Twentieth-Century America.* Baltimore: Johns Hopkins University Press, 1988.

Bourke, Joanna. *Fear: A Cultural History.* Emeryville, CA: Shoemaker & Hoard, 2006.

Campbell, Colin. *The Romantic Ethic and the Spirit of Modern Consumerism.* London: Blackwell, 2005.

Demos, John. *A Little Commonwealth: Family Life in Plymouth Colony.* New York: Oxford University Press, 2000.

Elias, Norbert, and Edmund Jephcott. *The Civilizing Process.* Oxford: Blackwell Publishers Limited, 1994.

Eustace, Nicole. *Passion is the Gale: Emotion, Power, and the Coming of the American Revolution.* Chapel Hill: University of North Carolina Press, 2008.

Furedi, Frank. *Culture of Fear: Risk Taking and the Morality of Low Expectations.* Rev. ed., London: Continuum, 2002.

Glassner, Barry. *The Culture of Fear: Why Americans Are Afraid of the Wrong Things.* New York: Basic Books 1999.

Greven, Philip. *The Protestant Temperament: Patterns of Child-Rearing, Religious Experience, and the Self in Early America.* Chicago: University of Chicago Press, 1988.

Lambert, Christophe *La Société de la peur.* Paris: Plon, 2005.

Matt, Susan J. *Keeping Up with the Joneses: Envy in American Consumer Society 1890–1930.* Philadelphia: University of Pennsylvania Press, 2002.

Orr, Jackie. *Panic Diaries: A Genealogy of Panic Disorder.* Durham, NC: Duke University Press, 2006.

Salovy, Peter. *The Psychology of Jealousy and Envy.* New York: The Guilford Press, 1991.

Stearns, Carol Zisowitz, and Peter N. Stearns. *Anger: The Struggle for Emotional Control in America's History.* Chicago: University of Chicago Press, 1986.

———. *Emotion and Social Change: Toward a New Psychohistory.* New York: Holmes and Meier, 1989.

Stearns, Peter N. *American Fear: The Causes and Consequences of High Anxiety.* New York: Routledge, 2006.

———. *American Behavioral History: An Introduction.* New York: New York University Press, 2005.

———. *Revolutions in Sorrow: The American Experience of Death in Global Perspective.* Boulder, CO: Paradigm Publishing, 2007.

Stearns, Peter N., and Jan Lewis. *Emotional History of the United States.* New York: New York University Press, 1998.

Stone, Lawrence. *Family, Sex and Marriage in England 1500–1800.* New York: Harper and Row, 1977.

Wouters, Cas. *Sex and Manners: Female Emancipation in the West 1890–2000.* London: Sage, 2004.

———. *An Age of Informalization: Western Regimes of Manners and Emotions Since 1890: An International Comparison.* Thousand Oaks, CA: Sage, 2007.

Chapter 2

EMOTIONS AT WORK

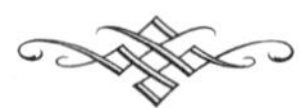

Potential and Perspectives of the History of Everyday Life

Alf Lüdtke

Concepts: The History of Everyday Life

HISTORIANS OF EVERYDAY life reconstruct practices by which people "make" their living. At issue are the ways individuals and groups deal with the world. Concretely, how do people cope with both the strain of demands and the promise of attractions they sense or encounter in their specific settings? Respective studies trace people's perceptions and sensations, actions and expressions, and their manifold material and symbolical registers.

Still, some researchers of the everyday confine themselves to the study of the (seeming) routines of daily life. The everyday, however, reverberates not only with repetition, oftentimes labeled "structure" or "institution." Instead, at the center are the individual's actions. Their range escapes any categorization, be it pursuit or reenactment of custom or, to the contrary, denial of tradition or any interrelationship with others. Thus, the everyday refers to and comprises continuity and rupture as well.

Notes for this section begin on page 42.

The focus on practices does not limit the researcher's attention to isolated contexts or brief incidents. Instead, this emphasis allows focusing on people's multilayered forms of appropriation. Because, when people cope with "given" realities they also (re)shape and, thus, appropriate the very conditions of their survival. At the same time, this view turns structures into temporal sequences and underlines "knots" of interaction (including strife or immediate clash). Hence, even institutions that claim a particularly *longue durée* like the Roman Catholic Church, or to a lesser extent bureaucracies or armies of the modern state, appear in a different light. Reconstructions of people's everyday show both adherents and opponents in their efforts to (re)produce or to block, if not to dismantle, such institutions. In turn, whatever forms of appropriation people pursued, the latter bred not only continuity but also transformation, if not sometimes revolution. In other words: the emphasis on practice enhances the sensitivity for the fluidity of what commonly goes as a longstanding "structural frame" and its "hard facts."

Deficits and Trends

Ironically, in their effort to unearth the multilayeredness of people's everyday, the practitioners of this approach have grossly neglected emotions. In this respect, they have ignored their claim and did not overcome the canonical limitations of established historiography.[1] Traditionally, historians were trained to consider individuals as "rational men" in pursuit of their interests and, by that very token, the best of mankind (Lucien Fèbvre, Johan Huizinga). Alternatively, encompassing cultural entities (Arnold Toynbee) or, more recently, "large" social processes (Charles Tilly) appeared as the driving forces of history. Such grand narratives have argued the uneven but progressive advent of rational behavior not only in the European and North American West but in other regions of the globe as well. In this vein, and notwithstanding their academic discipline, authors argued for the need of control if not suppression of all things emotional: unregulated emotions would instigate violence and, thus, not only cause suffering for the many but also delay the aspired "rationalization."[2]

Historians of the everyday have not been exempt from such views. On the contrary, in their research on, for instance, working people in factories or households, for decades they traced the "agency" of the exploited: the latter would propel people to ever more "rational" strivings for self-determination. This would lead, so the imagined future went, to powerful collective action.[3] Recently, however, studies of perpetrators or bystanders of the Holocaust and of war crimes in World War I and II have made a difference.

Microstudies on local or regional settings show the intricate interrelationship of rational calculation and emotional drive. Regional analyses of denunciation allude to a broad range of motives of those passing "information" on neighbors or workmates to the police if not to the Gestapo or other agencies of state, or even to the Nazi Party itself. At any rate, this widely spread practice seems fueled by intense longings of the respective individuals for the benevolence of authority.[4] Christopher Browning has traced the emotions at stake in the politics and practices of extermination in his study on a police battalion, and the behavior of its members in the killing operations in the occupied territories in Eastern Europe is a case in point.[5] Here, as elsewhere, the emotions among rank and file but also the officers involved ranged from "detachment" to hate (in diffuse ways perhaps spilling over into self-hate) and loathing for their victims. Even "emotional detachment" refers to a state of emotions: called for and displayed were not only "hot" but "cool" emotions.[6] However, not only the perpetrators of mass murder but also functional elites and even the broader masses show features of "cool" and "hot" emotions.[7]

Reports on public rallies in the 1930s coincide with secretly collected reports on the mood of the "many": the masses displayed an intense furor to accept but also to cooperate, if not fervently to support, the seclusion against and, finally, the destruction of presumed enemies to the Reich and its "people."[8] Especially any measures against Jewish "adversaries" to the "Aryan race" were met with inexhaustible emotion among those deemed "German"—who, in turn, rallied around the Führer admired if not loved by numerous people across the board of social milieu and gender backgrounds.[9] Such furor also fueled the letters of soldiers sent home from the various military fronts as it informed reciprocal writings of their relatives, mates, or superiors at home. By no means was this furor tied to victory. After the disaster at Stalingrad, letters indicate an even intensified determination: "coolness" enhanced![10]

The point is not to throw out the baby with the bathwater or to shift from "rational man" to the opposite—as if "emotional man" made it all. Needed are explorations of specific configurations of rational and emotional moments and their shifting if not meandering balances.[11] Here, historical actors appear as multifaceted individuals who follow not just one "line." Recent investigations of denunciation have provided important insights into the form of people's collisions with the powers that be and also the emotions that were pivotal. Accordingly, individuals rather selectively cooperated with authority. To "turn someone in" did not hinder people from keeping their distance to demands of the authorities of state and the Nazi Party, for instance when it came to verbally or physically attacking those marked as Jews. Still, most of these *Volksgenossen* were firmly convinced that the German Reich ought to "regain" previous power positions by military action. To that end, the vast majority of German "people's comrades" unconditionally supported the war effort of the Nazi empire, most of them until May 1945 and stubbornly ignoring suffering resulting from the deeds of this very regime.[12]

More generally, studies relating people's everyday to such configurations have successfully challenged structuralist approaches, for instance, regarding Nazism. For decades researchers had focused on socioeconomic processes and their dynamics. In this vein they explored the decay of political processes, and the ever-sharpened friend-foe antagonisms in the realm of ideologies. It was here they detected the determining forces having driven the "masses" towards acceptance of both the war of extermination and the destruction of European Jews and other peoples. In contrast, the emphasis of historians of everyday life on people's room for maneuvering showed practices of distancing. The overwhelming feature, however, emerging from these studies are the degrees of active cooperation, if not enthusiastic support, of the "many" for Nazi policies before and even more during the war. Thus, these studies put into question views of Nazism solely focusing on total control exercised on the "many" by institutions, ideologies, and power elites.

Against this background, even conventional studies of the political elites in the summer of 1914 display somewhat more sensitivity to the dimensions of the emotional than did studies occupied with "the masses" until recently. The lore is well known: in European capitals diplomats, ministers, and generals primarily concerned themselves with their protagonist's "nervousness or "anxiety" (or *Angst*).[13] However, it appears as if the impact of emotions for pushing the configuration of nations towards war urges the historians who narrate this story to treat the very sentiments they depict as deficient or premodern. And even a subtle analysis (as by Joachim Radkau in his study of "nervousness") presents emotions as obstacles hindering both politicians and the public from operating more rationally. Here, emotions blur people's vision and distract them from properly avoiding or solving their nations' if not mankind's problems.

The Study of Emotions: Foci and Methods

In their effort to put emotions on the agenda of historical research, Peter N. Stearns and Carol Z. Stearns have argued that the "real thing" (emotions and feelings) is beyond the reach of historical investigation. Instead, in their view historians should delineate "collective emotional standards of a society" and study their respective changes: this will constitute "emotionology."[14]

Of course, such caution is productive for two reasons. First, the emphasis on standards by which people and social groups or classes perceive and regulate emotions challenges the long-standing view as if they would be ahistorically "given". Emotionology is not interested in whether emotions are part of human nature situated seemingly "before" or "outside of" culture and, thus, possibly devoid of historical malleability. Second, by this token all efforts are discouraged from trying to retrieve "authentic" emotions of others or past historical actors. Traces, articulations, or expressions may refer to impulses, feelings, and emotions that triggered or shaped them. But what the impulses directly and immediately were must remain open. On the other hand, the emancipatory effects of such constructivist approaches should not obfuscate their possible blind spots or principle limits. One of them is perhaps that the either/or of culturally formulated standards vs. "authentic" emotions/feelings[15] is misleading.

In order to underline this, I want to refer to the recent works of historians Alain Corbin, Martina Kessel, and William M. Reddy. Their aim is to connect the study of articulations of emotions with the investigation of the contexts historical actors did encounter and, presumably, "felt". These authors follow the assumption that articulations of emotions like joy or boredom are both culturally constituted *and* actually and sensually encountered by those who articulate or express their emotions.

In his reconstitution of a "common life," Alain Corbin traces one villager in nineteenth-century rural France.[16] From detailed records from various archives, the historian pieces together the life-course of this man who in his adult years made his living as a maker of wooden shoes. Corbin mentions the emotions and feelings of this composite actor, Louis-François Pinagot. However, the historian claims time and again that Pinagot encountered certain feelings but does not go beyond these claims. The references and the concrete profile of these emotions remain vague. Instead, the historian provides a very nuanced analysis of patterns of property and of the demography and kinship system. From this basis Corbin rather speculatively approaches the "familiar relations of emotions," arguing that villagers like Pinagot found themselves in thick networks of such relations. But, at the same time, Corbin states that these "relations of emotions did not restrain people's freewheeling at that time".

In a rather different mode, Martina Kessel explores letters between husbands and wives of the early nineteenth century for their references to and evaluations of respective feelings and emotions.[17] She investigates the rhetoric women employ to articulate and complain about their boredom. These women emphasized the consequences: loss of energy, if not apathy, combined with the sense of a "slowdown" or a changed temporality. Kessel finds resonance with the sharpening and widening of distinctions between males and females in their respective role models. Males were consigned to wage work and public office, while females found "the private sphere and the family home" presented as their proper field of action. Kessel meticulously mines personal accounts, private letters, and diaries[18] in particular. The overall picture emerging shows women of a bourgeois background and milieu articulating their boredom—because they actually felt it. Still, references and distinctive features of these emotions remain diffuse.

For several years William Reddy has been exploring configurations of feelings and emotions in France throughout the eighteenth century. He shows the Enlightenment as much as a movement for rationality as a most intense stimulus for individuals to raise and, concomitantly, to encounter each other's sensitivity. It was only during the "Terreur" of the French Revolution in 1794, so Reddy claims, that the image of the Enlightenment was reshaped, thereby totally cut off from the realm of emotions and, in particular of sensitivity.

From here Reddy embarks on a more theoretical elaboration. He proposes to situate emotions in the context of producing and simultaneously translating cognition into action or utterance (one may add: expression).[19] In this view emotions "color" or "flavor" specific actions or utterances. The point is that utterances about, for instance, one's rage may contain descriptive elements. At the same time, though, these very utterances affect the state of mind they allude to: stimulating or calming down the speaker's or writer's rage. This is what Reddy, then, calls the "emotive" specifics of utterances on feelings/emotions. Or: statements about emotions do, in fact, manage and (re)mold emotions. Hence, before one can describe these emotions, they have still to be produced and felt.[20]

The focus on the emotive allows us to get beyond the conventional constructivist view. The latter would claim that, for instance, honor codes regulate and strictly control one's feelings. In this view, demands to behave in specific ways operate as emotive, thus stimulating "a certain style of emotion management". Accordingly, statements that mention if not depict emotions are *performative*. That is, terms about emotions always refer to ways in which individuals produce and practice, manage and feel them.

Emotions in Modern Times: The Case of Industrial Workers

Historical studies on modern societies overwhelmingly build on the notion that emotions are part and parcel of premodernity. Hence research concentrates on processes and practices of controlling or even erasing "things emotional". In contrast, I want to explore people under the spell of one of the features of modernity: capitalism. For wage workers in factory industry (but also for managers and entrepreneurs) emotions have been a nonissue, except when it comes to preindustrial or precapitalist behavior. Here I want to argue the changing but continuing impact of emotions in settings and (inter)actions of industrial workers.

Two Glimpses

In 1910 a weaver from the Lausitz area (in Eastern Saxony) stated that "after some days off" he felt a "desire" (*Sehnsucht*) for the "beautiful steadiness and repetitiveness" (*wunderschöne Gleichmäßigkeit*) of working his semi-automatic loom.[21] In his own words, this writer does not deny the very effect of repetitiveness. However, he leaves open whether or to what extent he encounters monotony as boredom, possibly causing anger or bitterness. At any rate, this man claims to successfully cope with what others of his contemporaries described as a decisive step to alienation. In this case, then, we see not dissatisfaction but even joy derived from mastering the strenuous side of daily work. In his own way this worker did cope with the toilsome aspects of his everyday at work.

Of course, this single sentence leaves open whether a religious subtext, probably informed by Protestant ethics, was at play, too. To be sure, such glorification of the daily burden of work might have charged the "desire" this man articulated in very specific ways.

In the late 1970s a female embroiderer recalled her life history.[22] She had been born in 1908 in Swabia; from age fourteen she had worked as an embroiderer in her home village. When she married in 1932, the couple acquired an embroidering machine. Summing up her experience in 1979, she said: "If I lose my machine, then I am finished with my life. ... So far, though, the machine never ever left me alone." Someone else had left her alone: her husband was killed in World War II in 1940. She had supported herself and her daughter from that time. Here, the machine stands for being independent and autonomous. At the same time, the machine does not appear as an impersonal object or tool. On the contrary, this woman imbued her machine with a personality of its own. In this interview the embroiderer displayed a strong attachment to "her" machine.

Emotions: Constantly "At Work"

Desire for machine operation and the appeal of its beauty, attachment to a machine: conventionally, labor historians ignore or, at best, ridicule such qualifications of industrial work.[23] Like the majority of historians dealing with the "modern era" and related societal changes, they underrate the constant impact of emotions on perceptions and practices of historical actors. In this view it is rationality that constitutes the "modern" human being and his or her behavior. Accordingly, such approaches render feelings that move (or activate) people—emotions (*emovere*)—as the epitome of the premodern. For example, studies of "collective protest" in the nineteenth and early twentieth centuries have portrayed rioters (in particular, machine-breaking protoindustrial weavers) as people stuck with irrational behavior and, thus, representing "traditional" codes of behavior.[24]

The following explorations are informed by the assumption that feelings and their emotional articulations did not recede in the process of industrialization of work. More generally, and in contrast to a view put forward by Nobert Elias, my point is that the processes of "civilizing" the modern human being did not fundamentally discipline his or her emotionality. To be sure, attitudes about and ways of dealing with emotions were transformed in multiple ways since the seventeenth and eighteenth centuries (in Central and West European societies). Still, albeit encountering vastly different settings, historical actors referred to and employed what to them were emotions and feelings (occasionally cherishing or despising them). This also holds for industrial workers. Looking closely, one does recognize that workers mentioned feelings time and again—regularly and in manifold forms.

The Survey of Adolf Levenstein

The statement of the weaver quoted above was published by Adolf Levenstein in his survey of the "psychophysical" impact industrial production bore on workers. In his book the author and publicist presented a selection from those approximately five thousand replies to a questionnaire he had sent to nine thousand workers in different industrial branches, representing various regions of the German Empire.[25] Levenstein, who was an author with theological and philosophical ambitions, had inquired about topics ranging from satisfaction with one's job to aspirations or anxieties about people's future.

The responses to Levenstein's questionnaire varied considerably. For instance, complaints about repetitive tasks were often connected to references of the flip side: repetition provided opportunity for letting one's own thoughts wander freely. A Berlin metal worker described attending to his drilling machine while he enjoyed pursuing freewheeling associations. He was no exception. He and others reported a distinct sense of "freedom" while clearly being tied to a flow of production. Others responded, however, by emphasizing their attachment to the distinct way of doing things in fulfilling their respective tasks—in particular, workers in machine construction reported about such "pride" in their jobs. Yet another response came from miners who articulated their attachment to their mates. These references to co-workers reflected the grinding working conditions and risks all of them had to bear "collectively". Such statements, however, also reflect the cruel ways of supervisors when dealing with those who actually bore the brunt of the labor in the pits.

Among the respondents, aspirations ranged from hopes for improvement for themselves or their children to longings for immediately overcoming the noise, smells, and heat (or cold, for that matter) one had to endure constantly, shift after shift. In fact, respondents repeatedly imagined themselves walking through forests or across spring meadows, thus enjoying "pure nature". Aspirations for "better times" also included spaces farthest away: one worker had put down his desire for earthy happiness—if he only would be able to watch the stars by that telescope he saved all his spare pennies for!

Interspersed into these observations one finds many references to people's rage and fury about their boss or the terrible noise of machinery, in particular at spinning and weaving machines. One-fifth of the respondents expressed their dislike (*Unlust*) of their particular job.[26] Most of these responses were rather specific—they "hated" the supervisor, or the factory hall, or "their" machine (and, yes, "its tiresome monotony"). However, every tenth of the respondents did *not* feel oppressed, and every other of this tenth mentioned his "joy in work." To be sure, the family as a site of "prospective" joy appeared more often than "joy in work." Family, though, was outnumbered by hopes for an increasing "impact" of unions and political labor movements. An even larger number of respondents turned to aesthetic pleasures. In their longings they envisioned hiking "in the woods" (*im Walde*) or, alternatively, the pleasure of reading "literature".

Summing up, Levenstein read these responses as variations of the diagnosis that had become widely acknowledged among social reformers of the time. In their view industrial workers suffered from estrangement.[27] They also held that both dire living conditions and degrading treatment by bosses would trigger a strong impulse for urgent change among the affected workers. In contrast, Levenstein did not refer to material hardship or structural constraints. His focus was on the mental and psychic situation of the industrial proletariat. In this vein, he juxtaposed "debts" and "credits," calculating that 55 percent of the responses displayed feelings of dissatisfaction. Although it remained unclear if the other 45 percent felt satisfied at work, Levenstein took these results as strong evidence for "pathological disharmony" among the industrial workers.[28]

Respondents employed terms circulating in contemporary newspapers and pamphlets as well as church meetings or, for that matter, political rallies. Of course, peer-group talk had picked up catchwords or phrases whether people chatted with drinking buddies, family, or kinsmen, or with the guys from the neighborhood (or among women with one's *Kaffeeklatsch*-friends). Levenstein himself relied on terms and rhetorical figures shaped by the debates of his time. While the idea of "moral statistics" began waning around 1900, people began to put emphasis on matters psychic. However, feelings and their emotional expression still remained marginal. In the effort to reveal the psychic dynamics of man, emotions appeared as surfaces to be decoded; they would refer to an underlying truth of people's "personae" if not of the societal structure, or of both.

What is missing in Levenstein's survey is the respective context of those who jotted down their toil, sacrifice, or indulgence and thus also referred to anxieties or rage as well as hopes or longings. In order to situate these articulations of feelings, one ought to get a clearer picture of both life courses and situational interactions in workshops and neighborhoods.

Joy of Working and Workers' Pride

Regarding life courses, autobiographical accounts of working people are rare but telling. To be sure, the autobiographical mold requires the author to present him- or herself as having mastered various adventures. Accordingly, he or she is well advised to display certain weaknesses or even previous misdeeds or, for that matter, emotional outbursts as long as they are clearly put "behind". In narrating such situations the author, then, shows that she or he has "learned" from the past. Reflective distance to strong emotions of former times enhances such claims of "having come of age" and forming a mature personality.

The few examples of autobiographical writings from those of working-class backgrounds mention and, in fact, display feelings. Here one finds feelings of attachment to mates and kin. At the same time, though, antipathy if not hatred of "them" are clearly articulated.

Theodor Bromme, for instance, a turner working for more than twenty years in metal workshops, described some of his mates as "devils" in his autobiography, in 1905: he was only too glad if they were out of sight, or if he could avoid them otherwise.[29] Still, these remarks are brief and rare. Such accounts were consistent with the code of collegial behavior on the shop floor. Recognition of ones mates required dexterity and reliability where working as well as seclusiveness towards superiors and bosses. Speed, rhythm, and a "good eye" were considered crucial to workers' daily practice. Only by performing well on these scores were workers able to retrieve or to protect time and space at the very point of production.

Working people sought to conceal the actual site of their labors from any examination by the bosses. Hence, pride about successful appropriation triggered joy; in turn, joy fueled pride about oneself and, not the least, one's product. Whether such experiences contributed to a long-term "build-up" of emotions, then also available in other arenas, is the focus of the following sections.

Work after 1918: Ultimate Resort for "Germanness"

Prior to 1914, German-built steamships had won the Blue Ribbon crossing the Atlantic; zeppelins designed and assembled in a German plant had in the air visually demonstrated "German craftsmanship" and engineering capabilities as well. During World War I, German long-distance artillery bombarding Paris, or the *"Dicke Bertha"* (a high-caliber howitzer referring by its very nickname to the major industrial armament complex in Germany owned by Bertha Krupp) demonstrated to friend and foe that "German quality work" was upheld, seemingly invincible in times of war.

However, at the same time misery in the trenches and hunger on the home front raised bitterness, which occasionally turned into rage.[30] Yet, such emotions did not dominate totally. At the same time people encountered—or produced—other feelings, too. Letters to and from wives, parents, or fiancées displayed pride, showing at least confidence in one's own capability to master hard times. These were not feelings that burst out loud; in contrast, they were rather subdued. Thus, they informed and shaped the intensity of people's behavior more in subtle ways. The furor of skillfully operating a lathe or a machine gun originated in the similarity of both practices.[31]

After World War I emotions of uncertainty (about endangered German superiority) as well as feelings of pride (about one's accomplishments) lost a major arena: the military battlefield. But already in 1919 authors pointed to an alternative: work would now be the only arena in which to fight the enemy and reestablish both individual and the nation's "honor".[32] This was certainly a terrain many Germans across the divides of class considered a particularly proper one. From now on, all energies of individuals and the assumed national collective had to be shifted to this new battleground, the "field of work".[33] Until 1923 masses of German workers (including revolutionaries of 1918) rallied to defend the fatherland against what to them were encroaching barbarians, whether these were *"Welsche"* (non-Germans, like Italians or French) or Russians or German Bolsheviks; African troops of the Allies or "Slaves" in the East or "Communists" within. In the years to follow, especially in the mid-1920s, German industry recovered and gained competitive strength; its output and profits boomed. Many of those workers who had employment saw slowly rising wages. Skilled workers, however, had to confront shrinking opportunities as managers increasingly relied on semiskilled hands. Of course, to the latter, rationalization meant more and better paid jobs.[34]

In contrast, the wider public increasingly tended to explicitly honor workers, not differentiating between skilled or semiskilled. Publications dwelt on photographs of male workers displaying dexterity as icons of "German quality work"; in fact, publishers used that media which itself was turning into an icon of modernity. Finished objects, machine tools, and workers were designed as representations of both modern industry and the nation. To be sure, depictions of fuming smoke stacks and shining machinery or their polished products closely resonated with the imagery of industry at the same time publicized and employed in the United States, France, or, for that matter, in the Soviet Union.

Articulations of emotions of pride centered on work can be traced elsewhere. Let us try a view from the margin. Skilled workers migrated from Germany to the Soviet Union in the late 1920s and early 1930s. Here, they saw job opportunities while the economy at home slumped. Some of these migrants were, of course, mostly driven by a commitment to socialism and communism. Their letters to the Moscow German-language daily newspaper *Deutsche Zentral-Zeitung* did, however, reflect mixed experiences.[35] Their accounts testify not only of individual distaste of the new environment in general but, even more, to feelings of increased bitterness and national cleavage revolving around the denial of respect and honor by their Russian mates.

One of these German workers in the USSR, Fritz Löw, wrote on 30 March 1933 to the editors. He told an appalling story of permanent harassment or, at least, improper treatment by superiors and mates alike. Suffering from hunger, he had, as he put it, still proposed improvements. For instance, the bosses of this locomotive factory had turned down his proposal to redesign the carts used to transport heavy objects. With his proposed cart, the object's weight was centered on the axle and the wheels, while the existing carts shifted all the weight on the worker who maneuvered it.

As Löw put it, Russians and especially those who called themselves technicians or engineers had turned down this idea. How could a "simple worker" claim to have better ideas than themselves? Löw added: "Our proposals are no inventions from thin air; they resemble practical experiences from Germany. The others [Russians] do not come by to ask for explanations. This they would consider dishonorable." (*Man hält dies unter seiner Würde.*) Bitterness and anger emerged among many of these Germans. In the end, a considerable number of them returned to Germany, even after the Nazi seizure of power.

Work in Fascism: "The Masses Can Express Themselves"?[36]

Tim Mason has argued that workers in Germany did nothing but pursue their wage interests when they staged or threatened industrial action during the armament boom after 1935–36. Workers pressed for better wages by industrial sabotage or undeclared strike. Still, the statement of a contemporary observer from the illegal SPD gives the gist of such activities beyond the shop floor: "The masses [more precisely: the proletarian masses, A.L.] remain quiet and accept everything."[37]

However, it was not just the glamour of the new powers that lulled those who, in the eyes of both socialist organizers and the Gestapo, were supposed to revolt. But the range of symbolical and material gratifications offered by the Nazis triggered or gave license to feelings of satisfaction (if not happiness) among "common people" in Germany.[38] The longing for "now being respected as a working man and, thus, as a human being" could be satisfied, at least once in awhile.

Such occasions could resonate with other encounters—such as the one a French intellectual staying in Frankfurt am Main in 1935–36 reported in his diary. Denis de Rougemont, thirty years of age, worked as a language teacher. He attended a Nazi rally on 11 March 1936 in a local assembly hall: "A floodlight focuses on a small man in brown clothes who appears at the entrance ecstatically smiling. Forty thousand people, forty thousand arms rose in one single movement. Slowly the man advances saluting the masses in slow movements like a bishop while the shouts of the people roar like thunder." He also observes the people around him: "They are standing upright and shout rhythmically and in a chorus, their eyes being fixated on this lighted dot in the distance, on this face smiling, while many are in tears watching him." Observing his own feelings, de Rougemont sees himself "rolled over" and "overpowered". To him this is a "sacred ceremony" exercising force that he feels is stronger than the collective body of tight bodies surrounding him. But looking around, he finds himself among ordinary people: "workers, labor service men, young girls and women from working-class background".[39]

Other recollections or reports refer to a wide and heterogeneous spectrum of feelings and emotions. The women interviewed by Margarete Doerr (1998) still mention feelings of embarrassment and "shame" while recalling such past situations and behaviors. Although some of them do recall irritation at the time, they recall turning away and going on to cooperate with or support the powers that be—they could not stand the anxiety of being disconnected from what they felt as an "embracing whole".

Melita Maschmann, born in 1918 and after 1938 employed by the compulsory "Association of Girls" (*Bund Deutscher Mädel, BDM*), reported in the late 1950s how she did cleanse her mind of perceptions of brutality against Jews she observed on 10 November 1938 in the streets of Berlin. She tried to tame the horror and shame about the brutalities by envisioning "the Germans" involved in a military struggle and herself as an active participant driven by a mixture of sacrifice and self-indulgence. Hence, she diagnoses "devotion" (*Hingabe*) as that highly charged attitude driving her until the very end of Nazism to ever new, excessive engagements and enormous workloads.[40]

In 1935, only some months prior to the March 1936 episode at Frankfurt mentioned above, Walter Benjamin had emphasized in his Paris exile that fascism would deny people their rights but did allow "the masses to express themselves".[41]

Warfaring as Working: Pleasures of Destruction?

Letters of soldiers have become an important source of understanding the ways of acceptance and corporation by which most Germans coped with Nazism and World War II. Particularly telling are those letters of soldiers who had been drafted or volunteered for the Wehrmacht from an industrial-proletarian background. Many of these soldiers wrote to their former employers: they expressed gratitude for occasional parcels, especially at Christmas; some of them wrote regularly. Here, the company or some particular person there was made part of, if not substituted for, this person's family. I draw on letters of workers/soldiers from Leipzig and Chemnitz respectively. These soldiers explicitly described striking similarities between industrial work and military service or military work. In other words, they felt in a specific way more "at home" with many of their comrades who had been recruited from other backgrounds.

To be sure, the role of the military is to prepare for killing. And if it comes to battle, the danger of being killed is imminent as is the likelihood that one might kill or wound others. The emotions of this setting were rarely articulated in these letters. Still, people often displayed a specific humor when it came to the ever-present dangers of soldiering. In September 1944 an Allied airplane had shot at a soldier stationed at the home front not far from the city of Chemnitz where he used to live and work. The bullet missed him by only a few meters—in his letter he dryly added that a long distance (referring to the distance between home and those serving in Russia or Italy, for example) is not a prerequisite for being killed in war. In the very same letter the author gave details about a hunt for "Russians", obviously escaped *Ostarbeiter.* The soldier explicitly delved into the joy of seeing these escapees trembling upon being caught.

Other previous employees now drafted sent letters to this company as well. A young woman had been conscripted (*dienstverpflichtet*) in early 1943; now she worked as a secretary for a member of the ordinance corps in the *Generalgouvernement.*[42] Some days prior, a "bandit" or a partisan had killed this man who had also previously cooperated with her at the Chemnitz company. She writes of her horror and sorrow. But in the very next sentence she adds: "His death causes a lot of extra work—although we got a new person to take over his job, this one has to get adjusted. … Nevertheless I enjoy very much my task (*Einsatz*), and I am almost ready to say that I do not want to come home now. Still I am truly fine."[43]

Concluding Remark

In the later nineteenth and early twentieth centuries, theoreticians from different viewpoints considered societal transformation as a shift from prerational to rational or from premodern to modern. In their everyday, however, people continued to intricately connect expressions of their emotions with the pursuit of their interests. Thus, the emotional was and remained interrelated with rational modes of orientation and practice. Put differently, the strivings of historical actors to become "modern" may have changed but did not erase their emotionality.

Still, the very wording of people's utterances may read to later observers and historians as devoid of any emotional charge. Must one, then, conclude that historical actors either had lost or never harbored or even sensed feelings? Or is it us, the observers in hindsight—are we blind or deaf and operate without the proper senses to detect the traces of past feelings and to unveil their specific features and moments of singularity?

Only contextualization on the microlevel can decode such realms of respective meaning(s). If the texts historians try to mine preserve "emotives" (Reddy) of and among historical actors, the focus might be put particularly on people's practices, whether verbal or physical. Hence, at the center of further explorations should be the specific configurations of practices and expressions that allowed for but may also have suppressed or silenced people's feelings.

For instance, how, to what extent, and in which rhythms did people change their treatment of both their environment and their task when confronted with tacit reminders or outright demands for "German quality work"? And more generally: Did people take note of or even entice emotional charges that might have "flavored" their very strivings for accomplishing a "good job" or their efforts to shy away from tasks? Such focus on the multiple worlds of behavior demands a sensitive eye for every trace of feelings. At any rate, it would trigger a move to bring back emotions to the agenda and work of historians. Foremost, however, such a wide angle could boost a sense of and for history among the historical actors at large.

Notes

1. Alf Lüdtke, "What is the History of Everyday Life and Who are its Practitioners?" in *The History of Everyday Life: Reconstructing Historical Experiences and Ways of Life*, ed. A. Lüdtke (Princeton, NJ: Princeton University Press, 1995), 3–40.
2. See on this the succinct assessment by B. H. Rosenwein, "Worrying About Emotions in History," *American Historical Review* 107 (2002): 821–45, esp. 826ff.
3. Anglo-Marxist works are prominent examples, for instance E. P. Thompson, *The Making of the English Working Class* (London: Penguin, 1963); E. Hobsbawm, *Labouring Men: Studies in the History of Labour* (London: Weidenfeld & Nicolson, 1972); E. Hobsbawm, *Worlds of Labour: Further Studies in the History of Labour* (London: Weidenfeld & Nicolson, 1984); for the United States see: D. Montgomery, *Workers' Control in America:*

Studies in the History of Work, Technology, and Labor Struggles (Cambridge: Cambridge University Press, 1979) and H. Gutman, *The Black Family in Slavery and Freedom: 1750–1925* (Oxford: Blackwell, 1976). For the second and third generation of researchers, see for instance in England, P. Joyce, *Work, Society, and Politics. The Culture of the Factory in Later Victorian England* (Brighton: Harvester Press, 1980); D. Vincent: *Poor Citizens: The State and the Poor in Twentieth-Century Britain* (London: Longman, 1991); for the United States see D. Roediger, *The Wages of Whiteness: Race and the Making of the American Working Class*, 2nd ed. (London: Verso, 1999).

4. G. Diewald-Kerkmann, *Politische Denunziation im NS-Regime—oder die kleine Macht der "Volksgenossen"* (Bonn: Dietz, 1995); R. Gellately, *The Gestapo and German Society: Enforcing Racial Policy, 1933–1945* (Oxford: Clarendon, 1990); G. Paul and K. Mallmann, eds., *Die Gestapo: Mythos und Realität* (Darmstadt: Wissenschaftliche Buchgesellschaft, 1995); for a comparative view see S. Fitzpatrick and R. Gellately, eds., *Accusatory Practices: Denunciation in Modern European History, 1789–1989* (Chicago: University of Chicago Press, 1997); A. Lüdtke and G. Fürmetz, eds., *Denunzianten in der Neuzeit: Politische Teilnahme oder Selbstüberwachung?* (Seelze: Friedrich, 1998); I. Marszolek, ed., *Denunziation im 20. Jahrhundert: Zwischen Komparatistik und Interdisziplinarität* (Cologne: Zentrum für Historische Sozialforschung, 2001).
5. See the exemplary study of C. Browning, *Ordinary Men: Reserve Police Battalion 101 and the Final Solution in Poland* (New York: HarperCollins, 1992).
6. H. Lethen, *Cool Conduct: The Culture of Distance in Weimar Germany* (Berkeley: University of California Press, 2002), German edition *Verhaltenslehre der Kälte: Lebensversuche zwischen den Kriegen* (Frankfurt am Main: Suhrkamp, 1994).
7. On functional elites: M. Wildt, *Generation des Unbedingten. Das Führungskorps des Reichssicherheitshauptamtes* (Hamburg: Hamburger Ed., 2002); U. Herbert, *Best: Biographische Studien über Radikalismus, Weltanschauung und Vernunft, 1903–1989* (Bonn: Dietz, 1996).
8. D. de Rougemont, *Journal aus Deutschland, 1935–1936* (Berlin: Aufbau Taschenbuch Verlag, 2001), 55f.
9. I. Kershaw, *The "Hitler Myth": Image and Reality in the Third Reich* (Oxford: Clarendon Press, 1987); cf. K. Mallmann and G. Paul, *Herrschaft und Alltag: ein Industrierevier im Dritten Reich* (Bonn: Dietz, 1991).
10. On cultural practices of "normalizing" cooperation with fascism and warfaring as work: A. Lüdtke, *Eigen-Sinn. Fabrikalltag, Arbeitererfahrungen und Politik vom Kaiserreich bis in den Faschismus* (Hamburg: Ergebniss Verlag, 1993), 283ff, 406ff; A. Lüdtke, "What Happened to the 'Fiery Red Glow'?" in Lüdtke, *History of Everyday Life*, 198–251. Cf. the collage from letters and diaries composed by the literary author W. Kempowski, *Das Echolot: Ein kollektives Tagebuch—Januar und Februar 1943* (Munich: Knaus, 1993); W. Kempowski, *Das Echolot: Fuga Furiosa—Winter 1945* (Munich: Knaus, 1999).
11. On the assumption of "emotional detachment", in this view characterizing "many of the Nazis' murderous thoughts and deeds", see D. F. Lindenfeld, "The Prevalence of Irrational Thinking in the Third Reich: Notes Toward the Reconstruction of Modern Value Rationality", *Central European History* 30 (1997): 365–85, esp. 370.
12. V. Klemperer, *Ich will Zeugnis ablegen bis zum letzten, Tagebücher I, II* (Berlin: Aufbau Verlag, 1995).
13. H.-U. Wehler, *Das deutsche Kaiserreich: 1871–1918*, 7th ed. (Göttingen: Vandenhoeck und Ruprecht, 1994); W. J. Mommsen, *Die Urkatastrophe Deutschlands. Der Erste Weltkrieg 1914–1918* (Stuttgart: Klett-Cotta, 2002); for a contrast see J. Radkau, *Das Zeitalter der Nervosität. Deutschland zwischen Bismarck und Hitler* (Darmstadt: Wissenschaftliche Buchgesellschaft, 1998).

14. P. N. Stearns and C. Z. Stearns, "Emotionology: Clarifying the History of Emotions and Emotional Standards", *American Historical Review* 90 (1985): 813–36; see the update J. Lewis and P. N. Stearns, "Introduction", in *An Emotional History of the United States,* ed. J. Lewis and P. N. Stearns (New York: New York University Press, 1998), 1–14. Here the authors attribute recent elaborations of the basic contructivist line Stearns and Stearns had emphasized to the impact of what academic short-shrift presents as "cultural turn"; in their reading the conventional claim of, for instance, psychologists that emotions pertain to the realm of nature is overcome by historicizing the categories of such analyses.
15. The neurobiologist Antonio Damasio makes the important distinction between a small number of background "emotions" and multiple "feelings" that he portrays as operating independently but in resonance to both each other and the "background" emotions. See his *The Feeling of What Happens* (London: Vintage, 2000).
16. A. Corbin, *Le monde retrouvé de Louis-François Pinagot* (Paris: Flammarion, 1998), German edition: *Auf den Spuren eines Unbekannten: ein Historiker rekonstruiert ein ganz gewöhnliches Leben* (Frankfurt: Campus-Verlag, 1999), 63f.
17. M. Kessel, "Balance der Gefühle. Langeweile im 19. Jahrhundert", *Historische Anthropologie* 4 (1996): 234–55; see also M. Kessel, *Langeweile. Zum Umgang mit Zeit und Gefühlen in Deutschland vom späten 18. bis zum frühen 20. Jahrhundert* (Göttingen: Wallstein Verlag, 2001).
18. Peter Gay has masterfully demonstrated the richness of such material for explorations of emotions and feelings in his *The Tender Passion* (New York: Oxford University Press, 1986).
19. W. M. Reddy, *The Navigation of Feeling: A Framework for the History of Emotions* (Cambridge: Cambridge University Press, 2001), 110f; for the following ibid., 108.
20. Cf. W. M. Reddy, "Sentimentalism and Its Erasure: The Role of Emotions in the Era of the French Revolution", *Journal of Modern History* 72 (2000): 113ff.
21. A. Levenstein, *Die Arbeiterfrage—mit besonderer Berücksichtigung der sozialpsychologischen Seite des modernen Großbetriebes und der psycho-physischen Einwirkungen auf die Arbeiter* (Munich: Reinhardt, 1912), 46.
22. H. Medick, *Weben und Überleben in Laichingen,* 2nd ed. (Göttingen: Vandenhoeck & Ruprecht, 1997), caption of photograph no. 7, between 264–65.
23. A rare exception is Leora Auslander, "Perceptions of Beauty and the Problem of Consciousness: Parisian Furniture Makers", in *Rethinking Labor History: Essays on Discourse and Class Analysis,* ed. L. R. Berlanstein (Urbana: University of Illinois Press, 1993), 149–81.
24. See, for instance, the works of social historians Charles, Louise, and Richard Tilly respectively (including their collective study *The Rebellious Century, 1830–1930* [Cambridge, MA: Harvard University Press, 1975]). As rich as these studies are, the authors categorize people's behavior solely along the line of "rational" vs. "irrational".
25. Levenstein, *Die Arbeiterfrage;* Levenstein had sent out his questionnaire in 1909.
26. Ibid., 405.
27. See also the thorough empirical investigations focusing on single factories in different branches of industry conducted by Alfred and Max Weber under the auspices of the *"Verein für Socialpolitik"* and published in several volumes between 1910 and 1913; cf. W. Schluchter, ed., *Zur Psychophysik der industriellen Arbeit: Schriften und Reden 1908–1912, Max Weber Gesamtausgabe I,* vol. 11 (Tübingen: Mohr (Siebeck), 1995).
28. Levenstein, *Die Arbeiterfrage,* 406.
29. M. Th. W. Bromme, *Lebensgeschichte eines modernen Fabrikarbeiters* (Frankfurt: Athenaeum Verlag, 1971 [1905]), 282; cf. Levenstein, *Die Arbeiterfrage,* 97, 129.

30. B. Davis, *Home Fires Burning: Food, Politics, and Everyday Life in World War I Berlin* (Chapel Hill: University of North Carolina Press, 2000); F. Schumann, ed., *"Zieh' Dich warm an!" Soldatenpost und Heimatbriefe aus zwei Weltkriegen. Chronik einer Familie* (Berlin: Verlag Neues Leben, 1989).
31. Even those who deserted in the midst of the disintegration of the German army since the spring of 1918, such as Dominik Richert, refer to feelings of satisfaction if not joy as to warfaring in their reports: feelings they experienced before deserting. See Dominik Richert, *Beste Gelegenheit zum Sterben: meine Erlebnisse im Kriege 1914–1918,* ed. A. Tramitz and B. Ulrich (Munich: Knesebeck & Schuler, 1989); see on the army's disintegration since spring 1918 W. Deist, "Verdeckter Militärstreik im Kriegsjahr 1918?" in *Der Krieg des kleinen Mannes: eine Militärgeschichte von unten,* ed. W. Wette (Munich: Piper, 1992), 146–67.
32. H. Pankow, *Vom Felde der Arbeit* (Leipzig: Dürr, 1920).
33. The furor of antibolshevik "Freicorps," as well as military activists of the Red Army in the Ruhrgebiet 1919–20 reflected, among others, feelings of hurt or endangered manhood. See on this in particular K. Theweleit, *Männerphantasien,* vols. I and II (Reinbek bei Hamburg: Rowohlt, 1980), English edition: *Male Phantasies* (Cambridge: Polity Press, 1987).
34. Cf. on this my piece "'Deutsche Qualitätsarbeit', 'Spielereien' am Arbeitsplatz und 'Fliehen' aus der Fabrik: industrielle Arbeitsprozesse und Arbeiterverhalten in den 1920er Jahren—Aspekte eines offenen Forschungsfeldes", in *Arbeiterkulturen zwischen Alltag und Politik,* ed. F. Boll (Vienna: Europa Verlag, 1986), 155–97.
35. GARF Moscow, Fonds 5451, Inventar 39, file 100 (1).
36. This section relies on my essay "Love of State—Love of Authority: The Politics of Mass Participation in the Twentieth Century," in *New Dangerous Liaisons,* ed. L. Passerini (New York: Berghahn Books, forthcoming).
37. Deutschland-Berichte der Sozialdemokratischen Partei Deutschlands (Sopade) 1934–1940, vol. 2 (1935), 355ff and vol. 4 (1937), 234f, 1238f, 1747, (Frankfurt am Main: 2001 [1980]).
38. See on the range of these efforts by the Nazi agencies my essays "What Happened to the 'Fiery Red Glow'?" in Lüdtke, *History of Everyday Life,* 198–251, and "The 'Honor of Labor': Industrial Workers and the Power of Symbols Under National Socialism," in *Nazism and German Society, 1933–1945,* ed. D. Crew (London: Routledge, 1994), 67–109.
39. Rougemont, *Journal aus Deutschland,* 65.
40. M. Maschmann, *Fazit: kein Rechtfertigungsversuch*, 4th ed. (Stuttgart, Deutsche Verlags-Anstalt, 1963).
41. W. Benjamin, "Das Kunstwerk im Zeitalter seiner technischen Reproduzierbarkeit" (2nd version), in *Gesammelte Schriften,* vol. I/2 (Frankfurt am Main: Suhrkamp, 1974), 471–508, 506.
42. This being the part of Poland that had not been incorporated into the Reich but merely designated as a colony and, in fact, the site of the Holocaust.
43. Sächsisches Staatsarchiv Chemnitz, Günter und Haussner, 260/261, 12 February 1944.

Bibliography

Auslander, Leora. "Perceptions of Beauty and the Problem of Consciousness: Parisian Furniture Makers." In *Rethinking Labor History: Essays on Discourse and Class Analysis,* edited by L. R. Berlanstein. Urbana: University of Illinois Press, 1993.

Benjamin, Walter. "Das Kunstwerk im Zeitalter seiner technischen Reproduzierbarkeit." 2nd version. In *Gesammelte Schriften,* vol. I/2, 471–508. Frankfurt am Main: Suhrkamp, 1974.

Bromme, Moritz Th. W. *Lebensgeschichte eines modernen Fabrikarbeiters.* Frankfurt: Athenaeum Verlag, 1971 (1905).

Browning, Christopher. *Ordinary Men: Reserve Police Battalion 101 and the Final Solution in Poland.* New York: HarperCollins, 1992.

Corbin, Alain. *Le monde retrouvé de Louis-François Pinagot.* Paris: Flammarion, 1998; German edition: *Auf den Spuren eines Unbekannten: ein Historiker rekonstruiert ein ganz gewöhnliches Leben.* Frankfurt and New York: Campus-Verlag, 1999.

Damasio, Antonio. *The Feeling of What Happens.* London: Vintage, 2000.

Davis, Belinda. *Home Fires Burning: Food, Politics, and Everyday Life in World War I Berlin.* Chapel Hill: University of North Carolina Press, 2000.

Deist, Wilhelm. "Verdeckter Militärstreik im Kriegsjahr 1918?" In *Der Krieg des kleinen Mannes: Eine Militärgeschichte von unten,* edited by Wolfram Wette, 146–67. Munich: Piper, 1992.

Deutschland-Berichte der Sozialdemokratischen Partei Deutschlands (Sopade) 1934–1940. Vols. 2 (1935) and 4 (1937). Frankfurt am Main: 2001 (1980).

Diewald-Kerkmann, Gisela. *Politische Denunziation im NS-Regime—oder die kleine Macht der "Volksgenossen."* Bonn: Dietz, 1995.

Doerr, Margarete. *"Wer die Zeit nicht miterlebt hat...": Frauenerfahrungen im Zweiten Weltkrieg und in den Jahren danach.* 3 vols. Frankfurt am Main: Campus, 1998.

Fitzpatrick, Sheila and Robert Gellately, eds. *Accusatory Practices: Denunciation in Modern European History, 1789–1989.* Chicago: University of Chicago Press, 1997.

Gay, Peter. *The Tender Passion.* New York: Oxford University Press, 1986.

Gellately, Robert. *The Gestapo and German Society: Enforcing Racial Policy, 1933–1945.* Oxford: Clarendon, 1990.

Gutman, Herbert. *The Black Family in Slavery and Freedom: 1750–1925.* Oxford: Blackwell, 1976.

Herbert, Ulrich. *Best: Biographische Studien über Radikalismus, Weltanschauung und Vernunft, 1903–1989.* Bonn: Dietz, 1996.

Hobsbawm, Eric. *Worlds of Labour: Further Studies in the History of Labour.* London: Weidenfeld & Nicolson, 1984.

———. *Labouring Men: Studies in the History of Labour.* London: Weidenfeld & Nicolson, 1972.

Joyce, Patrick. *Work, Society, and Politics: The Culture of the Factory in Later Victorian England.* Brighton: Harvester Press, 1980.

Kempowski, Walter. *Das Echolot: Ein kollektives Tagebuch—Januar und Februar 1943.* Munich: Knaus, 1993.

———. *Das Echolot: Fuga Furiosa—Winter 1945.* Munich: Knaus, 1999.

Kershaw, Ian. *The "Hitler Myth": Image and Reality in the Third Reich.* Oxford: Clarendon Press, 1987.

Kessel, Martina. "Balance der Gefühle: Langeweile im 19. Jahrhundert." *Historische Anthropologie* 4 (1996): 234–55.

———. *Langeweile: Zum Umgang mit Zeit und Gefühlen in Deutschland vom späten 18. bis zum frühen 20. Jahrhundert.* Göttingen: Wallstein-Verlag, 2001.

Klemperer, Victor. *Ich will Zeugnis ablegen bis zum letzten: Tagebücher I, II* (Berlin: Aufbau Verlag, 1995.

Lethen, Helmut. *Cool Conduct: The Culture of Distance in Weimar Germany* (Berkeley: University of California Press, 2002; German edition: *Verhaltenslehren der Kälte: Lebensversuche zwischen den Kriegen.* Frankfurt am Main: Suhrkamp, 1994.

Levenstein, Adolf. *Die Arbeiterfrage—mit besonderer Berücksichtigung der sozialpsychologischen Seite des modernen Großbetriebes und der psycho-physischen Einwirkungen auf die Arbeiter.* Munich: Reinhardt, 1912.

Lewis, Jan and Peter N. Stearns. "Introduction." In *An Emotional History of the United States,* edited by J. Lewis and P. N. Stearns, 1–14. New York: New York University Press, 1998.

Lindenfeld, David F. "The Prevalence of Irrational Thinking in the Third Reich: Notes Toward the Reconstruction of Modern Value Rationality." *Central European History* 30 (1997): 365–85.

Lüdtke, Alf. "'Deutsche Qualitätsarbeit', 'Spielereien' am Arbeitsplatz und 'Fliehen' aus der Fabrik: industrielle Arbeitsprozesse und Arbeiterverhalten in den 1920er Jahren—Aspekte eines offenen Forschungsfeldes." In *Arbeiterkulturen zwischen Alltag und Politik,* edited by F. Boll, 155–97. Vienna: Europa-Verlag, 1986.

———. *Eigen-Sinn. Fabrikalltag, Arbeitererfahrungen und Politik vom Kaiserreich bis in den Faschismus.* Hamburg: Ergebnisse, 1993.

———. "The 'Honor of Labor': Industrial Workers and the Power of Symbols Under National Socialism." In *Nazism and German Society, 1933–1945,* edited by D. Crew, 67–109. London: Routledge, 1994.

———. "What is the History of Everyday Life and Who are Its Practitioners?" In *The History of Everyday Life: Reconstructing Historical Experiences and Ways of Life,* edited by A. Lüdtke, 3–40. Princeton, NJ: Princeton University Press, 1995.

———. "What Happened to the 'Fiery Red Glow'?" In *The History of Everyday Life: Reconstructing Historical Experiences and Ways of Life,* edited by A. Lüdtke, 198–251. Princeton, NJ: Princeton University Press, 1995.

Lüdtke, Alf and Gerhard Fürmetz, eds. *Denunzianten in der Neuzeit: Politische Teilnahme oder Selbstüberwachung?* Seelze: Friedrich, 1998.

Mallmann, Klaus and Gerhard Paul. *Herrschaft und Alltag: ein Industrierevier im Dritten Reich.* Bonn: Dietz, 1991.

Marszolek, Inge, ed. *Denunziation im 20. Jahrhundert: Zwischen Komparatistik und Interdisziplinarität.* Cologne: Zentrum für Historische Sozialforschung, 2001.

Maschmann, Melita. *Fazit: kein Rechtfertigungsversuch.* 4th ed. Stuttgart, Deutsche Verlags-Anstalt, 1963.

Medick, Hans. *Weben und Überleben in Laichingen.* 2nd ed. Göttingen: Vandenhoeck & Ruprecht, 1997.

Mommsen, Wolfgang J. *Die Urkatastrophe Deutschlands: Der Erste Weltkrieg 1914–1918.* Stuttgart: Klett-Cotta, 2002.

Montgomery, David. *Workers' Control in America: Studies in the History of Work, Technology, and Labor Struggles.* Cambridge: Cambridge University Press, 1979.

Pankow, Herrmann. *Vom Felde der Arbeit.* Leipzig: Dürr, 1920.

Paul, Gerhard and Klaus Mallmann, eds. *Die Gestapo: Mythos und Realität.* Darmstadt: Wissenschaftliche Buchgesellschaft, 1995.

Radkau, Joachim. *Das Zeitalter der Nervosität. Deutschland zwischen Bismarck und Hitler.* Darmstadt: Wissenschaftliche Buchgesellschaft, 1998.

Reddy, William M. *The Navigation of Feeling: A Framework for the History of Emotions.* Cambridge: Cambridge University Press, 2001.

———. "Sentimentalism and Its Erasure: The Role of Emotions in the Era of the French Revolution." *The Journal of Modern History* 72 (2000): 109–52.

Richert, Dominik, *Beste Gelegenheit zum Sterben: Meine Erlebnisse im Kriege 1914–1918,* ed. A. Tramitz and B. Ulrich. Munich: Knesebeck & Schuler, 1989.

Roediger, David. *The Wages of Whiteness: Race and the Making of the American Working Class.* 2nd ed. London: Verso, 1999.

Rosenwein, Barbara H. "Worrying About Emotions in History." *American Historical Review* 107 (2002): 821–45.

Rougemont, Denis de. *Journal aus Deutschland, 1935–1936.* Berlin: Aufbau Taschenbuch Verlag, 2001.

Schluchter, Wolfgang, ed. *Zur Psychophysik der industriellen Arbeit: Schriften und Reden 1908–1912, Max Weber Gesamtausgabe I.* Vol. 11. Tübingen: Mohr, Siebeck, 1995.

Schumann, Frank, ed. *"Zieh' Dich warm an!" Soldatenpost und Heimatbriefe aus zwei Weltkriegen: Chronik einer Familie.* Berlin: Verlag Neues Leben, 1989.

Stearns, Peter N. and Carol Z. Stearns. "Emotionology: Clarifying the History of Emotions and Emotional Standards." *American Historical Review* 90 (1985): 813–36.

Theweleit, Klaus. *Männerphantasien.* Vols. I and II. Reinbek bei Hamburg: Rowohlt, 1980; English edition: *Male Phantasies.* Cambridge: Polity Press, 1987.

Thompson, Edward P. *The Making of the English Working Class.* London: Penguin, 1963.

Tilly, Charles, Louise Tilly, and Richard Tilly. *The Rebellious Century, 1830–1930.* Cambridge, MA: Harvard University Press, 1975.

Vincent, David. *Poor Citizens: The State and the Poor in Twentieth-Century Britain.* London: Longman, 1991.

Wehler, Hans-Ulrich. *Das deutsche Kaiserreich: 1871–1918,* 7th ed. Göttingen: Vandenhoeck und Ruprecht, 1994.

Wildt, Michael. *Generation des Unbedingten. Das Führungskorps des Reichssicherheitshauptamtes.* Hamburg: Hamburger Edition, 2002.

Emotions and War

Chapter 3

THE CORRUPTION OF CIVIC VIRTUE BY EMOTION

Anti-Imperialist Fears in the Debate on the Philippine-American War (1899–1902)

Fabian Hilfrich

THE SCHOLARLY ANALYSIS of the role of emotions in history has thus far mainly focused on the history *of* emotions, tracing the development and the changes of a certain emotion over time.[1] Much like recent psychosociological literature on the subject, these studies have shown that emotions are time- and culture-bound, that they are neither exclusively individual nor exclusively social, neither only cultural nor only natural. They depend on a "memory" of situation and circumstance, and their expression and manifestation can also be "socially constructed."[2]

In diplomatic history, however, emotions have thus far hardly figured as a matter of systematic scholarly interest, although they clearly have impacted foreign policy matters. Without the primary emotion of fear, for example, we can hardly appreciate the success of the superpowers' Cold War strategies or the relative success of the 1950s antinuclear movements in the Western world. Without the presence of fear or hate, some wars throughout history would seem unthinkable or at least unlikely. Quite obviously, in po-

Notes for this section begin on page 63.

litical discourse, policy makers have made extensive use of emotion management at the grassroots level to advance their strategic objectives.

This essay analyzes such argumentative strategies of instrumentalizing fears and examines the scare tactics of the so-called anti-imperialists in their fight against overseas expansion in the aftermath of the Spanish-American War of 1898. In general, the critics of empire warned that the policy they referred to as "imperialism" would inevitably undermine democratic institutions at home. While they focused primarily on the unconstitutionality of colonial rule and on the dangers "from above," namely, that of executive tyranny, they also offered another scenario of the destruction of democracy, namely "from the bottom up," by the people. Anti-imperialists believed that constant warfare and an atmosphere of crisis, deemed certain to follow an imperialist policy, would change the temper of the American people, at best distracting them from their civic duties and, at worst, increasing their aggressiveness to levels at which mob rule and revolution would be imminent.

The anti-imperialist portrayal of fear was important on two separate, yet closely interconnected levels. Arguably, the foreign policy critics tried to invoke fear of the decline of democracy in order to achieve the political end of obstructing overseas expansion. A closer analysis of their argument, however, reveals that these particular scare tactics could hardly have been designed to convince a majority of Americans because they were predicated on the insulting assumption that "the people," the sovereign of democratic government, were the gravest danger to its continued existence. Therefore, the argument is more appropriately read as a representation of the anti-imperialists' *own* fears rather than as scare tactics. More importantly, the fear of the people implicit in the antiexpansionist argument predated the fear of the negative consequences stemming from imperialism, and it actually existed quite independently of the foreign policy question at hand. From this fear, moreover, we can deduce the anti-imperialists' positive conception of popular government and gain insight into their social background, and into the audiences they most likely addressed—the latter two being observations that we would usually only gain from a thorough sociological analysis.

Hence, the analysis of emotions in anti-imperialist rhetoric takes a different approach than that usually taken by scholars who deal with emotions in history. It does not attempt to follow the development or the differences of a certain emotion over time, but rather focuses on one argument in a given historical context to gain insights into the anti-imperialist movement and the culture surrounding it.

Finally, it is important to note that the words *fear* and *emotion* are actually somewhat misplaced in this context. Emotions are usually described as immediate reactions to external events, and, as such, they are rather short-lived. The anti-imperialist fear of a decline of democratic government, whether prompted by imperialism or by even deeper root causes, was certainly not an emotion in that sense, but rather a mood or an "emotional disposition." Therefore, it would be more appropriate to replace the word *fear* by the German term *angst,* and it is only for purposes of legibility that fear is used more frequently throughout this study.

The Corrosive Effects of War (on the Human Psyche)

The "imperialism debate" around the end of the nineteenth century erupted in the wake of the Spanish-American War of 1898, prompted by the decision of Republican President William McKinley to acquire Puerto Rico, Cuba, and—most importantly—the Philippine Islands from Spain. As in most debates on American foreign policy, it quickly transcended the immediate policy questions, and the dispute between the so-called imperialists and anti-imperialists revolved around the heart of the United States' self-perception and character, in particular the question of whether the expansionist policies abroad corresponded to American ideals of democracy and morality.

In this context, the anti-imperialists warned that expansion abroad fundamentally contradicted democratic ideals and undermined democracy at home. In conjuring up their scenarios of an end of American democracy, the opponents of overseas expansion generally concentrated on the perceived abuses of power by the executive. They emphasized that the rule over subject territories was a purpose not envisioned by the Constitution and that the colonial practice would thus subvert this most hallowed of democratic institutions. When war broke out in the Philippines without Congress authorizing it either before or after the fact, the anti-imperialists warned that a tyrannical executive was already violating the separation of powers by waging an undeclared war. Underlying this phenomenological evidence was the conviction that colonial rule was logically incompatible with democracy, and that the requirements of the former would turn the United States into an empire, comparable to the monarchies of the Old World.

This brief summary of anti-imperialist thought indicates how much their overall argument relied on the element of striking fear into the hearts of their audience. In part, this reliance on fear, or scare tactics, was due to the specific discursive structure of the imperialism debate. The imperialists were proposing something deemed "novel," a more assertive and aggressive foreign policy that would even include at least the temporary annexation of foreign and densely populated territory. This position almost forced the imperialists to paint a positive picture and to emphasize the advantages of a departure from the presumably isolationist foreign policy of the nineteenth century. The anti-imperialists, on the other hand, were in a defensive or conservative position from the very beginning. They sought to convince their audiences to remain committed to the traditional course of foreign policy, and from this vantage point, it was only logical that they emphasized the dangers of empire.

In warning that imperialism would undermine democracy, the anti-imperialists not only perceived dangers arising from a tyrannical executive but also emphasized the possibly destructive effect of a public infatuated with imperial self-aggrandizement. Using metaphors of alcoholic intoxication, the opponents of territorial expansion warned of the "half-drunken condition into which war plunged about half the population"[3] already on the eve of the Spanish-American War. With all its promises of glory, sacrifice, and conquest, war could easily corrupt the spirit of a people at the grassroots level, just as an expansionist and belligerent executive could "militarize" the society from above. The enthusiastic popular response to the call to arms against Spain and the nationwide celebration of victory only seemed to confirm the anti-imperialists' worst fears. At the same time, the outbreak of war in the Philippines in February of 1899 seemed to prove the critics' claim that an imperialist policy would result in an endless series of armed conflicts. Hence, the "militarization" of the people's spirit would not be a fleeting phenomenon, but a constant feature of American society.

In detailed analyses the anti-imperialists outlined the detrimental impact of a belligerent mood on social relations. They maintained that war would corrupt the character of American soldiers stationed abroad, accustoming them to violence and brutality and thereby obstructing their reintegration into civilian life. In 1902, when news of torture and atrocities committed by American troops in the Philippines dominated public discussion in the United States, critics of empire found their worst predictions about the negative impact of war on the human character vindicated and heavily criticized the public for its complacency.[4]

In addition, discourses of race played a large role in the war and in its treatment at home. In this context, the anti-imperialists predicted that the war would instill in soldiers a feeling of racial superiority towards nonwhites in general. Such attitudes, the opponents of expansion insisted, would not only destroy the imperialist plans for a benevolent "civilizing" mission abroad, but—brought home in the soldiers' packs and transmitted by the media—would also obstruct the goal of integrating racial minorities in the United States. To prove their point, the anti-imperialist leagues across the country published a number of pamphlets with excerpts from soldiers' letters that were pervaded by racist prejudice.

The anti-imperialists did not believe that the brutalizing effects of war would be limited to the soldiers. Social reformer Jane Addams, for example, perceived a clear connection between the recent war against Spain and what she described as a brutalization of the society around her:

> The humane instinct, which keeps in abeyance the tendency to cruelty, the growing belief that the life of each human being—however hopeless or degraded, is still sacred—gives way, and the barbaric instinct asserts itself. It is doubtless only during a time of war that the men and women of Chicago could tolerate whipping for children in our city prison, and it is only during such a time that the introduction in the legislature of a bill for the re-establishment of the whipping post could be possible. National events determine our ideals, as much as our ideals determine national events.[5]

War, she intimated, was numbing the people toward the spectacle of violence in their own neighborhoods and violence became once again accepted as a solution to social ills. Other anti-imperialists attributed the upsurge in racially motivated lynching and recent Southern attempts to reinstitute white domination to the same popular attitudes and apathy presumably resulting from the "race war" in the Philippines. "This is not to be marveled at," commented Republican stalwart Senator George F. Hoar on Jim Crow measures in the South, "when the party of justice and freedom [the Republicans] is engaged in this unrighteous attempt to crush a people fighting for their freedom in the Eastern hemisphere."[6] On one level, then, war would simply rearrange the priorities of society and lead to a neglect of domestic ills and much-needed reforms. On another level, the anti-imperialists warned, violence abroad would also breed violence at home—or, at best, apathy towards it—thereby undermining social harmony and peace.

Underneath this phenomenological "evidence" of the negative impact of war on the public psyche was a much deeper fear that *all* popular passions, not only violent ones, were anathema to the democratic process as a whole. At some length, Georgia senator Augustus Bacon summarized society's brutalization resulting from war and the deep changes it wrought on popular attitudes toward democracy,

> not simply because [war] involves death and bloodshed, but because it accustoms our people and familiarizes them with scenes of violence and of blood; because it accustoms them to the idea of military rule rather than the peaceful agencies of civil government; because it weakens our reverence for and obedience to the great constitutional limitations which have been set up as the guardians of personal and political liberty.[7]

Applied to the examples chosen by Jane Addams, one could conclude that the anti-imperialists feared war would accustom the people to quick and irrational responses, to the view that impulsive and drastic reactions, rather than patient discourse and democratic decision making could serve as patent solutions to difficult problems. More than the immediate destructive effects of war, the anti-imperialists warned of its corrosive effects on the temper of the people, that it would arouse emotions that were difficult to tame. By its adverse impact on public temper and political discourse, war would not only negatively affect day-to-day relations and social harmony, but it would ultimately undermine the democratic order on the whole—and the people themselves, the core of democratic government, would act as its gravediggers.

Based on this premise, the anti-imperialists outlined a number of possible scenarios for the prophesied end of democracy—scenarios that once again involved the negative impact of emotions. In the most benign narrative, the people would be so distracted by the promise of glory and riches abroad that they would not even notice or care about the encroachments of a tyrannical executive upon their liberties, as long as it provided for the material well-being and the adventurism of an emotionalized society. Or they would actively hail (and elect) a military commander turned dictator, a new Caesar, because they would be more impressed with his military exploits than with a civilian's political, yet less flamboyant accomplishments. When a victorious Admiral Dewey returned from the Philippines, and when his potential fortunes as a presidential candidate were briefly discussed in public, some anti-imperialists felt that the people were ready to accept a military dictator.[8]

Alternatively, in a third scenario, some foreign-policy critics predicted a violent revolution and mob rule as a combined consequence of the brutalization of society and of the neglect of domestic ills that they were sure would follow an undue concentration on external matters. Proceeding on the assumption that imperialism would only benefit the few while taxing the many, the anti-imperialist William Lloyd Garrison, descendant of the famous abolitionist, openly evoked the specter of revolution: "When the duped people awake to a sense of their deception, how long will your puerile trade calculations and national glory pretenses prevent 'the whirlwind?'"[9]

The common denominator of these prophesies about a disruption of social harmony or the eventual destruction of democracy was their link to irrational and emotional behavior on the part of the people. In this argument war and imperialism would overwhelm rational thought and make the individual citizen violence-prone, unreflective, and emotional.

Anti-Imperialist Pessimism and Imperialist Optimism (Fear and Promise)

The potential mass appeal of this argument as a scare tactic must have been rather ineffectual, as none of the scenarios concerned the very survival of the country or possessed any of the individual and universal immediacy inherent in the fear of nuclear war, for example. If, as many psychologists claim, fear frequently results from the uncontrollable and the unknown,[10] then the anti-imperialist scare tactics appear even more puzzling because the audiences were invited to fear a known quantity (if one exempts, of course, the more modern notion of one's own psyche as the unknown), namely, themselves. The imperialist senator Albert J. Beveridge ingeniously picked up on this fundamental weakness of the anti-imperialist argument: "Militarism! Imperialism! Young men of America, will you strike your colors to a fear, and that fear a fear of yourselves? Your future is in your own hands."[11] More offensively even, the imperialists accused their opponents of committing "a slander against the American people" by questioning their instincts, while they themselves reiterated their "profoundest faith in the American people."[12] In imperialist rhetoric, fear had no place. Instead, proponents of empire assured their compatriots of their infinite capability to accomplish anything they set out do, to both uphold democracy and to rule subject populations abroad, and dismissed all scenarios by which anti-imperialists predicted a demise of American democracy. While the anti-imperialists implicitly insulted the people with their scare tactics, the imperialists praised them.

The "Antidemocratic" Origins of Anti-Imperialism

If it is therefore unlikely that the anti-imperialists devised their argument as calculated scare tactics with mass appeal, it might be more profitable to read it as an expression of their *own* fears and belief system. Viewed in this light, the fear of, or angst about uncontrollable popular passions yields important insights into most anti-imperialists' ideology, even into their social status and their prospective audiences.

First of all, we can deduce the anti-imperialists' positive understanding of democracy and its relation to emotions from their doomsday scenarios. They were first and foremost convinced that emotions had to be scrupulously kept out of the business of government. Politicians were supposed to avoid evoking popular emotions because these could easily get out of control and obstruct, if not destroy, the difficult process of democratic (deliberative) government. To Edwin Lawrence Godkin, editor of *The Nation,* the "hysteria" surrounding the Spanish-American War perfectly illustrated Gustave Le Bon's famous and devastating judgment on the psychology of the masses. Le Bon had essentially claimed that masses, once set in (e)motion, invariably behaved in an irrational and destructive manner and were impossible to stop by reason(ing).[13] While Godkin may have been the most pessimistic among anti-imperialists, many in this group shared the fear that it was particularly dangerous and detrimental to a democratic form of government to arouse popular emotions. Given this understanding of emotions in politics, incidentally, it appears all the more cynical that initially, in another, and arguably their most successful, argumentative strategy, many anti-imperialists deliberately instrumentalized widespread racial fears in their fight against colonial rule over the so-called inferior races.[14]

The anti-imperialist understanding of popular government was guided by a republican conception, which postulated a carefully calibrated and constantly threatened equilibrium not only between the different branches of government, but also between different forces in society. From the individual citizen, the republican order demanded the exercise of civic virtue, the reasoned and rational devotion of each individual to the ideals and institutions of the polity. In this context, Carl Schurz, for example, warned of the potentially corrosive and corrupting effect of war on civic virtue and morality: "War makes military heroes, but it makes civic cowards. No wonder that war has always proved so dangerous to the vitality of democracies, for a democracy needs above all things the *civic virtues*, which war so easily demoralizes, to keep it alive."[15]

If war was only considered the catalyst for the release of destructive popular emotions, it is safe to conclude that the anti-imperialists believed that the "seed of destruction" had to reside within the people themselves. They held a rather bleak view of humanity, or at least of a segment of it—the so-called masses Le Bon and Godkin had described. As Akira Iriye has pointed out: "The anti-imperialists often feared mob psychology as much as a powerful government, and sought to preserve what they considered to be an ideal constitution that had served the country well. Certainly after the Civil War there had been agrarian uprisings and industrial strife, but imperialism would not only not solve these domestic problems but would make matters worse by catering to mass violence and militarism."[16] To the anti-imperialists, the majority of human beings were still essentially ruled by base impulses and instincts under a thin veneer of "civilization." Consequently, democracy was a particularly delicate and threatened form of government because the people, its sovereign, could always upset it with their "natural" passions.

The fear the critics of empire purported to have *for* democracy was partially a fear *of* democracy, or, at least, a particular form of it. Many anti-imperialists' disgust with the current foreign policies thus pointed to a much deeper unease about the rise of modern mass democracy. Bernard Bailyn's judgment about the American Founding Fathers could easily be applied to a large segment of the anti-imperialists: "If 'republic' conjured up for many the positive features of the Commonwealth era and marked the triumph of virtue and reason, 'democracy'—a word that denoted the lowest order of society as well as the form of government in which the commons ruled—was generally associated with the threat of civil disorder and the early assumptions of power by a dictator."[17] In this instance *fear* is more appropriately described as *angst*, where the immediate trigger of the antiannexationist critique, "imperialism," was superseded by a long-standing unease about the value of democratic government.

Given this view of the people, it is not surprising that the anti-imperialist discourse placed so much emphasis on the Constitution. With its safeguards against majority tyranny and the abrogation of democratic/republican government, the Constitution was considered the most important institutional arrangement that contained and disciplined the irrational impulses of the people. In keeping with his negative view of "the masses," Godkin characterized the Constitution as "the only bridle [the people] has ever borne with patiently."[18] The anti-imperialists feared that the American public would lose their traditional reverence for the Constitution as elected leaders, the imperialists, disregarded or violated the war powers provisions and ruled subject populations against their will.

Concomitantly, the other prerequisite for upholding popular government, according to the anti-imperialists, was responsible and dispassionate leadership. That the imperialists ignored this precept and presumably incited and instrumentalized popular emotions in order to gain support for their own foreign policy plans was resented by the critics as much as the foreign policy itself. Apparently, they considered themselves members of a dispassionate elite, able to resist the "base impulses" of greed and glory and thus naturally destined to lead the people and to control their disruptive potential.

Emotions and Class

Such discursive evidence, assembled through a focus on emotions in anti-imperialist rhetoric, is supported by the sociological background of the anti-annexationists. To be sure, their movement was highly heterogeneous and included Southern Democrats and Northern abolitionists, Western populists as well as a minority of congressional Republicans, progressives and a vocal minority of the African American community. The so-called mugwumps, however, organized in a number of local leagues throughout the country, constituted its most vocal and prominent part. This was a loose association of fierce political independents, most of whom had bolted the Republican Party in the 1880s because they considered it too corrupt and immoral. The group was comprised of former abolitionists, Civil War–era generals and politicians, civil service reformers, and former industrial magnates. Accordingly, their median age was quite high in the 1890s, and their political clout had peaked during or immediately after the Civil War. The mugwumps saw themselves as moral authorities and spoke out on a variety of issues, which they regarded as examples of the moral depravity and decay of their age:

> The Mugwumps cherished their minority privileges. They acknowledged obligations only to their public principles and to their personal integrity. ... They had no stomach for the compromises that responsibility to a majority demanded. Their function as they saw it was to stand in the teeth of the wind and wait for the possible to bend to their ideal.[19]

By the late 1890s these individuals had lost much of their influence and suffered from a sense of displacement by the new elites of the Gilded Age. The issue of imperialism thus offered them a final opportunity to voice their frustrations with the recent sociopolitical changes and the advent of mass democracy.[20] To the anti-imperialists, the emotional tactics and strategies of their opponents, the "dangerous game" of evoking people's emotions, only proved the new elites' inability at national leadership.

Viewed from the vantage point of the mugwump anti-imperialists' social background, their fears about the dangers of emotions in politics appear to have been directed more at their fellow independents rather than at a mass-based audience. Except for the propagandists who served as congressmen or newspaper editors and enjoyed easy access to the larger public, the politically independent anti-imperialists chose smaller and "respectable" venues for their campaign against overseas expansion. Commenting on the first and most famous meeting of the New England Anti-Imperialist League in Boston's hallowed Fanueil Hall, the imperialist senator Henry Cabot Lodge reassured the Boston Brahmin Brooks Adams: "I am strongly of the opinion that we ought to take no notice of it. As far as I can judge from the papers it seems to have been very small, utterly ineffectual, and chiefly composed of elderly people." Even the initially anti-imperialist *Boston Evening Transcript* inadvertently confirmed both the elitism and the limited popular impact of the mugwump opponents of expansion. Conceding that the meeting could not match the numbers achieved in election campaigns, the paper characterized "the large audience [as] a thoroughly representative one, holding to an eminent degree the *best of the intelligence and character of this community.* On all sides could be seen the well-known faces of leaders of good causes among us."[21] It is thus highly likely that the anti-imperialists' discourse on the detrimental impact of emotions in politics was primarily directed at fellow travelers who presumably shared the critics' fundamental disposition.

Those elitist attitudes kept the anti-imperialists from waging a successful fight against the policy of expansion. Their habit of talking *about*—and even insulting—the people instead of talking *to* them reinforces the impression that they were out of touch with the demands of a modern style of mass democracy. The Republican George Hoar—anti-imperialist by persuasion, but never a friend of the mugwumps—intimated as much early on in the campaign when he criticized his allies that "they [did not] care ... to succeed so much as to show their own wisdom and their great disrespect for other people."[22]

But the mugwumps remained stubbornly proud of their minority status and presumed righteousness. In the election of 1900, many of them objected to the political expediency of an alliance with the anti-imperialist Democratic Party because they despised the populism of its presidential candidate, William J. Bryan.[23] When the imperialist Republicans carried the elections, their adversaries remained unwilling to accept either the verdict of the people or the fallacies of their own political strategies. On the contrary, the results only seemed to confirm their low esteem of their countrymen and "the ignorance and venality of the masses."[24] On this occasion, moreover, the disappointment with the people was not limited to mugwump anti-imperialists as even a staunch Democrat and Bryan supporter concluded: "That my predictions did not prove correct, I hold to be a reflection upon the people rather than upon myself, since they should have been true by every consideration of right and justice."[25] These anti-imperialists were apparently unwilling to accept the judgment of the majority on the issue of imperialism—the outcome of *procedural* democracy—and instead invoked a *substantive* understanding of democracy, proclaiming to have privileged knowledge of what was "right" and "just." In other words, democracy (or the republic) had to be defended against its agent, the people.

The analytical focus on the anti-imperialists' fear of an emotionalized people subverting American democracy has yielded important insights into the mindset, make-up, and failure of the movement. It appeared initially that their warnings were scare tactics, designed to convince audiences of just one of the dangers inherent in an expansionist and belligerent foreign policy. Yet, a closer look proved the logical and actual ineffectiveness of the argument for public consumption, unless it was designed for a highly limited "elite audience" in the first place. But if read as a representation of the anti-imperialists' own emotions—their fears and frustrations—their arguments make more sense. Having witnessed the labor and agrarian uprisings of the 1880s and early 1890s, they were positively afraid of emotionalized masses and the accompanying specter of revolution. Their view of humanity was bleak, insisting that human beings were instinctive and irrational, prone to erratic, even violent behavior. They believed that an orderly and democratic society needed emotional restraint and containment of vulgar impulses. War and a constant atmosphere of crisis, however, might bring out the worst in people and result in the destruction of the republic itself.

Given their suspicion of human emotions, it is ironic to observe that their own critique of foreign policy partially resulted from an entire host of emotions, some of them quite unrelated to the immediate issue of overseas expansion. Fear or, to be more precise, angst was foremost among these emotions or moods. Certainly, the anti-imperialists feared an aggressive foreign policy in its own right, but in the context analyzed here, they rejected expansion and war because they feared the American people. Whereas they cherished a more or less republican style of government, they were skeptical about the more modern conception of mass-based democracy. In addition to fear, the critics also experienced emotions of frustration and alienation with their own political decline and displacement by the new and younger elites of the Gilded Age, whom the mugwumps, at least, considered vulgar and careless, since they catered to and even incited emotions for their political purposes. By implication, there was also melancholy in the repertoire of anti-imperialist emotions, the yearning for an idealized passing order, in which quasi-aristocratic virtuous elites wisely controlled the emotions of the many.

In this regard, the imperialists' success and the anti-imperialists' failure also opens a window on the prevailing emotional and cultural climate of the time. Only ten years earlier, cataclysmic literature and predictions had been widespread in the United States, projecting scenarios of the decline of American democracy not unlike those of the anti-imperialists. But while the mugwump critics of empire remained concerned, large segments of society felt inspired by economic progress and victory in the "splendid little war" with Spain. Even Brooks Adams, who had theretofore been one of the most pessimistic doomsayers, considered imperialism a way out of the presumed cycle of the rise and decline of great nations.[26] The feeling that imperialism changed the historical laws, that overseas expansion provided a new outlet for both American industries and the "energies" of its people, pervaded the thoughts of the leading imperialists[27] and, at least for a brief moment in time, fueled the imagination of the American public as well.

The focus on the emotions inherent in anti-imperialist rhetoric thus furnishes a more complete picture of an important American protest movement and the culture surrounding it. In this respect, emotions history adds to the field of international history and complements the ever-widening analytical matrix with categories of culture, race, gender, and mutual perceptions. With respect to the study of emotions *in* history, the analysis of anti-imperialist fears validates the assumption that emotions are time- and culture-bound. While fear or angst may be universal emotions or moods among individuals worldwide, their triggers and specific manifestations can still be very specific and culturally determined. More than that, the elitist bent of anti-imperialist angst illustrates that emotions or moods can also be class bound.

Notes

1. For two of the best examples of this approach see Carol Zisowitz Stearns and Peter N. Stearns, *Anger: The Struggle for Emotional Control in America's History* (Chicago: University of Chicago Press, 1986); Peter N. Stearns, *Jealousy: The Evolution of an Emotion in American History* (New York: New York University Press, 1989).
2. Compare Heinz-Günter Vester, *Emotion: Gesellschaft und Kultur, Grundzüge einer soziologischen Theorie der Emotionen* (Opladen: Westdeutscher Verlag, 1991). The idea that emotions are socially and culturally constructed and defined is generally referred to as "emotionology." For an analysis of this view in historiographical perspective, see Peter N. Stearns with Carol Z. Stearns, "Emotionology: Clarifying the History of Emotions and Emotional Standards," *American Historical Review* 90 (October 1985): 813–36.
3. Carl Schurz, "The Issue of Imperialism," Convocation address before the University of Chicago, 4 January 1899, in Schurz, *Speeches, Correspondence and Political Papers of Carl Schurz,* ed. Frederic Bancroft, 6: 35 (New York and London: Putnam, 1913). Compare also E. L. Godkin, "The President's Popularity," *The Nation* 68 (6 April 1899): 252.
4. For the contemporary discussion of war crimes committed by American forces, compare Stuart Creighton Miller, *"Benevolent Assimilation: The American Conquest of the Philippines, 1899–1903* (New Haven, CT: Yale University Press, 1982), chapter 12.
5. Jane Addams, "Democracy or Militarism," Address at the Central Anti-Imperialist League, *Chicago Liberty Meeting*, 30 April 1899 (Chicago: CAIL, 1899), 37–39.
6. George F. Hoar to Caroline Putnam, 19 May 1900; Box 207, General Correspondence, Hoar Papers; Massachusetts Historical Society (hereafter cited as MHS), Boston. On the link between lynchings and the war in the Philippines, which many anti-imperialists perceived, compare Daniel B. Schirmer, *Republic or Empire: American Resistance to the Philippine War* (Cambridge, MA: Schenkman Publ., 1972), 101–2, 146–47.
7. Bacon in *Congressional Record,* 55th Congress, 3rd session, 1899: 739.
8. Compare E. L. Godkin, "The Moral of the Dewey Reception," *The Nation* 69 (19 October 1899), 292–93; George F. Hoar, "Cuba and the Philippines: Both Entitled to Independence," Letter to the Editors, *Journal, Advertiser, Herald, Globe* (all Boston), n.d.; report in the *Congressional Record,* 56th Congress, 1st session, 1900, Appendix: 163. The anti-imperialists failed to mention, however, that the United States had already had its share of military heroes turned presidents prior to "imperialism." In no small measure, George Washington, Andrew Johnson, Zachary Taylor, and Ulysses S. Grant owed their election to their previous military exploits.
9. William Lloyd Garrison, "Imperialism," Address at the Annual Meeting of the Progressive Friends, Longwood, PA, 10 June 1899; Anti-Imperialist Leaflets and Broadsides, Widener Library, Harvard University.
10. Vester, *Emotion,* 148.
11. Albert J. Beveridge, "The Young Men of America," Speech at Tomlinson Hall, Indianapolis, 18 October 1900, Box 297, Addresses and Articles, Beveridge Papers, Library of Congress, Washington, DC.
12. Charles H. Grosvenor in *Congressional Record,* 55th Congress, 3rd session, 1899: 1091; Henry Cabot Lodge, Speech at Convention, 6 October 189,, Newspaper Clipping, Box 99, Bound Volumes, Henry Cabot Lodge Papers, MHS, Boston.
13. Godkin to Charles Eliot Norton, 1 July 1899, bms Am 1083, Godkin Papers, Houghton Manuscript Library, Harvard University; Gustave Le Bon, *The Crowd: A Study of the Popular Mind* (New York: Viking Press, 1960 [1895]).

14. For the assumption that many anti-imperialists made use of racial stereotypes in a calculated and deliberate fashion, and that many of them stopped using the argument when it was no longer convenient or consistent, compare Fabian Hilfrich, "'Nation' and 'Democracy': Representations of the American Self in the Debates on American Imperialism (1898–1900) and on the Vietnam War (1964–1968)," PhD diss., Free University of Berlin, 2000 (microfilm).
15. Schurz, "Militarism and Democracy," Address at the American Academy of Political and Social Science, April 4, 1899; excerpts in *New York Times,* 8 April 1899 (emphasis mine). On the theory of republicanism and its persistence in the United States compare J. G. A. Pocock, *The Machiavellian Moment: Florentine Political Thought and the Atlantic Republican Tradition* (Princeton, NJ: Princeton University Press, 1975); Dorothy Ross, "The Liberal Tradition Revisited and the Republican Tradition Addressed," in John Higham and Paul K. Conkin, eds., *New Directions in American Intellectual History* (Baltimore: John Hopkins University Press, 1979), 116–31. On the republican traits in anti-imperialist thought, see Fabian Hilfrich, "Falling Back into History: Conflicting Visions of National Decline and Destruction in the Imperialism Debate around the Turn of the Century," in *The American Nation—National Identity—Nationalism,* ed. Knud Krakau (Münster: Lit, 1997), 149–166.
16. Akira Iriye, *From Nationalism to Internationalism* (London: Routledge & Paul, 1977), 146.
17. Bernard Bailyn, *The Ideological Origins of the American Revolution* (Cambridge, MA: Harvard University Press, 1967), 282.
18. Godkin, "The Old Constitution," *The Nation* 68 (12 January 1899): 22.
19. Geoffrey Blodgett, "The Mind of the Boston Mugwump," *Mississippi Valley Historical Review* 48 (1962), 633. For a description of the mugwump mindset, compare also Robert L. Beisner, *Twelve Against Empire: The Anti-Imperialists 1898–1900,* 2nd ed. (Chicago: University of Chicago Press, 1985), chapter 1.
20. The sense of displacement, termed a "status revolution," is a central explanatory tool for Richard Hofstadter's thesis on the rise of the progressive movement from the origins of mugwumpery. Hofstadter, *The Age of Reform: From Bryan to F.D.R.* (New York: Vintage Books, 1955), chapter 4. To explain the anti-imperialist movement on the whole, however, this explanation is insufficient because it leaves out the very real dangers to democracy that the opponents of expansion perceived from expansion abroad.
21. Henry Cabot Lodge to Adams, 20 June 1898, Box 39, Letterbooks, Lodge Papers; "The Fanueil Hall Protest," *Boston Evening Transcript,* 16 June 1898.
22. Hoar to Atkinson, 16 December 1898, Box 187, Correspondence, Hoar Papers.
23. On the anti-imperialist strategies for the election of 1900, compare Beisner, *Twelve Against Empire,* chapter 6.
24. Senator Benjamin Tillman to William J. Bryan, 5 December 1900, Box 26, General Correspondence, William J. Bryan Papers, Manuscript Division, Library of Congress, Washington, DC.
25. S. E. DeRockin [name hardly legible] to Bryan, 8 November 1900; compare Chamberlain to Bryan, 19 November 1900, Box 25, General Correspondence, Bryan Papers.
26. Frederic Cople Jaher, *Doubters and Dissenters: Cataclysmic Thought in America, 1885–1918* (London: Free Press of Glencoe, 1964). On the changing views of Brooks Adams, compare chapter 9.
27. For the argument that imperialism would transcend the "historical laws" of growth and decline compare Hilfrich, "'Nation' and 'Democracy,'" chapter 5.

Bibliography

Addams, Jane. "Democracy or Militarism," Address at the Central Anti-Imperialist League, *Chicago Liberty Meeting,* 30 April 1899. Chicago: Chicago Anti-Imperialist League, 1899.

Bailyn, Bernard. *The Ideological Origins of the American Revolution.* Cambridge, MA: Harvard University Press, 1967.

Beisner, Robert L. *Twelve Against Empire: The Anti-Imperialists 1898–1900.* 2nd ed. Chicago: University of Chicago Press, 1985.

Blodgett, Geoffrey. "The Mind of the Boston Mugwump." *Mississippi Valley Historical Review* 48 (1962): 614–34.

Congressional Record. 1898–1902.

Godkin, Edwin Lawrence. "The Moral of the Dewey Reception." *The Nation* 69 (October 19, 1899): 292–93.

———. "The Old Constitution," *The Nation* 68 (12 January 1899), 22.

———. "The President's Popularity." *The Nation* 68 (April 6, 1899): 252.

Hilfrich, Fabian. "'Nation' and 'Democracy': Representations of the American Self in the Debates on American Imperialism (1898–1900) and on the Vietnam War (1964–1968)." PhD diss., Free University of Berlin, 2000.

———. "Falling Back into History: Conflicting Visions of National Decline and Destruction in the Imperialism Debate around the Turn of the Century." In *The American Nation—National Identity—Nationalism,* edited by Knud Krakau, 149–66. Münster: Lit, 1997.

Hofstadter, Richard. *The Age of Reform: From Bryan to F.D.R.* New York: Vintage Books, 1955.

Iriye, Akira. *From Nationalism to Internationalism.* London: Routledge & Paul, 1977.

Jaher, Frederic Cople. *Doubters and Dissenters: Cataclysmic Thought in America, 1885–1918.* London: Free Press of Glencoe, 1964.

Le Bon, Gustave. *The Crowd: A Study of the Popular Mind.* New York: Viking Press, 1960 (1895).

Miller, Stuart Creighton. *"Benevolent Assimilation: The American Conquest of the Philippines, 1899–1903.* New Haven, CT: Yale University Press, 1982.

Pocock, J. G. A. *The Machiavellian Moment: Florentine Political Thought and the Atlantic Republican Tradition.* Princeton, NJ: Princeton University Press, 1975.

Ross, Dorothy. "The Liberal Tradition Revisited and the Republican Tradition Addressed." In *New Directions in American Intellectual History,* edited by John Higham and Paul K. Conkin, 116–31. Baltimore: John Hopkins University Press, 1979.

Schirmer, Daniel B. *Republic or Empire: American Resistance to the Philippine War.* Cambridge, MA: Schenkman, 1972.

Schurz, Carl. *Speeches, Correspondence and Political Papers of Carl Schurz.* Edited by Frederic Bancroft, 6 vols. New York and London: Putnam, 1913.

Stearns, Carol Zisowitz and Peter N. Stearns, *Anger: The Struggle for Emotional Control in America's History.* Chicago: University of Chicago Press, 1986.

Stearns, Peter N. *Jealousy: The Evolution of an Emotion in American History.* New York: New York University Press, 1989.

Stearns, Peter N., and Carol Zisowitz Stearns. "Emotionology: Clarifying the History of Emotions and Emotional Standards." *American Historical Review* 90 (October 1985): 813–36.

Vester, Heinz-Günter. *Emotion: Gesellschaft und Kultur, Grundzüge einer soziologischen Theorie der Emotionen.* Opladen: Westdeutscher Verlag, 1991.

Chapter 4

THE MOBILIZATION OF EMOTIONS

Propaganda and Social Violence on the American Home Front during World War I

Jörg Nagler

War as a Catalyst for Emotion

WAR AND EMOTIONS form an inherent symbiosis. Though the Prussian military analyst Carl von Clausewitz claimed in his famous quotation that war is merely a "continuation of policy ... by other means," the French Revolution and the Napoleonic Wars changed the course of how wars were conducted. The phenomenon of *levée en masse* or people's war became the principle of warfare, and with it came a new way of viewing war that had repercussions on the emotional dimension of war. Whereas earlier conflicts had almost been a rational undertaking, emotions now partly replaced reason in war making. Those who argued for the rational behavior of statesmen, however, did not exclude the emotional side of warfare. Whereas leaders perceived wars almost like a game of chess, people still were killed on the battlefield, wives became widows, children lost their fathers. In other words, deep emotional experiences of grief and sorrow, to name just a few feelings, were experienced by civilians in their everyday life. The mobilization of citizen-soldiers left its mark on the emotions of the families and the men themselves, and hence on the collective national consciousness, since the

Notes for this section begin on page 84.

personal decision to participate in a war was directly linked to the notion of enmity. The enemy as "the other" was primarily an emotional experience, individually felt but also collectively shared by all affected by the war; this identification of the enemy harnessed deep-rooted emotions such as hatred and fear, just to name a few.

Although war as a major national event is a strong catalyst for emotional expression, we still lack any sort of systematic research on the relationship between war and emotions.[1] For example, we still do not know enough about the relationship of prewar emotions and emotions in war, and how the emotional transformations effect postwar developments.

World War I as a "total war"[2] was a watershed in the history of warfare and led to a dramatic new assessment of the human impulse to war. This article deals with that war and emotions on a macrocosmic level; to be more precise, it examines the mobilization of emotions of noncombatants on the American home front in the age of total war. Social psychologists, among others, have emphasized that civilian morale is one crucial aspect of any war effort. The success of warfare hinges on the participants' mental processes, and emotions creating a war spirit play a pertinent role in enduring inevitable hardships. How did the emotional mobilization spurred on by propaganda on the American home front during World War I inspire nationalism and patriotism, and by what means was this achieved—and with what consequences? In this essay I will not concentrate on individual emotions, e.g., who felt what under what circumstances, but rather on the purposeful governmental "production" of emotions, created by people who were also touched by the emotions of their time. On a broader theoretical level, this subject questions whether emotions serve as a "possible causal agent in conflict" and lead to social violence and aggression.[3]

Nationalism has been one of the most powerful agents for generating emotions in public life ever since the late eighteenth century, and was even more effective in the twentieth century. Michael Howard has rightly emphasized that nationalism from its beginning was "almost indissolubly linked, both in theory and practice, with the idea of war."[4] When we describe nationalism as a sentimental state of mind in which the supreme loyalty of the individual belongs to the nation-state, and then link it up with the inherent tendency of nationalism towards war, it is simple to conclude that individual emotions may lead to the collective endeavor of war. Nationalism had always been nurtured by particular grievances, fears, and ambitions of nations worldwide. In the American case, nationalism possessed an exceptionally deep emotional involvement ("love or leave it") in the early 1900s. Americanism, interconnected with the emotional side of the individual's relationship with the state, was most outwardly symbolized by affection for the American flag. Additionally, the "pursuit of happiness" in the American

Declaration of Independence became a deeply embedded national ideology that each individual needed to pursue; any other ideology that endangered this principle fell into the Manichaean trap[5] of the juxtaposition of good versus evil with deep religious ramifications.

In every modern war, loyalty becomes the psychological touchstone upon which national cohesion is based: the ability to motivate civilians to become soldiers; to leave their families, homes, friends, and communities; and to risk the ultimate sacrifice—death—for a cause, a nation, or both. Loyalty includes an emotional attachment to the nation and is intimately connected to matters of patriotism, nationalism, and ideology. Disloyalty, or even the charge of it, is the gravest moral failing in the ideology of nationalism, as it threatens the necessary consensus for the war on the home front. Fostering loyalty is regarded, on one hand, as a positive, preventative measure, a streamlining of the national effort, and on the other, as reaction against domestic dissent.[6] Loyalty, then, is an emotional attachment to the nation, or a "passionate devotion"[7] that may vary in perceived emotional intensity. It is, however, not instinctive but rather learned or acquired, and is both a state of mind and a form of behavior.

The Consequences of Warfare

In an interview shortly before America's entry into World War I, President Wilson revealed his anxieties about the likely disruptive social effects of the war on the American people. To Frank Cobb, the editor of the *New York World,* he observed:

> Once lead this people into war, and they'll forget there ever was such a thing as tolerance. To fight you must be brutal and ruthless, and the spirit of ruthless brutality will enter into the very fiber of our national life, infecting Congress, the courts, the policeman on the beat, the man in the street.[8]

Concerning our subject of emotions in war time, it is important to point out that what Wilson described as tolerance is the central societal standard that could prevent the regression toward basic negative emotions such as hate, anger, and aggression in society. Wilson, a trained historian and political scientist, was quite aware of America's past wars and their disruptive social and emotional effects, and he foresaw that in order "to make the world safe for democracy," democratic structures and thus the tradition of tolerance might have to suffer at home. And indeed under the stress of modern wars, complex and sophisticated democratic political structures tend to become less complex, and, in order to fight the enemy, more primitive, atavistic, or even tribal instincts reemerge under the umbrella of nationalism and patriotism. Collective and individual fear become the central emotion within this regressive development spurred on by war. It was thus not surprising when, on 4 April 1917, conservative Republican senator Henry Cabot Lodge rendered the following remarks on the imminent American involvement in the war:

> We have never been a military nation; we are not prepared for war in the modern sense; but we have vast resources and unbounded energies, and the day when war is declared we should devote ourselves to calling out those resources and organizing those energies so that they can be used with the utmost effect in hastening the complete victory. The worst of all wars is a feeble war. War is too awful to be entered half-heartedly. If we fight at all, we must fight for all we are worth. It must be no weak, hesitating war. The most merciful war is that which is most vigorously waged and which comes most quickly to an end.[9]

These reflections on the pending American participation in the world conflict from two major—albeit very different—political figures represent pertinent perspectives on the anticipated nature and consequences of warfare Americans might experience. Although antagonists in terms of their political thinking, both Wilson and Lodge shared the view that in order to gain victory, the scope of warfare had to be decisive and full scale. Lodge, a fervent nationalist and proponent of a militarily well-prepared America, had no second thoughts about the social dimension and emotional impact of the war to be fought. His statements regarding the nature of the coming war sound astoundingly "modern" and reverberate with notions of total war. Lodge's call for the employment of all available resources—social and economic—in order to achieve "complete victory" indicate a close structural resemblance with the concept and elements of total war. Since Wilson and Lodge represented two very different political cultures prevailing in the United States at the time of the entry into the war, their views and perceptions gain a representative significance for our subject.

Pre–World War I US Society and Its Challenges

Wars are the products of the societies that lead them[10] and hence, in order to explain the emotional forces and motives behind the "war for the American mind," we have to examine the social components and makeup of American society before World War I.

Once America had regained its self-confidence after the trauma of its Civil War, consolidation in terms of economic strength encompassed the quest for a national culture, independent from European influences. While a strong American nationalism called increasingly for self-definition, in the global context a growing imperialistic competition occurred that manifested itself in the United States as diverging diplomatic and economic spheres of interests.[11] In the context of the Spanish-American war of 1898, jingoism and a form of bellicose nationalism were accompanied by a martial spirit affecting certain strata of American society. The British economist John A. Hobson defined jingoism as follows: "That inverted patriotism whereby the love of one's own nation is transformed into the hatred of another nation, and the fierce craving to destroy the individual members of that other nation."[12]

The United States at the time of its entry into World War I in 1917 was heterogeneous and ethnically and socially fragmented. The demographic shockwaves of the New Immigration that began in the 1890s combined with accelerated industrialization and rapid urbanization to foster social dislocation and unrest. The multiple frustrations engendered in this process led to frustrated desires—a precondition for the formation of negative emotions, which, in turn, caused social violence within a society involved in a "search for order."[13] At the root of this violence was the struggle of old stock Americans against the massive flood of immigrants, which signaled a profound social and cultural change in American life.[14] Nativism, the fear of aliens, has historically accompanied disorder in American society; in general, it is fostered by the fear of finding a coherent answer to the challenges of the political, economic, and ideological future. John Higham has correctly emphasized that for the history of nativism, "the big changes were not so much intellectual as emotional. The same idea might be mildly innocuous at one time and charged with potent feelings at another. For the history of nativism, therefore, emotional intensity provided the significant measurement of change."[15] In other words the intensity of emotions became the measuring stick for change.

Progressivism represented one attempt during the prewar era to answer the challenges of massive social change. With its moralistic demands for social reform, it resembled a modern evangelical awakening. The fight against social ills, which were allegedly caused by monopolists and industrial bosses, was tantamount to a struggle against the forces of evil and indeed achieved an almost religious dimension. Concerns that the melting pot had not worked, that old ethnic allegiances had survived in the minds of many immigrants, were omnipresent in contemporary discussions about the national crisis of identity. Entry into the war reformulated these concerns into a domestic security problem that was intimately connected with collective fears of subversion.[16] The social and political antagonisms reflected deep conflicts of interest, and they seemed to pose a threat to the emergence of a common civic identity, a successful molding of the American mind, and hence to effective mobilization for war.

Once the United States had decided to declare war in April 1917 against Imperial Germany, the government struggled to find a plausible justification for the intervention and to define war aims that would be supported by the public. The war declaration symbolized a radical departure from a long tradition of American isolation from European power politics. The reason for leading the American people into war had to be noble: "a war to end all wars" and to "make the world safe for democracy" were just two of many slogans with which Wilson justified American involvement in the war. These high moralistic ideals and radical war aims could presuppose—partly nurtured by the American ideal of mission—a unified nation ready for sacrifice in their name.

Though the "German menace" was juxtaposed to American liberal values, the hesitancy of the population was evident. And indeed, World War I was the second most unpopular war in American history, surpassed only by the Vietnam War, and it therefore required "correction" of public opinion by the means of propaganda.[17]

A paradoxical situation prevailed in the United States during the war that might explain certain emotional reactions toward the conflict: unlike other belligerents, the United States, the latecomer to the conflict, was not directly exposed on any fronts, nor was it subject to any immediate threat of attack by enemy forces. On the contrary, the enemy was distant and safely separated by the Atlantic. As Mark Sullivan, the keen observer of his times, noted: "The war did not come to America as it came to Europe. … It was not in the shape of violence of any sort that the war … came to us. Its coming took a form far away, far away in distance and even farther away in spirit.[18] In other words, the war was remote both in a spatial as well as emotional sense. The distance from the fighting made it even more essential to create a war spirit among people living in the American hinterland, where provincial attitudes made Washington DC just as remote as Europe. This challenge required a great propagandistic effort to build up the aggressive potential in the human mind by "implanting" the distant enemy into the minds and emotions of the people and to make him more immediate—a precondition for hating and fighting the enemy.

The projection of the distant enemy was eased by the presence of substantial numbers of immigrants from the Central Powers. In April 1917, out of the total US population of approximately 100 million, more than 14.5 million had been born in foreign countries. More than one hundred languages and dialects were spoken on the streets of America, and there were approximately 1,600 foreign-language newspapers and magazines, with a circulation of over 11 million. Over 8 million citizens were first- and second-generation Germans who considered Germany their land of origin; 2.5 million of this group had been born in Germany, almost 4 million had two German parents, and the rest had one German parent.[19] The substantial groups of Irish and German immigrants were already well known for their opposition against an American involvement in the European war.[20] In December 1917 with the declaration of war against Austria-Hungary, the substantial group of roughly 7 million persons born within the boundaries of the Central Powers loomed as a threat to national security, since it was assumed by old-stock Americans that this group would act as willing "fifth columnists." The concern that the concept of the "melting pot" had not worked, and that old national allegiances still existed in the minds of many immigrants, was an omnipresent topic in contemporary discussions about the national crisis of identity. The war then changed these concerns into a potential domestic security problem.[21]

The physical proximity of these groups made it tempting to accuse them of disloyalty.[22] Indirectly, the violence of the European war thus affected the body politic through its own propagandistic tendencies. Projecting the remote menace of Imperial Germany onto the internal (alien) "fifth column" exemplified by German Americans reflected increasing nativism and fed the xenophobia that exploded after America's entry into the war.

The pro-British bias in American society, especially among East-Coast elites, was easily nurtured by Imperial Germany's invasion of a neutral Belgium, which British propaganda exploited by depicting German soldiers as baby killers—the bloodthirsty Huns.[23] German submarine warfare and the sinking of the *Lusitania* in May 1915, killing 128 Americans—among them women and children—increased the negatively charged image of Germans and became one of the key emotional events that served as a matrix for the evocation of anti-German feelings in American society.

The fateful Zimmermann telegram and unrestricted submarine warfare finally led to the rupture of diplomatic relations and subsequently to the US declaration of war against Imperial Germany. Doubtless German propaganda, intrigues, and sabotage in the United States during the neutral period also contributed to a widespread and deeply anchored suspicion of a German menace within the United States, but this can only partly explain the phenomenon of "spy fever" that developed during the war.[24]

Propaganda and Emotional Mobilization

Although it is important to discuss by what means a society at war is militarily and economically organized and disciplined to meet the objective of victory, we tend to neglect the central dimension of how a society is emotionally mobilized for war. This is a paramount consideration—particularly in nontotalitarian, democratically structured nations—for a successful and effective mobilization, in which public support is essential and the decision-making process is based on the voters' choice. Once the national will to pursue a war is supported by the majority, however, the identification with the state and its policies becomes an individual and often emotional attachment, but only when the state is capable of creating a linkage between the collective and the individual. As Quincy Wright pointed out in his seminal study on war: "The moral identification of the individual with the state has given the national will priority over humanitarian considerations. The civilian's morale and industry support the national will."[25]

The central means to achieve an individual emotional identification with the national will is propaganda. Ever since its inception in the late eighteenth century, nationalism has been accompanied by government-sanctioned propaganda, and this was especially true in the twentieth century. Propaganda as the manipulation of collective attitudes[26] is the best means to achieve the individual's emotional allegiance, which consequently lodges itself deep within each person's psyche and becomes internalized. Words, symbols, and other visual presentations are the primary vehicles for the creation of strong negative emotions and the imagination necessary for most people to kill on the battlefield. On the home front these emotions, through their unifying aspects, are intended to create social homogeneity in order to implement a successful mobilization.

With the beginning of the twentieth century, however, the technological means of communication to change attitudes and behavior became much more advanced and a more subtle methodology had to be employed in the age of modern warfare. Fighting total war now called for an absolute enemy, which needed to be created in the minds and imaginations of the people—a precondition for a thorough mobilization. By creating or inventing the enemy, basic emotions were necessarily unleashed. The central negative emotion was fear, and fear is intrinsically intertwined with danger.

Although every propaganda effort has to base its approach on certain elements that preexist in the public mind, it can also create new emotions where no previous stereotype existed or only very little was known by the public.[27] In other words, democracies need not impose upon their citizenry the will to fight with direct measures, but rather can awaken the individual desires of each citizen for mobilization. Propaganda was the vehicle for this emotional mobilization.

Propaganda is also strongly connected with the psychological aspects of war's impact upon society and hence influences the course of emotional change. Most propaganda is concerned with the stimulation of hope and fear and not merely with the transmission of readily verifiable information. The emotional disorder called hysteria, often caused by war, is both a social and individual phenomenon that is dialectically interwoven and is a universal indication of the socially disruptive nature of warfare—the kind of popular infection to which Wilson had alluded in his remarks to Frank Cobb. Like war fever or war paranoia, which are also common terms in the historiography of total war, war hysteria derives from psychoanalysis and medicine; it emphasizes the correlation between the individual and the collective emotional experience of war.[28] As in other forms of human interaction, to work properly propaganda must also strike a balance between reason and emotion. Propaganda is aimed at increasing collective nationalism and patriotism though individual emotions can vary and thus must possess a core set of values everybody can agree with.

Moral Stereotypes and the Home Front

At the beginning of the twentieth century, propaganda could exploit new technological means of communication to change attitudes and arouse a war spirit. But in what respects was the Wilson administration prepared to meet the objective of mental mobilization and forming public opinion into one monolithic block, without using coercive powers? In the realm of domestic propaganda—as in other governmental spheres—surprisingly little preparation for the momentous task of leading a people into war was being made in the winter and spring of 1917.

When the war began, it seemed that people everywhere were filled with Victorian ideas about innocence and romanticism. But in March 1917 the muckraking journalist Arthur Bullard published a book with the title *Mobilizing America*. Bullard propagated a total national commitment that would require a mobilization of emotions, should the United States enter the European conflict. He then prophesied that "the effectiveness of our warfare will depend on the amount of ardor we throw into it." The precondition of military mobilization and fighting spirit had to be, Bullard insisted, "an inward, spiritual mobilization." Democracies were not to generate the will to fight by means of direct, forceful measures; they were to evoke the individual desire of each citizen to support mobilization. The vehicle for this "spiritual and emotional mobilization" was propaganda.

Bullard favored publicity over censorship, the technique of "constantly giving the man in the street something wholesome to think about."[29] Informing citizens about the war would make it popular. "Something wholesome" might also, however, include the ugly face of the enemy. Bullard additionally emphasized that in case of an American involvement in the European conflict, the people would require "some motive of sufficient force to completely revolutionize our habits and our attitude towards life." Bullard, not surprisingly, became the intellectual godfather of America's first propaganda agency and was instrumental in planning the Committee on Public Information (CPI) through his relationship to the president's personal adviser Col. Edward House (who recommended the plan for this agency to Wilson).

Established on 14 April 1917, the CPI was significantly the first step toward a new bureaucracy of mobilization. The CPI's leaders recognized that to be successful, propaganda had to appeal primarily to emotions, not to the intellect. The fundamental question facing them was how the creation of the primary emotion—hatred for the enemy—could be implemented. Was it possible to create the image anew, or should it be built upon emotions and stereotypes that existed prior to the war? In the case of the German enemy, preexisting, often latent negative stereotypes were activated for this purpose. Transforming the images of things German from positive to negative had already begun in the 1890s when increasing criticism of Prussian autocracy made German *Kultur* synonymous with German militarism and imperialism. Immigrants of German origins suffered under these misconceptions. But this phenomenon also reflected social and cultural tensions, popular resentments against the custodians of highbrow culture in the United States, the East Coast elites, who were ironically perceived by many as willing followers of German culture despite the fact that they were overwhelmingly Anglophilic. During the two and a half years in which the United States was neutral, British propaganda also played a role, stirring the anti-German emotions of millions of Americans.

The key events implanted into the national psyche that inspired the most outrage were the "rape of Belgium" and the *Lusitania* disaster. Both events became an effective emotional appeal in the later recruitment campaigns, and the CPI distributed hundreds of thousands of posters that reverberated with notions of Old Testament justice and a permanent reference to the violation of international law by Germany.[30] The depiction of cruelty and violent acts committed against women with explicit scenes of rape and sexual mutilation served as central components in the mobilization of emotions on the home front and how the war was imagined by the public.[31] Children, like women, also often appeared in posters as victims of war—innocent bystanders who suffered needlessly and through no fault of their own. Images of children bring out powerful emotions in most people, and this was certainly true of Americans in 1917. Poster artists were particularly adept at using pictures of children to encourage thrift and patriotism. Some images of children were designed to shame adults into a contribution toward the war effort.[32]

The CPI became the government's vehicle for the war of words and emotions. Both consciously and unconsciously it channeled the moralistic energy of Progressivism against German militarism and Prussian autocracy. Many former progressive reformers participated in the CPI, where they transformed their domestic crusade for social reform into a holy war for democracy on a global scale. The crusade turned into a cultural war on the American home front, a "clash of civilization." Germany was portrayed as a pariah among civilized nations, the embodiment of the evil that threatened the Christian world. In the House of Representatives, Billy Sunday captured this sentiment in a prayer: "Thou knowest, O Lord, that no nation so infamous, vile, greedy, sensuous, bloodthirsty ever disgraced the pages of history." He added that "if you turn hell upside down, you will find 'Made in Germany' stamped on the bottom."[33] German *Kultur* was equated with barbarism, militarism, authoritarianism, and the drive for world hegemony. Hence it was portrayed as the antithesis of the American or Anglo-American value system, which was associated in turn with freedom and democracy.

Posters as clear visual representations of a message made the use of language almost superfluous and thus were most important in the mobilization of emotions. This may explain why no other belligerent nation produced as many war posters as the United States did in World War I. One could argue that the enormous output of war posters demonstrated the government's great concern about the nation's full commitment to the war effort. Emotional appeals and simplistic caricatures of the enemy influenced many Americans, but the CPI recognized that certain social groups had to be targeted with more complex propaganda, such as academics and journalists.

Propaganda often functions best with the juxtaposition of positive and negative emotions. On the constructive side of the coin, the CPI posters' major messages were American idealism combined with sanitized Victorian sexual conduct in contrast to the alleged German cruelty against women. On other posters these American ideals were often compared with direct allusions to sexuality through the depiction of brutal, ape-like German soldiers about to rape American women and heroines.[34] The basic theme in many of these posters was "What if Germany invaded America?" and the horrible scenarios of what could happen if Americans let the Hun run amok (often combined with the prospect of sexual molestation). The caption "Hun or Home?" on one of the most widely distributed posters implied that the viewer had two behavioral choices: either remain passive and let German *Kultur* conquer the world or become active to prevent this. Very often the posters depicted exactly this juxtaposition of passive and active behavior and its consequences. The propaganda always emphasized that the individual's commitment to participate in the struggle of good versus evil counted. But the most active role one could take was to become a soldier and fight the Hun's grasp for world hegemony.

Besides recruiting an army, the government faced the problem of finding a way to finance the war. Almost immediately the US Treasury Department asked individual Americans to loan money to the federal government from their personal savings and current income. The loans took the form of interest-bearing bonds that purchasers could redeem in the future. In two years Americans loaned the government (by purchasing bonds) some $21 billion. This was about two-thirds of the cost of the war effort. Perhaps as important as the financial results of this impressive contribution, the personal decisions of millions of Americans to buy bonds gave each person a feeling that he or she had a stake in the outcome.

In order to facilitate this financial commitment, the creation of a collective fear about German victory first had to be successfully implanted by propaganda.[35] The great public interest in atrocity stories, of German soldiers "raping Belgium" in a most detailed manner, expressed an astounding American fear of German military victory. With each Liberty Bond campaign, the emotion of hate became even more intense, as people gradually became accustomed to the depiction of the cruelty and atrocities of the Hun. The CPI consequently had to increase the dose of propaganda. The four Liberty Bond drives that took place during the war between May 1917 and October 1918 were accompanied by circus-like shows that Senator Warren C. Harding criticized at the time as "hysterical and unseemly."[36] Secretary of Treasury William Gibbs McAdoo planned and organized these large-scale campaigns, which were so successful because they effectively evoked patriotic emotions—either visually, by posters or movies, or by speeches. The purchase of Liberty Bonds became a litmus test for 100-percent Americanism and a synonym for national loyalty. During the second Liberty Bond campaign, for example, McAdoo explained to an audience in California the significance of Liberty Bonds: "Every person who refuses to subscribe or who takes the attitude of let the other fellow do it, is a friend of Germany and I would like nothing better than to tell it to him to his face. A man who can't lend this government $1.25 at the rate of 4 percent interest is not entitled to be an American citizen."[37]

The negative emotions so strongly generated became counterproductive, however, and led to superpatriotic excesses. The posters illustrated the highest level of emotion as the fighting continued into its fifth year. Calls for money became more strident and images more grotesque. By constantly emphasizing the need for voluntary commitment to the war efforts, the CPI created an atmosphere of denunciations. For example, in the CPI pamphlet "The German Whisper," Harvey O'Higgins warns of German propagandists, and the author solicits the reader to report the names and addresses of persons suspected of spreading such propaganda to the Justice Department. This publication was one of the best known pamphlets during the war.[38]

Besides the visual propaganda, the spoken word also mobilized emotions, and the CPI utilized the voluntaristic energy of the 75,000 voluntary amateur speakers known as Four Minute Men[39] even between reels in movie shows. Though the CPI appealed to the Four Minute Men to direct their rhetoric more toward reason and facts rather than to emotions and fabricated stories, the individual speakers tended to concentrate on atrocity stories and emphasized a threat scenario that contributed to the public's mushrooming emotions of fear and hate.[40] In their publication, the *Four Minute Men Bulletin,* a critical component of the message included stirring up fear among the civilian population. It was clearly difficult to unite a people by talking only on the highest ethical plane. The fight for the ideal had to be coupled with baser thoughts of self-preservation.[41]

The organizational demands of warfare makes the expansion of the state's role and function mandatory. Due to the peculiarities of the history of the traditionally "weak" American state and the strong tradition of voluntarism, however, the government's reaction towards war rendered a very ambivalent attitude towards the expansion of the state and in certain places created a void that was filled by self-mobilizing grass-roots groups that took the law into their own hands.

Since the several governmental intelligence agencies were constantly overburdened by the number of dissenters and enemy aliens to monitor and investigate, especially the Justice Department with its Bureau of Investigation (BI) turned to voluntary vigilante groups. Here it reacted to the obvious self-mobilization of the population on the American home front. The largest and most organized among these vigilante groups was the American Protective League (APL), which was organized by a Chicago businessman in March 1917. This army of more than 250,000 amateur investigators and spies became the official BI's auxiliary for investigations and detecting disloyalty in general.[42] By the end of the war, the APL could boast more than 3 million investigations[43] forwarded to the Justice Department and later, during the war at home, also to Military Intelligence.[44] Although the Justice Department praised the APL in public, the free-wheeling activities of the volunteers during the first year often embarrassed it.[45] The already deep-seated social fears were instrumentalized by the APL in order to prevent subversive activities. The official historian of the American Protective League defined the central emotion that was used to achieve its "obvious success": "It was *fear* that held our enemy population down—*fear* and nothing else. It was the League's silent and mysterious errand to pile up good reason for that fear."[46]

Extralegal Social Violence

In respect to the overall emotional and social climate on the home front, what were the consequences of the massive mobilization of emotions through patriotic propaganda and the government's call for voluntarism? Since the government's appeal to patriotism and nationalism was largely based on hate and fear, it led, most directly, to an outburst of extralegal violence. The CPI evidently miscalculated the disruptive psychological effects of its propaganda. The men at the head of this agency were less adept in handling mass psychology than their World War II–era successors would be later on. In 1917 to 1918, they created a monster that they found difficult to control. George Creel and his staff had not realized that grassroots superpatriotism already existed to a considerable degree, and was already directed against loosely defined "alien elements." For these groups propaganda served merely as a match to start their home front flames. Like Theodore Roosevelt, many Americans were convinced that "either a man is a good American, and therefore is against Germany ... or he is not an American at all."[47] This litmus test of Americanism, the black and white dichotomy of friend or foe—proved to be an effective weapon in the fight against domestic dissenters, but it also increased the existing nationalistic mood and inevitably led to social violence. Interestingly, as David Kennedy has pointed out, the cries for full-blown Americanism were most remarkable in the mouths of the "cultivated classes, the elites supposedly inoculated by education against base emotional appeals."[48]

Just one week after the American declaration of war, the nation began to see such eruptions of extralegal violence in all of its ugly shades. The *Tulsa Daily World* reported, "Everywhere throughout the country men of foreign birth and allegiance are being compelled by judges and infuriated citizens to kiss the flag, to wear it, and to swear renewed allegiance to it."[49] The various government-sponsored propaganda led to an ominous synthesis of existing social predilections and the specific war-related aggression against dissenters of all shades. This fusion of emotion gained a momentum that needed few stimuli to explode and even led to public questioning of state authority. The extralegal social violence with its rituals of public flag-kissing, tar and feathering, and lynchings became an almost daily phenomenon in many sections of the country. Members of specific ethnic groups and adherents of certain beliefs (socialists, German Americans, pro-Germans, pacifists, Wobblies, and Mennonites—basically anyone opposed to America's participation in the war) became the victims.[50]

When this extralegal violence became a frequent occurrence throughout the United States, it bred overall social unrest and endangered mobilization efforts. These unanticipated results overwhelmed and surprised the Wilson Administration. The violence on the home front was not in any respect directly orchestrated by the administration, nor was it officially supported. It was more a synthesis between spontaneous and arbitrary mob actions that received their momentum from specific local, cultural, and political circumstances, and organized aggression sponsored by superpatriotic groups.

In the case of lynch justice, it had been mainly masterminded and organized by local elites—often members of the respected Council of Defense[51]—and then implemented by superpatriotic mobs composed of underclass participants. This combination of elite leadership and proletarian action preserved social control and maintained the local preestablished social hierarchy.[52] Latent and bottled-up aggressions that stemmed from the neutrality period fully emerged during these unfortunate occasions, and the more vociferous German Americans, who had publicly argued for American neutrality, now became the special targets of patriotic aggression. Even Lutheran ministers were tarred and feathered. Extralegal violence such as lynching had had a long tradition in America and was nothing new. During the War of Independence, for instance, patriotic mobs chased down Tories and disciplined them in this manner.[53] These acts of public violence symbolized, as the cultural anthropologist Clifford Geertz once expressed it, "a metasocial commentary ... [for] organizing collective existence."[54] Tarring and feathering was a folk practice that had European as well as American roots. The situation of war thus only amplified ingrained cultural tendencies and provided certain persons and groups an opportunity to experience feelings of fraternity and power in acting out repressed fantasies that could not be performed in ordinary circumstances—the fantasies of those who stripped, lashed, tarred, feathered, and murdered people, humiliated them and painted them yellow, clipped locks from their hair, poured oil on their heads, or made them kiss flags.

The overly negative emotions and the quest for a war spirit ultimately became counterproductive and indeed opened Pandora's box for the American government: extralegal social violence against dissenters became such a daily phenomenon that social unrest endangered mobilization efforts. The administration, to say the least, was shocked.

The propaganda-inspired hatred against all things German—including German books, which were publicly burned in some places—increased the threshold of violence against German Americans and enemy aliens. As Theodore Roosevelt pointed out, Germans as well as German Americans represented a culture that was "precisely analogous to a 'culture' of cholera germs."[55] Analogies like this one, attributed to famous personalities, seemed to legitimize violence against individuals who were genetically disposed to evil, morally perverted, and dishonorable barbarians. Americans who appeared to be "infected" by the German bacillus of *Kultur* received similarly aggressive treatment. Posters, as clear visual representations, made the use of language almost superfluous and thus were most important in the American mobilization of emotions. No other belligerent nation produced as many war posters as did the United States in World War I. The explanation of this phenomenon is multifaceted and can be partly found in the general "paranoid style" (Richard Hofstadter) in American history combined with a longing for social and cultural homogeneity that has deep roots in the American past. The enemy who threatens this alleged societal consensus stimulates the reservoir of negative emotions. War hysteria also afforded some the chance to avert suspicion of their own loyalty. A few German Americans tried to demonstrate fidelity to the United States by joining or assisting mobs that harassed people of their own national origin.[56]

Events in the far distant European theater of war had their effect upon the increased hysteria and social violence. The quest for social and political conformity became stronger the longer the conflict lasted and reached its climax in the spring of 1918. There are several reasons for this phenomenon that demonstrate the close interdependence between the battlefield and the home front. In March 1918 the Soviet Congress signed the Treaty of Brest-Litovsk with Kaiser Wilhelm II, granting him immense territorial gains and releasing scores of German divisions from duty in the east. These troops were quickly rushed westward and subsequently attacked the Western Front with renewed vigor. These events led to a deep disillusionment in the United States and added to the frustrations of a long winter and the sacrifices already made for a war that appeared no closer to final victory. More and more soldiers left for Europe, and American casualty lists began to rise alarmingly. Although the words and actions expressed during this period were not unlike those of earlier months, the tones were more severe, the tempo accelerated, and the meanings more ominous for those considered the enemy within.[57]

From the very beginning of the war there had been attacks upon things German. Now the cries of hate rose to a crescendo. In the historiography of the American home front of World War I, the spring of 1918 has been called "The American Reign of Terror."[58] The tabloid press increased the hysteria with reports of an imminent German invasion, among other false rumors. In the resulting climate of nervous watchfulness these unreal and unsubstantiated stories unequivocally left their mark on the collective imagination.

The delimitation of base emotions also affected race relations in a dramatic way. Rumors of a German conspiracy to incite the African American population against the government had already spread in the neutrality period. After the declaration of war, however, these fears became more real. In the first months of war the Bureau of Investigation (later Federal Bureau of Investigation) as well as other Secret Service agencies received numerous reports about the imminent danger of race riots sparked by German agents. The general mood was a state of paranoia, and the potential danger caused by an alleged unified attempt by aliens and African Americans to undermine national security was only made more plausible by the deeply embedded (and historically reoccurring) fear of aliens and blacks among old-stock

Americans. The war fever created a symbolic symbiosis that explains the increased hysteria.[59] In the prevailing racism of the South, the rumors of German subversive activities were accepted a priori and African Americans were automatically suspected of spreading German propaganda.[60] These fears of black revolts were then confirmed by race riots, such as that in East St. Louis on 2 July 1917, where thirty-nine blacks and eight whites were killed.[61] These violent eruptions were immediately interpreted as the influence of German propaganda and intrigue.[62]

Consequently, the war accelerated the crisis of already tense race relations. Racism and anti-German political hysteria coalesced into a frightening synthesis that proved fatal for some victims of the social violence caused by this phenomenon. In Georgia alone, thirty-nine African Americans were lynched between 1918 and 1919 for their suspected pro-German activities.[63] Again such violent eruptions were immediately interpreted as the influence of German propaganda.

The "enemy within" is a topos that seems to be characteristic of societies at war. For many Americans the representatives of dissent in their society fulfilled the function of a projection of external enemies onto the internal home front. The persons who stayed "home" could develop a sense of war participation by fighting the internal enemy. This "substitute war" led to an emotional overcompensation, and took place on a large scale in the realm of an imagined menace, which was amplified by propaganda. The initial demonization of the external enemy was steadily applied to the internal one through various conspiracy scenarios, which were based on preexisting archetypes of internal menaces. This theory explains why the American administration, represented by its intelligence apparatus and the populace in general, took the rumors about German agents and their subversive activities among African Americans at their face value. Old anxieties and fears of slave revolts that had haunted the popular imagination in the South for years were easily evoked. David Brion Davis has rightly emphasized that "Americans have long been disposed to search for subversive enemies and to construct terrifying dangers from fragmentary and highly circumstantial evidence."[64] On a subconscious level, this idea may explain the root of American war hysteria in World War I, created by the unleashing of negative emotions and all-too-effective employment of propaganda.

In conclusion we can come back to President Wilson's prophetic fears concerning the disruptive forces of war that were confirmed by the events on the home front. Indeed "the spirit of ruthless brutality" and war hysteria entered into the fabric of American society during the war. Wilson himself, however, seldom undertook the necessary steps to maintain the spirit of tolerance he had spoken of. Under the stresses and demands of warfare, one might ask, how much tolerance of dissent was really possible.

The American response to total war resembled a crusade or a holy war against the forces of evil—quite in the tradition of Manichaeism. This time Prussian militarism and autocracy were caught in this "trap."[65] The strong current of pacifism in the United States prior to the American entry into the war was transformed into a "military pacifism," which meant fighting a war for a lasting peace and democracy. In order to guarantee this outcome and hence absolute victory, the war had to be fought with all available resources. This was the message American propaganda constantly poured out in posters, pamphlets, movies, and speeches by the Four Minute Men. In order to fight militarism abroad, the national psyche became affected by a degree of martiality that surpassed anything before in American history—with the exception of the Civil War.

To put this phenomenon in the larger context of the national history of the United States in the beginning of the twentieth century: the country not only was in a "search for order," but also in a search for identity that embraced questions of its new role in world politics. Only through this interpretation can we fully understand the highly emotional nationalistic ardor and the inevitable disruptive social and psychological forces that always seem to accompany nationalism supported by propaganda in times of war.

All attempts to explain the eruption of violence on the home front must be placed in the context of the mobilization of emotions of the government, and beyond this contextual framework we must look for causation in the matrix of prewar American political culture. The yearning for national homogeneity and the discovery of a political consensus existed ever since the founding of the nation. Alexis de Tocqueville had reported about these phenomena in his observations on American democracy in the early 1800s.[66]

The belligerency of the "100-percent Americanism" demanded universal conformity organized through complete national loyalty. Nothing in this demand was wholly new in American history—certainly not loyalty and certainly not conformity. Partly because of the great social, political, and ethnic diversity within the country in the early 1900s and the deliberate avoidance of the usage of the government's coercive powers during the war, social conformity became enforceable through unprecedented extralegal violence. Never before World War I had the urge for conformity blended so neatly with the spirit of nationalism. Never before had propaganda sparked such excesses in self-regulatory patriotic groups, based upon hate emotions.[67] While the quest for making the world "safe for democracy" served as legitimization for the external war, the American home front suffered from a repressive atmosphere that often collided with the American democratic tradition.

War and emotion in a specific nation and specific time as a subject should lead to comparative studies between the United States (and comparison to other national wars) and other nations. For example: is there a purely American emotional style and standard in the conduct of war? Only with the publication of such innovative work will we be able to identify particular emotions in a nation at war at a specific time, and to analyze more deeply the power of the modern state to intensify emotional reactions.

Notes

1. See as rare examples: Thomas J. Scheff, *Bloody Revenge: Emotions, Nationalism, and War* (Boulder and San Francisco: Westview Press, 1994); Barbara Ehrenreich, *Blood Rites: Origins and History of the Passions of War* (New York: Holt, 1997); Rose McDermott, "Emotions and War," in *Handbook of War Studies III,* ed. Manus Midlarsky (Ann Arbor: University of Michigan Press, forthcoming). The papers of the conference "Politics of Fear in the Cold War," that took place at the Hamburg Institute for Social Research in Hamburg, Germany, are now published. See *Angst im Kalten Krieg,* ed. Bernd Greiner, Christian Th. Müller and Dierk Walter (Hamburg: Hamburger Edition, 2009).
2. See Roger Chickering and Stig Förster, eds., *How Total was the Great War?* (New York: Cambridge University Press, 2000).
3. Scheff, *Emotions, Nationalism, and War,* 7.
4. Michael Howard, *The Lessons of History* (New Haven, CT: Yale University Press 1991), 39.
5. See Detlef Junker, *The Manichean Trap: American Perceptions of the German Empire, 1871–1945* (Washington, DC: German Historical Institute, 1995).
6. See for this subject Jörg Nagler, "Loyalty and Dissent: The Home Front in the American Civil War," in *On the Road to Total War: The American Civil War and the German Wars of Unification,* ed. Stig Förster and Jörg Nagler (Washington, DC: German Historical Institute, 1996), 329–55. See also John H. Schaar, *Loyalty in America* (Westport, CT: Greenwood Press, 1982); Harold Guetzkow, *Multiple Loyalties: Theoretical Approach to a Problem in International Organization* (Princeton, NJ: Princeton University Press, 1955); Merle Curti, *Roots of American Loyalty* (New York: Columbia University Press, 1946).
7. See Schaar, *Loyalty in America,* 5.
8. Wilson cited in John Milton Cooper, Jr., *The Warrior and the Priest: Woodrow Wilson and Theodore Roosevelt* (Cambridge, MA: Belknap Press, 1983), 320. On the Cobb interview with Wilson see Arthur Link, "That Cobb Interview," *Journal of American History* 72 (1985): 7–17.
9. Henry Cabot Lodge, *War Addresses, 1915–1917* (Boston: Houghton Mifflin, 1917), 301.
10. See also Clausewitz's dictum, "All wars are the products of the societies that fought them," cited in Michael Howard, *Clausewitz* (Oxford: Oxford University Press, 1983), 48; Hans Speier, "Klassenstruktur und totaler Krieg," in *Krieg und Frieden im industriellen Zeitalter,* ed. and intro. by Uwe Nerlich, 2 vols. (Gütersloh: Bertelsmann, 1966), 1:247.
11. See Jörg Nagler, "From Culture to *Kultur:* American Perceptions of Imperial Germany, 1871–1914," in *Transatlantic Images and Perceptions: Germany and America since 1776,* ed. David E. Barclay and Elisabeth Glaser-Schmidt (New York: Cambridge University Press, 1997), 134–35.
12. John A. Hobson, *The Psychology of Jingoism* (London: G. Richards, 1901), 1.

13. Stressed by Robert H. Wiebe in his seminal study *The Search for Order, 1877–1920* (New York: Hill and Wang, 1967).
14. See Richard Maxwell Brown, "Historische Muster der Gewalt in Amerika," in *Gewalt in den USA,* ed. Hans Joas and Wolfgang Knöbl (Frankfurt am Main: Fischer Taschenbuch Verlag, 1994), 101–3.
15. See John Higham, *Strangers in the Land: Patterns of American Nativism 1860–1925,* 2nd ed. (New York: Atheneum, 1984), ii.
16. See Volker Bischoff and Marino Mania, "*Melting Pot*-Mythen als Szenarien amerikanischer Identität zur Zeit der *New Immigration,*" in *Nationale und kulturelle Identität. Studien zur Entwicklung des kollektiven Bewußtseins in der Neuzeit,* ed. Bernhard Giesen (Frankfurt am Main: Suhrkamp, 1991), 513–36.
17. See Samuel Walker, *In Defense of American Liberties: A History of the ACLU* (New York: Oxford University Press, 1990), 12; Seymour Lipset, *Exceptionalism: A Double-Edged Sword* (New York: Norton, 1996), 65.
18. Mark Sullivan cited in David M. Kennedy, "American Political Culture in a Time of Crisis: Mobilization in World War I," in *Confrontation and Cooperation: Germany and the United States in the Era of World War I, 1900–1924,* ed. Hans-Jürgen Schröder (Providence, RI: Berg, 1993); Kennedy, "American Political Culture," 214.
19. *U.S. Bureau of the Census, Thirteenth Census of the United States Taken 1910,* 11 vols. (Washington, DC: Government Printing Office, 1912–1914), vol. 1:875–79. Altogether, about one-third of America's foreign born were from enemy countries.
20. Stephen Vaughn, *Holding Fast the Inner Lines: Democracy, Nationalism, and the Committee on Public Information* (Chapel Hill, NC: University of North Carolina Press, 1979), 105.
21. See Bischoff and Mania, "*Melting Pot*-Mythen," 513–36.
22. On national minorities and the thread of internal security on the American home front during the First World War, see Jörg Nagler, *Nationale Minoritäten im Krieg. 'Feindliche Ausländer' und die amerikanische Heimatfront während des Ersten Weltkriegs* (Hamburg: Hamburger Edition, 2000).
23. For British propaganda during World War I in the United States, see M. L. Sanders and Philip M. Taylor, *British Propaganda during the First World War, 1914–1918* (London: Macmillan, 1982), 167–207.
24. For German intelligence operations and sabotage during the neutrality period, see the studies of Reinhard R. Doerries, "The Politics of Irresponsibility: Imperial Germany's Defiance of United States Neutrality during World War I," in *Germany and America: Essays on Problems of International Relations and Immigration,* ed. Hans L. Trefousse (New York: Brooklyn College Press, 1980), 3–20; Doerries, "Empire and Republic: German-American Relations before 1917," in *America and the Germans: An Assessment of a Three-Hundred-Year History,* ed. Frank Trommler and Joseph Mc Veigh, 2 vols. (Philadelphia: University of Pennsylvania Press, 1985), 2:3–17; Doerries, "The War of Words: Imperial German Propaganda Efforts in the United States, 1914–1917," in *The Mirror of History: Essays in Honor of Fritz Fellner,* ed. Solomon Wank, Heidrun Maschl et al. (Santa Barbara, CA: Abc-Clio, 1988), 395–410. See also Friedhelm Koopmann, *Diplomatie und Reichsinteresse. Das Geheimdienstkalkül in der deutschen Amerikapolitik 1914 bis 1917* (Frankfurt am Main: Lang, 1990).
25. Quincy Wright, *A Study of War,* 2nd ed. (Chicago: University of Chicago Press, 1965), 307.
26. As for total war, there is no concise definition of "propaganda." Some students of propaganda argue that all persuasive communication is propagandistic, while others suggest that only dishonest messages can be considered propaganda. Political activists of all stripes

claim that they speak the truth while their opponents preach propaganda. The literature on propaganda is immense and cannot be listed here. For the specific Anglo-American situation in World War I, see H. D. Lasswell, *Propaganda Technique in the World War* (Cambridge, MA: MIT Press, 1927); Horace C. Peterson, *Propaganda for War: The Campaign against American Neutrality* (Port Washington, NY: Kennikat, 1939); James Read, *Atrocity Propaganda for War: The Campaign against American Neutrality, 1914–1917* (New Haven, CT: Yale University Press, 1941); M. L. Sanders and Philip M. Taylor, *British Propaganda during the First World War, 1914–1918* (London: Macmillan, 1982); Peter Buitenhuis, *The Great War of Words: British, American, and Canadian Propaganda and Fiction, 1914–1933* (Vancouver: University of British Columbia Press, 1987); Burton Dunbar and Richard McKinzie, *Art and Propaganda: Images of Ourselves and Our Enemies* (Kansas City, MO: Liberty Memorial Museum, 1987). For a useful historical survey of the usage of propaganda in the European context see Ute Daniel and Wolfram Siemann, eds., *Propaganda. Meinungskampf, Verführung und politische Sinnstiftung 1789–1989* (Frankfurt am Main: Fischer Taschenbuch-Verlag, 1994). See also Eberhard Demm, "Propaganda and Caricature in the First World War," *Journal of Contemporary History* 28 (1993): 163–92.

27. See Nagler, "From Culture to *Kultur*," 133.
28. I use the term *hysteria* in the widest sense as a type of social-psychological disorder that has affected the body politic.
29. Vaughn, *Holding Fast the Inner Lines,* 13.
30. On these posters see George Theofiles, *American Posters of World War I* (New York: Dafran House, 1973).
31. Susan Kingsley Kent, "Love and Death: War and Gender in Britain, 1914–1918," in *Authority, Identity and the Social History of the Great War,* ed. Frans Coetzee and Shevin Coetzee (Providence, RI: Berghahn Books, 1995), 159.
32. Dunbar and McKinzie, *Art and Propaganda,* 18.
33. Billy Sunday, cited in Robert H. Ferrell, *Woodrow Wilson and World I, 1917–1921* (New York: Harper & Row, 1985), 205.
34. Buitenhuis, *The Great War of Words,* 70.
35. See Dunbar and McKinzie, *Art and Propaganda,* 15.
36. The first war loan campaign took place in May–June 1917, the second in October 1917, the third in April–May 1918, and the fourth in September–October 1918; *Congressional Record,* Senate, 65th Congress, 1st session, vol. 55, part 4, 8 June 1917, 3325, cited in Kennedy, "American Political Culture," 224.
37. William Gibbs McAdoo, *Crowded Years* (Boston: Houghton Mifflin, 1931), 374–79; Kennedy, "American Political Culture," 224.
38. See Vaughn, *Holding Fast the Inner Lines,* 26–27.
39. See ibid., 116.
40. See ibid., 140.
41. *Four Minute Men Bulletin,* 2 January 1918, 10.
42. See Frank J. Donner, *The Age of Surveillance: The Aims and Methods of America's Political Intelligence System* (New York: Knopf, 1980), 32–33; Joan M. Jensen, *The Price of Vigilance* (Chicago: Rand McNally, 1968), 158, 175–76; Richard Gid Powers, *Secrecy and Power: The Life of J. Edgar Hoover* (New York: Free Press, 1987), 45.
43. See Harold M. Hyman, *To Try Men's Souls: Loyalty Tests in America History* (Berkeley: University of California Press, 1959), 278.
44. Higham, *Strangers in the Land,* 211.
45. *Annual Report of the Attorney General* (Washington, DC: GPO, 1918), 83.
46. Emerson Hough, *The Web* (Chicago: Reilly & Lee, 1919), 59.

47. Theodore Roosevelt, *The Foes of Our Own Household* (New York: Scribner, 1917), 30.
48. See David Kennedy, *Over Here: The First World War and American Society* (New York: Oxford University Press, 1980), 73.
49. *Tulsa Daily World*, 15 April 1917, cited in James H. Fowler, "Tar and Feather Patriotism: The Suppression of Dissent in Oklahoma During World War I," *The Chronicles of Oklahoma* 56 (1978–79): 411.
50. Roosevelt, *The Foes*, 293–94.
51. There are numerous regional studies on the respective Councils of Defense. For the national organization see William Breen, *Uncle Sam at Home: Civilian Mobilization, Wartime Federalism, and the Council of National Defense, 1917–1919* (Westport, CT: Greenwood Press, 1984).
52. See Brown, "Historische Muster der Gewalt," 76, 92. Mob violence against Mennonites in Kansas was initiated and organized by "well-respected" members of the community. See James Juhnke, "Mob Violence and Kansas Mennonites in 1918," *Kansas Historical Quarterly* 43 (1977): 334–50.
53. See Brown, "Historische Muster," 77. For a historical analysis of American social violence see especially Richard Maxwell Brown, *Strain of Violence: Historical Studies of American Violence and Vigilantism* (New York: Oxford University Press, 1975); Brown, *No Duty to Retreat: Violence and Values in American History and Society* (New York: Oxford University Press, 1991); Ted Robert Gurr, ed., *Violence in America*, 2 vols. (Newbury Park, CA: Sage, 1989); Robert Brent Toplin, *Unchallenging Violence: An American Ordeal* (Westport, CT: Greenwood Press, 1975); David Ammerman, *In the Common Cause: American Response to the Coercive Acts* (Charlottesville: University Press of Virginia, 1974); Dirk Hoerder, *Crowd Action in Revolutionary Massachusetts, 1765–1780* (New York: Academic, 1977).
54. Clifford Geertz, *The Interpretation of Cultures: Selected Essays by Clifford Geertz* (New York: Basic Books, 1973), 448.
55. Theodore Roosevelt, *The Great Adventure* (1917), reprinted in *The Works of Theodore Roosevelt: National Edition*, 20 vols. (New York: Scribner, 1926), 19:327. See also Paul Finkelman, "The War on German Language and Culture, 1917–1925," in Schröder, *Confrontation and Cooperation*, 177–205. For the equation of immigrants and germs see Allan Kraut, *Silent Travellers: Germs, Genes, and the Immigrant Menace* (New York: Basic Books, 1994).
56. See Ronald Schaffer, *America in the Great War: The Rise of the War Welfare State* (New York: Oxford University Press, 1991), 26.
57. H. C. Peterson and Gilbert C. Fite, *Opponents of War, 1917–1918* (Madison: University of Wisconsin Press, 1957), 194.
58. Ibid., 195.
59. For a genesis and history of these fears see David Brion Davis, *The Fear of Conspiracy: Images of Un-American Subversion from the Revolution to the Present* (Ithaca, NY: Cornell University Press, 1971). The press stirred up these fears. See for example the report in the *New York Times*, 7 April 1917, 3, from Birmingham, Alabama entitled "Evidence of Movements by German Agents to incite Negroes in the South"; or the *Literary Digest*, 21 April 1917, 1153: "German Plots Among Negroes." On the general aspects of fears as a social construction see, e.g., D. L. Altheide, *Creating Fear: News and the Construction of Crisis* (New York: Aldine De Gruyter, 2002), 24. For superb historical and cultural analysis of fear see, e.g., Joanna Bourke, *Fear: A Cultural History* (London: Virago Press, 2005), and Corey Robin, *Fear: The History of a Political Idea* (New York: Oxford University Press, 2004). See also Richard Hofstadter, "The Paranoid Style in American Politics," *Harper's Magazine* (November 1964): 77–86.

60. See William Fitzhugh Brundage, *Lynching in the New South: Georgia and Virginia, 1880–1930* (Urbana: University of Illinois Press, 1993), 228.
61. On this race riot see Elliott Rudwick, *Race Riot at St. Louis, 2 July 1917* (Carbondale: Southern Illinois University Press, 1964).
62. See the enclosed letter in the correspondence between Wilson and Joseph Patrick Tumulty, *Washington Post*, 5 July 1917, cited in *The Papers of Woodrow Wilson*, ed. Arthur S. Link, 69 vols. (Princeton, NJ: Princeton University Press, 1966–1994), 43:103. See also Mark Ellis, "Federal Surveillance of Black Americans during the First World War," *Immigrants and Minorities* 12 (1993): 9.
63. See Brundage, *Lynching in the New South*, 228.
64. Davis, *The Fear of Conspiracy*, xix.
65. See Junker, *The Manichean Trap*, 16, 19.
66. See Kennedy, *Over Here*, 46, 138, 142.
67. Higham, *Strangers in the Land*, 205.

Bibliography

Altheide, D. L. *Creating Fear: News and the Construction of Crisis.* New York: Aldine De Gruyter, 2002.

Ammerman, David. *In the Common Cause: American Response to the Coercive Acts.* Charlottesville: University Press of Virginia, 1974.

Annual Report of the Attorney General. Washington, DC: GPO, 1918.

Bischoff, Volker and Marino Mania. "*Melting Pot*-Mythen als Szenarien amerikanischer Identität zur Zeit der *New Immigration.*" In *Nationale und kulturelle Identität. Studien zur Entwicklung des kollektiven Bewußtseins in der Neuzeit,* edited by Bernhard Giesen, 513–36. Frankfurt am Main: Suhrkamp, 1991.

Bourke, Joanna. *Fear: A Cultural History.* London: Virago Press, 2005.

Breen, William. *Uncle Sam at Home: Civilian Mobilization, Wartime Federalism, and the Council of National Defense, 1917–1919.* Westport, CT: Greenwood Press, 1984.

Brown, Richard Maxwell. "Historische Muster der Gewalt in Amerika." In *Gewalt in den USA,* edited by Hans Joas and Wolfgang Knöbl, 75–121. Frankfurt am Main: Fischer Taschenbuch Verlag, 1994.

———. *No Duty to Retreat: Violence and Values in American History and Society.* New York: Oxford University Press, 1991.

———. *Strain of Violence: Historical Studies of American Violence and Vigilantism.* New York: Oxford University Press, 1975.

Brundage, William Fitzhugh. *Lynching in the New South: Georgia and Virginia, 1880–1930.* Urbana: University of Illinois Press, 1993.

Buitenhuis, Peter. *The Great War of Words: British, American, and Canadian Propaganda and Fiction, 1914–1933.* Vancouver: University of British Columbia Press, 1987.

Chickering, Roger and Stig Förster, eds. *How Total was the Great War?* New York: Cambridge University Press, 2000.

Cooper, John Milton, Jr. *The Warrior and the Priest: Woodrow Wilson and Theodore Roosevelt.* Cambridge, MA: Belknap Press, 1983.

Curti, Merle. *Roots of American Loyalty.* New York: Columbia University Press, 1946.

Daniel, Ute and Wolfram Siemann, eds. *Propaganda. Meinungskampf, Verführung und politische Sinnstiftung 1789–1989.* Frankfurt am Main: Fischer Taschenbuch Verlag, 1994.

Davis, David Brion. *The Fear of Conspiracy: Images of Un-American Subversion from the Revolution to the Present.* Ithaca, NY: Cornell University Press, 1971.

Demm, Eberhard. "Propaganda and Caricature in the First World War." *Journal of Contemporary History* 28 (1993): 163–92.

Doerries, Reinhard R. "Empire and Republic: German-American Relations before 1917." In *America and the Germans,* 2 vols., edited by Frank Trommler and Joseph Mc Veigh, 2:3–17. Philadelphia: University of Pennsylvania Press, 1985.

———. "The Politics of Irresponsibility: Imperial Germany's Defiance of United States Neutrality during World War I." In *Germany and America: Essays on Problems of International Relations and Immigration,* edited by Hans L. Trefousse, 3–20. New York: Brooklyn College Press, 1980.

———. "The War of Words: Imperial German Propaganda Efforts in the United States, 1914–1917." In *The Mirror of History: Essays in Honor of Fritz Fellner,* edited by Solomon Wank, Heidrun Maschl et al., 395–410. Santa Barbara, CA: Abc-Clio, 1988.

Donner, Frank J. *The Age of Surveillance: The Aims and Methods of America's Political Intelligence System.* New York: Knopf, 1980.

Dunbar, Burton and Richard McKinzie. *Art and Propaganda: Images of Ourselves and Our Enemies.* Kansas City, MO: Liberty Memorial Museum, 1987.

Ehrenreich, Barbara. *Blood Rites: Origins and History of the Passions of War.* New York: Holt, 1997.

Ellis, Mark. "Federal Surveillance of Black Americans during the First World War." *Immigrants and Minorities* 12 (1993): 1–20.

Ferrell, Robert H. *Woodrow Wilson and World I, 1917–1921.* New York: Harper & Row, 1985.

Finkelman, Paul. "The War on German Language and Culture, 1917–1925." In *Confrontation and Cooperation: Germany and the United States in the Era of World War I, 1900–1924,* edited by Hans-Jürgen Schröder. Providence, RI: Berg, 1993.

Four Minute Men Bulletin. 2 January 1918.

Fowler, James H. "Tar and Feather Patriotism: The Suppression of Dissent in Oklahoma During World War I." *The Chronicles of Oklahoma* 56 (1978–79): 409–30.

Geertz, Clifford. *The Interpretation of Cultures: Selected Essays by Clifford Geertz.* New York: Basic Books, 1973.

Greiner, Bernd, Christian Th. Müller and Dierk Walter, eds. *Angst im Kalten Krieg* (Hamburg: Hamburger Edition, 2009).

Guetzkow, Harold. *Multiple Loyalties: Theoretical Approach to a Problem in International Organization.* Princeton, NJ: Princeton University Press, 1955.

Gurr, Ted Robert, ed. *Violence in America,* 2 vols. Newbury Park, CA: Sage, 1989.

Higham, John. *Strangers in the Land: Patterns of American Nativism 1860–1925.* 2nd ed. New York: Atheneum, 1984.

Hobson, John A. *The Psychology of Jingoism.* London: G. Richards, 1901.

Hoerder, Dirk. *Crowd Action in Revolutionary Massachusetts, 1765–1780.* New York: Academic, 1977.

Hofstadter, Richard "The Paranoid Style in American Politics." *Harper's Magazine* (November 1964): 77–86.

Hough, Emerson. *The Web.* Chicago: Reilly & Lee, 1919.

Howard, Michael. *Clausewitz.* Oxford: Oxford University Press, 1983.

———. *The Lessons of History.* New Haven, CT: Yale University Press, 1991.

Hyman, Harold M. *To Try Men's Souls: Loyalty Tests in America History.* Berkeley: University of California Press, 1959.

Jensen, Joan M. *The Price of Vigilance.* Chicago: Rand McNally, 1968.

Juhnke, James. "Mob Violence and Kansas Mennonites in 1918." *Kansas Historical Quarterly* 43 (1977): 334–50.

Junker, Detlef. *The Manichean Trap: American Perceptions of the German Empire, 1871–1945*. Washington, DC: German Historical Institute, 1995.

Kennedy, David M. "American Political Culture in a Time of Crisis: Mobilization in World War I." In *Confrontation and Cooperation: Germany and the United States in the Era of World War I, 1900–1924*, edited by Hans-Jürgen Schröder. Providence, RI: Berg, 1993.

———. *Over Here: The First World War and American Society*. New York: Oxford University Press, 1980.

Kent, Susan Kingsley. "Love and Death. War and Gender in Britain, 1914–1918." In *Authority, Identity and the Social History of the Great War*, edited by Frans Coetzee and Shevin Coetzee, chapter 7. Providence, RI: Berghahn Books, 1995.

Koopmann, Friedhelm. *Diplomatie und Reichsinteresse. Das Geheimdienstkalkül in der deutschen Amerikapolitik 1914 bis 1917*. Frankfurt am Main: Lang, 1990.

Kraut, Allan. *Silent Travelers: Germs, Genes, and the Immigrant Menace*. New York: Basic Books, 1994.

Lasswell, H. D. *Propaganda Technique in the World War*. Cambridge, MA: MIT Press, 1927.

Link, Arthur. "That Cobb Interview." *Journal of American History* 72 (1985): 7–17.

———., ed. *The Papers of Woodrow Wilson*, 69 vols. Princeton, NJ: Princeton University Press, 1966–1994.

Lipset, Seymour. *Exceptionalism: A Double-Edged Sword*. New York: Norton, 1996.

Lodge, Henry Cabot. *War Addresses, 1915–1917*. Boston: Houghton Mifflin, 1917.

McAdoo, William Gibbs. *Crowded Years*. Boston: Houghton Mifflin, 1931.

Nagler, Jörg. *Nationale Minoritäten im Krieg. 'Feindliche Ausländer' und die amerikanische Heimatfront während des Ersten Weltkriegs*. Hamburg: Hamburger Edition, 2000.

———. From Culture to *Kultur*: American Perceptions of Imperial Germany, 1871–1914." In *Transatlantic Images and Perceptions: Germany and America since 1776*, edited by David E. Barclay and Elisabeth Glaser-Schmidt, 131–54. New York: Cambridge University Press, 1997.

———. "Loyalty and Dissent: The Home Front in the American Civil War." In *On the Road to Total War: The American Civil War and the German Wars of Unification*, edited by Stig Förster and Jörg Nagler. Washington, DC: German Historical Institute, 1996.

Peterson, H. C., and Gilbert C. Fite. *Opponents of War, 1917–1918*. Madison: University of Wisconsin Press, 1957.

Peterson, Horace C. *Propaganda for War: The Campaign against American Neutrality*. Port Washington, NY: Kennikat, 1939.

Powers, Richard Gid. *Secrecy and Power: The Life of J. Edgar Hoover*. New York: Free Press, 1987.

Read, James. *Atrocity Propaganda for War: The Campaign against American Neutrality, 1914–1917*. New Haven, CT, Yale University Press, 1941.

Robin, Corey. *Fear: The History of a Political Idea*. New York: Oxford University Press, 2004.

Roosevelt, Theodore. *The Foes of Our Own Household*. New York: Scribner, 1917.

———. *The Great Adventure* (1917). Reprinted in *The Works of Theodore Roosevelt: National Edition*, vol. 19. New York: Scribner, 1926.

Rudwick, Elliott. *Race Riot at St. Louis, 2 July 1917*. Carbondale: Southern Illinois University Press, 1964.

Sanders, M. L. and Philip M. Taylor. *British Propaganda during the First World War, 1914–1918*. London: Macmillan, 1982.

Schaar, John H. *Loyalty in America*. Westport, CT: Greenwood Press, 1982.

Scheff, Thomas J. *Bloody Revenge: Emotions, Nationalism, and War.* Boulder, CO: Westview Press, 1994)

Schaffer, Ronald. *America in the Great War: The Rise of the War Welfare State.* New York: Oxford University Press, 1991.

Speier, Hans. "Klassenstruktur und totaler Krieg." In *Krieg und Frieden im industriellen Zeitalter,* edited and introduction by Uwe Nerlich, 2 vols. Gütersloh: Bertelsmann, 1966.

Theofiles, George. *American Posters of World War I.* New York: Dafran House, 1973.

Toplin, Robert Brent. *Unchallenging Violence: An American Ordeal.* Westport, CT: Greenwood Press, 1975.

U.S. Bureau of the Census, Thirteenth Census of the United States Taken 1910, 11 vols. Washington, DC : Government Printing Office, 1912–1914, vol. 1.

Vaughn, Stephen. *Holding Fast the Inner Lines: Democracy, Nationalism, and the Committee on Public Information.* Chapel Hill: University of North Carolina Press, NC, 1979.

Walker, Samuel. *In Defense of American Liberties: A History of the ACLU.* New York: Oxford University Press, 1990.

Wiebe, Robert H. *The Search for Order, 1877–1920.* New York: Hill and Wang, 1967.

Wright, Quincy. *A Study of War,* 2nd ed. Chicago: University of Chicago Press, 1965.

Chapter 5

Hanoi Jane, Vietnam Memory, and Emotions

Andreas Etges

Pretty little Jane in her go-go boots
made her claim to fame
when she betrayed her roots.

Went on over to Hanoi
climbed up on her soap box
filled with the corpse of
the boy from down the block.

Sided with the commies,
filled young hearts with pain,
earned herself the title
"That bitch, Hanoi Jane."

Heard you say you're sorry,
well Jane, I'm sorry too.
There's just no way the USA
should have to live with you.

The poem "Plain Jane" by Barbara Pope, the wife of a Vietnam veteran, is one of several poems, songs, and stories about Jane Fonda's controversial visit to North Vietnam in 1972.[1] Veterans' stands on the Mall in Washington still sell stickers like these: "Jane: Call Home 1-800-Hanoi" and "I'm

Notes for this section begin on page 104.

JANE: CALL HOME
1-800-HANOI

Figure 5.1. Sticker: "Call home Fonda."

not Fond'a Hanoi Jane." Another sticker reads: "I'll forgive her when the Jews forgive Hitler." An internet search produces many thousand hits for "Hanoi Jane," most of them unforgiving for Fonda's alleged treason. The actress is pictured on these websites in prison or in a cage, as a snake, or as a sample for target practice. Someone sells a dart board with her face on it, others show an animated little man urinating on a Fonda picture or her grave, and finally one can order special "urinal stickers" showing the actress in workout tights in her famous aerobic pose with her legs spread.[2] During the presidential election campaign of 2004, the antiwar activism of Fonda was linked to that of Democratic candidate John Kerry. A forged photograph that was widely distributed showed them side by side at a rally, t-shirts featured "Hanoi Jane" and "Hanoi John" on separate images.[3]

Despite a general sense of reconciliation on the national level, Jane Fonda remains a focus of hate for many veterans of the Vietnam War. Why does Fonda still trigger such violent expressions of emotions among many veterans, so long after the war? Richard Lazarus and Joseph Ledoux have argued that "emotional information can … be stored as a memory," and that memories of a "prior emotional encounter" can help trigger an emotion.[4] Fonda is such a "trigger." In order to understand the special role the actress plays in the emotional memory of many veterans, this essay will examine her political emergence in the late 1960s, her brief visit to North Vietnam in July 1972, the ensuing public controversy, the changing veterans' relation-

Figure 5.2. Sticker: "Not Fonda."

ship with Fonda until today, and the multiple connections between Vietnam memory, emotions, and Jane Fonda's role.

From "Liberal" to "Revolutionary"

The prominent actress Jane Fonda spent much of the 1960s in Paris with her then husband, the French director Roger Vadim. "I didn't think women could change anything, except sheets," she later described that period of her life.[5] At first she was only a distant observer of the political situations that were unfolding in Paris, Berlin, and in many places in the United States. But she soon became more interested, and finally—after returning to America in early 1970—involved. After protesting with Native Americans on Alcatraz Island, she left for a three-month political cross-country trip in March 1970 that transformed her into one of America's most visible activists. She traveled all over the United States, supporting the Black Panthers, Native Americans, and the women's movement: "When I left the West Coast I was a liberal. When I landed in New York I was a revolutionary."[6]

Fonda's prominence immediately gained her national visibility. She became an icon of the protest movement, even making the cover of *LIFE*.[7] Her ubiquity was criticized by her political opponents, and not always appreciated by those active in the movements she supported, who were afraid that her lack of knowledge and her naiveté often damaged rather than furthered their causes. Furthermore, others doubted her sincerity as she often seemed to say lines that had been fed to her. "It is as though the Weatherman faction kidnapped Barbarella and then turned her loose again with the movement tape recorder running in her throat," the *Detroit Free Press* wrote in the second half of 1970.[8]

Her outrage at injustice and her will to change "the American system" were sincere, though. She was arrested several times, spent most of her money on these issues, and certainly neglected, if not jeopardized, her Hollywood career. She was, in her own words, "a Socialist. But without a theory, without an ideology." And she later admitted that being emotional and not always well informed made her defensive and overreactive.[9]

Finally Fonda became very active in the antiwar movement, supporting critical soldiers, draft resisters, and veterans against the war in Vietnam. She helped organize the Winter Soldier Investigations in Detroit in February 1971, where Vietnam veterans admitted their guilt and told their stories, and she was a major sponsor of Fred Gardner's United States Servicemen's Fund, which opened coffee houses near bases and tried to organize internal opposition within the US forces. There Fonda picked up the idea to put together an alternative to the official entertainment shows for soldiers that featured Bob Hope and others. In mid-February 1971 she announced: "The time has come for entertainers who take a different view on the war to reach our servicemen, too. Antiwar shows are what today's soldiers want." That year the FTA ("Free Theater Association," "Free the Army," "Fun, Travel, Adventure," or "Fuck the Army") consisting of Fonda, Donald Sutherland, and other actors and singers offered highly popular shows near military bases inside and outside the United States criticizing the military and making fun of it.[10]

All these activities soon caught the attention of the FBI and its notorious director, J. Edgar Hoover. From March 1970 on Fonda was under observation, her phone was tapped for years, and the FBI launched a systematic campaign to discredit the actress in the public eye, such as her arrest on drug charges at Cleveland airport in November 1970.[11] Although much of this maneuvering was uncovered in the wake of the Watergate scandal, the FBI succeeded at least in part in questioning her patriotism and political reliability in substantial segments of public opinion long before she embarked on her visit to the "enemy" in the summer of 1972, just a couple of months after she had received her first Academy Award for *Klute* that April.[12]

Jane Fonda in Hanoi, July 1972

In historical perspective, Jane Fonda's two-week trip to North Vietnam from 8–22 July 1972 surely was one of the least important episodes of the Vietnam War. A major reason for her visit was to protest the bombing of dikes, which many believed Nixon was planning and which might have caused immense damage and possibly killed tens of thousands of people.[13] She met Vietnamese from different social backgrounds, including Vice President Nguyen Duy Trinh, visited factories and kindergartens, watched plays and ballet, listened to songs and poetry, and witnessed the widespread destruction caused by US bombardments.[14]

But this did not make her visit memorable. During her trip Fonda recorded a number of statements for Radio Hanoi.[15] In these transmissions, the American actress described her impression of the country and its people and criticized the American war against Vietnam. She also repeatedly urged soldiers—including American prisoners of war who had to listen to the broadcasts—to end their destructive work. Fonda asked questions and urged American servicemen to think about the consequences of their actions. "Why? Why do you do this? Why do you follow orders telling you to destroy a hospital or bomb the schools?" "All of you in the cockpits of your planes, on the aircraft carriers, those who are loading the bombs, those who are repairing the planes, those who are working on the 7th Fleet, please think what you are doing." Fonda accused the US Army of using illegal weapons such as napalm bombs. Their deployment and the bombing of the dikes, she argued, not only made the American leaders but also the soldiers war criminals, just like the Germans and the Japanese in World War II, some of whom had been executed for their crimes: "Some day we're going to have to answer to our children for this war." The United States, led by President Richard Nixon, whom Fonda even characterized as "a new-type Hitler," was responsible for a "mass genocide." And that made the war in her eyes "the most terrible crime that has ever been created [*sic*] against humanity."[16]

Even more than the broadcasts, two other "events" defined the way in which public memory of the visit was shaped in the long run. The first one was a staged meeting with seven American POWs in Hanoi who got a chance to talk to Fonda during her visit. In one of her radio messages she described the meeting as a free exchange of ideas. The soldiers told her that they were treated well and were in good health. Supposedly they now condemned the war and felt bad about what they had done. They even wanted her to tell their relatives to join the antiwar movement.[17] It is not clear whether some of them really told Fonda that they now opposed the war or if she just read statements that had been prepared for her by the North Vietnamese. In any case, Fonda obviously was naively unaware that the soldiers had not volunteered to meet her and could not speak openly in the presence of their guards.[18]

The second event that enshrined her image as a "traitor" was the famous film clip and resulting photographs, capturing Fonda, smilingly wearing a helmet in the midst of North Vietnamese soldiers, pretending to operate an antiaircraft gun, used to shoot down American planes.[19]

Immediately after her return to the United States, Fonda was greeted by a wave of criticism in the American press. That summer her opponents coined the moniker "Hanoi Jane"—a name that has stuck until today.[20] She was accused of siding with the enemy at a time when "our boys" were dying in Vietnam, for playing a part in communist propaganda efforts, while American POWs had to grin and bear it. In short: she was a "traitor," and her broadcasts were compared to the World War II Japanese propagandists named "Tokyo Rose" (one of whom was identified as Iva Toguri D'Aquino), of Radio Tokyo. Many people, among them a number of congressmen, demanded that she be tried for treason or sedition.[21] For Fonda, however, antiwar protesters like herself were the true patriots. They were the ones who really cared about this "American tragedy," while Nixon was a "traitor," "who is committing the most heinous crimes I think have ever been committed."[22]

Fonda was also "blacklisted" by the government and while still in North Vietnam was officially reprimanded by the Department of State.[23] On 10

August 1972, the House Internal Security Committee, which had discussed her trip, decided not to subpoena her at that time but turned her case over to the Department of Justice, which then put the FBI on the case.[24] In September, the committee, which investigated "communist and other subversive activities affecting the internal security of the United States," started its own hearings.[25] At the same time experts of the Passport Office of the State Department discussed if Fonda had violated passport laws by traveling into an enemy country without permission.[26]

The investigations of the committee ran into a number of problems. In order to protect political opposition and to prevent misuse of the law, Art. 3, Sec. III of the Constitution defines treason rather narrowly. A person has to levy war or at least actively support the enemies of the United States. In addition, clear proof of treason is necessary either in the form of a confession of the accused in court or through the testimony of two witnesses. There was no doubt that Fonda had been in North Vietnam, that she had recorded speeches critical of the United States' conduct of war, that these speeches had been broadcasted via Radio Hanoi, and that they had been listened to by American soldiers. But could she be convicted of treason or illegal use of her passport?

Representatives of the Department of Justice doubted that they could prove she had committed treason. While it was clear that she had supported the enemy, Fonda definitely would not confess what she had done. It seemed impossible to find two witnesses who had been present when the speeches were taped in North Vietnam. Surely, the Founding Fathers could not have foreseen the possibility of electronic recordings in the future, but the Constitution was unambiguous: without confession or witnesses to the deed there was no case for treason.[27]

The attempt to charge her with violation of the passport laws proved equally futile. As the Deputy Director of the Passport Office explained to the committee members, the federal government could and did restrict traveling into countries that were in a state of war with the United States or that were declared enemies. For those countries US citizens needed special permission, and the records indicated that Fonda had not applied for such permission before visiting North Vietnam. Upon reentering the United States, immigration officers had checked her passport for North Vietnamese visa stamps but had found none. It was assumed that she had gotten a visa on a separate piece of paper, as local authorities were aware of the judicial consequences for Americans traveling to North Vietnam. While there were lots of photos and other evidence that she had actually been there, it was nearly impossible to prove that she had used her passport to get in. Her presence in North Vietnam alone was not punishable. A number of prominent dissidents such as Noam Chomsky, Abbie Hoffman, Jerry Rubin, Eldridge Cleaver, and

Stokeley Carmichael had traveled to Vietnam without special permit, as had relatives of American POWs. If Fonda was to be tried, so were they.[28]

In order to measure the effects of Fonda's broadcasts on the morale of American soldiers in Vietnam, the House Internal Security Committee invited testimony from three experts of psychological warfare.[29] The publisher and editor of "Tactics," Edward Hunter, a leading American specialist on psychological warfare "who put the word 'brainwashing' into our language," was the first to testify. For Hunter, Fonda's broadcasts were masterpieces of "psywar": "Rarely did even Goebbels go to greater extremes of calculated distortion and propaganda lying against the United States than Fonda did." In his estimate they even surpassed those of Tokyo Rose in World War II. Not only was the war propaganda highly professional, but the North Vietnamese had chosen an American celebrity to deliver it. As an actress, Fonda, who in Hunter's view had a "brainwashed mind," functioned extremely effectively. The witness concluded that the broadcasts had "seriously assaulted the stamina" of "an incalculable number" of American soldiers listening to them. The damage to the soldier as "the target of this practically unprecedented form of war" was like that of a real wound, like "a bullet shot from behind him, from his own side, when the paralyzing or killing words are uttered through the mouth of an American."[30] According to Hunter's testimony, Jane Fonda's broadcasts were a kind of "traumatic assault" on those American soldiers who listened to her. While the other two experts agreed that the broadcasts were rather good propaganda, their evaluation of effects was inconclusive.[31] The Justice Department lacked substantial evidence to further pursue the case and dropped all further charges against Fonda.[32] But this was only the end of the judicial story. Anger soon flared up again.

Trying to prevent Nixon's reelection and wanting to inform the American public about the history of Vietnam and the reality of war, Fonda and her future husband, Tom Hayden, started the "Indochina Peace Campaign" in September of 1972. During extensive lecture tours throughout the country, Hayden, Fonda, and their friends distributed tens of thousands of copies of excerpts from the Pentagon Papers and illustrated their presentations with slides taken by Fonda during her recent trip to North Vietnam.[33]

After the peace treaty was signed in January 1973, the Nixon administration staged "Operation Homecoming" ceremonies for returning POWs. Still outraged by the infamous and internationally condemned Christmas bombings of the North just a few weeks before, Fonda dismissed POWs returning with tales of torture as "liars, hypocrites, and pawns of President Nixon." Coming home "looking like football players," these "professional killers" did not tell the truth. Fonda soon regretted her overreaction and admitted that there had been "incidents of torture," while still denying that systematic torture of American POWs had taken place; but that did not prevent a new series of vicious reactions.[34]

Several state legislatures discussed her visit and some publicly denounced her. In Colorado, a resolution to declare the "foul-mouthed offensive little Vassar dropout" (Representative Michael Strang) unwelcome in the state was countered by an amendment proposed by the only black woman in the legislature, declaring John Wayne unwelcome, "unless, by act of God, he were to become black, brown or poor." Maryland legislator William Burhead was against executing her, "But I think we should cut her tongue off to keep her mouth quiet." In Washington, Republican congressman Robert Steele suggested to nominate her for a new award as "the rottenest, most miserable performance by any one individual American in the history of our country." And after a speech at the University of Southern California, students hanged Fonda in effigy. But having already concluded that they had no real case, the House Internal Security Committee as well as the Justice Department rejected renewed efforts to bring her to court.[35]

"Ms. America"

In July–August 2001, Jane Fonda made the cover of *American Heritage* with two photographs, one from the 1968 movie "Barbarella," and the other from 2001. According to Peter Braunstein's article, Fonda, now in her mid-sixties, represented the epitome of "Ms. America," a "mirror of the nation's past forty years" from a young and sexy actress in the early sixties, to a political radical, to a fitness-crazed businesswoman, who sold two million copies of her workout book in the 1980s. In 1991 she married media tycoon Ted Turner and finally became religious.[36] By that time, mainstream American society had come to embrace her and women celebrated her as a role model and one of the country's outstanding female personalities.[37] By April 1999, Jane Fonda was even included in Barbara Walters's ABC show "One Hundred Years of Great Women." A few months later, the American Association of University Women's Legal Advocacy Fund honored her with the "Speaking Out for Justice" award. And yet, this step-by-step embrace was accompanied by surges of intense hatred and anger among conservatives and especially among veterans, who even organized boycott campaigns against Fonda products like her exercise videos.

While the chameleon-like change described by Braunstein is a somewhat crude simplification, Fonda evolved her political views and publicly regretted some of the things she had said and done in the past. A first indirect attempt at public reconciliation was the film *Coming Home* of 1978. Inspired by the disabled Vietnam veteran Ron Kovic, whose bestselling autobiography *Born on the Fourth of July* was later made into a film by Oliver Stone, it is both a story of healing and of hurting. Jane's character Sally Hyde is married to an uptight and dominating officer who is sent off to Vietnam. Alone among her middle-class friends, Sally volunteers to help disabled veterans and falls in love with a severely traumatized serviceman. The relationship turns him from an asocial and tyrannical human being into a loving and affectionate person as he becomes actively engaged in the antiwar movement. Through the film Fonda had dared to again publicly associate herself with the Vietnam War and the veterans, though this time as a "healer," the typical role expected from women. She and her co-star Jon Voight were rewarded with Academy Awards for their performances the following year, but *Coming Home* definitely did not help make people forget about "Hanoi Jane"—if they needed any reminder.[38]

Jane Fonda's name was repeatedly associated with the initial debate about the design of the Vietnam Veterans Memorial in Washington, as early critics called the "wall" a "degrading ditch," a "black gash of shame and sorrow" in a city of white monuments. For Phyllis Schlafly, the prominent opponent of the Equal Rights Amendment, it was a "tribute to Jane Fonda." On the tenth anniversary of the monument in 1992, veterans burned "Hanoi Jane" in effigy.[39] And the POW movie *Hanoi Hilton* of 1987 about the infamous Hao Lo Prison in Hanoi even includes a character based on Fonda.[40]

Not until 1988 did Fonda apologize for her visit to North Vietnam. That year, MGM planned to film *Stanley and Iris* with Jane Fonda and Robert De Niro in a small New England town. Much to everybody's surprise, local veterans of Waterbury, Connecticut, organized protests against "Hanoi Jane" that soon made national headlines.[41] In an interview with Barbara Walters on ABC's *20/20* on 17 June 1988, Fonda finally apologized "to men who were in Vietnam whom I hurt, or whose pain I caused to deepen because of the things I said or did. I feel that I owe them an apology. My intentions were never to hurt them or make their situation worse. It was the contrary. I was trying to help end the killing and the war, but there were times when I was thoughtless and careless about it and I'm very sorry that I hurt them. And I want to apologize to them and their families."

The following day, Fonda met with some of her critics, among them Joseph Griggs of the "Veterans Coalition Against Hanoi Jane." While she did not apologize for her participation in the antiwar movement or for her visit of Hanoi, the actress found words of regret for having called veterans who claimed to have been tortured "liars" and for having posed with the antiaircraft gun: "It's the most stupid, naive thing I could have done."[42]

Since then, she has repeatedly voiced strong self-criticism: "I will go to my grave regretting the photograph of me in an antiaircraft (gun) carrier, which looks like I was trying to shoot at American planes." "It hurt so many soldiers. It galvanized such hostility. It was the most horrible thing I could possibly have done. It was just thoughtless."[43]

Her detractors proved to be less forgiving, then and now. The annual "Veterans of Foreign Wars" convention in Chicago in August 1988 adopted resolutions to investigate her "treasonable actions." Congress, the delegates demanded, should try her for treason and in true "Christian" spirit, televangelist Jerry Falwell commented on the occasion of the "Speaking Out for Justice" award: "Responsible Americans must never forget the intentional treachery Jane Fonda displayed toward her nation. ... Hanoi Jane spoke out against her own nation. And we must never forget." That same year, actor Charlton Heston, one of the National Rifle Association's most prominent spokesmen, called Barbra Streisand, who had produced a TV movie with an antigun message "Hanoi Jane of the Second Amendment." London's *Sunday Telegraph* talked about Fonda as the "head cheerleader for Ho Chi Minh." For many she has remained the traitorous young woman, sitting in an anti-aircraft gun, and fraternizing with the enemy. Because of people like Fonda, they argue, the war was prolonged and many American soldiers died.[44]

Her rejection reached a new level with the circulation of a particularly libelous account of Fonda's meeting with POWs in North Vietnam that is featured on many websites about American prisoners in Vietnam. Conservative journalist William F. Buckley, Jr. incorporated this highly questionable account about the meeting between Fonda and the American POWs in a widely circulated article: "Each man secreted a tiny piece of paper, with his serial number on it, in the palm of his hand. They were ... paraded before Ms. Fonda and a cameraman, and she walked the line, shaking each man's hand and asking little encouraging snippets like: 'Aren't you sorry you bombed babies?' and 'Are you grateful for the humane treatment from your benevolent captors?' Believing this had to be an act, they each palmed her their sliver of paper." She allegedly "took them all without missing a beat. At the end of the line, and once the camera stopped rolling, to the shocked disbelief of the POWs, she turned to the officer in charge ... and handed him the little package of papers."[45] The soldiers, the story continues, were beaten and three of them died, while others never fully recovered from the injuries inflicted by their North Vietnamese guards.

Much of this account is a fabrication. Two of the soldiers named in the story have denied the charges as some veterans' groups have distanced themselves from such efforts to publicly discredit Fonda. Mike McGrath, president of NAM-POWs, has denied that POWs were tortured in connection with Fonda's visit. On the contrary, Fonda carried many letters to POWs and returned their answers to their families in the United States. McGrath concluded: "To my knowledge, the worst that happened to the rest of us was that we had to listen to the camp radio ... with the Fonda propaganda. It pissed us off, but I doubt you can call that 'torture'."[46] However, individual allegations of torture as a consequence of talking frankly to Fonda about the conditions of captivity persist to this day.[47]

Hanoi Jane, Vietnam Memory, and Emotions

In his autobiography, Tom Hayden ponders the history of hostility towards his former wife Jane Fonda by many veterans: "Was it because she was a woman? A sex symbol turned into an accuser of macho men? A successful American rejecting the system that rewarded her? Why the hate?"[48] And why this hate and anger nearly thirty years later, one might add? What does Fonda represent?

The Vietnam War was a watershed in American history. The crimes committed by American troops belied the nation's perceived moral strength and innocence, while ultimate defeat undermined any notion of military superiority. The war left America deeply divided over fundamental aspects of the nation's core values and identities.[49]

Remembering Vietnam mainly as a personal tragedy for American families, the nation has finally found a way to deal with it. This national reconciliation and memorialization comes at the price of forgetting: forgetting that it was a *war*, forgetting why and how it was fought, forgetting how American politicians and generals lied to the public, and, above all, forgetting that there were millions of victims in Southeast Asia.

The debate whether the Vietnam War is an open wound, if the wound has healed, or if the scars can easily tear open again, rages on. And even though there are indications of a national "healing process," the violent reactions to Jane Fonda indicate the traumatic persistence of anger and hate.

A war shatters emotional restraints in fundamental ways and brings out extreme emotional experiences like fear or anger, often regarded as so-called basic emotions, which in many ways violate the soldier's sense of order and ethical standards. While this is probably true of every war, Vietnam differs in at least one major respect: this time the violence and atrocities were not justified by a just cause, by a victory, or at least by the unanimous support of the home front. The soldiers witnessed, "survived," and inflicted death, but their guilt was often neither resolved nor cushioned by societal support.

In his novel *A Rumor of War,* Philip Caputo talks about "the things men do in war and the things war does to them": "We had survived, but in war, a man does not have to be killed or wounded to become a casualty."[50] The prominent psychiatrist Robert Jay Lifton has worked with many such "casualties," Vietnam veterans as well as Holocaust survivors. His attempt to explain the effects of traumatic experiences and to develop analytical categories for treatment has been highly influential, and helps to understand the ongoing hate and anger of Vietnam veterans. Lifton writes that "unresolved death guilt can also be expressed through feelings of rage and impulses toward violence."[51]

A central experience for American soldiers in Vietnam and afterwards was a keen sense of betrayal: betrayal by the government, by the military, by the Veterans' Administration, by courts, and by their own people, especially the protesters—among them, Jane Fonda. A former POW described his feelings after he had heard a speech by the American actress: "I wept. I did not believe it. I felt betrayed."[52] Lifton found that the more soldiers initially believed in their mission, the greater their fantasies of revenge once confronted with disillusionment and defeat. "We swore they would pay, the hippies and draft card burners. They would pay if we ever ran into them," as Ron Kovic later described his feelings. For many, this day of reckoning has yet to come.[53] At the veterans' stands on the Washington Mall, "Hanoi Jane" stickers are still sold side-by-side with bitter accusations of betrayal and neglect by the US government.

In the eyes of many veterans and their families and friends, Jane Fonda epitomizes all that was wrong with America in those years: She was part of the antiwar movement, denouncing the war effort and the soldiers' sacrifices. Even more, she made friends and laughed with the enemy and showed solidarity, even sitting in an antiaircraft gun as if pretending to shoot down American planes. In radio announcements she called Americans criminals and compared their deeds to those of the Nazis. This amounted to the ultimate form of betrayal in an hour of crisis: treason.

The fact that this was an attractive woman, the daughter of Henry Fonda, the actress who had played "Barbarella," who many considered a sex symbol and whose pin-up some probably even carried to Vietnam with them only heightened the feeling of betrayal and rebuff.[54] "She was the pinup who went AWOL—something for which she must forever be pursued and nailed back to the wall."[55]

She stayed in the spotlight after the war, became even more famous, got many honors, and married Ted Turner. While Jane Fonda seemed to have emerged from the conflict unscathed, many of the soldiers returned psychologically or physically harmed. Aerobics made her body even more perfect, while disabled veterans still suffered from their injuries. Fonda herself recognized that having transcended her prescribed role, she sent out confusing messages: "I was on soapboxes, and *Barbarella* was playing down the street."[56]

The gender factor is very important. With everything Fonda did, she betrayed not only America but also her sex. Instead of being a nurse or healer—like Sally Hyde in *Coming Home*—she had figuratively killed some of her own countrymen.[57] Posing with the antiaircraft gun is the enshrined image of Jane Fonda/Hanoi Jane in the minds of countless veterans, reproduced on innumerable web pages, regardless of what she did or said afterwards. Fonda herself later had trouble understanding how she as an actress, as a public figure—"I know the power of images"—could have been so unaware of the possible effects of her image.[58]

Issues of betrayal and guilt, class, ideology, and gender all matter, and so Jane Fonda, who never actually used the antiaircraft gun, has turned into a "trigger," periodically unleashing the hate and anger stored in the veterans' emotional memories. But the last presidential campaign also showed that there are people and groups who deliberately pull this "trigger," hoping to profit politically and hurt their opponents by invoking the memory of Hanoi Jane. And there are those who profit financially from selling stickers and t-shirts. "I don't think we've ever resolved what the war meant—there are still festering wounds and a lot of pain, and for some I've become a lightning rod," Fonda said in the ABC interview in 1988.[59] Her words remain true today as the damage inflicted by the Vietnam War is still present in its physical and emotional marks.

Notes

1. Cf. the song "Hanoi Jane" http://www.nic0lesullivan.org/darlenemcbride.html; poem "Ms. Fonda" by the former Marine Ernesto Gomez, http://www.hmm-364.org/fondapoem.html. I'd like to thank Henry Wend, Stephen Aranha, and Alice Orth for comments and corrections.
2. http://www.ioffer.com/i/FORGIVE-HANOI-JANE-WHEN-HITLER-12x18-METAL-SIGN-VietNam-5313468; http://www.restoringamerica.org/archive/veterans/hanoi_jane.html; http://members.tripod.com/~itsamarinething/HanoiJane.html; http://www.firstmarines.net/Hanoi_Jane.html; http://itsjustanamthing.com/janefonda.htm; http://www.raskys.com/07.html; http://www.timjacobs.com/Hanoi%20Jane.htm; http://members.tripod.com/~chopchop3/fonda.html; (these and all other links accessed 24 March 2005).
3. The forged photo, which merged images of Kerry and Fonda and different events, was wrongly credited as an AP image. Cf. http://www.snopes.com/photos/politics/kerry2.asp. The t-shirts are sold online: http://0cents.com/Merchant2/merchant.mv?Screen=PROD&Store_Code=0CP&Product_Code=2119&Category_Code=TS.
4. Richard Lazarus, "The Past and the Present in Emotion," in *The Nature of Emotion: Fundamental Questions,* ed. Paul Ekman and Richard J. Davidson (New York: Oxford University Press, 1994), 306–10; Joseph E. Ledoux, "Memory Versus Emotional Memory in the Brain," in ibid., 311–12.

5. Quote in Tom Hayden, *Reunion: A Memoir* (New York: Random House, 1988), 451.
6. John Frook, "Busy Rebel: Jane Fonda, Pusher of Causes," *Life*, 23 April 1971, 52D. Cf. Fred Lawrence Guiles, *Jane Fonda: The Actress in Her Time* (Garden City, NY: Doubleday, 1982), 163–75, 181–214; Christopher Andersen, *Citizen Jane: The Turbulent Life of Jane Fonda* (New York: Holt, 1990), 193–224; Michael Freedland, *Jane Fonda* (New York: Weidenfeld and Nicolson, 1988), 148–71; Thomas Kiernan, *Jane: An Intimate Biography of Jane Fonda* (New York: Putnam, 1973), 278–99; Tessa Perkins, "The Politics of 'Jane Fonda'," in *Stardom: Industry of Desire,* ed. Christine Gledhill (London: Routledge, 1991), 237–50.
7. *Life,* 23 April 1971. See also "The Cause Celeb," *Newsweek,* 16 November 1970, 65–66; "Typhoon Jane," *Time,* 3 January 1972, 71; Margaret Ronan, "Whatever Happened to Baby Jane," *Senior Scholastic,* 29 November 1971, 20, 36.
8. Jeanne Zeidler, "Speaking Out, Selling Out, Working Out: The Changing Politics of Jane Fonda," in *Women and American Foreign Policy: Lobbyists, Critics, and Insiders,* ed. Edward C. Crapol (New York: Greenwood Press, 1987), 138–39; Kiernan, *Jane,* 305. Detroit Free Press quoted in Freedland, *Jane Fonda,* 159–60. Activist Saul Alinsky called her "a hitchhiker on the highway of causes." Quoted in Kiernan, *Jane,* 326. In 1968 Fonda played the title role in *Barbarella.* The movie "based on a French comic book character, was the first sexy, camp, science fiction-adventure film. ... It stamped me as a sex symbol." *Jane Fonda's Workout Book* (London: Simon & Schuster, 1981), 18. The *Los Angeles Times* suggested "2002: A Space Idiocy" as a subtitle. Quoted in Andersen, *Citizen Jane,* 161.
9. Fonda quotes in Zeidler, "Speaking Out, 140; Kiernan, *Jane,* 325.
10. Kiernan, *Jane,* 310, 329–43, 330. Cf. Andersen, *Citizen Jane,* 238–45; Freedland, *Jane Fonda,* 178–80; Zeidler, "Speaking Out," 141; Gary Arnold, "FTA: The Fonda Way," *Washington Post,* 28 June 1972, E9; "The Show the Pentagon Couldn't Stop," *Ramparts,* September 1972, 29–32.
11. Cf. *New York Times,* 16 December 1975, 26; Kiernan, *Jane,* 310–24; Guiles, *Actress in Her Time,* 169–70; Freedland, *Jane Fonda,* 143–44, 161–62; Zeidler, "Speaking Out," 142. The FBI considered her "subversive" and "anarchist." A fake but damaging letter to *Variety* that had been authorized by Hoover, but had never been sent, is reprinted in Andersen, *Citizen Jane,* 229.
12. The feeling of estrangement was also felt by her first husband Roger Vadim, who was getting more and more unhappy with their relationship that soon ended in a divorce: "I prefer being married to someone soft and vulnerable than to an American Joan of Arc." Quoted in Andersen, *Citizen Jane,* 214.
13. Art Buchwald discussed the question whether the dikes were bombed by the Americans with a humoristic note: "Both Sides, Now," *Washington Post,* 1 August 1972, B1.
14. On the visit see Guiles, *Actress in Her Time,* 197–214; Kiernan, *Jane,* 344–51; Freedland, *Jane Fonda,* 181–85. Her future husband Tom Hayden, the main author of the "Port Huron Statement" of the "Students for a Democratic Society" (1962), had used his contacts to help her organize the trip. Guiles, *Actress in Her Time,* 186–87, and Zeidler, "Speaking Out," 144, write that she had already made arrangements to visit Hanoi in February 1971, but that the federal government, knowing about this trip, made travel to North Vietnam illegal, one week before her planned departure. However, hearings of the Committee on Internal Security regarding Fonda and possible violations of passport laws do not mention that she had planned an earlier trip or make a connection between that trip and new travel restrictions. The latter were announced in the Federal Register on 24 March 1972. Fonda's passport, which explicitly listed those restrictions, was only issued

on 23 June 1972. Cf. US Congress, House Committee on Internal Security, Hearings Regarding H.R. 16742: Restraints on Travel to Hostile Areas. 92nd Congress, 2nd session, 19 and 25 September 1972 (Washington, DC: Government Printing Office, 1972), esp. 7562–80 (hereafter Committee on Internal Security, H.R. 16742).

15. The list of the twenty broadcasts, their transcripts, as well as a theme analysis can be found in Committee on Internal Security, H.R. 16742, 7642–78.
16. Ibid., 7646, 7648–50, 7653, 7667.
17. Ibid., 7670. Cf. *Washington Post,* 25 July 1972, A3; 26 July 1972, A14. The travel itinerary in Committee on Internal Security, H.R. 16742, 7639, puts this meeting on 18 July 1972. In a radio broadcast, Fonda herself dated it 19 July.
18. How the meeting is described by those who are ill disposed towards Fonda will be discussed below.
19. French directors Jean-Luc Godard and Jean-Pierre Gorin, with whom Fonda had worked a few months before going to Vietnam, even made a film about it. Inspired by a photograph in the French paper *L'Express* showing Fonda during her visit to North Vietnam, *Lettre à Jane* (Letter to Jane, 1972) discusses the role of Western intellectuals in the international revolution. "The star in militant activity" is heavily criticized by Godard and Gorin who analyze the image and Fonda's "function." See the text in Jean-Luc Godard, *Jean-Luc Godard par Jean-Luc Godard* (Paris: Cahiers du Cinéma, 1985), 350–62. Cf. Guiles, *Actress in Her Time,* 207; Michael Anderegg, "Hollywood and Vietnam: John Wayne and Jane Fonda as Discourse," in *Inventing Vietnam: The War in Film and Television,* ed. Michael Anderegg (Philadelphia: Temple University Press, 1991), 23–24.
20. Kiernan describes that protesters shouted "Hanoi Jane" when Fonda arrived in New York in July 1972. He used it as a title for a chapter of his book, which was published in 1973. Kiernan, *Jane,* 338, 347. William F. Buckley, Jr. called her "Secretary Fonda"—the future secretary of state of the Democratic presidential nominee George McGovern. William F. Buckley, Jr., "Secretary Fonda," *National Review,* 18 August 1972, 918–19.
21. In 1949 D'Aquino was convicted for treason and sentenced to ten years in prison plus a high fine. She was paroled after six years in prison.
22. *New York Times,* 25 July 1972, 8; 29 July 1972, 9.
23. *New York Times,* 15 July 1972, 9; *Washington Post,* 15 July 1972, A3.
24. *Washington Post,* 11 August 1972, A18; 26 August 1972, A2; *New York Times,* 11 August 1972, 59. The letters by the committee and the Department of Justice are reprinted in Committee on Internal Security, H.R. 16742, 7539–41.
25. Committee on Internal Security, IV. Its forerunner was the House Un-American Activities Committee.
26. At the time the committee was debating a new bill (H.R. 16742: Restraints on Travel to Hostile Areas) that should make it easier to punish traveling to hostile states. Cf. Committee on Internal Security, H.R. 16742, 7603–24, 7633–37. Some called it the "Fonda Amendment" to the House Internal Security Act of 1950. Cf. Peter Braunstein, "Ms. America: Why Jane Fonda Is a Mirror of the Nation's Past Forty Years," *American Heritage,* July–August 2001, 36.
27. Committee on Internal Security, H.R. 16742, 7539–54. See also the memorandum on the treason and sedition laws by Assistant Attorney General A. William Olson, 7625–32.
28. Ibid., 7561–80. In 1972 travel to Cuba, North Korea, and North Vietnam was restricted.
29. Ibid., 7581–602.
30. Ibid., 7581–97, quotes 7581–83, 7588, 7590, 7592, 7597. The writer Nelson DeMille, a Vietnam veteran, recently "confirmed" Hunter: "People like her succeeded very well in lowering troop morale, and as any combat vet will tell you, low morale leads to lowered

effectiveness, and that leads to battlefield deaths." http://www.henrymarkholzer.com/hanoijane.net/endorsements.htm.

31. Committee on Internal Security, H.R. 16742, 7597–602; quote 7585.
32. Kiernan, *Jane*, 349, and Guiles, *Actress in Her Time*, 206, wrongly believe that Fonda was not charged with treason because the United States was not officially at war with North Vietnam, which made the military actions illegal.
33. Two hundred additional sets of slides were made for local organizers. Cf. Hayden, *Reunion*, 448–50; Kiernan, *Jane*, 351–52. In 1974 IPC produced its first film: *Introduction to the Enemy*, a sixty-minute documentary of Fonda's and Hayden's trip to North Vietnam in April 1974. Cf. Guiles, *Actress in Her Time*, 233–35; Andersen, *Citizen Jane*, 273–74.
34. Quotes in *New York Times*, 7 April 1973, 11; Peter N. Carroll, *Famous in America: The Passion to Succeed. Jane Fonda, George Wallace, Phyllis Schlafly, John Glenn* (New York: Dutton, 1985), 163.
35. *New York Times*, 6 April 1973, 37; 7 April 1973, 11; 14 April 1973, 21; *Washington Post*, 13 April 1973, A11; Freedland, *Jane Fonda*, 184–85; Guiles, *Actress in Her Time*, 228. A recent book focusing on Fonda's visit to North Vietnam argues that she could have been successfully tried for treason. See Henry Mark and Erika Holzer, *"Aid and Comfort": Jane Fonda in North Vietnam* (Jefferson, NC: McFarland, 2002), and the related website: http://www.henrymarkholzer.com/index.php?subPageN=&mainPageN=Hanoi%20Jane&UprPageN=henrymarkholzer.
36. Cf. Braunstein, "Ms. America." Kiernan in 1973 and Jane Leavy of the *Washington Post* in 1985 had made similar arguments about Fonda mirroring her times. Kiernan, *Jane*, 357; Jane Leavy, "Jane Fonda, Good as Old," *Washington Post*, 26 January 1985, C1. On Fonda's changing popular image see Susan McLeland, "Barbarella Goes Radical: Hanoi Jane and the American Popular Press," in *Headline Hollywood: A Century of Film Scandal*, ed. Adrienne L. McLean and David A. Cook (New Brunswick, NJ: Rutgers University Press, 2001), 232–52.
37. Cf. Zeidler, "Speaking Out," 137, 149.
38. Cf. Andersen, *Citizen Jane*, 283–87; Anderegg, "Hollywood and Vietnam," 22; Hayden, *Reunion*, 456; The film, set in 1968, was produced by IPC. It came out the same year as Michael Cimino's *Deer Hunter*, which got the prize for best film. An example of negative reactions among veterans is William B. Guidry, *Radical Leaders: Tom Hayden and Hanoi Jane, American Opinion*, June 1979, republished at http://www.jbs.org/vietnam/below/hanoi_jane.htm (4 January 2001). Anderegg, "Hollywood and Vietnam," 29, is wrong that only with the reinterpretation of Vietnam in the Reagan years was "Hanoi Jane" rediscovered, as the next paragraphs will prove.
39. Kristin Ann Hass, *Carried to the Wall: American Memory and the Vietnam Veterans' Memorial* (Berkeley: University of California Press, 1998), 16, 112. Mark Steyn, "The Heart Doesn't Grow Fonda," *Sunday Telegraph* (London), 28 December 1997, 11.
40. The *Washington Post* called it an "anti-Jane Fonda POW drama." Rita Kempley, "The Hanoi Hilton," *Washington Post*, 19 June 1987.
41. Cf. Andersen, *Citizen Jane*, 3–13. Aldermen in Holyoke, MA even voted against Fonda filming in town. Cf. *New York Times*, 4 August 1988, B1.
42. See the text of the interview in Andersen, *Citizen Jane*, 8–11. Cf. Ron Rosenbaum, "Dangerous Jane," *Vanity Fair*, November 1988, 142–47, 208–15.
43. Quoted in Michael Ellison, "Fonda Sorry for Hanoi Jane Image," *The Guardian*, 22 June 2000, 16. Fonda is thinking of writing down her version of the story. "Fonda's Next Exercise: Hanoi Jane's War Diary," *Daily Telegraph* (London), 10 February 2001, 16.
44. Andersen, *Citizen Jane*, 332; *Falwell Confidential*, 25 June 1999, http://www.falwell.com/confiden/fc990625.htm; Margot Hornblower, "Have Gun, Will Travel," *Time*, 6 July

1998 http://www.time.com/time/magazine/1998/dom/980706/box1.html; Mark Steyn, "The Heart Doesn't Grow Fonda," *Sunday Telegraph,* 28 December 1997, 11. Cf. Myra MacPherson, *Long Time Passing: Vietnam and the Haunted Generation* (Garden City, NY: Doubleday, 1984), 466; John Elvin, "The Vietnam War Is Over, but 'Hanoi Jane' Lives On," *Insight on the News,* 25 November 1996, 20–21; Steve Dunleavy, "Blame This on Hanoi Jane," *New York Post,* 18 June 1998, 2; Richard Roeper, "The Jane Fonda Follies: Much Ado over Nothing," *Denver Post,* 8 December 1999, B11; "Remembering Hanoi Jane," *New Hampshire Sunday News,* 13 August 2001; Ted Sampley, "Hanoi Jane: Yesterday's Fiery Communist Revolutionary. She's today's very rich capitalist," *U.S. Veteran Dispatch,* October–December 1996, http://www.usvetdsp.com/story8.htm; Jonah Goldberg, "Plain Jane," *National Review,* 26 July 1999 http://www.nationalreview.com/goldberg/goldberg072799.html.

45. William F. Buckley, Jr., "Top 100: Does Fonda Belong?" *Omaha World-Herald,* 9 November 1999.
46. Mike McGrath http://www.rt66.com/~korteng/SmallArms/hanoijan.htm#falseinfo. Cf. Urban Legends http://www.snopes.com/military/fonda.asp; http://urbanlegends.about.com/library/weekly/aa110399.htm?terms=jane+fonda. On the letters see *New York Times,* 8 July 1972, 15. Cf. *Washington Post,* 19 May 1973, A4.
47. Cf. *Washington Post,* 13 April 1973, A11; Michael Benge, "Shame on Jane," *Advocacy and Intelligence Index,* 28 April 1999 http://www.pray4pows.org/controversies/100%5Fgreat%5Fwomen%5Ffonda/objections%5Fbenge.html; Guiles, *Actress in Her Time,* 205–6. In his memoirs even Nixon writes that "one POW had his arm and leg broken because he refused to meet Miss Fonda." Richard Nixon, *The Memoirs of Richard Nixon* (New York: Grosset & Dunlap, 1978), 862.
48. Hayden, *Reunion,* 450.
49. Cf. Jerry Lembcke, *The Spitting Image: Myth, Memory, and the Legacy of Vietnam* (New York: New York University Press, 1998); G. Kurt Piehler, *Remembering War the American Way* (Washington, DC: Smithsonian Institutions Press, 1995), esp. 154–82.
50. Philip Caputo, *A Rumor of War* (London: Holt, Rinehart & Winston, 1999 [1977]), xiii, 207.
51. Robert Jay Lifton, *Home From the War: Vietnam Veterans—Neither Victims nor Executioners* (New York: Simon & Schuster, 1973), 65.
52. POW Ted Gostas quoted in Guiles, *Actress in Her Time,* 206.
53. Ron Kovic, *Born on the Fourth of July* (New York: McGraw-Hill, 1976), 134.
54. Cf. Carol Burke, "Why They Love to Hate Her," http://www.duckdaotsu.org/lovetohateher.html. The July 1968 issue of *Leatherneck, Magazine of the Marines* showed a pin-up style photo of Fonda as Barbarella.
55. J. Hoberman, "G.I. Jane: A Hollywood Daughter's Radical Past Winds up on the Cutting Room Floor," *Village Voice,* 2–8 May 2001, http://www.villagevoice.com/issues/0118/hoberman.php.
56. Quoted in Zeidler, "Speaking Out," 141.
57. Cf. ibid.; Anderegg, "Hollywood and Vietnam," 22–24.
58. Quoted in Andersen, *Citizen Jane,* 8. In a press conference after her Vietnam visit, she even showed a twenty-minute silent film that included the now famous scene. Hoberman fittingly called it "the greatest sign crime."
59. Quoted in Andersen, *Citizen Jane,* 8. Tom Hayden calls the ongoing attention and emotions directed towards Fonda "a diversion from a larger battlefield" Tom Hayden, "You Gotta Love Her," *The Nation,* 22 March 2004.

Bibliography

Anderegg, Michael. "Hollywood and Vietnam: John Wayne and Jane Fonda as Discourse." In *Inventing Vietnam: The War in Film and Television,* edited by Michael Anderegg, 15–32. Philadelphia: Temple University Press, 1991.

Andersen, Christopher. *Citizen Jane: The Turbulent Life of Jane Fonda.* New York: Holt, 1990.

Arnold, Gary. "FTA: The Fonda Way." *Washington Post,* 28 June 1972, E9.

Benge, Michael. "Shame on Jane." *Advocacy and Intelligence Index,* 28 April 1999. http://www.pray4pows.org/controversies/100%5Fgreat%5Fwomen%5Ffonda/objections%5Fbenge.html.

Braunstein, Peter. "Ms. America: Why Jane Fonda Is a Mirror of the Nation's Past Forty Years." *American Heritage,* July–August 2001, 30–39.

Buchwald, Art. "Both Sides, Now." *Washington Post,* 1 August 1972, B1.

Buckley, William F., Jr. "Secretary Fonda." *National Review,* 18 August 1972, 918–19.

———. "Top 100: Does Fonda Belong?" *Omaha World-Herald,* 9 November 1999.

Burke, Carol. "Why They Love to Hate Her." http://www.duckdaotsu.org/lovetohateher.html.

Caputo, Philip. *A Rumor of War.* London: Holt, Rinehart & Winston, 1999 [1977].

Carroll, Peter N. *Famous in America: The Passion to Succeed. Jane Fonda, George Wallace, Phyllis Schlafly, John Glenn.* New York: Dutton, 1985.

"The Cause Celeb." *Newsweek,* 16 November 1970, 65–66.

Dunleavy, Steve. "Blame This on Hanoi Jane." *New York Post,* 18 June 1998, 2.

Ellison, Michael. "Fonda Sorry for Hanoi Jane Image." *The Guardian,* 22 June 2000, 16.

Elvin, John. "The Vietnam War Is Over, but 'Hanoi Jane' Lives On." *Insight on the News,* 25 November 1996, 20–21.

Falwell Confidential, 25 June 1999. http://www.falwell.com/confiden/fc990625.htm.

Fonda, Jane. *Jane Fonda's Workout Book.* London: Simon & Schuster, 1981.

"Fonda's Next Exercise: Hanoi Jane's War Diary." *Daily Telegraph* (London), 10 February 2001, 16.

Freedland, Michael. *Jane Fonda.* New York: Weidenfeld and Nicolson, 1988.

Frook, John. "Busy Rebel: Jane Fonda, Pusher of Causes." *Life,* 23 April 1971, 50–52D.

Godard, Jean-Luc. *Jean-Luc Godard par Jean-Luc Godard.* Paris: Cahiers du Cinéma, 1985, 350–62.

Goldberg, Jonah. "Plain Jane." *National Review,* 26 July 1999. http://www.nationalreview.com/goldberg/goldberg072799.html.

Gomez, Ernesto. "Ms. Fonda." http://www.hmm-364.org/fondapoem.html.

Guidry, William B. *Radical Leaders: Tom Hayden and Hanoi Jane. American Opinion,* June 1979. http://www.jbs.org/vietnam/below/hanoi_jane.htm (4 January 2001).

Guiles, Fred Lawrence. *Jane Fonda: The Actress in Her Time.* Garden City, NY: Doubleday, 1982.

"Hanoi Jane." http://www.nic0lesullivan.org/darlenemcbride.html.

Hass, Kristin Ann. *Carried to the Wall: American Memory and the Vietnam Veterans' Memorial.* Berkeley: University of California Press, 1998.

Hayden, Tom. "You Gotta Love Her." *The Nation,* 22 March 2004.

———. *Reunion: A Memoir.* New York: Random House, 1988.

Hoberman, J. "G.I. Jane: A Hollywood Daughter's Radical Past Winds up on the Cutting Room Floor." *Village Voice,* 2–8 May 2001. http://www.villagevoice.com/issues/0118/hoberman.php.

Hornblower, Margot. "Have Gun, Will Travel." *Time,* 6 July 1998. http://www.time.com/time/magazine/1998/dom/980706/box1.html.

http://0cents.com/Merchant2/merchant.mv?Screen=PROD&Store_Code=0CP&Product_Code=2119&Category_Code=TS.

http://itsjustanamthing.com/janefonda.htm.

http://members.tripod.com/~chopchop3/fonda.html.

http://members.tripod.com/~itsamarinething/HanoiJane.html.

http://urbanlegends.about.com/library/weekly/aa110399.htm? terms=jane+fonda.

http://www.firstmarines.net/Hanoi_Jane.html.

http://www.henrymarkholzer.com/hanoijane.net/endorsements.htm.

http://www.ioffer.com/i/FORGIVE-HANOI-JANE-WHEN-HITLER-12x18-METAL-SIGN-VietNam-5313468.

http://www.raskys.com/07.html.

http://www.restoringamerica.org/archive/veterans/hanoi_jane.html.

http://www.snopes.com/photos/politics/kerry2.asp.

http://www.timjacobs.com/Hanoi%20Jane.htm.

Kempley, Rita. "The Hanoi Hilton." *Washington Post,* 19 June 1987.

Kiernan, Thomas. *Jane: An Intimate Biography of Jane Fonda.* New York: Putnam, 1973.

Kovic, Ron. *Born on the Fourth of July.* New York: McGraw-Hill, 1976.

Lazarus, Richard. "The Past and the Present in Emotion." In *The Nature of Emotion: Fundamental Questions,* edited by Paul Ekman and Richard J. Davidson, 306–10. New York: Oxford University Press, 1994.

Leavy, Jane. "Jane Fonda, Good as Old." *Washington Post,* 26 January 1985, C1.

Ledoux, Joseph E. "Memory Versus Emotional Memory in the Brain." In *The Nature of Emotion: Fundamental Questions,* edited by Paul Ekman and Richard J. Davidson, 311–12. New York: Oxford University Press, 1994.

Lembcke, Jerry. *The Spitting Image: Myth, Memory, and the Legacy of Vietnam.* New York: New York University Press, 1998.

Lifton, Robert Jay. *Home From the War: Vietnam Veterans—Neither Victims nor Executioners.* New York: Simon & Schuster, 1973.

MacPherson, Myra. *Long Time Passing: Vietnam and the Haunted Generation.* Garden City, NY: Doubleday, 1984.

Mark, Henry, and Erika Holzer. *"Aid and Comfort:" Jane Fonda in North Vietnam.* Jefferson, NC: McFarland, 2002. Related website: http://www.henrymarkholzer.com/index.php?subPageN=&mainPageN=Hanoi%20Jane&UprPageN=henrymarkholzer.

McGrath, Mike. http://www.rt66.com/~korteng/SmallArms/hanoijan.htm#falseinfo.

McLeland, Susan. "Barbarella Goes Radical: Hanoi Jane and the American Popular Press." In *Headline Hollywood: A Century of Film Scandal,* edited by Adrienne L. McLean and David A. Cook, 232–52. New Brunswick, NJ: Rutgers University Press, 2001.

New York Times, 8. July 1972, 15.

New York Times, 15 July 1972, 9.

New York Times, 25 July 1972, 8.

New York Times, 29 July 1972, 9.

New York Times, 11 August 1972, 59.

New York Times, 6 April 1973, 37.

New York Times, 7 April 1973, 11.

New York Times, 14 April 1973, 21.

New York Times, 16 December 1975, 26.

New York Times, 4 August 1988, B 1.

Nixon, Richard. *The Memoirs of Richard Nixon.* New York: Grosset & Dunlap, 1978.
Perkins, Tessa. "The Politics of 'Jane Fonda.'" In *Stardom: Industry of Desire,* edited by Christine Gledhill, 237–50. London: Routledge, 1991.
Piehler, G. Kurt. *Remembering War the American Way.* Washington, DC: Smithsonian Institutions Press, 1995.
"Remembering Hanoi Jane." *New Hampshire Sunday News,* 13 August 2001.
Roeper, Richard. "The Jane Fonda Follies: Much Ado over Nothing." *Denver Post,* 8 December 1999, B11.
Ronan, Margaret. "Whatever Happened to Baby Jane." *Senior Scholastic,* 29 November 1971, 20, 36.
Rosenbaum, Ron. "Dangerous Jane." *Vanity Fair,* November 1988, 142–47, 208–15.
Sampley, Ted. "Hanoi Jane: Yesterday's Fiery Communist Revolutionary. She's today's very rich capitalist." *U.S. Veteran Dispatch,* October–December 1996. http://www.usvetdsp.com/story8.htm.
"The Show the Pentagon Couldn't Stop." *Ramparts,* September 1972, 29–32.
Steyn, Mark. "The Heart Doesn't Grow Fonda." *Sunday Telegraph* (London), 28 December 1997, 11.
"Typhoon Jane." *Time,* 3 January 1972, 71.
US Congress. House. Committee on Internal Security, Hearings Regarding H.R. 16742: Restraints on Travel to Hostile Areas. 92nd Congress, 2nd session, 19 and 25 September 1972. Washington, DC: Government Printing Office, 1972.
Urban Legends http://www.snopes.com/military/fonda.asp.
Washington Post, 15 July 1972, A3.
Washington Post, 25 July 1972, A3.
Washington Post, 26 July 1972, A14.
Washington Post, 11 August 1972, A18.
Washington Post, 26 August 1972, A2.
Washington Post, 13 April 1973, A11.
Washington Post, 19 May 1973, A4.
Zeidler, Jeanne. "Speaking Out, Selling Out, Working Out: The Changing Politics of Jane Fonda." In *Women and American Foreign Policy: Lobbyists, Critics, and Insiders,* edited by Edward C. Crapol, 137–51. New York: Greenwood Press, 1987.

Emotions, Art, and the Media

Chapter 6

"Stop Them Damned Pictures"

Political Cartoons, the Study of Emotions, and the Construction of the Anglo-American Relationship

Stefanie Schneider

Introduction

"Stop them damned pictures; I don't care so much what the papers say about me. My constituents can't read. But, damn it, they can see pictures!" raged Tammany Hall Boss William Tweed, facing a veritable cartoon campaign by Thomas Nast against his corrupt practices in the courthouse of New York City in the 1870s.[1] His angry exclamation illustrates one of the most famous reactions to political cartoons by the beholder in general, and by those attacked in pictorial satire in particular. It not only shows how "emotional" a person reacted to witty, fitting cartoons but also demonstrates his fear of its impressive and influential effect on other readers.[2]

Cartoons have generally been judged as manipulative in their "shock value of raw emotional impact," although "it is impossible to ascertain precisely how a cartoon achieves its impact."[3] Unfortunately, the reaction to and reception of a cartoon is rarely easy to determine.[4] If—in exceptional cases—it has been handed down through generations, as we can see in the

Notes for this section begin on page 129.

case of Boss Tweed's reaction, it has turned into a myth. That it shows and addresses emotions, though, is undoubtedly the case.[5]

This essay focuses on the potential of political cartoons as historical sources for the analysis of emotions and how this bears on the perception of international relations. I would like to show first, in what way cartoons address and visualize emotions, and second, how emotions can be used as a category of analysis for the study of changing patterns of Anglo-American relations symbolically represented in political cartoons of the nineteenth century.

In the nineteenth century, the relationship between Great Britain and the United States underwent a profound change: it developed from a hostile relationship at its beginning into a friendly alliance at its close. This essay's objective is to analyze whether such a surprising fundamental change in diplomatic relations was prepared on the symbolic level.

Human perception, interpretation, and action in international relations and foreign policy is embedded in and channeled by a symbolically transmitted cultural background, which is coded in repetitive patterns as social rules for human orientation and behavior. Visual, textual, and ritual representations can thus be regarded as influential (f)actors even in political spheres of action. Based on the cultural approach to diplomatic history developed by Akira Iriye,[6] it is my aim to pick out one of several interpretative patterns and visual contextualizations of the relationship, which I have called "ties that bind," and to examine its changing or continuous interpretations in the light of diplomatic historians' findings concerning the Anglo-American friendship. This symbolic image presents itself as a love-hate relationship with diverse roots, which leaves ample space for the visualization of short-term conflict *and* long-term cooperation between the two nations; at the same time it constructed an in-group excluding other countries, and thus laid the mythological foundation of the twentieth-century "special relationship."

Political Cartoons: Constructing—Addressing—Appealing to Emotions?

What can be more obvious, yet just as challenging, for the historical analysis of change in or caused by emotions than to draw upon a source—the political cartoon—that itself is working with and heavily drawing on emotions to achieve its enormous appeal? Only relatively recently have cartoons been paid the researchers' attention they deserve. Originally judged to be of ephemeral, popular, and artistically low in character and thus neither worth an art historian's analysis nor a historian's close study, their function seems to have remained reduced to an illustrative quality for conference papers and published studies that kept focusing mainly on the diplomatic historian's "real" sources, such as state papers and administrative documents.[7] It is only in recent years that mainly students of cultural studies have elaborated on more fruitful analyses of cartoons in search for their significance regarding culture and mentality aspects.[8] Cartoon analyses for the study of emotions history, though, have yet to be presented.

Why did Boss Tweed lose his temper at the sight of the Nast cartoons? Why do we generally react emotionally to pictures, cartoons in particular? According to Matravers, this is because of the representational content of how to understand human situations.[9]

Cartoons are prime media of symbolic representation: they combine abstract and concrete qualities in the visualization of an idea or concept.[10] By its capacity to present a complex problem visually in its entirety, the cartoon triggers an immediate pang of understanding and thus affects the emotional state of the beholder.[11] The cartoon has the power to activate emotions with the use of certain symbols and to attribute political events or figures with emotions in order to shape them in the eye of the beholder. As pictorial and communicative systems, cartoons thus visualize otherwise invisible political, social, and historical interrelations and collective attitudes in society. The cartoonist's combination of emotionally laden cultural symbols, visual patterns, and contrasts with political issues and events leads to the construction of a new perception of the world around him. In carrying political and cultural symbols of identification and transforming their relationship and context, they not only produce values, attitudes, and interpretations of the world but they also have the potential to disseminate and change them. Thus, they make a major contribution to the construction of political culture and national identity in the nineteenth century.[12]

The double function of emotions in society, Vester holds,[13] is of direct relevance to the production and reception of cartoons. First, emotions represent a modus of information processing, i.e., they influence the choice of codes for the perception and storage of information. Emotionally attached or appealing material such as cartoons will probably catch the eye (short-term effect) and be remembered (long-term effect) more easily than other material because "only the emotional-laden symbolic processing of percepts gives the infinite number of pieces of the perceived world some kind of integrated unity."[14]

Second, emotions are coded in cartoons. Emotions are learned in a particular context and essentially tied to the community and its conceptual apparatus. The codes represent the collective social knowledge about emotions, emotional standards, sanctioning, and the appropriate expression of emotions. Rules on the manifestation and (de)legitimization of emotions are then promoted by social organizations and institutions and coded in collective pictorial systems such as cartoons, which represent models of behavior toward events and actions according to which people can orient themselves.[15] Emotional patterns for political problems and cultural values are thus formed with the help of cultural symbols in cartoons to represent appropriate ways of dealing with and acting in new social situations.

Emotions, Cartoons, and the Construction of the Anglo-American Relationship

The Diplomatic Historian's Story

Why are we interested at all in studying the emotional, representative, and visual dimension of nineteenth-century Anglo-American relations? Is there a new side to their relationship to be reconstructed from political cartoons that traditional diplomatic history has not been able to shed light on so far?

From the point of view of diplomatic historians, all is crystal clear. They have meticulously studied state papers and administrative documents of the period to determine that the alleged "special relationship"[16] between Great Britain and the United States never really existed; on the contrary, it can be regarded as a myth, a social construction by the British side to compensate for the fact that, at the turn of the twentieth century, its imperial world power declined whereas the influential position of the United States was on the rise:

> Since the beginning of this century, the dominant factor in the relationship between Britain and America has been a steely British determination to assume that there is between the two powers an underlying common interest, more important than the often sharp clashes of particular interests, or sharp differences of interpretation of particular situations. ... Whether any reality has matched these assumptions is another question. ... The other immediate point is that it has been the *British* choice of assumptions that was, or is, decisive.[17]

The thesis of the existence of a special relationship, it was alleged, would save the British from facing their declining influence in world politics. If the special relationship is a British myth, then why did those cartoons visualizing that special bond of equality, harmony, and long-term attachment appear *not* in British, but without exception in American magazines? Is the special relationship thus a construction from the American side? And if so, what function did it serve? The United States as a rising, enormous world power had no need of encouragement by a declining British nation.

Yet, the question remains as to why, when, and how the originally hostile relationship between Great Britain and the United States had changed fundamentally. In the course of the nineteenth century it developed toward an ambiguous if not mostly friendly alliance at the end, growing even into a "special relationship" in the twentieth century.[18] What diplomats' correspondence still cannot answer satisfactorily is how this change in the mentality of the two nations was prepared and transmitted, which side it was initiated by, and when it was fundamentally enforced. I argue that it was mainly by the symbolic representation of this relationship in cultural artifacts such as texts, rituals—and of course, images—that this change was not only visualized but actively prepared.

Anglo-American National Symbols and Interpretative Patterns

In what way are the interpretative and visual patterns of the special relationship different from the interpretations by diplomatic historians? The interactive relationships or patterns that crop up regularly in cartoons vary between conflict and cooperation, aversion and acceptance, hierarchy or equality, and finally similarities and differences. They emerge from cartoons through visualized patterns[19] such as family constellations[20] and are already bound up with emotions through their allusion to everyday life situations and their emotional standards. Thus, the categorization and analysis of these patterns in regard to their implicit emotional quality enable the student of international relations to trace the change in attitudes, perceptions, and the construction of images, constellations, and relationships such as the Anglo-American friendship as it evolved from cartoons in the course of the nineteenth century.

At the time, nations were often symbolized in cartoons not by their political leaders, but by personification in national symbols. The predominant symbols used in British and American cartoons were John Bull and Uncle Sam.[21] These figures reduced complex national entities to ordinary human beings; consequently, the cartoonist not only attributed certain actions and characteristics but also emotions to them. The latter were visualized in the cartoons by body language, i.e., gesture and mimicry; by language, i.e., their alleged comments; and lastly by their meaning-laden actions with or against their fellow nations. Thus, they were set in an interactive and interrelational context with other countries, which was presented as emotionally laden. There, nations are personified as living people; they are acting in real-life situations and portrayed as *having emotions:* "In international relations, the symbolic image of the nation is of extraordinary importance. ... Cartoons ... continually reinforce the image of roles of nations as real personalities—lions, bears, and eagles, *loving, hating, embracing, rejecting, quarrelling, fighting.*"[22]

Yet, for the study of the special relationship, an analysis of the choice and the (dis)continuity of these symbols alone did not turn out to be useful as they do not allow any conclusions on the basis and the character of their relationship. Instead, it proved to be much more revealing to look at the contextualization, the situation and relationships these symbols were portrayed in, and to draw conclusions from the indirect comparison and the thus constructed parallels between a political event and the distorted situation chosen. The repetition and variation of these contexts allow a systematization of visual patterns, which shed some light on the constructed basis and quality of the special relationship. This is mostly done by a transference of a political to an everyday situation or a social context to facilitate the reader's understanding of a complex political constellation, and to enable the reader to decode the message of the cartoon: These situations are context based, culture and time specific, as well as connected to the profile of the satirical magazine in which the cartoon was published.

"Ties That Bind"

The five political cartoons chosen for an exemplary analysis of the underlying interpretation of nineteenth-century Anglo-American relations are grouped around the visual pattern "ties that bind." Linguistically speaking, "ties that bind" can refer to different contexts as well as to different nations: neither is it special for the Anglo-American or for a political context, nor does it exclusively allude to separation or combination of two elements. On the positive side, one might count ties of friendship, family ties, ties of blood, or business ties, all of which refer to the establishment of cooperation, close links, or relationships, to the exchange of communication or to bonding in the sense of emotional attachment. On the negative side, ties can be understood as chains limiting space, hindering actions, thwarting intentions. They can be interpreted as burdens or responsibilities, in shackles of marriage or other family ties. An interesting third connotation mainly used in sports contexts is "tie" for being equal. It remains to be seen if all three connotations of "tie" had their influence on the production of these cartoons.

Even though few in number, the pattern visible in these American cartoons is interesting because it directly addresses the foundations of the Anglo-American relationship, understood as an ambivalent relationship oscillating between conflict and cooperation, hierarchy and equality, similarities and differences, acceptance and resentment. This is illustrated by the use of (a) differently specified tie(s) binding both nations closely together, partly in spite of their quarrelling and discomfort. Taken as a metaphor as such, "tie" is generally neutral; it contains neither positive nor negative interpretations and attitudes, which makes an analysis of its further differentiation depending on the context all the more interesting. Thus, the analysis has to focus not only on changes in the pattern over time but also on changes in the visualization of the interpretative pattern as such.

The cartoons were taken from the big American national satirical magazines of the time, *Judge, Puck,* and *Life.*[23] They appeared in the period between 1896 and 1904, a fourth "imperial" phase in Anglo-American relations, so characterized in his periodization scheme by Herbert G. Nicholas in his study *Great Britain and the United States* from 1972.[24] Although originally it was the aim of this study to compare the British and American cartoons using this pattern, the search only produced American cartoons containing it. How far this is a specifically American attitude toward the special relationship is a question that also has to be dealt with in the following analysis.

My cartoon analysis will address the following questions: Which emotions are represented in the cartoons and thus predominantly used to characterize the long-term and short-term condition of their relationship? What value judgment is attributed to the relationship between Great Britain and the United States by using this pattern? What does this reveal about the nature of the Anglo-American relationship as constructed in the cartoons in question? In what way is the interpretive pattern complementary or opposed to interpretations of traditional diplomatic history?[25]

Coded Emotions

The cartoon "They can't fight"[26] of 1896 (see figure 6.1) shows the national symbols Uncle Sam and John Bull engaged in an impending fight. They face each other, threatening their opponent with fists, mad looks, imperial gestures, and authoritative body language. Uncle Sam is slim, but tall: he seems to tower over John and thus to dominate the conflict.[27] Yet, due to several bonds tying their hands and feet together, the threatening conflict will not break out. Hence the title of the cartoon, "They can't fight." Holding them together, preventing them from leaving and obstructing their actions at the same time, the bonds are qualified as social (ties of friendship, international marriages, social ties), cultural (ties of literature and art), ideological (conservatism, civilization), and business related (mutual commercial benefits, trade interests, property interests, financial ties). Neither John nor Sam can loosen their ties as the knots are out of reach for them.

The cartoon is not commenting on a specific historical event, but on the state of affairs in Anglo-American relations at the end of the nineteenth century in general. Although there is no direct reference to diplomatic incidents, relations were tense mainly because of territorial and economic disputes in Latin America and Asia.[28] These were not lived by military conflict, but settled by diplomatic activity, i.e., communicative measures, which is illustrated by the verbal conflict in the cartoon. Emotions are explicitly

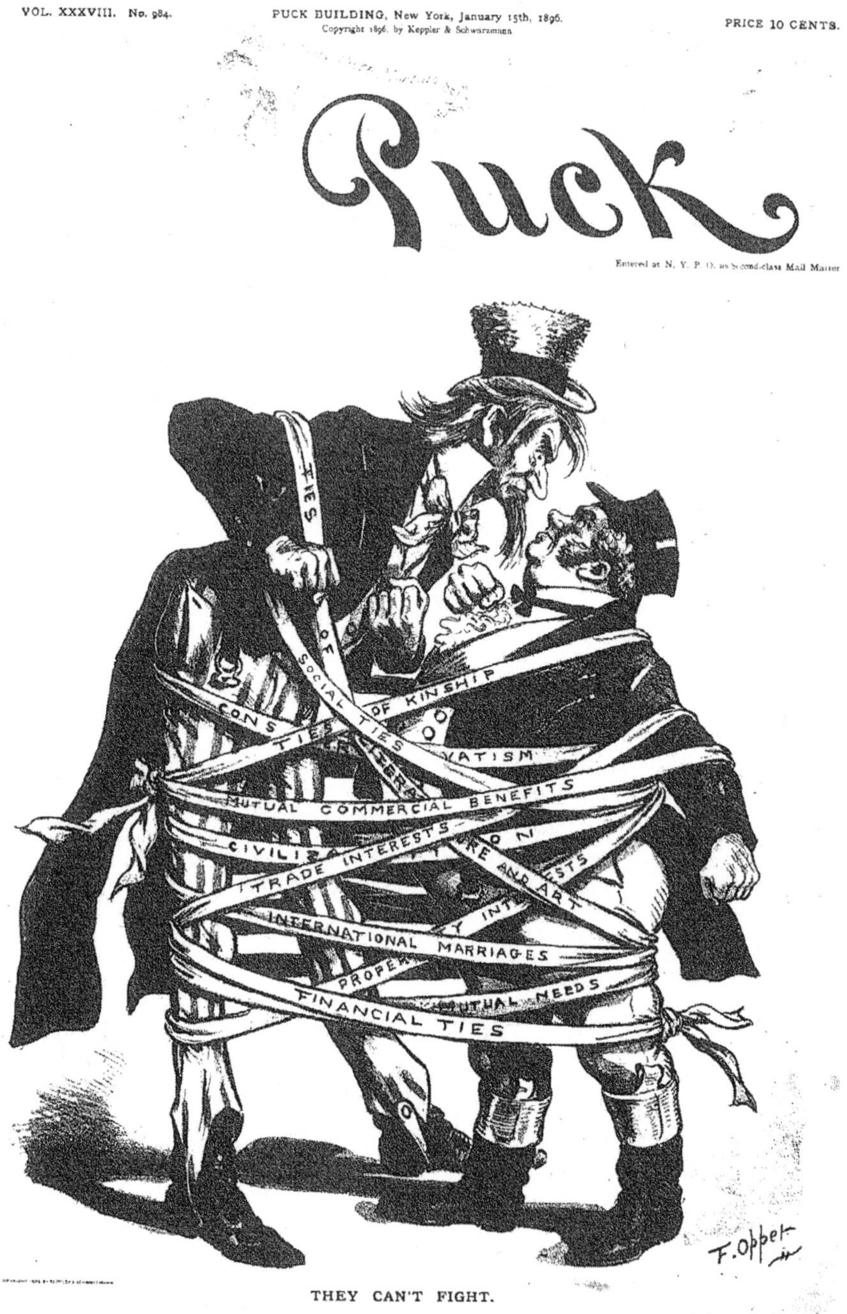
VOL. XXXVIII. No. 984.
PUCK BUILDING, New York, January 15th, 1896.
Copyright 1896, by Keppler & Schwarzmann
PRICE 10 CENTS.
Puck
Entered at N. Y. P. O. as Second-class Mail Matter
SOCIAL TIES
OF KINSHIP
MUTUAL COMMERCIAL BENEFITS
TRADE INTERESTS
INTERNATIONAL MARRIAGES
FINANCIAL TIES
F. Opper
THEY CAN'T FIGHT.

Figure 6.1. Cartoon: Frederick B. Opper, "They can't fight," *Puck*, 15 January 1896.

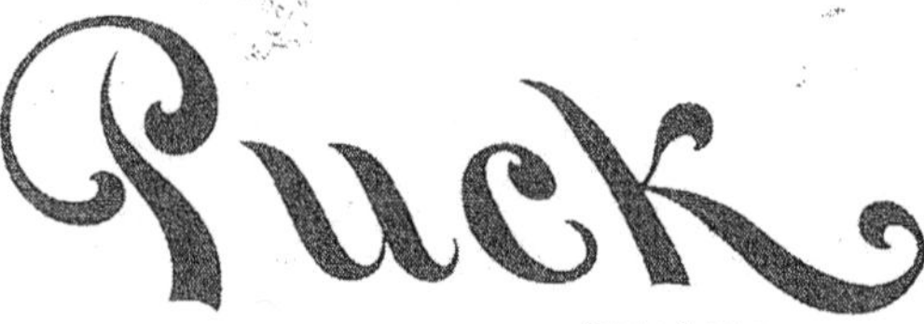

and implicitly addressed in this cartoon. Emotive gestures and body language representing anger and aggression strike the eye at once and point to the stressed atmosphere of a short-term conflict on edge. Yet, on the other hand and much more subtly alluded to by the inscription on the ties, some common features such as cultural and family ties suggest some "irrational" long-term attachments of belonging together, which must be differentiated from other rational and profitable mercantile or ideological ties. It is vital that the last-mentioned ties are the persisting ones that prevent a war.

The cartoon "Quite a strain on the Anglo-Saxon alliance"[29] of 1901 (see figure 6.2) shows a similar situation of temporary conflict. Again, both national symbols are bound together against their will, this time by their coats' sleeves. They are prepared for conflict, as a baton and a pickaxe lie ready for use at their feet. Standing on the beach, they try to distance themselves from each other, watch each other suspiciously over their shoulders while pretending to study the documents named after the diplomats responsible for the arbitration, Clayton-Bulwer and Hay-Pauncefaute respectively. These papers contextualize the cartoon as a comment on the Venezuela crisis, a boundary dispute between Great Britain and Venezuela concerning British Guyana. The United States successfully forced Great Britain to accept American mediation in the conflict on the grounds of the Monroe Doctrine, which can be interpreted as an indication of a changing structure of power in the Western Hemisphere.

QUITE A STRAIN ON THE ANGLO-SAXON ALLIANCE.

Figure 6.2. Cartoon: Schweitz, "Quite a strain on the Anglo-Saxon alliance," *Life*, 14 May 1901.

Although not visible in the cartoon and not publicly accepted at the time either, the compromise was also of interest to the British because they were heavily burdened by military operations in the Boer War and in an arms race with other European powers. Although compromise (diplomatic papers) and aggression (weapons) are symbolized both visually and textually ("quite a strain" and "alliance") in the cartoon, it is the long-term aspect of the relationship that wins over the controversy: again, it is the Anglo-Saxon alliance, i.e., the racial or kinship aspect that is decisive for the prevention of violent action here.

The cartoon "The International Siamese Twins"[30] of 1902 (see figure 6.3) stands in stark contrast to the two pictures previously analyzed. It shows the national animals, the British lion and American eagle, sitting together on the beach in harmony. Their bond is now entitled "Business interests—friendship"; it consists of material as well as affective elements, joined by the expression *twins* in the title, which alludes to the family interpretation of the relationship. In this case, the bond does not represent conflict between both parties, but an alliance against the unhappy-looking German kaiser, who is lingering in the background with his back turned on both, raising a knife entitled "envy" because of "US trade relations with England." The animals seem to be ignoring him completely, but the satisfied expression in their faces might also be interpreted as schadenfreude toward him. Their identical mimicry and body language to the side of the eagle—another sign of US dominance?—mirrors complementary attitudes and actions (concerning foreign policy), which is fittingly expressed in the use of the "international Siamese twins" metaphor. This metaphor points to the interpretation of common cultural as well as historical origins as family in addition to economic and friend-related bonds.

In their outward appearance, though, they do not resemble each other at all: whereas the eagle is dressed in striped trousers and starred shirt, smoking a cigar, the lion is dressed in typical aristocratic garb, a majestic ermine coat combined with a smoking pipe, a monocle, and a bowler hat. Despite their foreign-policy similarities, their domestic conditions still vary greatly. Yet, concentrating on the international arena of politics by also showing the German kaiser, the cartoon focuses on multilateral power constellations with a harmonious Anglo-American couple, as opposed to the preceding cartoons on strained Anglo-American bilateral relations.

In the cartoon "How could they quarrel when their interests are so interwoven"[31] of 1903 (see figure 6.4), Uncle Sam and John Bull hold a big flag with British and American colors merging over a small rill of a river symbolizing the Atlantic. Great Britain and the United States intend to put the flag down between them, symbolizing a bridge across the sea between

THE INTERNATIONAL SIAMESE TWINS.

Figure 6.3. Cartoon: Victor Gillam, "The International Siamese Twins," *Judge*, 21 June 1902.

Figure 6.4. Cartoon: Victor Gillam, "How could they quarrel when their interests are so interwoven," *Judge,* 21 February 1903.

the two powers in emotional attachment and communication ("relationship," "friendship," "wireless telegraphy," "language," "steamships"), business relations ("business" and "commerce"), and ideological aims ("desires," "Anglo-Saxonism"), although the ties mentioned here use more emotive language than the cartoon "They can't fight" of 1898. Both nations are displayed in identical actions; again, they seem to be content and ignore the European powers Germany, Russia, and France who are watching them suspiciously and unhappily from the continental coastline. The setting is a multilateral one; consequently, emphasis is put on the harmony aspect of the Anglo-American transatlantic relationship as an in-group in the quarreling international family of nations. Geographical distance between Great Britain and the United States is no issue here; the mental proximity generated by identical ideological aims such as Anglo-Saxonism is decisive.

Although the theoretical possibility of a conflict is alluded to in the caption, "How could they quarrel," it is not mirrored in the picture, which is a perfect example of mutual harmony. According to the subtitle, the reason for this lies in the interlocking interests of the two powers mentioned in the flag. It is interesting that the qualification of the reasons for harmony is denoted with a neutral, matter-of-fact, rational expression, "interests," whereas the enumeration of interests is not profit bound, but rather mentions irrational reasons such as "desire," "friendship," and "wireless telegraphy."

Finally, the cartoon "If they only could, they would—force them apart"[32] of 1904 (see figure 6.5) shows the perception of the Anglo-American friend-

IF THEY ONLY COULD THEY WOULD—FORCE THEM APART.

Figure 6.5. Cartoon: Eugene Zimmerman, "If they only could, they would—force them apart," *Judge,* 16 April 1904.

ship from the perspective of the European continental powers Germany, Russia, and France who, visible in their firm facial expression, seem to be determined to separate Great Britain and the United States by pushing them away from each other. Standing on a world map and looking extremely unhappy, the latter are both clinging to a document entitled "Exponents of civilization," which is nearly ripped in two. This document represents their connection. Their closeness is again symbolized by a narrowed Atlantic Ocean and by their ideological similarities. Looking at the picture without the title evokes the impression that the attempt at separation is successful. The caption then proves the beholder's first impression wrong: "If they only could," The picture represents a dream vision, wishful thinking of the European powers. This enforces the impression that in their eyes, the relationship between the United States and Great Britain is in fact unbreakable—from within due to strong ideological foundations as well as from the outside because of military action by scheming nations.

Emotions as Codes

Although emotions as codes for information processing are naturally not visible in the cartoons, it is still possible to discern the different techniques in the cartoons that ensure an attentive and memorable effect in the receiver.

The cognitive dissonances thus caused have an effect on the "cogmotion" side of perception.

It is important to pay attention to the construction of contrasts and similarities in the cartoons as they allow conclusions on the interpretive patterns of the relationship: alliances and opponents, conflict and cooperation, similarities and differences, sympathy and antipathy, hierarchies and equality. Metaphors of contrasts are those formal elements of interest for the analysis of the Anglo-American relationship, as they are based on comparison between two actors in the cartoon; therefore, they qualify not the figures as such, but their interdependent relationship.

The division of the picture into foreground and background can create contrasts, by colors, height, activity and passivity, speech(lessness), and naming strategies. Although John Bull and Uncle Sam or the British lion and American eagle are very different in their outward appearances, it is striking that their actions in the cartoons mirror each other, no matter if they act in accordance or fight, if they think differently or agree, if they face or turn their back on each other, if they look happy or dissatisfied. Their positions are identical, they are both the active protagonists of the cartoons, while the other international actors mainly watch sulkily on account of their outsider status. This points to a perceived nonhierarchical, equal relationship between Great Britain and the United States. In addition, it does not allow any negative or positive attributions: we cannot determine who started an argument or caused disagreement. Emotional quality is thus attached to both; negative feelings are channeled toward "outsiders" like the other European powers. The family metaphor of the "Siamese twins" used on the title page of the *Judge* issue in 1902 thus fits perfectly into the evolving picture. Moreover, the third connotation of ties as equal comes back sneaking through the back door while one has already forgotten its significance for the visual pattern of "ties that bind." It seems important not only that Uncle Sam and John Bull share the same attitudes and intentions, but also that they are doing this on the same footing.

Conclusion

To conclude, all five cartoons can be classified as commenting on the special relationship as a long-term emotionally and rationally based phenomenon, which cannot be shaken to its very foundations by other nations' intrigues or short incidents of political disagreement. In its wide interpretative and visual scope of conflict and cooperation, the "ties that bind" metaphor is ideal to illustrate Anglo-American relations and its inconsistencies. It becomes obvious that the interpretation and visualization of the Anglo-American relationship ambiguously vacillates between resentment and rapprochement. In an outward-oriented setting, they seem to demonstrate harmony and an unbreakable, impermeably closed group; concentrating on the relationship as such without other intruding actors, they like to quarrel despite their conscious long-term attachment. This is visible in actions on the one hand and attitudes and intentions on the other.

The emotions side of the illustration visible in gestures, mimicry, and body language of the portrayed entities as well as in the choice of language mainly reveals information on the second aspect mentioned above. The differentiation between affects as short-term emotions and long-term positive or negative attitudes toward a person or an event has to be kept in mind here. Long-term attachments have been symbolized by entitled ties, short-term conflicts by facial expressions and threatening gestures. Long-term emotions have been characterized as emotional attachment through cultural and family ties and rational common interests such as trade and business relations. The text-image relation and its contrastive value have to be kept in mind for a comprehensive reading of the cartoon.

Considering once again the interpretive value of these cartoons for the construction of the special relationship, it seems to me ever more striking that, first, they were not produced by British, but solely by American cartoonists, and second, bearing in mind that most visual patterns used in cartoons were imitated over and over again, the British equivalent of American satirical magazines, *Punch* or the *London Charivari*, did not come up with a similar interpretation of the "ties that bind" metaphor. It is the American side that seems to have actively constructed an image of close Anglo-American relations. Of course, other visual patterns oscillating between conflict and cooperation such as family, gender, or sports remain to be analyzed in this respect. Yet, in view of the present findings, the results on the character of the special relationship formulated by diplomatic historians seem no longer convincing. Rather, they have to be revisited in the light of the evidence based on an emotion-centered cultural approach to diplomatic history, exemplified here by "them damned pictures."

Notes

1. This particular reaction was possibly caused by viewing Thomas Nasts's well-known cartoon, "Who stole the people's money?" in *Harper's Weekly*, 19 August 1871, e.g., printed in Roger A. Fischer, *Them Damned Pictures: Explorations in American Political Cartoon Art* (North Haven, CT: Archon Books, 1996), 2–3.

2. Emotional in the sense of spontaneous (due to its wholesome impression), angry (of its distortion), fearful (of its effect on others), intuitive (due to its appealing quality).
3. Fischer, *Them Damned Pictures,* 14.
4. Although the reactions to cartoons have been measured by psychologists in numerous studies, they are not dealing with the cultural specificity of beholder's reactions, but rather with the universality of emotions. Paul Ekman, *The Face of Man: Expressions of Universal Emotions in a New Guinea Village* (New York: Garland STPM Press, 1980); Paul Ekman and Richard J. Davison, *The Nature of Emotions: Fundamental Questions* (New York: Oxford University Press, 1994); Paul Ekman and Klaus Scherrer, eds., *Approaches to Emotion* (Hillsdale, NJ: L. Erlbaum Associates, 1984). On studies on humor in particular see Hans Jürgen Eyseneck, "The Appreciation of Humor: An Experimental and Theoretical Study," *British Journal of Psychology* 32 (1942): 295–309 and "National Differences in Sense of Humor: Three Experimental and Statistical Studies," *Character and Personality* 13 (1944): 37–56; Paul Ekman and Wallace V. Friesen, *Unmasking the Face: A Guide to Recognizing Emotions from Facial Clues* (Englewood Cliffs, NJ: Prentice-Hall, 1975).
5. Another possibility to find out about readers' reactions for a contemporary or relatively recent study of cartoons might lie in an analysis of letters to the editor. That cartoons are consulted for an interpretation of today's events and also examined in regard to mirroring a certain political atmosphere or contemporary mentality is clearly demonstrated by the reaction of a reader of a daily German newspaper, stressing the cartoonist's ability to "ban the *moods of the nation* on paper with short, precise, striking sketches." (Karl Harkot, Letter to the editor, *Westdeutsche Allgemeine Zeitung,* 9 February 2002, my translation and emphasis. The original quote reads "mit kurzen, treffenden Strichen ... *den Seelenzustand der Nation* aufs Papier gesetzt.")
6. On the cultural approach to diplomatic history see Akira Iriye, "Culture and International History," in *Explaining the History of American Foreign Relations,* ed. Michael J. Hogan and Thomas G. Paterson (Cambridge: Cambridge University Press, 1991), 214–25 and "Culture and Power: International Relations as Intercultural Relations," *Diplomatic History* 3, no.1 (1979): 115–28. On the cultural approach and traditional diplomatic history see Michael H. Hunt, "Die lange Krise der amerikanischen Diplomatiegeschichte und ihr Ende," in *Internationale Geschichte: Themen—Ergebnisse—Aussichten,* ed. Wilfried Loth and Jürgen Osterhammel (Munich: R. Oldenbourg Verlag, 2000), 61–93. For a criticism of Iriye's concept see Ursula Lehmkuhl, "Entscheidungsprozesse in der internationalen Geschichte. Möglichkeiten und Grenzen einer kulturwissenschaftlichen Fundierung außenpolitischer Entscheidungsmodelle," in *Internationale Geschichte. Themen—Ergebnisse—Aussichten,* ed. Wilfried Loth and Juergen Osterhammel (Munich: R. Oldenbourg Verlag, 2000), 187–208.
7. It was only the Warburg circle of scholars who, by broadening the canon of art history to a more broadly understood "Bildwissenschaft," brought political cartoons to the attention of students of the letters. Already in 1963, Ernest Gombrich, who—together with Ernst Kris—had been working on a theory of caricature since the 1940s and has published widely on the matter, judged highly on the potential of the political cartoon for the history of mentalities: "The professional art historian ... is quite happy to leave these puzzling and often ugly images [i.e., caricatures] to the historian who may know how to unriddle their recondite allusions to long-forgotten issues and events. But historians in their turn usually think they have more important and more relevant documents to study in the state papers and speeches of a period, and generally they leave the old cartoons to the compilers of popular illustrated histories where these crude and often enigmatic scrawls jostle uneasily with portraits, maps, and pictures of pageantries and assassinations.

[... It is well worth, though,] to look at these strange configurations with puzzled curiosity, not so much for what they can tell about historical events *as for what they may reveal about our own minds.*" Ernest H. Gombrich, "The Cartoonist's Armoury," *South Atlantic Quarterly* 62 (1963): 189–228, my emphasis. Theoretical studies on the cartoon include William A. Coupe, "Observations on a Theory of Political Caricature," *Comparative Studies in Society and History* 11, no.1 (1969): 79–95; Lawrence H. Streicher, "On a Theory of Political Caricature," *Comparative Studies in Society and History* 9, no.4 (1967): 427–45; Thomas Milton Kemnitz, "The Cartoon as a Historical Source," *Journal of Interdisciplinary History* 4, no.1 (1973): 81–93; Charles Press, *The Political Cartoon* (London: Associated University Presses, 1981).

8. Interesting studies include Volker Sellin, "Maskierung und Demaskierung. Kriegskarikaturen des Simplicissimus in der Weimarer Republik als Quellen der Mentalitätsgeschichte," in *Bild und Geschichte. Studien zur politischen Ikonographie. Festschrift für Hansmartin Schwarzmaier zum fünfundsechsigsten Geburtstag*, ed. Konrad Krimm and John Herwig (Sigmaringen: Jan Thorbecke Verlag, 1997), 301–17; Lester C. Olson, *Emblems of American Community in the Revolutionary Era: A Study in Rhetorical Iconology* (Washington, DC: Smithsonian Institution Press, 1991); Michaele Siebe, *Von der Revolution zum nationalen Feindbild. Frankreich und Deutschland in der politischen Karikatur des 19. Jahrhunderts. Kladderadatsch und Charivari* (Münster: LitVerlag, 1995); Raymond N. Morris, *Behind the Jester's Mask: Canadian Editorial Cartoons about Dominant and Minority Groups, 1960–1979* (Toronto: University of Toronto Press, 1989); Raymond N. Morris, *The Carnivalization of Politics: Quebec Cartoons on Relations with Canada, England and France, 1960–1979* (Montreal: McGill-Queen's University Press, 1995).
9. In his study *Art and Emotion* (Oxford: Clarendon Press, 1998), Matravers concentrates on this question in regard to fiction.
10. Studies on symbolic representation mainly concentrate on visual representation and (twentieth-century) symbolic politics as a conscious staging of politics by the mass media, e.g., in architecture or celebrations. Martin Warnke, "Politische Ikonographie. Hinweise auf eine sichtbare Politik," in *Wozu Politikwissenschaft? Über das Neue in der Politik*, ed. Claus Leggewie (Darmstadt: Wissenschaftliche Buchgesellschaft, 1994), 170–78. The most interesting studies include Marion G. Müller, *Politische Bildstrategien im amerikanischen Präsidentschaftswahlkampf, 1828–1996* (Berlin: Akademischer Verlag, 1997), Andreas Dörner, *Politischer Mythos und symbolische Politik: Sinnstiftung durch symbolische Formen am Beispiel des Hermannsmythos* (Opladen: Westdeutscher Verlag, 1995) and the collection of essays edited by Rüdiger Voigt, *Symbole der Politik—Politik der Symbole* (Opladen: Leske & Budrich, 1989).
11. Before the reader can actually feel an emotion, he has to "understand" the message the cartoonist tries to convey to the beholder. "Writer [or, for that matter, caricaturist] and reader are active participants in a process which ... is always double-sided, always interactive. Representation functions less like the model of a one-way transmitter and more like the model of a dialogue." Stuart Hall, *Representation: Cultural Representations and Signifying Practices* (London: Sage/Open University, 1997), 10. A successful process of communication also depends on the activation of this combination of knowledge and emotions. Thus the kind of person the reader is, his or her dislikes, preferences, personal history, and cultural origins determine and channel his reaction to a cartoon.
12. These assumptions are based on Assmann's theory of cultural memory. Jan Assmann, *Das kulturelle Gedächtnis. Schrift, Erinnerung und politische Identität in frühen Hochkulturen* (Munich: Beck 1997).
13. As emotions have been demonized and mystified as the intuitive, immediate, and intensive counterpart of cold and impartial "rationality," they have generally been neglected in

research until approximately twenty years ago, when a renewed interest in the individual and its subjective point of view resurged in the social sciences. Since then, there has been an ongoing debate between psychologists, biologists, and anthropologists about the nature of emotions. Whereas the natural scientists stress the universality of individually experienced emotions, cognitive anthropologists and constructivist psychologists understand emotions as conceptual social constructions of society. According to them, emotions are context bound, culture specific, and historically developed. For a sociologist's approach to emotions and their place in culture and society see the following enlightening studies: Heinz-Günter Vester, *Emotionen, Gesellschaft und Kultur. Grundzüge einer soziologischen Theorie der Emotionen* (Opladen: Westdeutscher Verlag, 1991); Jürgen Gerhards, *Soziologie der Emotionen. Fragestellungen, Systematik und Perspektiven* (Weinheim: Juventa Verlag, 1988); Amelie von Griessenbeck, *Kulturfaktor Emotion. Zur Bedeutung von Emotionen für das Verhältnis von Individuum, Gesellschaft und Kultur* (Munich: Akademischer Verlag, 1997); Ansgar Klein and Frank Nullmeier, eds., *Masse—Macht—Emotionen. Zu einer politischen Soziologie der Emotionen* (Munich: Westdeutscher Verlag, 1999).

14. Robert I. Levy, "Emotion, Knowing, and Culture," in *Culture Theory: Essays on Mind, Self, and Emotion,* ed. Richard A. Shweder and Robert A. LeVine (Cambridge: Cambridge University Press, 1984), 218. One might object that this is valid for all visual sources. Yet, in what way do cartoons still differ? What is the extraordinary characteristic of cartoons in this respect? The answer is obvious: their main attraction lies in their quality to be ironic, witty, and funny. Caricatures ridicule the occurrences of the time, and thus make them memorable. For the explanation of immediate attention and memorability of cartoons, Ernest H. Gombrich draws on Sigmund Freud's work *Wit and its Relation to the Unconscious* (1916). Parallel to the interpretation of dreams, wit is explained as the melting of two seemingly disparate elements into a whole. The unexpected and incomplete "riddle" in cartoons creates cognitive disharmony in the individual's mind. The attention and the surprise effect needed to solve the riddle by puzzling together preknowledge, beliefs, attitudes of symbols, context, and culture will ensure that it remains in the reader's mind longer than a conventional picture. Ernst Kris and Ernst H. Gombrich, "The Principles of Caricature," in Ernst Kris, *Psychoanalytic Explorations in Art* (New York: International University Press, 1965), 189–204.

    The question then remains as to which elements create this lasting and emotive impression in cartoons. In which elements are wit, fun, and irony represented? It is Gombrich again who draws our attention to the most important features of caricature. He argues that oversimplification, distortion, metamorphosis, figures of speech, and metaphors of contrast aim at reducing the topic's complexity by visualizing condensation and comparison and by combining "pictorial symbolism" and "artistic transformation," i.e., contextualization. These formal elements add to the characterization of events or individuals and thus to one-sided negative or positive emotions toward the topic portrayed. Ernst H. Gombrich, "The Principles of Caricature," *British Journal of Medical Psychology* 17 (1938): 319–42. Ernst H. Gombrich, "Psycho-Analysis and the History of Art" and "The Cartoonist's Armoury," in *Meditations on a Hobby Horse and Other Essays on the Theory of Art* (London: Phaidon, 1971), 30–45, 127–43.

15. These issues have undoubtedly influenced considerations formulated by Peter and Carol Stearns for the study of emotions in history. They point to the importance of differentiating between emotionology—i.e.. the collective emotional standards of society—and emotions of individuals and certain groups in society by stressing that "we can see not only that actual experience sometimes differs markedly from notions about how people ought to behave and feel, but also that these prescriptions for emotional life often have important cultural, social, and political functions. Emotional standards are woven into

the fabric of the discourses, belief systems and ideologies that explain and attempt to structure our lives." According to them, the aims of a historical study of emotions are first, to point to discrepancies between emotions and emotionology, second, to analyze changes in emotional standards over time, and third, to examine the impact of emotional standards on other areas of social and political life. The last two aims are aspects that cartoons as historical sources could shed some light on. Peter Stearns and Carol Zisowitz Stearns, "Introduction," in *An Emotional History of the United States,* ed. Peter Stearns and Jan Lewis (New York: New York University Press, 1998), 2. Also see Peter Stearns and Carol Zisowitz Stearns, "Emotionology: Clarifying the History of Emotions and Emotional Standards," *American Historical Review* 90 (1985): 813–36; Carol Zisowitz Stearns and Peter Stearns, eds., *Emotion and Social Change: Toward a New Psychohistory* (New York: Holmes & Meier, 1988); Carol Zisowitz Stearns and Peter Stearns, *Anger: The Struggle for Emotional Control in America's History* (Chicago: University of Chicago Press, 1986); Peter Stearns, *Jealousy: The Evolution of an Emotion in American History* (New York: New York University Press, 1989).

16. On the special relationship see Coral Bell, "The Special Relationship," in *Constraints and Adjustments in British Foreign Policy,* ed. Michael Leifer (London: Allen & Unwin, 1972), 103–19; Alexander Elmslie Campbell, "The United States and Great Britain: Uneasy Allies," in *Twentieth Century American Foreign Policy,* ed. John Braeman, Robert Hamlett Bremner, and David Brody (Columbus: Ohio State University Press, 1971), 471–501; Geoffrey Warner, "The Anglo-American Special Relationship," *Diplomatic History* 13, no. 4 (1989): 479–99; Steve Smith, "The Special Relationship," *Political Studies* 38 (1990): 126–36; Max Beloff, "The Special Relationship: An Anglo-American Myth," in *A Century of Conflict, 1850–1950: Essays for A.J.P. Taylor,* ed. Martin Gilbert (London: Hamilton, 1966), 151–71.
17. Bell, "The Special Relationship," 103 (emphasis by the author).
18. On the Anglo-American relationship in the nineteenth century see Henry Cranbrook Allen, *Great Britain and the United States: A History of Anglo-American Relations, 1783–1952* (New York: St. Martin's Press, 1955); Alexander Elmslie Campbell, *Great Britain and the United States, 1895–1903* (London: Longmans, 1960); Frank Thistlethwaite, *The Anglo-American Connection in the Early Nineteenth Century* (Philadelphia: University of Pennsylvania Press, 1959); Charles S. Campbell, *From Revolution to Rapprochement: The United States and Great Britain, 1783–1900* (New York: Wiley, 1974); Charles S. Campbell, *Anglo-American Understanding, 1898–1903* (Baltimore: John Hopkins Press, 1957); William Clark, *Less Than Kin: A Study of Anglo-American Relations* (London: Hamilton, 1957).
19. A theory of these interpretive patterns (*Deutungsmuster*) was first developed by Ulrich Oevermann in an unpublished conference manuscript that was then unofficially circulating through sociology departments and conferences until a revised version was finally published in *Sozialer Sinn* in 2001, which renewed the discussion of the character of interpretative patterns. Ulrich Oevermann, "Die Struktur sozialer Deutungsmuster—Versuch einer Aktualisierung," *Sozialer Sinn* 1 (2001): 35–81; Christine Plaß and Michael Schetsche, "Grundzüge einer wissenssoziologischen Theorie sozialer Deutungsmuster," *Sozialer Sinn* 3 (2001): 511–36; Ulrich Oevermann, "Kommentar zu Christine Plaß/Michael Schetsche, Grundzüge einer wissenssoziologischen Theorie sozialer Deutungsmuster," *Sozialer Sinn* 3 (2001): 537–46. Further probed and elaborated on by Plaß and Schetsche, the concept developed into a useful category of analysis as it stressed the patterns' potential for continuity and change through their dissemination via the mass media, such as journals, newspapers, and magazines. The only indication of a successful cartoon (also see footnote 5 and 6) might be taken from these patterns, which can be regarded as

accepted and thus effective if they are used several times in consecutive cartoons and thus form a certain category according to which a topic can be analyzed. Once such a pattern has been successfully established, its references might become more and more indirect, but still understood. The slighter a reference in a picture, the higher its acceptance in the receptionist culture. For example, from the beginning of colonial times, the Anglo-American relationship has often been portrayed as a family relationship with Britannia or John Bull as the parents of Uncle Sam. Toward the end of the nineteenth century, John Bull and Uncle Sam increasingly appeared as cousins, brothers, or even twins, thus moving, on a hierarchical scale, toward an ever closer and equal blood relationship. Using this well-known pattern at the end of the nineteenth century, it is no longer necessary for the cartoonist to portray both in a family setting, but it suffices to let the national symbols address each other as Brother Jonathan or Cousin Bull, while additionally setting them up in a totally different situation, such as at the business counter, in a fight, or as rivals in a sport competition, thus adding another dimension to the construction of an already complicated multilayered relationship.

20. On the family metaphor for Anglo-American relations see Jennifer Clark, "The War of 1812: American Nationalism and Rhetorical Images of Britain," *War & Society* 12, no. 1 (1994): 1–26; Jennifer Clark, "John Bull's American Connection: The Allegorical Interpretation of England and the Anglo-American Relationship," *Huntington Library Quarterly* 53, no.1 (1990): 15.
21. On Uncle Sam as a national symbol see Alton Ketchum, *Uncle Sam: The Man and the Legend* (New York: Hill and Wang, 1959); Kendall B. Mattern, Jr., "America's Favorite Relative: The Birth and Long Life of Uncle Sam," *Target: The Political Cartoon Quarterly* 1, no. 3 (1982): 15–19; on Jonathan see Winifred Morgan, *An American Icon: Brother Jonathan and American Identity* (London: Associated University Presses, 1988); on John Bull see for example Peter Mellini and Roy T. Matthews, "John Bull's Family Arises," *History Today* 37 (1987): 17–23.
22. Kenneth Boulding, *The Image: Knowledge in Life and Society,* 17th ed. (Ann Arbor: University of Michigan Press, 1987), 110–11.
23. On satirical magazines in the United States see Frank Luther Mott, *A History of American Magazines* (Cambridge, MA: Harvard University Press, 1957); David E. E. Sloane, ed., *American Humor Magazines and Comic Periodicals* (New York: Greenwood Press, 1987); Maurice Horn, "A History of *Puck*, *Judge*, and *Life*," in *The World Encyclopedia of Cartoons,* ed. Maurice Horn, 2 vols. (New York: Chelsea House, 1980), 705–44.
24. Nicholas divided nineteenth-century Anglo-American relations into four phases: up to 1861, the American Civil War (1861–1865), Reconstruction (ca. 1866–1895), and 1895–1914. Herbert G. Nicholas, *The United States and Britain* (Chicago: University of Chicago Press, 1972).
25. Although this does not apply to the "ties that bind" metaphor, some of the visual patterns used in cartoons are applicable for all nations, constellations, or events; in this case, the specificity of the Anglo-American context and its continuity or change has to be determined in comparison to other nations. Some cartoon motifs explicitly or implicitly refer to other well-known cartoons, but change protagonists or visual makeup. For example, the cartoon by James Gillray, "The plum-pudding in danger; or state epicures taking a petit souper," 26 February 1805, printed in *Drawn and Quartered: The History of American Political Cartoons,* ed. Stephen Hess and Sandy Northrop (Montgomery, AL: Elliott & Clark, 1996), 35, has inspired many following cartoons going back to a dinner scene of "sharing" a country, territory, or colony by dividing a map or globe of it with the help of a sword; this motif can also be found in several variations in the Anglo-American context.
26. Frederick B. Opper, "They can't fight," *Puck,* 15 January 1896.

27. This might be one main statement of the cartoon, but on the other hand, their bodily features—John's well-fed, wealth-signaling body and Uncle Sam's skinny appearance—already belong to their stock appearance as cartoon symbols.
28. On these territorial and economic disputes see Robert George Neale, *Great Britain and United States Expansion, 1898–1900* (East Lansing: Michigan State University Press, 1966); Robert George Neale, *Britain and American Imperialism, 1898–1900* (St. Lucia: University of Queensland Press, 1965); Hans-Heinrich Jansen and Ursula Lehmkuhl, eds., *Großbritannien, das Empire und die Welt: Britische Außenpolitik zwischen Größe und Selbstbehauptung, 1850–1990* (Bochum: Brockmeyer, 1995); Lionel Gerber, *The Rise of the Anglo-American Friendship: A Study in World Politics, 1898–1906* (Hamden, CT: Archon Books, 1966); Richard Heathcote Heindel, *The American Impact on Great Britain, 1898–1914: A Study of the United States in World History* (New York: Octagon Books, 1968); Edward P. Crapol, *America for Americans: Economic Nationalism and Anglophobia in the Late Nineteenth Century* (Westport, CT: Greenwood Press, 1973); Joseph Smith, *Illusions of Conflict: Anglo-American Diplomacy Toward Latin-America, 1865–1896* (Pittsburgh, PA: University of Pittsburgh Press, 1979).
29. Schweitz, "Quite a strain on the Anglo-Saxon alliance," *Life,* 14 May 1901.
30. Victor Gillam, "The International Siamese Twins," *Judge,* 21 June 1902.
31. Victor Gillam, "How could they quarrel when their interests are so interwoven," *Judge,* 21 February 1903.
32. Eugene Zimmerman, "If they only could, they would—force them apart," *Judge,* 16 April 1904.

Bibliography

Allen, Henry Cranbrook. *Great Britain and the United States: A History of Anglo-American Relations, 1783–1952.* New York: St. Martin's Press, 1955.

Assmann, Jan. *Das kulturelle Gedächtnis. Schrift, Erinnerung und politische Identität in frühen Hochkulturen.* Munich: Beck, 1997.

Bell, Coral. "The Special Relationship." In *Constraints and Adjustments in British Foreign Policy,* edited by Michael Leifer, 103–19. London: Allen & Unwin, 1972.

Beloff, Max. "The Special Relationship: an Anglo-American Myth." In *A Century of Conflict, 1850–1950: Essays for A.J.P. Taylor,* edited by Martin Gilbert, 151–71. London: Hamilton, 1966.

Boulding, Kenneth. *The Image: Knowledge in Life and Society,* 17th ed. Ann Arbor: University of Michigan Press, 1987.

Campbell, Alexander Elmslie. "The United States and Great Britain: Uneasy Allies." In *Twentieth Century American Foreign Policy,* edited by John Braeman, Robert Hamlett Bremner, and David Brody, 471–501. Columbus: Ohio State University Press, 1971.

———. *Great Britain and the United States, 1895–1903.* London: Longmans, 1960.

Campbell, Charles S. *Anglo-American Understanding, 1898–1903.* Baltimore: John Hopkins Press, 1957.

———. *From Revolution to Rapprochement: The United States and Great Britain, 1783–1900.* New York: Wiley, 1974.

Clark, Jennifer. "John Bull's American Connection: The Allegorical Interpretation of England and the Anglo-American Relationship." *Huntington Library Quarterly* 53, no. 1 (1990): 15.

———. "The War of 1812: American Nationalism and Rhetorical Images of Britain." *War & Society* 12, no. 1 (1994): 1–26.

Clark, William. *Less Than Kin: A Study of Anglo-American Relations.* London: Hamilton, 1957.

Coupe, William A. "Observations on a Theory of Political Caricature." *Comparative Studies in Society and History* 11, no. 1 (1969): 79–95.

Crapol, Edward P. *America for Americans: Economic Nationalism and Anglophobia in the Late Nineteenth Century.* Westport, CT: Greenwood Press, 1973.

Dörner, Andreas. *Politischer Mythos und symbolische Politik: Sinnstiftung durch symbolische Formen am Beispiel des Hermannsmythos.* Opladen: Westdeutscher Verlag, 1995.

Ekman, Paul. *The Face of Man: Expressions of Universal Emotions in a New Guinea Village.* New York: Garland STPM Press, 1980.

Ekman, Paul, and Richard J. Davison. *The Nature of Emotions: Fundamental Questions.* New York: Oxford University Press, 1994.

Ekman, Paul, and Wallace V. Friesen. *Unmasking the Face: A Guide to Recognizing Emotions from Facial Clues.* Englewood Cliffs, NJ: Prentice-Hall, 1975.

Ekman, Paul, and Klaus Scherrer, eds. *Approaches to Emotion.* Hillsdale, NJ: L. Erlbaum Associates, 1984.

Eyseneck, Hans Jürgen. "National Differences in Sense of Humor: Three Experimental and Statistical Studies." *Character and Personality* 13 (1944): 37–56.

———. "The Appreciation of Humor: An Experimental and Theoretical Study." *British Journal of Psychology* 32 (1942): 295–309.

Fischer, Roger A. *Them Damned Pictures: Explorations in American Political Cartoon Art.* North Haven, CT: Archon Books, 1996.

Gerber, Lionel. *The Rise of the Anglo-American Friendship: A Study in World Politics, 1898–1906.* Hamden, CT: Archon Books, 1966.

Gerhards, Jürgen. *Soziologie der Emotionen. Fragestellungen, Systematik und Perspektiven.* Weinheim: Juventa Verlag, 1988.

Gombrich, Ernest H. "The Cartoonist's Armoury." *South Atlantic Quarterly* 62 (1963): 189–228.

———. "Psycho-Analysis and the History of Art" and "The Cartoonist's Armoury." In *Meditations on a Hobby Horse and Other Essays on the Theory of Art,* edited by Ernst H. Gombrich, 30–45, 127–43. London: Phaidon, 1971.

———. "The Principles of Caricature." *British Journal of Medical Psychology* 17 (1938): 319–42.

Griessenbeck, Amelie von. *Kulturfaktor Emotion. Zur Bedeutung von Emotionen für das Verhältnis von Individuum, Gesellschaft und Kultur.* Munich: Akademischer Verlag, 1997.

Hall, Stuart. *Representation: Cultural Representations and Signifying Practices.* London: Sage/Open University, 1997.

Heindel, Richard Heathcote. *The American Impact on Great Britain, 1898–1914: A Study of the United States in World History.* New York: Octagon Books, 1968.

Hess, Stephen, and Sandy Northrop. *Drawn and Quartered: The History of American Political Cartoons.* Montgomery, AL: Elliott & Clark, 1996.

Horn, Maurice. "A History of Puck, Judge, and Life." In *The World Encyclopedia of Cartoons,* edited by Maurice Horn, 705–44. New York: Chelsea House, 1980.

Hunt, Michael H. "Die lange Krise der amerikanischen Diplomatiegeschichte und ihr Ende." In *Internationale Geschichte: Themen—Ergebnisse—Aussichten,* edited by Wilfried Loth and Jürgen Osterhammel, 61–93. Munich: R. Oldenbourg Verlag, 2000.

Iriye, Akira. "Culture and International History." In *Explaining the History of American For-*

eign Relations, edited by Michael J. Hogan and Thomas G. Paterson, 214–25. Cambridge: Cambridge University Press, 1991.

———. "Culture and Power: International Relations as Intercultural Relations." *Diplomatic History* 3, no. 1 (1979): 115–28.

Jansen, Hans-Heinrich and Ursula Lehmkuhl, eds. *Großbritannien, das Empire und die Welt: Britische Außenpolitik zwischen Größe und Selbstbehauptung, 1850–1990.* Bochum: Brockmeyer, 1995.

Kemnitz, Thomas Milton. "The Cartoon as a Historical Source." *Journal of Interdisciplinary History* 4, no. 1 (1973): 81–93.

Ketchum, Alton. *Uncle Sam: The Man and the Legend.* New York: Hill and Wang, 1959.

Klein, Ansgar, and Frank Nullmeier, eds. *Masse—Macht—Emotionen. Zu einer politischen Soziologie der Emotionen.* Munich: Westdeutscher Verlag, 1999.

Kris, Ernst, and Ernst H. Gombrich. "The Principles of Caricature." In *Psychoanalytic Explorations in Art,* edited by Ernst Kris, 189–204. New York: International University Press, 1965.

Lehmkuhl, Ursula, "Entscheidungsprozesse in der internationalen Geschichte. Möglichkeiten und Grenzen einer kulturwissenschaftlichen Fundierung außenpolitischer Entscheidungsmodelle." In *Internationale Geschichte. Themen—Ergebnisse—Aussichten,* edited by Wilfried Loth and Jürgen Osterhammel, 187–208. Munich: R. Oldenbourg Verlag, 2000.

Levy, Robert I., "Emotion, Knowing, and Culture." In *Culture Theory: Essays on Mind, Self, and Emotion,* edited by Richard A. Shweder and Robert A. LeVine. Cambridge: Cambridge University Press, 1984.

Matravers, Derek. *Art and Emotion.* Oxford: Clarendon Press, 1998.

Mattern, Kendall B., Jr. "America's Favorite Relative: The Birth and Long Life of Uncle Sam." *Target: The Political Cartoon Quarterly* 1, no. 3 (1982): 15–19.

Mellini, Peter, and Roy T. Matthews. "John Bull's Family Arises." *History Today* 37 (1987): 17–23.

Morgan, Winifred. *An American Icon: Brother Jonathan and American Identity.* London: Associated University Presses, 1988.

Morris, Raymond N. *Behind the Jester's Mask: Canadian Editorial Cartoons about Dominant and Minority Groups, 1960–1979.* Toronto: University of Toronto Press, 1989.

———. *The Carnivalization of Politics: Quebec Cartoons on Relations with Canada, England and France, 1960–1979.* Montreal: McGill-Queen's University Press, 1995.

Mott, Frank Luther. *A History of American Magazines.* Cambridge, MA: Harvard University Press, 1957.

Müller, Marion G. *Politische Bildstrategien im amerikanischen Präsidentschaftswahlkampf, 1828–1996.* Berlin: Akademischer Verlag, 1997.

Neale, Robert George. *Britain and American Imperialism, 1898–1900.* St. Lucia: University of Queensland Press, 1965.

———. *Great Britain and United States Expansion, 1898–1900.* East Lansing: Michigan State University Press, 1966.

Nicholas, Herbert G. *The United States and Britain.* Chicago: University of Chicago Press, 1972.

Oevermann, Ulrich. "Die Struktur sozialer Deutungsmuster—Versuch einer Aktualisierung." *Sozialer Sinn* 1 (2001): 35–81.

———. "Kommentar zu Christine Plaß/Michael Schetsche, Grundzüge einer wissenssoziologischen Theorie sozialer Deutungsmuster." *Sozialer Sinn* 3 (2001): 537–46.

Olson, Lester C. *Emblems of American Community in the Revolutionary Era: A Study in Rhetorical Iconology.* Washington, DC: Smithsonian Institution Press, 1991.

Plass, Christine, and Michael Schetsche. "Grundzüge einer wissenssoziologischen Theorie sozialer Deutungsmuster." *Sozialer Sinn* 3 (2001): 511–36.

Press, Charles. *The Political Cartoon.* London: Associated University Presses, 1981.

Sellin, Volker. "Maskierung und Demaskierung. Kriegskarikaturen des Simplicissimus in der Weimarer Republik als Quellen der Mentalitätsgeschichte." In *Bild und Geschichte. Studien zur politischen Ikonographie. Festschrift für Hansmartin Schwarzmaier zum fünfundsechsigsten Geburtstag,* edited by Konrad Krimm and John Herwig, 301–17. Sigmaringen: Jan Thorbecke Verlag, 1997.

Siebe, Michaele. *Von der Revolution zum nationalen Feindbild. Frankreich und Deutschland in der politischen Karikatur des 19. Jahrhunderts. Kladderadatsch und Charivari.* Münster: LitVerlag, 1995.

Sloane, David E. E., ed. *American Humor Magazines and Comic Periodicals.* New York: Greenwood Press, 1987.

Smith, Joseph. *Illusions of Conflict: Anglo-American Diplomacy Toward Latin-America, 1865–1896.* Pittsburgh, PA: University of Pittsburgh Press, 1979.

Smith, Steve. "The Special Relationship." *Political Studies* 38 (1990): 126–36.

Stearns, Carol Zisowitz, and Peter Stearns. *Anger: The Struggle for Emotional Control in America's History.* Chicago: University of Chicago Press, 1986.

———, eds. *Emotion and Social Change: Toward a New Psychohistory.* New York: Holmes & Meier, 1988.

Stearns, Peter. *Jealousy: The Evolution of an Emotion in American History.* New York: New York University Press, 1989.

Stearns, Peter, and Carol Zisowitz Stearns. "Emotionology: Clarifying the History of Emotions and Emotional Standards." *American Historical Review* 90 (1985): 813–36.

———. "Introduction." In *An Emotional History of the United States,* edited by Peter Stearns and Jan Lewis. New York: New York University Press, 1998.

Streicher, Lawrence H. "On a Theory of Political Caricature." *Comparative Studies in Society and History* 9, no. 4 (1967): 427–45.

Thistlethwaite, Frank. *The Anglo-American Connection in the Early Nineteenth Century.* Philadelphia: University of Pennsylvania Press, 1959.

Vester, Heinz-Günter. *Emotionen, Gesellschaft und Kultur. Grundzüge einer soziologischen Theorie der Emotionen.* Opladen: Westdeutscher Verlag, 1991.

Voigt, Rüdiger. *Symbole der Politik—Politik der Symbole.* Opladen: Leske & Budrich, 1989.

Warner, Geoffrey. "The Anglo-American Special Relationship." *Diplomatic History* 13, no. 4 (1989): 479–99.

Warnke, Martin. "Politische Ikonographie. Hinweise auf eine sichtbare Politik." In *Wozu Politikwissenschaft? Über das Neue in der Politik,* edited by Claus Leggewie, 170–78. Darmstadt: Wissenschaftliche Buchgesellschaft, 1994.

Chapter 7

EMOTIONS OF COMPARISONS

Perceptions of European Anti-Americanism in US Magazines of the 1920s

Adelheid von Saldern

Introduction

COLLIER'S MAGAZINE OPENED its edition of 19 September 1926 with an article entitled "Why They Hate Us." The headline's juxtaposition between "they" and "us" describes a classic subject of inquiry for historians, philosophers, psychologists, and other social scientists as well. It also highlights the importance of perceptions in transatlantic relations and reminds us of the yet insufficiently explored power of emotions in Euro-American relations.

Research on emotions provides historians with unique insights into the foundations of society and culture. It is a key to understanding social norms and values and enables a better grasp of society's cohesive forces.[1] According to French sociologist and philosopher Emile Durkheim, emotions are fundamental for the spiritual construction of social realities. Emotions structure the way in which society and the world are perceived, they build up mental maps of orientation, and in doing so construct differences.[2] Emotions are thus an integral part of comparison as perceptions of otherness are central to individual, group, or national self-interpretation. This emotional dimension is referred to as "emotions of comparisons."[3]

Notes for this section begin on page 151.

This chapter examines the emotions of comparisons between the United States and Europe through an analysis of American perceptions of European anti-Americanism, published in US magazines during the 1920s. As the interpretation of other countries involves and demands reference to one's own country, this analysis encompasses the reconstruction of debates over American identity in the 1920s and thus contributes to the growing historiography of interwar political culture in the United States. To be sure, the working assumption of a national identity affected by emotions is not new. Yet a subtle analysis based on highly differentiated questions and interpretations promises novel insights into the emotional history of comparison. Let me begin with four observations on emotions.

First, prototypical emotions such as fear, sadness, fury, joy, and love are culturally formed, socially constructed and encoded. Any historical analysis requires a more thorough differentiation of these prototypical emotions,[4] whereby figurative terms have also to be taken into consideration.[5]

Second, work on the history of emotions requires an acknowledgment that the cognitive and affective dimensions of human behavior are not mutually exclusive but interwoven in a complex way.[6] Therefore terms such as *rationality of emotion* or *emotional rationality* make sense. This insight indicates the complexity of the topic: emotions cannot only be considered by themselves but must be discussed together with their contrary terms—the cognitive, the rational, the unemotional, the "coolness." To be sure, at first glance, a rational tone seems to be the opposite of emotionality. As already mentioned above, no one, however, holds that these "cognitive processes," characteristic of the magazines referred to in this chapter, were "irrelevant to emotion."[7]

Third, the expressions of emotions are anchored in history. The extreme difficulties in reconstructing the peculiarities of emotional expressions of the past lower our expectations of the possibilities of historical research and remind us that all statements on emotions are nothing but vague approaches.

Finally, the characteristics of emotional expressions, anchored in history, are the product of a complex set of sources. They are shaped by family background, education, experiences in daily and communal life, rituals, festivals, and texts. They demonstrate the challenges of the complexity of the past.

Texts and Emotions

Texts often serve as mediators in transmitting existing or desired emotions from writers to individual or group recipients.[8] As the issue of hate speech indicates, texts can also evoke or stimulate powerful emotions on a public issue.[9] At the same time, they can improve the emotional competence and the emotional intelligence of their readers. Similar to ritual and symbolic practices, texts give expression to emotions, while also producing, stimulating, legitimizing, and controlling them. In doing so, texts both express and produce the ways in which emotions are coded in a given society. Furthermore, emotions expressed in a text are often used just as means to an end to provide a meaningful interpretative framework for events and actions, or in order to foster the creation of socially and culturally dominant attitudes and interpretations.

Media texts have played a central role in the encoding and stimulation of public emotions in twentieth-century history. While public acceptance of media-produced social codes of perceptions, experiences, and emotions can never be guaranteed, at most permanent reiteration of an idea might lead to the intended reception by the public and thus the creation of a dominant discourse. The multiple diversities of the recipients as to ethnicity, class, and gender complicate a simple action-reaction scheme of discursive hegemony.[10] In addition, research in the field of *cultural studies* indicates the complexities of information transmission. The appropriation of media texts is not pure and simple adoption but a complex process that depends to a large degree on the recipient's mental disposition and situation. The importance of media texts in the history of emotions depends on how well texts affected the mentality of their readership.[11] As a rule, however, direct or indirect references to the audience's experience or ideas are a prerequisite for emotional stimulation.[12] But writers can also produce emotions beyond the realm of personal experience as long as the recipient's interest and curiosity are stimulated.[13] Any acquaintance with conditions in interwar Europe was thus no prerequisite for an American recipient's opposition to European cultural anti-Americanism.[14]

During the 1920s so-called quality magazines published an average of 50,000 to 100,000 copies.[15] These magazines saw themselves simultaneously as opinion leaders and representatives of the American public. Their target audience consisted of the expanding middle classes with a college or university education and the small minority of intellectuals. To be sure, this media-related public was a social construction. Above all, this public was defined as national and this definition superseded the identities that were traditionally based on local communities.[16]

The following analysis complements current research on the history of an emerging Atlantic community[17] with respect to magazine discourses on European anti-Americanism and American national identity during the 1920s.

Emotional Background: The Search for American National Identity

American perceptions of the Old World, in particular European cultural anti-Americanism,[18] played an important role in the social construction of American national identity. Such interconnections between perceptions of the "other" and definition of the "self" confirm Benedict Anderson's paradigm of the nation as "imagined political community."[19] Initially the nation is imagined,[20] but it assumes a special kind of reality in people's minds, experiences, and deeds fostered, for example, by media texts.[21] Such an ongoing process of persistent nation building is highly dependent on emotionality.[22] It reaches maximum effect with the inclusion of emotional components and the development of a visionary dimension of the nation's future.[23]

In the United States, the 1920s were a decade characterized by extensive debate over national identity. Harold Stearns, editor of *Civilization in the United States,* for example, argued in 1922: "No headway can be made unless we begin to achieve genuine nationalistic self-consciousness."[24] In some respects such a debate was new, as British political scientist George E. G. Catlin, who taught at Cornell University, emphasized in 1927.[25] It differed from earlier debates in its intensity as Warren Susman retrospectively comments: "There was something special and excessive about it in this period."[26]

The rise of the United States to a world power and the nation's transformation to a consumer and machine society were at the root of this interwar discourse. It was a period strongly shaped by memories of the Progressive Era and the Great War. During World War I, the societal consensus about the necessity of reforms broke down, and victory in 1918 did not lead to new reform impulses.[27] As a consequence some intellectuals drifted towards socialism and radicalism while others focused on the debate over the nation's future. In some respects, the debates on American identity formed a bridge between the Progressive Era and the era of the New Deal and recognized the impact of transitions on American society. These shifts had a lasting impact on the way in which national identity was imagined and emotions were directed.

The 1920s were characterized in part by a desire to escape from the complexities of modernity coupled with a "web of ambivalence" in societal attitudes towards the nation's present and past. There were many signs that "Americans found it far easier to come to terms with the new if it could be surrounded somehow by the aura of the old."[28] Philosopher-journalist Walter Lippman spoke of the "acids of modernity" that transformed society, but historian Lawrence W. Levine correctly emphasized American society in this decade as all but an already-transformed one. According to Levine, the 1920s were "marked by furious struggles waged over prohibition, religion, the rights of Catholics and Jews, the very nature of morality and ethos that would define and guide Americans in the years to come."[29]

The inherent emotional ambiguity towards past and present also influenced the tensions between notions of national superiority and feelings of inferiority vis-à-vis Europe.[30] In contrast to the so-called expatriates, such as Ernest Hemingway, who clearly favored life in Europe over that in the United States, and in contrast to radical American writers and critics like Sinclair Lewis and H. L. Mencken,[31] many Americans searched for a pragmatic and realistic orientation with respect to national identity in the postwar decade of modernity. The quality magazines of the time such as *Atlantic Monthly, Nation, New Republic, Forum, Scribner's Magazine,* and *Harper's Magazine* played an important role in this discourse as their contributions simultaneously offered severe criticism of life in America and productive empathy designed to improve conditions in the United States.[32]

African American views of national development were largely absent in these magazine discourses. The Harlem Renaissance exerted a powerful influence on interwar culture, arts, and daily life but failed to produce social reform, racial integration, or black participation in mainstream debates over the nation's identity.[33]

Emotional European Anti-Americanism

European views of the United States were prominently featured in American interwar magazines. In particular the Old World's cultural anti-Americanism generated heated debates reflected in emotionally charged headlines such as "Does England Dislike America?"[34] "Why They Hate Us,"[35] "Does France Hate America?"[36] or "Nobody Loves Us"[37]—titles designed to stimulate the readers' interest. Especially towards the end of the 1920s, an increasing number of magazine articles emphasized that hate and fear of America were widespread in Europe and increasingly replaced any sense of admiration and friendship.

To be sure, a number of contributors marginalized European's anti-Americanism.[38] Some articles, for example, questioned the differing characteristics of Europeans and Americans.[39] Walter Lippmann even contradicted conventional assumptions of Old World anti-Americanism and argued that the "greatness of America is better appreciated throughout Europe than it is here."[40] Lothrop Stoddard, racist author of the successful books *The Revolt against Civilization, The Rising Tide of Color,* and *The New World of Islam,* traveled "to England determined to unearth the sources of anti-Americanism there." He soon made a disconcerting discovery: "No Englishman would admit that he was an anti-American! A few did say they thought there was a certain amount of ill feeling here and there on specific points like our period of entry into the war and the debt settlement," but he "was unable to get any tangible evidence. The redoubtable editor of the *National Review* told [him] … that, in his opinion, the sole obstacle to more cordial relations between the two countries was the numerous anti-Britishers in the United States,"[41] referring mainly to anti-British sentiment among Irish-Americans. Reversing Old World sentiment into an emotion of Irish immigrants, the story explicitly marginalized British anti-Americanism and implicitly pushed the common features of Anglo-American civilization.

But despite those critical voices, articles on European anti-Americanism were more common and, in any case, more conspicuous. Although the *Forum* published a series of articles in 1928 explaining the loss of American popularity in Europe,[42] most contributions focused on perceptions of the United States in individual countries, in particular Great Britain and France, but not Germany. While the tradition of a special relationship with England and an American fascination with French culture explained the interest in those two nations, Germany's absence was largely the result of the nation's responsibility for the Great War.

The intensity of French anti-Americanism varied, according to English novelist Ida A. R. Wylie, who had lived in Belgium, Germany, and the United States.[43] Another author complained in the *Forum* that French admiration for Americans had given way to dislike.[44] And while Charles Lindbergh's transatlantic flight of May 1927[45] incited widespread admiration not only for the pioneer but America at large, resentment rekindled in France later that year when the Sacco and Vanzetti trial shocked the French public.[46]

Bernard Fay, professor of French literature at Clermont-Ferrand, characterized American perceptions of French resentment as a shock. In his article "The French Mind and the American," published in *Harper's Magazine* in 1931, he argued, "Today, little more than a decade after the war enthusiasm, Americans are struck by the hostility against their country which they sense in Europe." Fay insisted that France had not forgotten the American intervention in the Great War but suggested that domestic policies in both countries "fan the flame of an apparent bitterness between the two nations and accentuate some few real factors of discord."[47] In addition, Fay argued that America was interpreted by many French contemporaries "as the symbol of a hateful future and the agent of an atrocious universal metamorphosis."[48]

A different view of anti-Americanism was diagnosed in Great Britain. Political scientist George E. G. Catlin argued that the United States was fast becoming the "best hated nation in Europe"—a fate that only the English had suffered until then.[49] Catlin located British apprehensions about America in a mixture of jealousy and intimidation by the nation's industrial power: "Jealousy of America as wealthy has been politely converted into a professed contempt for wealth as American."[50] Envy of American wealth was, according to Charles E. Payne, complemented by a strong sense of colliding Anglo-American global interests, prompted by naval competition as well as Washington's strategy of debt settlement which placed a heavy burden on the interwar British economy.[51]

Unemotional American Responses

Much of the magazine discourse on the decline of American prestige characterized Europeans as highly emotional people and contrasted their hate and dislike of the United States with a relatively unemotional analysis of the sources for the transatlantic rift. Such an approach, which allocated the affective to Europe and the cognitive to the United States, was to create and sustain a sense of American intellectual superiority. It consisted at least of four major arguments.

The first was presented by Sir Philip Gibbs, a British writer with much empathy towards the United States. He suggested that the rising world power was favored by evolutionary-historical processes and urged Americans to accept their ensuing global responsibilities. In contrast to Europe, which was considered a declining madhouse, the United States was equated with progress and advances in human evolution.[52] Such emphasis on driving forces of history implied of course that such a development was beyond human influence. If historical development was believed to work in favor of America, there was no need for the American nation to become unduly concerned about European cultural anti-Americanism. A reserved and unemotional response to the decline of American prestige in the Old World was thus the clearest expression of the New World's superiority.

This thinking in long-term dimensions was not a superficial and merely tactical way of responding to European criticism, but was—secondly—rhetorically substantiated by a rediscovery of the American past. Poet and critical essayist John Peale Bishop suggested such a new look at the nation's history in *Vanity Fair:*

> We are like a youth who on coming of age is suddenly aware of his own identity, and hence curious of everything which serves to set him apart from his fellows. It is in order to establish our character more clearly in our minds that we have begun to look into our past. The consciousness of a race, like that of an individual, is composed of memory and desire; we cannot, if we are to know ourselves, ignore either our childhood or our ancestry. And both belong to the past.[53]

Bishop's analysis clarified the inner connection between the laconic argument of evolutionary development and the discoveries of the past. Time received a new dimension in which the constructed collective memories were to be incorporated. History and future achieved a new meaning for the interpretation of the present. Bernard Fay argued along similar lines and suggested, "Apart from material interests and social discipline, the one great force which upholds the national unity of the United States is history."[54] History provided Americans with national pride and complemented the traditional set of instruments of symbolic integration, such as symbols, a festive culture, and national icons.

Not surprisingly, historians played an important role in the interwar discourse on national identity. The new interest in the nation's past emphasized its independence from Europe and celebrated national accomplishments. Bernard Fay, for example, evoked Frederick Jackson Turner and argued: "He neither feared or hated Europe, but he loved America. To him that love was no system but a fact, a fact so real that he drew inspiration from it first, and only later a theory which will undoubtedly remain the most original and satisfying view of American development."[55] This statement reveals the direction of arguments: there ought not to be a dislike of Europe as a reaction to European anti-Americanism but an empathetic feeling for the United States and a discovery of America's genuine roots and achievements. It was Turner who stood for the conviction that America was "wholly original, uniquely virtuous, and self-sustaining" and had a monopoly of democracy.[56]

The third argument in reaction to Old World apprehensions emphasized America's economic power and wealth. Historian Thomas J. Wertenbaker stressed that high wages in the United States and a constant stream of inventions provided ample evidence for American superiority without the necessity of any emotional undertones at all.[57] And distinguished essayist Agnes Repplier observed that the "condescension which Americans now daily display" was based on "superiority of wealth"—in comparison to Europe.[58] Finally, Barton W. Currie distanced himself from all the "sentimentalists," who "have overrated" Europe in many areas.[59]

A fourth argumentative cluster reinvoked notions of mystical-religious exceptionalism and national destiny. One author rejected the charge of American imperialism and simultaneously praised not only the traditional wisdom of "manifest destiny," but slid into the mystic-divine when he wrote, "The United States follows a well defined plan of wisdom taken from the balance of history,—the only one which will continue making of the American Continent the home of harmony and the refuge of the 'brave and the free'."[60]

Some criticized this attitude of superiority towards Europe. Agnes Repplier, for example, was shocked by her audience's approval of her recital of a particularly condescending quote from the *Ladies' Home Journal:* "There is only one first-class civilization in the world today. It is right here in the

United States and the Dominion of Canada. Europe's is hardly second-class, and Asia is about fourth- to sixth-class." Repplier dismantled the superiority and efficiency complex as a perilous way of defining American identity, warned that the "superiority complex" was as "imperious to fact as to feeling" and insisted that admiration for efficiency had to be balanced with emotional life.[61]

Her warnings were amplified by authors who utilized fear of declining international prestige as a tool for criticism of US foreign relations and American hypocrisy and self-assertiveness.[62] In this argumentative context, frequent references to possibly negative international reactions to American actions were incorporated in a strategy designed to foster the quest for national identity.

Emotionality and the American Nation

While the arguments presented in magazine articles against European emotionally laden anti-Americanism were conspicuously unemotional, the American people themselves were not characterized as unemotional. Some explanations for their emotional state of mind appropriated a typical European characterization of America as young and inexperienced but replaced the condescending negative with a celebratory positive connotation: "It is no wonder that a youthful giant who is still uncertain about what his manhood is likely to be and who is overflowing with an impetuous and mobile temper should bewilder the outsider and startle him into extravagant admiration or despair. It is no wonder that he can spring from affection to enmity in an instant."[63]

Despite acknowledgement of the emotionality of Americans, many authors rejected any charge of the effeminate American male as "emotional America" became discursively synonymous with a society dominated by women.[64] This gendered discourse was complemented by racial considerations. The association of emotionality and inferiority was extended to African Americans as well. Although excluded from most debates on national identity, black culture in general and the Harlem Renaissance in particular were regarded as fascinating phenomena, as "self-expression of a primitive race" that, however, should not be imitated by whites in the search for national identity.[65]

Instead Yale president emeritus Arthur T. Hadley recommended a rediscovery of the contributions of the conquest of the American West to the development of a "national character."[66] And historian Frederick Jackson Turner pleaded for the creation and sustenance of well-balanced "national emotions" that were to be achieved through further national integration and the containment of sectional economic interests.[67] While Turner's argument focused on the economic interests, the distinguished New York neurologist Joseph V. Collins warned of excessive emotional ties of the public to political parties.[68] According to Collins, "excessive partisanship" in the United States with its reliance on the party machine system and allegiance to a strong boss-client system was the dangerous emotional counterpart to European "excessive patriotism."[69] Other authors emphasized the potential contributions of American art and literature in the renewed quest for national identity and rejected any European claim to cultural hegemony.[70] Finally, a number of contributions examined the processes of immigrant integration into American society but questioned the instructive value and "noisy aggressiveness" of the Americanization discourse for the issue of national identity.[71]

In sum, magazine texts stimulated a moderate and reasonable national feeling among its readers. Neither female emotionality nor the so-called primitive emotionality of African Americans, nor the emotional fury of the "100-percent Americans" were deemed acceptable as models for the national consciousness of the future. A moderate and reasonable national feeling was to be based on the balanced integration of economic interests, artistic developments, political party interests, and immigration to alleviate anxieties and enable the sustenance of confidence. The "cool" and cognitive responses to European anti-Americanism served as examples of how a self-confident nation should react towards exaggerated emotionality.

Beyond Emotionality: The Transatlantic Elite

Many of the magazine articles were written by Europeans and Americans who had lived on both sides of the Atlantic and used their knowledge as "cultural capital" (Bourdieu). Their writings displayed a genuine interest in transatlantic understanding and their personal biographies made them well suited as intermediaries for American academic readers. These European-American members of an emerging transatlantic elite hoped to expand the transatlantic network and regarded themselves as unemotional transmitters of cultural matters and public affairs. As Bernard Fay wrote: "It is indispensable for France and the United States to possess an élite capable of understanding and of interpreting to each other their respective countries. … Artists, men of letters, diplomats, leaders of industry, and great promoters are in duty bound to contribute."[72]

The concept of a transatlantic network was based on highly elitist views. Fay wished for "intelligent, educated people, who will be needed to guide and stem popular passions on both sides of the Atlantic."[73] Such a network was to be free of emotional apprehensions: "Certainly England hates America—as America hates England, as all herds hate each other," but not—as can be added—the transatlantic elite.[74]

Implicit in this vision of an integrated North Atlantic community was the differentiation between the cognitive capabilities of members of the respective elite and the uncontrolled emotional masses. Such a view was based on insights provided by the emerging discipline of psychology and a double discourse "which blurred divides between natural and constructed, between the agentic and determined."[75] While the new academic psychologists advocated the idea of psychological beings as determined and therefore limited in their power to alter themselves, others regarded modern humans as independent of nineteenth-century conventional moralism. These two opinions shaped a double discourse and produced a mixed rhetoric that allocated emotionality on the basis of class membership. It operated on the premise that "emotional experiences and expressions vary according to a social hierarchy: emotions are distributed, experienced, and managed differently by different persons and *classes* of persons."[76]

In our case, emotional expressions were attributed to the lowest, indefinable strata, characterized as a "herd" with limited creative power. In contrast, members of the transatlantic elite were regarded as self-determinable individuals obliged to guide the masses and control their "popular passions" and "half-instinctive mental habits."[77] This conceptual approach enjoyed popularity among the respective elites whose members felt threatened by the potentially violent consequences of the rapid transformations in Euro-American industrial societies. Gustave LeBon addressed many of those fears in his study *Psychology des foules,* which was also known in the United States.[78]

The concept of a transatlantic elite was complemented by the rise of a Euro-American epistemic community of professional experts, social reformers, and architects who were interested in mutual learning, international cooperation, and mutual appreciation.[79] In the 1920s those new transatlantic professionals were part of a growing international community of scientists, technicians, engineers, businessmen, writers, and diplomats who developed an intense network of communication and exchange and remained largely aloof (at least in their official relations) from the nationalist antagonisms of their home countries.[80]

The contributors to the magazine discourse on European perceptions of America widely ignored this already existing epistemic North Atlantic community. They were interested in neither exploring the intensity of mutual interaction nor ignoring the persistent decline of American prestige in the Old World. Their writings on emotionalized European anti-Americanism were to strengthen their own interpretative position in the transatlantic network, attract readership in the United States, and shape the contours of the renewed discourse on national identity.

Clearly, the authors were less interested in the ongoing transatlantic learning processes but in the development of genuine understanding for the respective cultures, especially for educated European views of the United States. This promotion of such an acceptance corresponded with the authors' claim to a central role as mediators, transmitters, and interpreters. From today's view, both groups, the professional experts and the men of letters, were determined to become the transatlantic transmitters of the future.

Conclusions

The relationship between the United States and Europe has always been influenced by notions of respective inferiority or superiority. The intensity and importance of this *longue durée,* however, has varied according to specific historical circumstances. During the 1920s American learned magazines interpreted European anti-Americanism as extremely emotional. The contributors to this discourse avoided anti-European emotions but instead drafted their articles as unemotional statements designed to reveal their nation's superiority based on evolution, history, wealth, and mission to cover up the American inferiority complex towards Europe.

This discourse not only encompassed intensive debate over America's position vis-à-vis Europe but entailed reflection on the nation's identity and strongly affected American self-interpretations.[81] This magazine discourse drew heavy attention to the Old World's rejection and mistrust of America, fostered the emancipation of the United States from an allegedly emotionalized Europe, and aided in the construction of an American nation. The authors discussed here developed a concept of nation and nationality best described by the terms *rationalized emotion* or *emotional rationality.*

In this context most authors operated on the prejudice and assumption that members of the emerging transatlantic elite were to contain and control the emotionality of the Euro-American "masses." They were consequently not interested in a strong American anti-Europeanism at all and used the magazines as a forum for discussion to shape the readers' mental map of Europe.[82] While this mental map changed after the Wall Street crash of 1929 and the subsequent Great Depression and the New Deal era, the quest for national identity remained a central and defining feature of American magazine analyses of conditions in the Old World.[83]

The contemporary elite discourse was highly engendered at the time and rested on the mute equation between masses and women, both deemed easily seducible. Although women displayed as much patriotism as men, their contribution to serious discourses on nation and nation building had traditionally been limited since the New Nationalism of the Progressive Era. Not surprisingly, most articles on European anti-Americanism in quality magazines were written by men. Their texts revealed a powerful desire for the international recognition and acceptance of their nation and utilized the "emotions of comparisons" for shaping a future based on a self-confident and culturally emancipated United States as precondition for transatlantic understanding and cooperation.

Notes

1. Jürgen Gerhards, *Soziologie der Emotionen. Fragestellungen, Systematik und Perspektiven* (Weinheim: Juventa, 1988), 40; Amelie von Griessenbeck, *Kulturfaktor Emotion. Zur Bedeutung von Emotion für das Verhältnis von Individuum, Gesellschaft und Kultur* (Munich: Akademie Verlag, 1997), e.g., 100–101. I warmly thank Jessica Gienow-Hecht, Norbert Finzsch, Frank Schumacher, and Jacob Jones for their advice and criticism.
2. See Gerhards, *Soziologie der Emotionen,* 37–38; Heinz-Günter Vester, *Emotion, Gesellschaft und Kultur. Grundzüge einer soziologischen Theorie der Emotionen* (Opladen: Westdeutscher Verlag, 1991).
3. Jon Elster, *Alchemies of the Mind: Rationality and the Emotions* (Cambridge: Cambridge University Press, 1999), 141. See Ansgar Klein, Frank Nullmeier, and Oliver von Wersch, "Zum künftigen Umgang mit 'Emotionen' in der Politikwissenschaft," in *Masse—Macht—Emotionen. Zu einer politischen Soziologie der Emotionen,* ed. Ansgar Klein, Frank Nullmeier, and Oliver von Wersch (Opladen: Westdeutscher Verlag, 1999), 345–59; see also the introduction by the editors, 9–27.
4. Vester, *Emotion, Gesellschaft, Kultur,* 29–30. The many differentiations that need to be made indicate the complexity involved in applying such a multilayered concept of emotion to history. In addition, core meaning must be distinguished from peripheral meaning.
5. This is a serious problem of quantitative analyses that requires prior identification of the emotional terms under consideration.
6. See Gary B. Palmer and Debra J. Occhi, "Introduction: Linguistic Anthropology and Emotional Experience," in *Languages of Sentiment: Cultural Constructions of Emotional Substrates,* ed. Gary B. Palmer and Debra J. Occhi (Amsterdam: Benjamins, 1999), 3–4.
7. Unfortunately there is "marked disagreement about the nature of those processes, and the precise role of cognition in determining which emotion occurs and the subjective experience of emotion"—a gap that also can not be filled in this paper. Klaus R. Scherer and Paul Ekman, "Questions About Emotion: An Introduction," in *Approaches to Emotion,* ed. Klaus R. Scherer and Paul Ekman (Hillsdale, NJ: Erlbaum, 1984), 3; Elster, *Alchemies of the Mind,* 408–9.
8. The same can be said with respect to pictures.
9. See Judith Butler, *Hass spricht. Zur Politik des Performativen* (Berlin: Berlin Verlag, 1998), esp. 19.

10. Jan Lewis and Peter N. Stearns, "Introduction," in *An Emotional History of the United States,* ed. Jan Lewis and Peter N. Stearns (New York: New York University Press, 1998), 15–32.
11. Kenneth J. Gergen, "History and Psychology: Three Weddings and a Future," in Stearns and Lewis, *Emotional History,* 15–32. There is no clear border between the private and the public sphere; instead both spheres are entwined. Emotions and the access to emotionality are constructed in both the private and the public spheres; emotions motivate attitudes in both spheres—along the lines of class, genders and ethnicity. Vice versa, media texts are important for both spheres; they are produced in the public sphere and in the case of quality magazines focus on public affairs on the one hand and penetrate the private sphere of the readers on the other.
12. Many inspirations come from Catharine A. Lutz and Lila Abu-Lughod, "Introduction: Emotion, Discourse, and the Politics of Everyday Life," in *Language and the Politics of Emotions,* ed. Catharine A. Lutz and Lila Abu-Lughod (Cambridge: Cambridge University Press, 1990), 1–23.
13. The relevance of authentic experiences to generating emotions has been the subject of debate among scholars. There is an agreement, however, that the production of societal codes and standards for emotions have the best chances of succeeding when they are related to the recipients' experiences.
14. In the course of the twentieth century, the number of media available increased, leading to an expansion of emotions and emotional experiences mediated by the media. Such an increase in medially transmitted emotions—e.g., about war events—can, however, be counterproductive, inducing emotional apathy.
15. For more see: Theodore Peterson, *Magazines in the Twentieth Century,* 2nd ed. (Urbana: University of Illinois Press, 1974); Adelheid von Saldern, "Amerikanische Magazine. Zur Geschichte gesellschaftlicher Deutungsinstanzen (1880–1940)," *Archiv für Sozialgeschichte* 41 (2001): 171–204.
16. In this context, Warren I. Susman mentions that the 1920s were marked by concern about the survival of local communities. Warren I. Susman, *Culture as History: The Transformation of American Society in the Twentieth Century* (New York: Pantheon Books, 1965), 257; see also Casey Nelson Blake, *Beloved Community: The Cultural Criticism of Randolph Bourne, Van Wyck Brooks, Waldo Frank, & Lewis Mumford* (Chapel Hill: University of North Carolina Press, 1990).
17. Daniel T. Rodgers, *Atlantic Crossings: Social Politics in a Progressive Age* (Cambridge, MA: Harvard University Press, 1998).
18. German anti-Americanism is the focus in Adelheid von Saldern, "Überfremdungsängste. Gegen die Amerikanisierung der deutschen Kultur in den zwanziger Jahren," in *Amerikanisierung. Traum und Alptraum im Deutschland des 20. Jahrhunderts,* ed. Alf Lüdtke, Inge Marssolek, and Adelheid von Saldern (Stuttgart: Steiner, 1996), 213–45. The French anti-Americanism is described in Richard F. Kuisel, *Seducing the French: The Dilemma of Americanization* (Berkeley, CA: University of California Press, 1993). See also Egbert Klautke, *Unbegrenzte Möglichkeiten. "Amerikanisierung" in Deutschland und Frankreich (1900–1933)* (Stuttgart: Steiner, 2003). Some points of the British anti-Americanism are elaborated on in D. L. LeMahieu, *A Culture for Democracy: Mass Communication and the Cultivated Mind in Britain Between the Wars* (Oxford: Clarendon, 1988).
19. Benedict Anderson, *Die Erfindung der Nation. Zur Karriere eines folgenreichen Konzepts* (Frankfurt: Campus, 1996); Eric Hobsbawm and Terence Ranger, eds., *The Invention of Tradition* (Cambridge: Cambridge University Press, 1983).
20. Hobsbawm and Ranger, *Invention of Tradition.*

21. In general: Rudolf Speth, "Nation und Emotion. Von der vorgestellten zur emotional erfahrenen Gemeinschaft," in Klein, Nullmeier and von Wersch, *Masse—Macht—Emotionen: Zu einer politischen Soziologie der Emotionen,* 287–307.
22. This can be created best by rituals.
23. With respect to the prewar and wartime period see Cecilia E. O'Leary, *To Die For: The Paradox of American Patriotism* (Princeton, NJ: Princeton University Press, 1999).
24. Cited in Susman, *Culture as History,* 115.
25. George E. G. Catlin, "America under Fire: A European Defense of Our Civilization," *Harper's Magazine* (1927): 222–27.
26. Susman, *Culture as History,* 115.
27. Manfred Henningsen, "Das amerikanische Selbstverständnis und die Erfahrung des Großen Kriegs," in *Kriegserlebnis. Der Erste Weltkrieg in der literarischen Gestaltung und symbolischen Deutung der Nationen,* ed. Klaus Vondung (Göttingen: Vandenhoeck & Ruprecht, 1980), 368–86, esp. 384.
28. Lawrence W. Levine, *The Unpredictable Past: Explorations in American Cultural History* (New York: Oxford University Press, 1993), 204, see also 200–203.
29. Ibid., 195.
30. The inner ties between foreign relations and the construction of national identity "at home" have been explored in the past decades. See e.g., Emily S. Rosenberg, "Turning to Culture," in *Close Encounters of Empire; Writing the Cultural History of U.S.-Latin American Relations,* ed. Gilbert M. Joseph, Catherine C. LeGrand, and Ricardo D. Salvatore (Durham, NC: Duke University Press, 1998).
31. H[enry] L[ouis] Mencken (1880–1956), editor of *Smart Set* and from 1924 of *American Mercury,* was well known because of his pungent and sarcastic view of American cultural life.
32. At that time *Reader's Digest* only reprinted articles from other magazines, quite often from so-called qualitative magazines, though they were condensed.
33. The Ku Klux Klan had 2 million members. See Norbert Finzsch, James O. Horton, and Lois E. Horton, *Von Benin nach Baltimore. Die Geschichte der African Americans* (Hamburg: Hamburger Ed., 1999), 409.
34. C. E. M. Joad, "Does England Dislike America?" *The Forum* (November 1928): 692–98.
35. Frederick Palmer, "Why They Hate Us," condensed from *Collier's, The National Weekly* (September 1925), *Reader's Digest* (September 1925): 439–40.
36. Pertinax (anonymous), "Does France Hate America?" *The Forum* (December 1928): 871–77.
37. Barton W. Currie, "Nobody Loves Us." A Condensation from *The Ladies' Home Journal, Reader's Digest* (September 1922): 425. Currie, who wrote in the *Ladies' Home Journal,* regretted that "nobody loves us for ourselves or for our deeds."
38. For example: Lothorp Stoddard, "Impressions of England," condensed from *Scribner's Magazine* (September 1923), *Reader's Digest* (September 1923): 402 and James Truslow Adams, "Home Thoughts from Abroad," condensed from *Atlantic Monthly* (October 1927), *Reader's Digest* (December 1927): part 2, 467.
39. James Truslow Adams, "Home Thoughts," 467.
40. Cited in Henry James Forman, "What's Right with America?" condensed from *McCall's Magazine* (November 1929), *Reader's Digest* (December 1929): 705–6.
41. Stoddard, "Impressions of England," 401–2, *Scribner's.* Stoddard reported not only from Europe but also from the Far East. In 1919 he began a department called "The World as It Is" in the magazine *World's Work.*
42. Joad, "Does England," 692–98.

43. Ida A. R. Wylie, "Anglo-American Joadism: A Reply to C.E.M. Joad," *The Forum* (February 1929): 107.
44. Charles Henry Metzler, "The Post-War Psychology of Europe," *The Forum* (November 1920): 384.
45. Lindbergh's first nonstop transatlantic flight impressed the Americans and Europeans alike by the technological progress and his appearance as a modern hero.
46. Nicola Sacco and Bartolomeo Vanzetti, two Italian immigrants and anarchists, were accused of murder and robbery. Despite little evidence and many protests, they were sentenced to death in 1927.
47. Fay, "The French Mind," 708. Fay, born in Paris in 1893 and educated at the Sorbonne and at Harvard, was well known because of his biography of Benjamin Franklin. He is also the author of *The Revolutionary Spirit in France and America* and of *George Washington.*
48. Fay, "The French Mind," 709.
49. Catlin, "America under Fire," 223.
50. Ibid., 222.
51. Charles E. Payne, "England and America," *The Nation* (July 1929): 8; naval competition existed between the two nations. At the Washington Conference in 1921–22 the US was allowed the same capacity in battleships as Great Britain. Parity was supposed to be achieved at the Geneva Conference in 1927 with respect to smaller ships, but this conference ended without results and with animosity on both sides of the Atlantic. Animosity also existed because of the debt settlement, by which the former European war allies were obliged to pay all their debts to the United States. See also William MacDonald, "Portrait of America," *The Nation* (February 1929): 259.
52. Philip Gibbs, "America's New Place in the World," *Harper's Monthly Magazine* (December 1919): 89–97. Gibbs also wrote from abroad in prewar *Cosmopolitan.*
53. John Peale Bishop, "America Becomes 'Past' Conscious," condensed from *Vanity Fair* (February 1925), *Reader's Digest* (March 1925): 668. Bishop also wrote about Princeton University in *Smart Set.*
54. Bernard Fay, "An Invitation to American Historians," *Harper's Magazine* (December 1932): 22.
55. Ibid., 30.
56. For Turner see Richard Hofstadter, *The Progressive Historians: Turner, Beard, Parrington* (New York: Knopf, 1968), esp. 47–166, here 149.
57. See e.g., Thomas Jefferson Wertenbaker, "What's Wrong with the United States?" condensed from *Scribner's Magazine* (October 1928), *Reader's Digest* (November 1928): 377–88.
58. Agnes Repplier, "On a Certain Condescension in Americans," condensed from *The Atlantic Monthly, Reader's Digest* (July 1926): 81.
59. Currie, "Nobody Loves Us," 426. Although the popular magazine, the extremely successful *Ladies' Home Journal,* did not belong to the group of quality magazines, the article on European anti-Americanism is nevertheless included.
60. Diòmedes Pereyra, "A South American Denial," *The Forum* (December 1927): 835.
61. Repplier, "On a Certain Condescension," 82. In the 1890s Repplier had contributed to the new department of "Art and Letters" in *Cosmopolitan* magazine.
62. Edwin L. James, "America's Moral Influence, If Any," condensed from the *New York Times* (19 August 1930), *Reader's Digest* (October 1930): 513–15. See also Walter Lippmann, "America as an Empire," condensed from *Vanity Fair* (April 1927), *Reader's Digest* (June 1927): 77–78. Lippmann was editor of *World* (New York) and author of *A Preface to Morals, Drift and Mastery,* and other books; Hiram Motherwell, "The Ameri-

can Empire," *The Forum* (December 1929): 372–77. Motherwell, correspondent in Europe for the *Chicago Daily,* became conscious of the intangible reality that he calls the American Empire; William J. McNally, "Is the United States Imperialistic?—A Debate," *The Forum* 78 (December 1927): 821–88.

63. Pertinax, "Does France Hate America?" 873–74.
64. Ira S. Wile and Mary Day Winn, "Emotional America," condensed from *The Outlook and Independent*, *Reader's Digest* (July 1929): 251–53.
65. Dr. Franz Damrosch (1924), quoted in Robert Walser, "Deep Jazz: Notes on Inferiority, Race and Criticism," in *Inventing the Psychological: Toward a Cultural History of Emotional Life in America,* ed. Joel Pfister and Nancy Schnog (New Haven, CT: Yale University Press, 1997), 275.
66. Arthur T. Hadley, "Our National Character," condensed from *Current History* (October 1923), *Reader's Digest* (Oct 1923): 493–95.
67. Frederick Jackson Turner, "Sections and Nation," excerpts from the Yale Review, *Reader's Digest* (November 1922): 523–24. The last sentence was set in quotation marks.
68. Joseph V. Collins, "The Mistakes of America," *The Forum* (June 1925): 836–37.
69. For the evolution of the American party system: Helmut Klumpjan, *Die amerikanischen Parteien. Von ihren Anfängen bis zur Gegenwart* (Opladen: Leske & Budrich, 1998), 239–42.
70. Robert Briffault, "What is Wrong with American Culture," *Scribner's Magazine* (October 1935): 207–9; for more see Norbert Finzsch, "Die Maler des amerikanischen Regionalismus der dreißiger Jahre zwischen Tradition und Moderne," in *Gesellschaft und Diplomatie im transatlantischen Kontext. Festschrift für Reinhard Doerris,* ed. Michael Wala (Stuttgart: Steiner, 1999), 142.
71. Anonymous, "The Timid American," *The Nation* (August 1923): 182.
72. Fay, "The French Mind," 415; see also Fay, "The Course," 437–55. Currie differentiated between the "appreciative judgements" of some [distinguished] people on the one hand and "the masses of Britishers and Continentals, to whom we are still far-off 'colonists', hewing our way through the wilderness." Currie, "Nobody Loves Us," 426.
73. Fay, "The Course," 455.
74. Wylie, "Anglo-American Joadism," 107.
75. Jill D. Morawski, "Educating the Emotions: Academic Psychology, Textbooks, and the Psychology Industry, 1890–1940," in *Inventing the Psychological: Toward a Cultural History of Emotional Life in America,* ed. Joel Pfister and Nancy Schnog (New Haven, CT: Yale University Press, 1997), 218. Morawski refers to Mark Seltzer.
76. Ibid., 219.
77. Fay, "The Courses," 455, 452.
78. For more see Robert A. Nye, *The Origins of Crowd Psychology: Gustave LeBon and the Crisis of Mass Democracy in the Third Republic* (London: Sage, 1975), especially the list of the reviews of this book, 203–19; Susanna Barrows, *Distorting Mirrors: Visions of the Crowd in Late Nineteenth-Century France* (New Haven, CT: Yale University Press, 1981).
79. Besides Rodgers see Thomas P. Hughes, *American Genesis: A Century of Invention and Technological Enthusiasm, 1870–1970* (New York: Viking, 1989). Hughes focuses nearly exclusively on the positive aspects of transatlantic relations.
80. I thank Jacob Jones for drawing my attention to this point. Cooperation was often organized by the various committees of the League of Nations. Akira Iriye, *The Cambridge History of American Foreign Relations* (Cambridge: Cambridge University Press, 1993), III: 82.
81. MacDonald, "Portrait of America," 258. This was a book review.

82. The reference to mental maps is based on the insight that aspects of the world are incorporated in one's head and that such maps serve as pictures of orientation.
83. Charles C. Alexander, *Nationalism in American Thought, 1930–1945* (Chicago: Rand McNally, 1969).

Bibliography

Alexander, Charles C. *Nationalism in American Thought, 1930–1945*. Chicago: Rand McNally, 1969.

Anderson, Benedict. *Die Erfindung der Nation. Zur Karriere eines folgenreichen Konzepts.* Frankfurt: Campus, 1996.

Barrows, Susanna. *Distorting Mirrors: Visions of the Crowd in Late Nineteenth-Century France.* New Haven CT: Yale University Press, 1981.

Blake, Casey Nelson. *Beloved Community: The Cultural Criticism of Randolph Bourne, Van Wyck Brooks, Waldo Frank, & Lewis Mumford.* Chapel Hill: University of North Carolina Press, 1990.

Butler, Judith. *Hass spricht: Zur Politik des Performativen.* Berlin: Berlin Verlag, 1998.

Elster, Jon. *Alchemies of the Mind: Rationality and the Emotions.* Cambridge: Cambridge University Press, 1999.

Finzsch, Norbert. "Die Maler des amerikanischen Regionalismus der dreißiger Jahre zwischen Tradition und Moderne." In *Gesellschaft und Diplomatie im transatlantischen Kontext. Festschrift für Reinhard Doerris,* edited by Michael Wala, 133–48. Stuttgart: Steiner, 1999.

Finzsch, Norbert, James O. Horton, and Lois E. Horton. *Von Benin nach Baltimore: Die Geschichte der African Americans.* Hamburg: Hamburger Ed., 1999.

Gergen, Kenneth J. "History and Psychology: Three Weddings and a Future." In *An Emotional History of the United States,* edited by Jan Lewis and Peter N. Stearns, 15–32. New York: New York University Press, 1998.

Gerhards, Jürgen. *Soziologie der Emotionen. Fragestellungen, Systematik und Perspektiven.* Weinheim: Juventa, 1988.

Griessenbeck, Amelie von. *Kulturfaktor Emotion: Zur Bedeutung von Emotion für das Verhältnis von Individuum, Gesellschaft und Kultur.* Munich: Akademie Verlag, 1997.

Henningsen, Manfred. "Das amerikanische Selbstverständnis und die Erfahrung des Großen Kriegs." In *Kriegserlebnis: Der Erste Weltkrieg in der literarischen Gestaltung und symbolischen Deutung der Nationen,* edited by Klaus Vondung, 368–86. Göttingen: Vandenhoeck & Ruprecht, 1980.

Hobsbawm, Eric, and Terence Ranger, eds. *The Invention of Tradition.* Cambridge: Cambridge University Press, 1983.

Hofstadter, Richard. *The Progressive Historians: Turner, Beard, Parrington.* New York: Knopf, 1968.

Hughes, Thomas P. *American Genesis: A Century of Invention and Technological Enthusiasm, 1870–1970.* New York: Viking, 1989.

Iriye, Akira. *The Cambridge History of American Foreign Relations.* Cambridge: Cambridge University Press, 1993.

Klautke, Egbert. *Unbegrenzte Möglichkeiten: "Amerikanisierung" in Deutschland und Frankreich (1900–1933).* Stuttgart: Steiner, 2003.

Klein, Ansgar, Frank Nullmeier, and Oliver von Wersch. "Zum künftigen Umgang mit 'Emotionen' in der Politikwissenschaft." In *Masse—Macht—Emotionen: Zu einer politischen So-*

ziologie der Emotionen, edited by Ansgar Klein, Frank Nullmeier, and Oliver von Wersch, 345–59. Opladen: Westdeutscher Verlag, 1999.

Klumpjan, Helmut. *Die amerikanischen Parteien: Von ihren Anfängen bis zur Gegenwart.* Opladen: Leske & Budrich, 1998.

Kuisel, Richard F. *Seducing the French: The Dilemma of Americanization.* Berkeley: University of California Press, 1993.

LeMahieu, D. L. *A Culture for Democracy: Mass Communication and the Cultivated Mind in Britain Between the Wars.* Oxford: Clarendon, 1988.

Levine, Lawrence W. *The Unpredictable Past: Explorations in American Cultural History.* New York: Oxford University Press, 1993.

Lewis, Jan, and Peter N. Stearns. "Introduction," in *An Emotional History of the United States,* edited by Jan Lewis and Peter N. Stearns, 15–32. New York: New York University Press, 1998.

Lutz, Catharine A., and Lila Abu-Lughod. "Introduction: Emotion, Discourse, and the Politics of Everyday-Life." In *Language and the Politics of Emotions,* edited by Catharine A. Lutz and Lila Abu-Lughod, 1–23. Cambridge: Cambridge University Press, 1990.

Morawski, Jill D. "Educating the Emotions: Academic Psychology, Textbooks, and the Psychology Industry, 1890–1940." In *Inventing the Psychological: Toward a Cultural History of Emotional Life in America,* edited by Joel Pfister and Nancy Schnog, 217–44. New Haven, CT: Yale University Press, 1997.

Nye, Robert A. *The Origins of Crowd Psychology: Gustave LeBon and the Crisis of Mass Democracy in the Third Republic.* London: Sage, 1975.

O'Leary, Cecilia E., *To Die For: The Paradox of American Patriotism.* Princeton, NJ: Princeton University Press, 1999.

Palmer, Gary B., and Debra J. Occhi. "Introduction: Linguistic Anthropology and Emotional Experience." In *Languages of Sentiment: Cultural Constructions of Emotional Substrates,* edited by Gary B. Palmer and Debra J. Occhi. Amsterdam: Benjamins, 1999.

Peterson, Theodore. *Magazines in the Twentieth Century,* 2nd ed. Urbana: University of Illinois Press, 1974.

Rodgers, Daniel T. *Atlantic Crossings: Social Politics in a Progressive Age.* Cambridge, MA: Harvard University Press, 1998.

Rosenberg, Emily S. "Turning to Culture." In *Close Encounters of Empire: Writing the Cultural History of U.S.-Latin American relations,* edited by Gilbert M. Joseph, Catherine C. LeGrand, and Ricardo D. Salvatore. Durham, NC: Duke University Press, 1998.

Saldern, Adelheid von. "Überfremdungsängste: Gegen die Amerikanisierung der deutschen Kultur in den zwanziger Jahren." In *Amerikanisierung. Traum und Alptraum im Deutschland des 20. Jahrhunderts,* edited by Alf Lüdtke, Inge Marssolek, and Adelheid von Saldern, 213–45. Stuttgart: Steiner, 1996.

———. "Amerikanische Magazine. Zur Geschichte gesellschaftlicher Deutungsinstanzen (1880–1940)." In *Archiv für Sozialgeschichte* 41 (2001): 171–204.

Scherer, Klaus R., and Paul Ekman. "Questions About Emotion: An Introduction." In *Approaches to Emotion,* edited by Klaus R. Scherer and Paul Ekman. Hillsdale, NJ: Erlbaum, 1984.

Speth, Rudolf. "Nation und Emotion. Von der vorgestellten zur emotional erfahrenen Gemeinschaft." In: *Masse—Macht—Emotionen. Zu einer politischen Soziologie der Emotionen,* edited by Ansgar Klein, Frank Nullmeier, and Oliver von Wersch, 287–307. Opladen: Westdeutscher Verlag, 1999.

Susman, Warren I. *Culture as History: The Transformation of American Society in the Twentieth Century.* New York: Pantheon Books, 1965.

Vester, Heinz-Günter. Emotion, Gesellschaft und Kultur: Grundzüge einer soziologischen Theorie der Emotionen. Opladen: Westdeutscher Verlag, 1991.

Chapter 8

Emotions and Nineteenth-Century American Art

Bettina Friedl

THE VISUAL ARTS traditionally seem to have an intense and complex association with emotions. In fact, much of what we perceive and treasure in a majority of art works appears to be directly connected either with the expression of emotions in or through the work of art itself, or with a specific emotional response to the art work by viewers.[1] In his seminal work *Art and Its Objects,* Richard Wollheim explains that "originally, it was claimed that works of art were expressive of a certain state if and only if they had been produced in, and were capable of arousing to, that state."[2] This rather narrow concept of art and emotion should, however, not be restricted to deliberate acts of creating or perceiving art, as Wollheim cautions us. It is futile, he argues, to deduce from a specific emotion expressed by an art work that the artist was conscious of this or that he (or she) was moved by a corresponding emotion: "There are feelings that a man has of which he is not conscious, and there are ways of being in touch with those which he has other than experiencing them in a primary sense: and a more realistic statement ... should not require more than that those states expressed by the work of art is among those states, conscious or unconscious, to which the artist and spectator stand in some possessive relation."[3]

Throughout the history of art, painters and sculptors have reconciled the supposedly conflicting domains of thematic representation in and recep-

---

Notes for this section begin on page 174.

tion of a work of art by selecting particular emotionally charged topics that both depict and evoke specific emotions. Feelings of maternal love are as easily elicited by moving representations of mothers and infants as are emotions of empathy, grief, and mourning at the sight of dying national heroes or other personages of rank. A popular art genre of the nineteenth century was that of the deathbed scenes of American presidents, widely distributed as inexpensive prints and thus readily available for patriotic households. As a result, emotions such as grief, affection, awe, or fear are often associated with those paintings that themselves present scenes that conventionally target these emotions in the audiences.

In the wake of 11 September 2001, the *New York Times* ran a series of articles examining the relation between grief and art, in which Bruce Weber pointed to the affinities between grief and the artistic sensibility.[4] In the same issue, Holland Cotter briefly summarized the long tradition of art work that has responded to deep feelings of grief, pain, and sorrow, which have "impelled Western art from the earliest time, from Classical Greece, with its vase paintings of Niobe weeping disconsolately over the bodies of her children, to Christianity, which has tragedy at its very core." Cotter refers to the numerous lamentations of Christ's crucifixion as examples of iconic emotion and then selects Picasso's *Guernica* (1937), with its monumental depiction of despair and mourning, as an outstanding document of grief in twentieth-century art.[5]

Eighteenth- as well as nineteenth-century Western art still consciously drew on respected traditions for selecting topics that could be closely associated with specific emotions, although it is not clear to what extent spectators' emotional responses corresponded to the "intention" of the topic.[6] It is important to note, however, that the expressiveness of most of the paintings and sculptures that appear to target particular emotional responses is a result either of a common iconology of emotions that relies on conventional visual symbols or the open involvement of familiar narratives—as in religious art and in genre painting—that refer the viewer to some nonvisual domain of cultural knowledge, be it religious, literary, or historical. Usually, the titles of such paintings serve as quotations by alluding to narratives underlying the particular thematic choice, or create their own narratives through anecdotal phrases. For instance, the mid-nineteenth century American artist Lilly Martin Spencer's paintings of domestic genre scenes rely on an immediate and primarily narrative emotional appeal that is delineated in the titles and themes of her works.[7]

Instead of selecting art works that overtly target direct emotional responses, especially through conventional and mostly sentimental usage of scenes, themes, or titles,[8] I will discuss six paintings—all well known and at the same time less obviously "emotional" than those of the sentimental school—that demonstrate how art works allow us to regard them as prime examples in the history of ideas and at the same time view them as expressing specific and important art-historical developments of the nineteenth century. In my discussions of well-known nineteenth-century paintings by Edward Hicks, Frederic Edwin Church, and Thomas Eakins, I will attempt to demonstrate how in the course of the nineteenth century conventionally expressive art gradually transformed both its emotional content and its emotional appeal into a premodern concept of displaying and responding to art that was more restrained, more intellectualized, and more private in character and scope than had been the case at the beginning of the century.

I begin my discussion of emotions in American paintings with a familiar early nineteenth-century depiction of piety, patriotism, and deeply felt desire for harmony (figure 8.1). This is one of well over a hundred known versions of the *Peaceable Kingdom* that the Quaker minister Edward Hicks (1780–1849) produced during his lifetime. Hicks was trained as an ornamental painter; his work is commonly regarded as folk art and thus as a valid expression of the vernacular, a mode of vaguely nonprofessional painting that, nonetheless, demands talent. The lack of academic training did not prevent him from eventually becoming one of the best known and most beloved

Figure 8.1. Edward Hicks, *Peaceable Kingdom*, 1832–1834. Oil on canvas, 17¼″ x 23¼″. Abby Aldrich Rockefeller Folk Art Center, The Colonial Williamsburg Foundation, Williamsburg, Va.

American painters well into the twentieth century. Like almost all of his paintings bearing the same title, this particular *Peaceable Kingdom* consists of two different scenic representations. On the right, and dominating the painting's foreground, is a serene group of animals, domestic as well as wild, lying placidly next to each other. Some are facing the viewer—especially the predators seem to be quite alert; others appear to be sleepily introspective or ruminating; all are entirely unafraid of the company in which they find themselves. Three infants in angelic garb are either embracing animals or pointing at the entire group as if to call attention to its unusual, and thus exemplary, character. This part of the *Peaceable Kingdom* is, of course, an illustration of the biblical passage from Isaiah 11:6–7: "The wolf also shall dwell with the lamb, and the leopard shall lie down with the kid; and the calf and the young lion and the fatling together; and a little child shall lead them. And the cow and the bear shall feed; their young ones shall lie down together; and the lion shall eat straw like the ox."

To the left and rear of this prominent and appealingly picturesque group—at first sight thematically unrelated to it—is the scenic presentation of William Penn's historic treaty with the Delaware Indians that accompanies the majority of the *Kingdoms.* A ship in the background refers to Penn's recent arrival on American soil; trees and the prospect of a bay provide the frame and the background for the group that is depicted as an integral part of a pastoral scene. Hicks not only succeeds in creating an impression of domestic and pastoral serenity and tranquility but also brings the illustration of the familiar biblical allegory of peace into physical contact with a scene from colonial history, reflecting the Quaker principle of extending harmonious cohabitation to the representatives of both wilderness and civilization. The expression of piety and patriotism visibly links harmony to an event in the American past as a reminder that peace and love are possible even under adverse conditions. The joint presentation of the two diverse scenes—one biblical and allegorical, one historical and political—in one frame calls on us to regard them as simultaneous events and sets them in a relation of mutual interpretation.

In order to specify how emotionally charged such an innocuous painting can be, it is important to establish some theoretical understanding of the character of emotions. Emotions, according to the philosopher Martha Nussbaum, are not "unthinking forces that have no connection with our thoughts, evaluations, or plans"; instead, an emotion like fear depends in its "identity as fear on its having some such object: take that away and it becomes a mere trembling or heart-leaping." She continues to explain: "the object is an *intentional* object: that is, it figures in the emotion as it is seen or interpreted by the person whose emotion it is. Emotions are not *about* their objects merely in the sense of being pointed at them and let go, the way an arrow is released toward its target. Their aboutness is more internal, and embodies a way of seeing."[9]

The *Kingdoms* were produced during a period of renewed political discord in the United States and of religious controversy within the Quaker community. Hicks clearly wished to remedy this rift through his biblical and historical allusions to peace and harmony by relating both scenes to similar concepts of Christian belief. Since the 1820s, the Primitive, or Hicksite, Quakers, named after the painter's cousin, minister Elias Hicks, had come under severe attack from Orthodox Quakers, especially those in England.[10] Hicksites regarded themselves as the true followers of George Fox and William Penn, a conviction that is illustrated by the visual and verbal references to Penn in the *Kingdoms*. In the terminology of Elias Hicks, the aggressiveness of the English Friends resembled that of "beasts of prey"; the enemy possessed "the carnivorous cruelty of the leopard," while "the redoubtable English lion thundered out its excommunications."[11] In a letter to Edward Hicks, he asked the artist whether he "had to combat with Beasts at Ephesus."[12] Hicks's paintings show both the leopard and the lion as pacified beasts of prey that are no longer threatening the serenity of the group, thus documenting the artist's painterly attempt to evoke tolerance and respect for others, however strange or even "wild" in appearance, through his visual presentation.

The textual frames accompanying the so-called "bordered *Kingdoms*" (figure 8.2) serve as an even more explicit illustration of the painter's intent. The verses begin at the top with the couplet: "The leopard with the harmless kid laid down / And not one savage beast was seen to frown." They continue on the right and left margins with the lines: "The lion with the fatling on did move / A little child was leading them in love, / The wolf did with the lambkin dwell in peace / His grim carniv'rous nature there did cease." The use of words as a framing device for the visual presentation does not equal a translation of image into text. Instead, because it is a rhymed rendition of the biblical passage, it refers the viewer directly to the religious source of the allegory and emphasizes its textual authority. The privileged position directly under the picture of the couplet devoted to the history event—"When the great PENN his famous treaty made / With indian chiefs beneath the elm tree's shade."—gives it the status of title and heightens the emblematic significance of the occasion. Its appeal is a clear indication of the painter's desire for visible harmony in the nation—"as in the animal kingdom, so in the human," as Robert Hughes aptly states.[13]

There is a deliberate correspondence between the amiable animals, each of which represented specific traits of human nature to the painter,[14] and the cordial political act depicted in his work, on the one hand, and the desired emotional response on the part of the viewer, on the other hand. Both indi-

Figure 8.2. Edward Hicks, *The Peaceable Kingdom,* 1826–1828. Oil on canvas, 29¼″ x 35¼″. Abby Aldrich Rockefeller Folk Art Museum, The Colonial Williamsburg Foundation, Williamsburg, Va.

cate how the artist, accused of heresy,[15] wished to palliate existing religious strife and preempt upcoming political controversy by producing the emotions—on a personal, a religious, and a national level—that he felt to be an adequately positive response to the times. Adverse emotions, the artistic message suggests, could be influenced and reformed through visual allusion to the Christian prophecy. Using the venerable tradition of the medieval humors in his Goose Creek sermon, Hicks expresses his trust in the remedy of the Inward Light of Quaker belief for each character: "May the melancholy be encouraged and the sanguine quieted; may the phlegmatic be tendered and the choleric humbled; may self be denied and the cross of Christ worn as a daily garment; may his peaceable kingdom for ever be established in the rational, immortal soul."[16]

The reference to rationality in the context of religious belief and emotions may seem surprising because "emotions are notoriously supposed to be subjective," as de Sousa points out.[17] Yet as both Nussbaum and de Sousa argue, emotions are always "targeted" and thus in each case involve an object; most emotions, de Sousa explains, "such as anger, fear or love, appear to relate the emoter to something else, referred to by name or definite description. Sometimes (in fear or love) the something else need not be as the subject believes it to be. In some emotions (fear, but not so clearly love or anger) it need not even exist."[18] The fear of a division or dissolution of the Society of Friends was as real to Hicks, and therefore as rationally grounded, as the impending dissolution of the union was to Frederic Edwin Church (1826–1900). Contrary to the assumptions held by behavioral psychologists, philosophers have long reasoned that emotions, unlike mere affects, can be enduring and thus have far more lasting consequences for the individual.[19] A deeply felt emotion, such as grief, compassion, or love, can, in effect, determine entire phases in an individual's life without becoming diminished to a mere "mood."[20]

Landscapes may well express similar sentiments of piety and patriotism, yet they rarely allow as literal a reading as is possible in the case of emblematic religious paintings. By the time Church painted *Twilight in the Wilderness* in 1860 (figure 8.3), he had already produced a number of grandiose North American and South American landscapes that had earned him the title of "national artist."[21] This particular painting continues to draw on the iconography of the sublime both in the perception and the expression of nature that Church saw as the essential medium of a unifying nationalism.[22] The sulfurous light over the purple mountain tops and the stunning "phan-

Figure 8.3. Frederic Edwin Church, *Twilight in the Wilderness,* 1860. Oil on canvas, 101.6 x 162.6 cm. The Cleveland Museum of Art. Mr. and Mrs. William H. Marlatt Fund 1965.233.

tasmagoric"[23] colors of the sunset over a wilderness landscape are mirrored in a calm lake. A traditional Claudean framing of the entire vista is produced by gnarled, bare trees, a rock, and a stump; this framing indicates the artist's perspective and determines the viewer's position.[24] Although such colorful sunsets could e regarded as entirely realistic, if rare, the date of the painting suggests an additional symbolic meaning: this is the "eve *of* something—landscape as portent."[25] In fact, it has become standard practice among art historians to use the epithet *apocalyptic* in connection with this specific painting, although, in general, landscape painting of the decades before the Civil War had abandoned allegory for a more naturalist language. Comparing Thomas Cole's 1836 cycle *The Course of Empire,* a five-part allegory of the rise and fall of civilizations, to the works of later landscape painters, Miller argues that around "the middle of the 1850s bleak if disguised predictions of the nation's future began to appear, coinciding with the deterioration of compromise efforts. To artists searching for images with which to evoke a prospective sense of loss and cultural ruin, Cole's *Desolation* [the last panel of the allegory] summed up a generation's fears."[26]

My interpretation of the portentous meaning of Church's work of art is supported by a small oil painting entitled *Our Banner in the Sky* that Church produced in 1861. It shows a sunset quite similar to the one in *Twilight in the Wilderness,* with a similar reference to the end and the promise of a new beginning. This painting was subsequently turned into a chromolithograph: stars accompany the bright blue and red of the clouds and the barren trees become flagpoles. A flyer for this oil sketch "enthusiastically proclaimed [that] a 'sudden and simultaneous outburst of patriotism ... electrified the entire North, West, and East of America,' finding 'no more hearty or instant response among any class of our citizens than the Artist.'"[27] Indeed, it became an extremely popular decorative item in thousands of Northern homes. Of the two pictures, the far more ambitious and slightly earlier *Twilight in the Wilderness* reveals a patriotic quality that may be less evident than in the subsequent chromolithograph, yet that is nevertheless manifest to the discerning viewer. A knowledge of Church's artistic repertoire thus allows us to regard many of his landscapes as emotionally charged.

Art historians from Barbara Novak and John Wilmerding to Angela Miller have pointed out that Church's paintings in general had a national meaning and that this ominous twilight landscape in particular adumbrates the widespread fear of national conflict and Civil War, while his subsequent *Rainy Season in the Tropics* (1866) (figure 8.4), with a gigantic rainbow spanning the abyss between two radically contrasting views of nature, celebrates a renewal of hope for the union after the end of the war. The opposition between lush vegetation on the right and the group of sublimely ragged mountains rearing up on the left dramatizes prewar antagonism,

Figure 8.4. Frederic Edwin Church, *Rainy Season in the Tropics,* 1866. Oil on canvas, 142.9 x 214 cm; frame: 196.9 x271.8 x 15.3 cm. Fine Arts Museums of San Francisco, Museum purchase, Mildred Anna Williams Collection, 1970.9.

while the allegorical rainbow indicates the presence of divinity; it forms a monumental bridge that unites the opposites and provides for a frame that symbolizes national rebirth. There may no longer be anything original in such a patriotic reading of the two Church paintings; what makes it relevant in a discussion of emotions in art is not only the artist's obvious devotion to his country—he regards the American landscape as a potent symbolic space, capable of expressing emotions ranging from awe and foreboding to restored hope and belief in the nation's future—but also the powerful effect these and other landscapes by Church had on the American public.

Hicks's numerous *Peaceable Kingdoms* were never intended for public display. They were personal gifts by the artist to friends and fellow Quakers and were meant to be effective in the privacy of modest Pennsylvania homes. Church's grand landscapes, on the other hand, affected the American public far beyond the city limits of New York. His paintings were exhibited individually, enhanced by magnificent and elaborate wooden frames and decorated with flags; music accompanied the viewings; they toured the country (and were shown in Europe as well); they were regarded as national works of art and thus as visually representative of patriotic emotions as well as feelings of piety and humility in the presence of divine creation. Spectators found these landscapes elevating and inspiring; they experienced them collectively as symbolizing "the birth of a new mood of introspective self-awareness," as Miller suggests.[28] These collective emotional experiences are not surprising in situations of national distress or war because everyone is involved, if to varying degrees, in emotions generated by such momentous events. They result in a general cultural response that can be identified directly with the emotions defining a specific period or event in the cultural memory of the people.[29]

It is obvious that in the mid-nineteenth century, American landscape painting was emotionally charged, according to a majority of spectators, in a way that other genres were not. It elicited spirited debates about the state of the nation, the virtues of patriotism, and the value of politics or piety. It made visible the entire spectrum of attitudes towards nature and the land, past and present, by conflating landscape and history painting. And it could therefore confront viewers with novel vistas of America with which they were not familiar. The popularity of landscape painting in America, especially the monumental landscapes of painters beginning with Church and extending to Albert Bierstadt and Thomas Moran, equaled that of history paintings in Europe. The general interest in religious allegories, such as Hicks's, and in genre paintings usually relied on a recognition of the visual equivalent of narratives, as I stated earlier. They either refer to commonly known texts—e.g., the Bible, anecdotal history, or familiar domestic scenes—which they aim to illustrate by referring to such existing narratives, or they suggest a specific way of viewing that evokes events in a temporal sequence that in turn may be related to the sequence of narratives. Viewers are encouraged to imagine what is going on in the scenic representation and often begin to speculate about the further developments that might result from a particular scene. They are, in fact, invited to "read" such paintings. I do not here refer strictly to the act of interpretation but rather to the assumption that the visible scene is merely a segment of something comparable to a fictional representation with a past and a future. Viewers thus feel entitled to read beyond the moment represented in the actual picture frame.

Portrait painting is seemingly simpler than either landscape, allegory, or genre painting because of its limited subject matter. At the same time, however, it is more complicated for the spectator than the other genres because it is so restricted in its narrative quality: it is supposed to be expressive only of one individual's likeness and disposition. Viewers are not necessarily asked to empathize with the expression of the person portrayed, but instead are often required to attempt to identify the emotion of the sitter by scrutinizing a human face that refuses to reveal more than can be seen in a close encounter with a stranger. While early portrait paintings had frequently relied on conventions of posture and allegorical detail to express specific emotions, realistic painting rejects this approach. In the eighteenth century, for example, John Singleton Copley typically provided entire frameworks of appurtenances, from ledgers and books to furniture, dress, and flowers, to express the sitter's social status and education as well as his or her emotional state. Viewers, in turn, knew how to "read"—and here I do mean to interpret—and translate these signs into indications of such personality and emotion that the facial expression alone did not necessarily convey, because it usually depended on type more than on distinctions of individual countenance.

By contrast, the expression of the human face in portraiture of the second half of the nineteenth century tends to be less formulaic in its depiction than that of earlier centuries, and it no longer relies as heavily on specific symbolic meanings suggested by the background and props. Increasingly, the painted face alone gives a personal, individualized impression of a character; the expression in a portrait could be emotionally charged without resorting to older types of physiognomy stylization, on the one hand, or to any of the hyperbole familiar from caricature, on the other hand. This new artistic program of realism becomes particularly evident in Thomas Eakins's portraits (1844–1916). I will here focus on two of his late portraits and examine some of the possibilities of realistically representing the human face.

My first example is Eakins's portrait of Walt Whitman (1887–88) (figure 8.5).[30] What I have just described as an added difficulty for the general interpretation of portraits is, of course, a somewhat less compelling argument in the case of portraits of public personae of whom we often have different likenesses to compare. In the case of Whitman, we have early daguerreotypes and numerous photographs from various stages of his career, even a sequence of photographs taken by Eakins himself. We are familiar with Whitman's biography and can situate this particular portrait as a very late likeness, executed at a time in Whitman's life in which he had at long last turned into something like a celebrity. His house on Mickle Street in Camden "had become a virtual pilgrimage destination for Philadelphia's intelligentsia," as Fred B. Adelson writes in the catalogue of the 1993 Eakins retrospective.[31] Eakins was introduced to Whitman by a friend in the fall of 1887. Whitman later recalled that Eakins had seemed "careless, negligent, indifferent, and quiet: you would not say retiring, but amounting to that."[32] Yet the poet and the painter obviously realized that they had much in common and they remained close friends until Whitman's death in 1892.[33] David Shi, in his study on realism in America, speculates that perhaps "because of their shared reputation as rebels living under a cloud of public disapproval, Whitman and Eakins developed an intense comradeship in 1887–88." He names their Quaker background,[34] their scientific studies and admiration for the aesthetics of American technology, their enjoyment of outdoor life, and their reverence for the naked human figure as common

Figure 8.5. Thomas Eakins, *Walt Whitman*, 1887–88. Oil on canvas, 30⅛″ x 24¼″. Pennsylvania Academy of the Fine Arts, Philadelphia. General Fund.

interests, and then he adds: "The aspect of Whitman's writings that Eakins most admired ... was 'the realistic; the observation, the truth, the sense of coming direct out of life.'"[35]

Eakins began to work on his portrait of Whitman in November 1887, doing short sketches, as Whitman told Traubel, and then gave the finished portrait to Whitman (in whose possession it still was at the time of his death). The loose, sketch-like brush strokes, the undefined dark background and the strong light from the left, and the slightly reclining posture of the sitter as well as his ruddy face are somewhat reminiscent of the work of the Dutch portrait painter Frans Hals.[36] When the portrait was exhibited publicly for the first time in 1891, the *Philadelphia Press* praised it highly: "Mr Eakins' Walt Whitman is by odds and far the best portrait yet made of an heroic figure in our letters."[37] Whitman's response to the finished product was favorable as well, if for different reasons: "I like Eakins' picture (it's like sharp cold cutting true sea brine)."[38]

Our familiarities with Whitman's life and poetic work as well as with photographs of him make it extremely difficult to view Eakins's portrait as anything but the great poet's likeness. To us, the expression on his face is so much part of what we recognize as Whitman's persona from his poems that we view Eakins's portrait as if the face in the painting were informed by our familiarity with the poet's self-presentation. The emotions that are being expressed are—as is usually the case in paintings and especially in portraits—subject to interpretation, if not speculation. In the case of this particular portrait, however, the conflicting interpretations of sitter and viewer help to demonstrate how much the expression of emotions is really the result of a construction: Whitman himself regarded his portrait as somewhat reminiscent of an image of King Lear—the face of "a poor old blind despised & dying king."[39] Yet we now see far less melancholy or human tragedy in the poet's expression but rather a certain cheerfulness, or perhaps the wisdom or pensiveness of old age: his slack posture and somewhat disheveled appearance emphasize conscious informality and absence of pretension. These elements contrast sharply with contemporary formal portraits of eminent citizens, whose desire to impress viewers with their status and importance is so obviously part of the public and communicative function of representative portraiture. Background knowledge of Whitman's early career and the resistance with which his poetry was met clearly informs present-day viewers' understanding of the possible emotions represented via the painting, even beyond what might perhaps have been expressed or intended at the time.

Before I come to my final example, I would like to return to the distinction I drew earlier between the artist's appeal to the viewer that is intended to provoke an emotional response and the expression of a sitter's emotion as directly discernible in a portrait. The human face, as we all know, is especially expressive of emotions. Yet it is also particularly difficult to interpret the emotions expressed by the human face alone, without additional explanation or biographical context, unless these emotions are being exaggerated in their expression beyond that which is still deemed effective, let alone realistic. Acting in early silent films thus often resorted to an excessive theatricality, which we understandably regard as disturbing or amusing rather than as impressive and enlightening.

If we look at the face of a person whom we do not know as we know Whitman, and if there is no suggested narrative context to assist our perception, we find that our reading of emotion in a human face becomes almost completely speculative. We are continuously searching for some correspondence between outer and inner self, as Wollheim explains:

> Apart from a few primitive cases, no physiognomy perception will be independent of what is for us the supreme example of the relationship between inner and outer: that is, the human body as the expression of the psyche. When we endow a natural object or an artefact with expressive meaning, we tend to see it corporeally: that is, we tend to credit it with a particular look which bears a marked analogy to some look that the human body wears and that is constantly conjoined with an inner state.[40]

The difficulty of adducing an adequate interpretation of the inner state of a person through the contemplation of a face without access to any additional information is demonstrated by another late portrait by Eakins. Initially, we only see the pale face of an aging woman against a uniformly dark background (figure 8.6). Upon closer inspection, the different textures of an informally upturned collar of her black coat and the elegantly draped tie of her midnight-blue satin blouse framing her pale face become perceptible. Apart from a single white streak of hair, there are only two ornaments that lighten up the almost complete black-in-black presentation and therefore attract attention: a pin with a greenish gem—an opal, perhaps, or a turquoise—holding the tie of her blouse, and another gold pin adorning her hair. The sitter, painted in an undefined dark environment, with a slight tilt of her head that is emphasized by the off-center position of the hairpin, is facing us squarely.

This fact in itself is already somewhat unusual for Eakins, who more often did bust portraits of people in half or three-quarter profile and slightly averted gaze, as in the Whitman portrait. According to Wilmerding, "the bust portrait facing forward was an infrequent undertaking possibly because of its unnerving frankness in directly confronting the viewer's eyes."[41] The effect of the frontal pose is enhanced here by the view at the woman's face slightly from below and by the intense proximity of the face to the gaze of the viewer (and artist). To scrutinize and paint a human face at such intimate close range is rare and requires courage on the part of the sitter, because it exposes every nuance of expression. Nevertheless, it is difficult here to translate either pose or expression adequately: the slight tilt of the woman's head could indicate a certain inquisitiveness, or perhaps a critical distance, or even a silent appeal.

Figure 8.6. Thomas Eakins, *Portrait of Mrs. Thomas Eakins (Susan Macdowell Eakins)*, c. 1899. Oil on canvas, 20⅛″ x 16⅛″. Hirshhorn Museum and Sculpture Garden, Smithsonian Institution, Washington, DC. Gift of Joseph H. Hirshhorn.

The problem of reading her emotions correctly is underscored by the direct, almost piercing gaze that meets the painter's eyes and of course, vicariously, the spectator's as well. Wilmerding speaks "of the last and most difficult of the general categories, the frontal pose."[42] Such frontality, as well as the viewer's closeness to the woman's face, suggests a degree of privacy that makes thought and emotion the theme of the painting, even as we attempt to interpret it. For Meyer Schapiro, "the strict full-face [is] an extreme position." Comparing it to the first-person speaker addressing an observer, he says of such a frontal pose: "It seems to exist both *for* us and *for* itself in a space virtually continuous with our own, and is therefore appropriate to the figure as symbol or as carrier of a message."[43] While Schapiro is referring to religious paintings here, especially to the frontal figure of Christ, the symbol or message may be oblique or even absent in a secular frontal portrait such as this. Barbara Novak actually calls the late portraits by Eakins the equivalent of "a hermetic reverie," a phrase that indicates how difficult it is for the outside viewer to decode the thoughts and emotions of the individuals in these paintings.[44]

This particular portrait of the elderly woman no longer has a public function, as Whitman's portrait so obviously still does. If we begin to look for additional information to help us solve the enigma of the woman's emotions as expressed in the painting, the title informs us that it is a portrait of the painter's wife, Susan Macdowell Eakins. He had married Susan Macdowell, his former student and "a gifted painter in her own right who made great sacrifices to promote his career,"[45] in 1884. This knowledge does not, however, offer immediate access to the personality, the thoughts, or the emotions of the sitter; nevertheless, it is obvious that the portrait of her is not intended to be a mere "likeness," in the sense of "looking like" the person who sat for her portrait, but rather that the face expresses powerful feelings that appeal to the viewer although one would be hard pressed to find their verbal equivalents.

Comparing an earlier portrait of Eakins's wife from 1885 with this late painting, Wilmerding attempts to link the expression on her face to pain and disappointment: "[T]he reddened rims of Susan's eyes [are as] aching voices of encroaching pain." He argues that all this remains apparent in the late portrait as well: "[T]he same tilt of head and weighted eyelids now give even fuller expression to the intervening accumulation of adversity."[46] Because this particular portrait can be regarded as a dialogue between painter and sitter as well as that between husband and wife, there is a certain probability in Wilmerding's assumption that Susan Eakins expressed very private feelings, perhaps including those of sadness, disappointment, or grief. Yet there are also possibilities of seeing in her expression the probing look of a self-reliant and mature woman, or as illustrating affection, sensitivity, and compassion, or even all of these, instead of just a single emotion. This may be the reason why Daniel J. Strong, in his contribution on the portrait, merely points to "the weary yet unwavering eyes of Susan Eakins,"[47] and the Hirshhorn Museum website argues that the portrait is "completely unsentimental but captures her still reserve and inner strength."[48] Elizabeth

Johns concludes that "Susan Eakins alone is virtually unfathomable, and in that lies, we realize, her strength."[49]

While the discussion of the paintings by Hicks and Church has revealed that collective emotions of a period, be they religiously, nationally, or culturally grounded, can be assessed fairly accurately through a historical context of similarly expressed emotions, it becomes far more complicated, if not altogether impossible, to attempt to comprehend and evaluate an individual's private emotions through facial expression alone. Johns argues that Eakins, in his late portraits, shows

> that men and women were physical creatures, subject to the forces of nature beyond their control. These forces included aging and disease; but they also included the forces of urban life—of "modern life," of disappointment, of competition, of tension. He showed in his sitters' faces not only the aging that was the natural "wear" of the body, but the carefully composed set of the head against "tear"—against emotional outburst, against exhaustion of one's physical, irreplaceable resources.[50]

Realism in art, with its emphasis on the individuality of each person, thus seems to put an end to the representation of collective expressions of emotions in the arts and refers us to the new privacy of emotions that turn out to be of a more individual quality and are therefore almost impossible to decipher verbally, even if we confront a convincing visual rendering of them.

Notes

1. The art historian James Elkins identifies a number of periods in history during which an open emotional response to the fine arts seemed entirely appropriate to viewers. Crying in front of paintings or statues, according to Elkins, was considered as a natural response to particularly moving themes; see *Pictures & Tears: A History of People Who Have Cried in Front of Paintings* (New York: Routledge, 2001).
2. Richard Wollheim, *Art and Its Objects* (Cambridge: Cambridge University Press, 1980), 28.
3. Wollheim, *Art and Its Objects,* 29.
4. Bruce Weber et al., "The Expression of Grief and the Power of Art," *New York Times,* 13 September 2001.
5. Holland Cotter, "A Cry That Inspires and Heals," *New York Times,* 13 September 2001.
6. Wollheim refers to this direct emotional response as "natural expression," distinguishing it from the nineteenth-century term "correspondence" as "expressive of a certain condition because, when we are in that condition, it seems to us to match, or correspond with,

what we experience inwardly: and perhaps when the condition passes, the object is also good for reminding us of it in some special, poignant way, or for reviving it for us." Wollheim, *Art and Its Objects,* 31.

7. One of her paintings of a young woman with flowers bears the title *We Both Must Fade;* another, of a mother and child, uses a line from a nursery rhyme for a title: *This Little Pig Went to Market; Listening to Father's Watch* accurately describes the subject matter of father and son. On the sentimental value of such literal captions of her art, see also the exhibition catalogue *Lilly Martin Spencer (1822–1902): The Joys of Sentiment* (Washington, DC: Smithsonian Institution Press, 1973).
8. For the distinction between emotion and sentimentality, see esp. Ronald de Sousa, *The Rationality of Emotions* (Cambridge, MA: MIT Press, 1987), 320: "An emotion is mere sentimentality if, in the face of opportunities for action, it reveals itself to have been merely a species of contemplative *self-indulgence.*" De Sousa then proceeds to analyze Oscar Wilde's famous aphorism: "A sentimentalist is one who desires to have the luxury of an emotion without paying for it."
9. Martha C. Nussbaum, *Upheavals of Thought: The Intelligence of Emotions* (Cambridge: Cambridge University Press, 2001), 26–27.
10. In her exhibition catalogue, Carolyn J. Weekley summarizes the conflict: "Chief among the issues were the distinctions that had evolved between the English Quaker Church and the Society [of Friends] as it emerged in colonial America. By Edward's lifetime, the two bodies were not closely connected. ... Although as a Quaker he was also a pacifist, Edward Hicks ardently upheld the social philosophy of the new nation and even praised and painted its principal hero, George Washington. For Quakers such as Edward, arbitrary authority would be intolerable and unbearable, and thus was a reason for debate." *The Kingdoms of Edward Hicks* (Williamsburg, VA: Colonial Williamsburg Foundation, 1999), 35–36.
11. Quoted from ibid., 36.
12. Quoted from ibid., 34.
13. Robert Hughes, *American Vision: The Epic History of Art in America* (New York: Knopf, 1997), 38.
14. See Weekley, *Kingdoms of Edward Hicks,* 53.
15. Ibid., 40.
16. Quoted from ibid., 51.
17. De Sousa, *Rationality of Emotions,* 110.
18. Ibid., 109.
19. Behaviorism and its theory receives short shrift in Nussbaum's book. She regards most psychological theories of emotion as inadequate and summarizes their shortcomings in a brief chapter entitled "The Decline of Reductionist Theories of Emotion"; Nussbaum, 93–100. Yet de Sousa cautions against a complete rejection of William James's early observations: "There was something right in James's claim that the emotion follows on, rather than causing the voluntary and involuntary bodily changes which are held to express it. ... [W]e can sometimes be caught in our own pretense." Ronald de Sousa, "Emotion." *Stanford Encyclopedia of Philosophy* (First published 3 February 2003; substantive revision 5 June 2007. <http//plato.stanford.edu/entries/emotion> (accessed 18 June 2007). Not even poststructural theory reduces emotion entirely to affect, as Rei Terada argues; see *Feeling in Theory: Emotion after the "Death of the Subject"* (Cambridge, MA: Harvard University Press, 2001), 110–127.
20. Horst Gundlach, in his original contribution to the 2001 conference on "Emotions in American History," oddly conflated the concepts of affects and emotions, regarding emotions as extremely short-lived sensations. What is terminologically even more confusing is

the fact that he relegated some of the seven Deadly Sins (vanity and pride) to emotions in an area that he dismissed as "Folk Psychology," a term that the philosopher and art historian Arthur Danto expressly wishes to save from abuse; see Arthur C. Danto, "Beautiful Science," in *The Body /Body Problem: Selected Essays* (Berkeley: University of California Press, 1999), 206–26; 215.

21. Hughes, *American Vision,* 162.
22. See Angela L. Miller, *The Empire of the Eye: Landscape Representation and American Cultural Polities, 1825–1875* (Ithaca, NY: Cornell University Press, 1993), 128.
23. Hughes, *American Vision,* 164.
24. Until well into the nineteenth century, feelings of reverence and awe in religious as well as in secular terms were still strongly dependent on Edmund Burke's idea of the sublime in nature, for which the point of view is essential.
25. Hughes, *American Vision,* 164. Church is, of course, not the first American painter to have responded to the impending crisis of the union. As Angela Miller points out, since the 1850s artists had employed pictorial elements that had soon become conventional expressions of fear and warning; reviews of paintings demonstrate "how standard, indeed hackneyed, the symbolism of the storm had become for conveying themes of national crisis." Miller, *Empire of the Eye,* 127.
26. Miller, *Empire of the Eye,* 127.
27. Ibid., 131. Another of Church's paintings from the same period, *Aurora Borealis* (1865), has also "been plausibly interpreted as a portent—triumphant and desolate, both—of the Union victory." See Kevin J. Avery, "Treasures from Olana," in *Treasures from Olana: Landscapes by Frederic Edwin Church* (Hudson, NY: The Olana Partnership/Ithaca, NY: Cornell University Press, 2005), 25–70; 48.
28. Miller, *Empire of the Eye,* 136.
29. These rather far-reaching ramifications have been part of a history of emotions investigating how and why emotions may obtain cultural significance. Historians François, Siegrist, and Vogel, in the introduction to their essay collection focusing on nation and emotion, wish to investigate "wie und warum Emotionen im Rahmen der jeweiligen Kultur (Kultur als System kollektiver Sinnkonstruktion und Symbole verstanden) ihre Bedeutung bekommen. Emotionen werden als Teil des Schemas der Weltinterpretation begriffen, mit dem die Menschen Wirklichkeit definieren und wahrnehmen." "Die Nation: Vorstellungen, Inszenierungen, Emotionen." Ed. Etienne François, Hannes Siegrist & Jakob Vogel, *Nation und Emotion: Deutschland und Frankreich im Vergleich—19. und 20. Jahrhundert.* Göttingen: Vandenhoeck & Ruprecht, 1995, 13–35; 21.
30. The painting is incorrectly dated 1887 on the upper right by the painter who finished the portrait in April 1888, after working on it for almost six months. The verso inscription is even more confusing because it reads: "Walt Whitman Painting from Life by Thomas Eakins 1897/1887." See Fred B. Adelson on the Whitman portrait in *Thomas Eakins,* ed. John Wilmerding (London: National Portrait Gallery; Washington, DC: Smithsonian Institution Press, 1993), 109–11.
31. Adelson, *Thomas Eakins,* 109.
32. Ibid.
33. Elizabeth Johns, in her book on Eakins, devotes an entire chapter to the Whitman portrait in which she explains in detail the similarities and distinctions between the two men as possible reasons for their late friendship. See Elizabeth Johns, *Thomas Eakins: The Heroism of Modern Life* (Princeton, NJ: Princeton University Press, 1983), 144–69.
34. It is interesting that this Quaker background would also directly connect Edward Hicks and Whitman, who seems to be referring to the *Peaceable Kingdom* when he writes: "I think I could turn and live with animals, they are so placid and self-contain'd." "Song of

Myself," 32, line 684. *Leaves of Grass,* ed. Harold W. Blodgett and Sculley Bradley (New York: New York University Press, 1965), 60.

35. David E. Shi, *Facing Facts: Realism in American Thought and Culture 1850–1920* (New York: Oxford University Press, 1995), 145–46.
36. It is surprising that most art historians note Eakins's admiration for Spanish portraits of the seventeenth century, especially those by Velasquez, but, with the exception of Robert Hughes, rarely remark on the striking similarity between Frans Hals and Eakins; see Hughes, 300.
37. Adelson, *Thomas Eakins,* 110.
38. Ibid.
39. David S. Reynolds, *Walt Whitman's America: A Cultural Biography* (New York: Knopf, 1995), 564.
40. Wollheim, *Art and Its Objects,* 32–33.
41. John Wilmerding, "Thomas Eakins's Late Portraits," in *American Views: Essays on American Art* (Princeton, NJ: Princeton University Press, 1991), 244–63; 246. Of course, Eakins also famously portrayed people in full figure; more often, however, he would paint either bust-length figures, or even choose the format of approximately three-quarters of the seated person, as in his well-known portrait of *Miss Amelia C. Van Buren* (1891).
42. Ibid., 254.
43. Meyer Schapiro, "Frontal and Profile as Symbolic Forms," *Words, Script, and Pictures: Semiotics of Visual Language* (New York: George Braziller, 1996), 73. It is interesting to note that Paul Ekman, renowned scholar in the study of facial expression of emotions, admits the inadequacy of artistic drawings in a scientific study of the human face as compared to photographs or movies because of the interference of the artist's own emotions: "Although drawings have the virtue of allowing control over demographic characteristics, lighting, and various physiognomic features, they have the enormous failing that they may include as facial behavior components that simply do not occur or cannot co-occur and possible idiosyncratic or stereotypic views of the artist." Paul Ekman, Wallace V. Friesen, and Phoebe Ellsworth, "Methodological Decisions," in *Emotion in the Human Face,* 2nd ed., ed. Paul Ekman (Cambridge: Cambridge University Press, 1982), 22–38; 36.
44. Barbara Novak, *American Painting of the Nineteenth Century: Realism and the American Experience* (New York: Harper & Row, 1979), 210.
45. Shi, *Facing Facts,* 147.
46. Wilmerding, "Thomas Eakins's Late Portraits," 259.
47. Daniel J. Strong's entry in *Thomas Eakins,* ed. John Wilmerding, 147.
48. "The American Vision." http://www.150.si.edu/150trav/imagine/m119.htm (accessed 14 July 2007).
49. Johns, *Thomas Eakins,* 168.
50. Ibid., 161.

Bibliography

Adelson, Fred B. "Walt Whitman." In *Thomas Eakins,* edited by John Wilmerding, 9–11. London: National Portrait Gallery/Washington, DC: Smithsonian Institution Press, 1993.

Avery, Kevin J. "Treasures from Olana." In *Treasures from Olana: Landscapes by Frederic Edwin Church,* 25–70. Hudson, NY: The Olana Partnership/Ithaca, NY: Cornell University Press, 2005.

Bolton-Smith, Robin. *Lilly Martin Spencer (1822–1902): The Joys of Sentiment.* Washington, DC: Smithsonian Institution Press, 1973.

Cotter, Holland. "A Cry That Inspires and Heals." *New York Times,* 13 September 2001.

Danto, Arthur C. "Beautiful Science." In *The Body/Body Problem: Selected Essays,* 206–26. Berkeley: University of California Press, 1999.

De Sousa, Ronald. *The Rationality of Emotions.* Cambridge, MA: MIT Press, 1987.

———. "Emotion." In *Stanford Encyclopedia of Philosophy,* http//plato.stanford.edu/entries/emotion (accessed 18 June 2007).

Ekman, Paul, Wallace V. Friesen, and Phoebe Ellsworth. "Methodological Decisions." In *Emotion in the Human Face,* 2nd ed., edited by Paul Ekman, 22–38. Cambridge: Cambridge University Press, 1982.

Elkins, James. *Pictures & Tears: A History of People Who Have Cried in Front of Paintings.* New York: Routledge, 2001.

François, Etienne, Hannes Siegrist, and Jakob Vogel, eds. "Die Nation: Vorstellungen, Inszenierungen, Emotionen." In *Nation und Emotion: Deutschland und Frankreich im Vergleich—19. und 20. Jahrhundert im Vergleich,* 13–35. Göttingen: Vandenhoeck & Ruprecht, 1995.

Hughes, Robert. *American Vision: The Epic History of Art in America.* New York: Knopf, 1997.

Johns, Elizabeth. *Thomas Eakins: The Heroism of Modern Life.* Princeton, NJ: Princeton University Press, 1983.

Miller, Angela L. *The Empire of the Eye: Landscape Representation and American Cultural Politics, 1825–1875.* Ithaca, NY: Cornell University Press, 1993.

Novak, Barbara. *American Painting of the Nineteenth Century: Realism and the American Experience.* New York: Harper & Row, 1979.

Nussbaum, Martha C. *Upheavals of Thought: The Intelligence of Emotions.* Cambridge: Cambridge University Press, 2001.

Reynolds, David S. *Walt Whitman's America: A Cultural Biography.* New York: Knopf, 1995.

Schapiro, Meyer. "Frontal and Profile as Symbolic Forms." In *Words, Script, and Pictures: Semiotics of Visual Language.* New York: George Braziller, 1996.

Shi, David E. *Facing Facts: Realism in American Thought and Culture, 1850–1920.* New York: Oxford University Press, 1995.

Terada, Rei. *Feeling in Theory: Emotion after the "Death of the Subject".* Cambridge, MA: Harvard University Press, 2001.

Weber, Bruce. "The Expression of Grief and the Power of Art." *New York Times,* 13 September 2001.

Weekley, Carolyn J. *The Kingdoms of Edward Hicks.* Williamsburg, VA: Colonial Williamsburg Foundation, 1999.

Whitman, Walt. *Leaves of Grass,* edited by Harold Blodgett and Sculley Bradley. New York: New York University Press, 1965.

Wilmerding, John. "Thomas Eakins's Late Portraits." In *American Views: Essays on American Art,* 244–63. Princeton, NJ: Princeton University Press, 1991.

———, ed. *Thomas Eakins.* London: National Portrait Gallery; Washington, DC: Smithsonian Institution Press, 1993.

Wollheim, Richard. *Art and Its Objects.* Cambridge: Cambridge University Press, 1980.

Emotions and Society

Chapter 9

A Horrifying Experience?

Public Executions and the Emotional Spectator in the New Republic

Jürgen Martschukat

"When the day of Execution comes, then, Multitudes, Multitudes flock together," observed Reverend Eliphalet Adams in 1738.[1] Thousands of people often gathered around the scaffold when capital punishment was executed in the small communities of colonial America. The crowd consisted of women and men, of boys and girls, and many had traveled a long way, by foot or carriage, to see one of their fellow men die. Before a hanging, at least in New England and the mid-Atlantic Colonies, the spectators listened to an execution sermon. Historians of punishment and social control glean from these sermons the conception of the death penalty in the seventeenth and eighteenth centuries.[2] In these moralizing speeches, the wrongdoer was described as a bad example for the community. The condemned was not depicted as an extraordinary type of person, but as indication of the general depravity of humankind and the ultimate consequence of a morally dissolute life or a lack of subordination. The execution on the scaffold thus fulfilled a dual function: it ended an unruly and immoral biography and simultaneously served as a powerful warning to all those present at the spectacle.

For example, in 1693 Reverend Cotton Mather addressed a convicted child murderess as well as the listening crowd by describing the successive

Notes for this section begin on page 193.

steps in her sinful life: "Your sin has been Uncleanness; Repeated Uncleanness, Impudent Uncleanness, Murderous Uncleanness."[3] According to Cotton Mather, "uncleanness" had to be understood as a first indication of criminal decay, and since almost every observer was somehow morally "unclean," a public execution was perceived as a moralizing and necessarily horrifying experience for the crowd. It was supposed to work as an awe-inspiring performance that reproduced the rules and the power of God and of the authorities on earth. It was considered a drama that taught the lessons of "good" and "bad" and finally convinced the spectators to lead a righteous life. A public execution was a ritualized answer to the evil in the world, and it was meant to have a cathartic effect on the spectators. Thus, in this conception, the execution of a death penalty needed a public. "Not only must the people know," as Michel Foucault has claimed, "they must see with their own eyes. ... They must to a certain extent take part in it."[4]

In the era of the early republic, this conception of the death penalty was subjected to numerous inquiries, and the capital punishment ritual underwent changes. Those reconsiderations climaxed during the 1830s and 1840s, when, in the northeastern part of the United States, the execution of a death penalty was moved behind prison walls. This change of venue was the consequence of numerous political, social, and cultural transformations, such as a new conceptualization of state and society and its power structure, or the creation of public and private spheres. In this essay I will elaborate on another major factor in the transformation of the capital punishment ritual, namely, the creation of the emotional spectator. I will argue that an emotional human being with interdependent outer and inner spheres was discursively shaped throughout the eighteenth century and that this new type of person implied a reconsideration of the impact of violent public executions on the character of the observer. This essay will trace the reevaluation of character, pain, suffering, and the execution process in the capital punishment discourse of the early republic, and it will also demonstrate how these discursive transformations (and especially the construction of the emotional spectator) were intertwined with a reorganization of the state and the criminal justice system. The sentimentalized body in pain and the new "humanitarian narrative," which were part of historically changing cultural attitudes towards the visual perception of human suffering and the possibly degenerating effects on the characters of the observers, enhanced the nineteenth-century transition of law and society. They contributed to the modification of permissible and impermissible forms of violence and affected the development of punishment in modern society, and thus modern society itself.[5]

I consequently do not locate this transition of the capital punishment procedure within the "civilizing process," which usually implies a progressive, teleological understanding of history as development towards a more sensitive, more rational, and less violent society.[6] Instead, the reorganization of the punishment procedure exemplifies the transformation into a society that dealt *differently* with violence, based on a different conceptualization of the human being and its emotionality. When the ceremonial execution of colonial times gradually gave way to bureaucratic procedure played out behind prison walls, in isolation from the community, this procedure was neither less nor more violent, but different: violence was supposed to be hidden. Feelings were, and they still are, suppressed in increasingly bureaucratically administered executions, as Robert Johnson has shown in his study on the modern execution process and as Austin Sarat has emphasized repeatedly.[7]

This essay therefore is less interested in the actual experience of "real" emotions within the observer of an execution in the early nineteenth century, but rather concentrates on the observation, description, and definition of the observers' emotions in historic discourses to better understand the conceptualization of the emotional spectator. The first part indicates the creation of this concept in discourses of medicine, philosophy, and law from the late seventeenth to the early nineteenth centuries; the second part analyzes how the idea of the emotional spectator contributed to the reevaluation of public punishments since the late eighteenth century. My analysis in this context will not adhere to a purely textual approach, but, following Peter Stearns's suggestion, will utilize emotional history as a "fulcrum" between the historic conceptualization of individual experience and larger historical developments. The essay's final part specifies how the definition of emotions and their supposed effects significantly influenced the shaping of the political, social, and cultural landscape of the early republic.[8]

The Creation of the Emotional Spectator

To reconstruct the creation of the emotional spectator, it is necessary to go back to the later seventeenth century, when medical scholars conducted intensive research on human anatomy. They were particularly interested in the brain and in the nervous system, as nerves and the senses seemed to transmit stimuli from the outer world to the interior body, and more specifically to the brain, which recently had been defined as the one and only seat of the soul. Consequently, the existence of this type of nervous system made the traditional dichotomy of mind and body at least unstable.[9]

As a result of the research of physicians like Thomas Willis and his contemporaries, a theory of sensory perception, learning, and the further association of ideas took shape. Senses and nerves were considered the basis of thoughts, feelings, and emotions, and therefore emotions had strong materialist roots. Intellectual historians and historians of medicine, such as Sergio Moravia, George S. Rousseau, or Roy Porter, have demonstrated how this new physiological paradigm diffused from medical discourse into the realm of philosophy, ethics, and politics. In general, the fields of philosophy and medicine were hardly distinguishable in the seventeenth and eighteenth centuries; many physicians of the enlightenment were philosophers and vice versa. John Locke, for example, was trained in medicine and practiced as a physician for a time, and his "Essay Concerning Human Understanding" (1690), which was paradigmatic in the realm of sensation, represented this typical mixture of philosophy, ethics, medicine, and science. Furthermore, eighteenth-century philosophers and political theorists often viewed themselves as doctors of a pathological society.

One major consequence of the new conceptualization of the inner and outer spheres of a human being as interrelated entities was that man seemed not to be thrown into an unalterable position in a divinely given cosmos anymore. Instead, he appeared to be more a product of his environment, and much less of a divine order. Climate, nature, education, and the social world—as exterior stimuli—now seemed to play a crucial role in the permanent process of shaping and reshaping a malleable human character.[10]

The theory of human perception was a central theme of a new eighteenth-century "science of man," and it defined sensibility to outer stimuli as the "natural" emotional state of the human mind or soul. Within this context the observation and perception of physical violence and its consequences was highly and controversially debated. On the one hand, the observation of human pain and agony was assumed to lead to a "strong sense of pity, and a great proneness to relieve," to quote the Scottish philosopher Francis Hutcheson, whose writings were widely approved of in America.[11] Such an observer empathized with the observed, showed a compassionate response, and strongly identified with the suffering fellow creature, as, for example, Adam Smith emphasized in his writings on the "Theory of Moral Sentiments": "We conceive ourselves enduring all the same torments, we enter as it were into his body, and become in some measures the same person with him, ... and even feel something which, though weaker in degree, is not altogether unlike them."[12] Among others, Thomas Jefferson stressed that this sort of experience followed from an innate "moral instinct ... that nature hath implanted in our breasts" and that irresistibly moved the observing man to alleviate the suffering of a fellow creature.[13]

On the other hand, the relationship between violence and the spectator was interpreted as highly ambiguous as a number of possibly degenerating effects of displays of violence on the moral qualities of human beings were debated. Sentimentalists seemed not only to experience pain and agony in the observation of violence, but some form of pleasure as well, as only spectators of cruel and violent acts could experience their moral and emotional qualities and demonstrate them towards themselves and others. Thus, the observation of violence and agony could at least lead to some degree of satisfaction, and the so-called cult of sensibility seemed to coincide with voyeurism and hypocrisy. The sheer number of increasingly graphic and detailed textual descriptions of violent acts and sufferings since the late eighteenth century, such as in John de Crèvecoeur's famous "Letters from an American Farmer" in the chapter on "Negro slavery,"[14] or in crime literature such as the "Brief Narrative of the Life and Confession of Barnett Davenport," were indicative of this trend. Almost every report claimed to convey "the most horrible murder ever committed," or "the most shocking, inhuman and unnatural" misdeeds. Moreover, the reader's appetite was often stimulated by the writer's confession of personal horror at the beginning of the report.

At the same time, some contemporaries criticized that spectators not only identified with the suffering human being but also with the torturer. Closely related was their concern over possibly negative effects of violent exterior stimuli, which prompted a number of questions, central to the discourse over public executions: Would not the observation of violence lead to violence? Could observers from the lower ranks of society really live up to high moral standards and feel pity and empathy for a fellow creature in agony, torture, and pain, or were they "entertained with dying agonies," as some voices had been warning since the late eighteenth century? And most importantly, would not the presentation of violence accustom large parts of the public to brutal behavior, and thus lead to individual and collective moral decay?[15]

Public Executions as Sources of Moral Decay

The evaluation of public punishments underwent substantial transformations in the old and new worlds as the concept of the emotional spectator gained prominence in the late eighteenth century. To be sure, the crowd had played a major role in the execution ritual in early modern Europe and in the American colonies, and some scholarly interpretations maintain a highly active and crucially important role for the audience, supposedly endowed with enormous "agency."[16] And yet, in the early modern *conceptualization* of the punishment rituals, spectators had been given a largely passive role. People were supposed to assemble around the scaffold to witness a demonstration of almighty power and to experience horror, fear, and a catharsis intended to stabilize collective obedience. In fact, the sources show that, generally speaking, as long as an execution was not botched but successfully performed by the executioner, the crowd did not stir up trouble or raise a protest but complied with its largely passive role.[17]

Only when the emotional spectator evolved in the course of the eighteenth century did the crowd and its behavior move to center stage in the capital punishment discourse. An influential author in this discourse was the Italian Cesare Beccaria. In 1764 in his essay "On Crime and Punishment," Beccaria not only questioned the effectiveness of public punishments but also considered them counterproductive. He argued that the presentation of cruelty was no deterrent at all and even hardened the public as it accustomed people to frequent violence and cruelty. For Beccaria then, public punishments intensified social violence and crime and produced popular disregard for the politically powerful. Almost immediately translated into English, Beccaria's essay reached a large audience in the American colonies. It was published in several editions and subsequently reprinted as a series in newspapers such as the *New Haven Gazette and the Connecticut Magazine.* Beccaria's arguments strongly impressed Thomas Jefferson, who ranked "On Crime and Punishment" among the six most important publications on the art of civil government.[18]

He also shaped the theories of Benjamin Rush, America's leading criminal justice theorist at the time. Rush had studied at the University of Edinburgh, which played a central role in the development of the fields of medicine and philosophy during the Enlightenment. One of the university's characteristic features was its concern with the interaction between mind and body, in the context of the Scottish Enlightenment and its philosophers such as Francis Hutcheson or Adam Smith. After his return from Europe, Rush became a professor of chemistry and medicine. He was one of the Founding Fathers of the American republic and remains *the* founding father of American medicine.

As a physician and philosopher, Rush wrote elaborately on the mode of human perception, on sensibility, and on character building. He generally considered it one of his chief tasks to bring the principles, morals, and manners of American citizens into conformity with republican institutions, and in this frame of thought he perceived the abolition of public punishments and of the death penalty as key to an ordered and morally superior new republic. Referring to the doctrine of the nerves and the concept of sensation and reaction, of environmentally given stimulus, and of emotional and behavioral response, Rush criticized the effects of public executions on the emotional spectator as personally and politically devastating.

Rush emphasized the lack of deterrence of capital punishments and warned of their morally degrading influence. He suggested that the observation of violent acts implanted a proneness to physical violence and cruelty in the individual and the collective character of the citizens. His critique was confirmed by observers of public executions and their assertion that the majority of spectators were unimpressed and rude during and after an execution as most people around the scaffold demonstrated neither exterior nor interior seriousness.

Neither did the very few spectators who behaved less rude at the scaffold perceive an execution as an act of both divine and secular justice. If they identified with the convicted person on the scaffold at all, according to Rush, they empathized with the fellow creature and felt disgust for the authorities. In this perception, a public execution portrayed neither the depravity of the specific sinner nor of mankind in general. Consequently, both types of reaction by emotional spectators (either being hardened on the one side, or feeling empathy with the victim on the other side) were politically destabilizing. They proved that the existing mode of public punishments was socially damaging and a major obstacle to a true republic that was to be founded on virtue, rationality, and respect for life in the "principles, opinions and manners" of the people, as Rush emphasized in a letter to Vice-President John Adams in 1789. The spirit of the citizens and the moral and virtuous character of society would form the prime measure of the success or failure of the new republic. Obviously, the crowds of public executions were neither virtuous nor controlled in their manners—not to mention the lack of respect for human life, while a republican government was supposed to reclaim its human capital rather than to destroy it.[19]

Benjamin Rush did not argue for the private execution of the death penalty, but for its abolishment. Around 1800, reformers made several efforts to abolish capital punishment, especially in the states of Pennsylvania and New York. But finally, none of the abolitionists was able to gather enough support to break with "that vestige of barbarism," as their efforts failed.[20] Still, one of the most promising and influential initiatives was undertaken by Edward Livingston in Louisiana. Livingston was a New Yorker, and he had been influenced by the New York reform movement of the late eighteenth and early nineteenth centuries. He moved to Louisiana, which became the eighteenth state of the Union in 1812, and eight years later was elected a member of Louisiana's legislative body. In 1822 he presented his first "Report on the Plan of a Penal Code" for the state of Louisiana to its legislative assembly. Although a second report followed in 1825, Livingston's concepts never became law in Louisiana. Nevertheless, he superbly formalized statements that had circulated in the criminal justice discourse for many years, and thereby he exerted a powerful influence on the reform movement of the 1830s.[21]

In his proposal to the assembly, Livingston maintained "that the punishment of death should find no place in the [new criminal] code" of Louisiana. To substantiate this claim, he unfolded three major arguments. First, he questioned the deterrence effect of the death penalty and suggested that a potential murderer's criminal energy was driven by either passion or by greed, and averred that both were stronger than the fear of death. Second, Livingston warned that in the case of a death penalty, a miscarriage of justice could not be revised. Even if capital punishment were the best and most effective of all possible punishments, a single mistaken decision would be enough to render its abolishment necessary.

His third major argument evolved into a cornerstone of the capital punishment controversy in the following years. Livingston followed arguments presented by Benjamin Rush and other contemporaries and asserted that the frequent "infliction of death ... loses its effect; the people become too familiarized with it ... ; it is changed into a spectacle, which must frequently be repeated to satisfy the ferocious taste it has formed." Consequently, the spectacle of public executions led into moral and emotional decay, into a whirl of blood and slaughter, into a whirl of an "atrocious passion for witnessing human agonies." A constant escalation of cruelty in punishments became necessary to satisfy the observers' needs. Livingston maintained that once the "natural repugnance" of human sufferings was conquered, the intellectual taste and the taste of the senses changed, and "we become most fond of those enjoyments." Thus, capital punishments created an "inhuman taste" and an "increasing curiosity," and the more frequently inflicted, the more they laid the foundation for a moral and emotional depravity of the people.

Such a development, Livingston warned, endangered the health of the republic which depended entirely on the character and the spirit of its citizens. Sooner or later, a moral and emotional decay of the people would have the gravest consequences for representative republican institutions, on the juries, the courts, and the government. On the other hand, in a system of rare capital punishments, "the sufferer, whatever be his crime, becomes a hero or a saint; he is the object of public attention, curiosity, admiration, and pity." In that case, "exalted emotions" were created by a public execution, the wrongdoer was turned into a martyr, and the republican government into a torturer. This kind of emotional response by the spectators, "it cannot be doubted, ... counteracts every good effect that punishment is intended to produce. ... Thus the end of the law is defeated, the force of example is totally lost, and the place of execution is converted into a scene of triumph for the sufferer, whose crime is wholly forgotten." According to Livingston, "the utter inutility of this waste of human life, its utter inefficiency as a punishment, and its demoralizing operation on the minds of the people," were more than proven. No matter how frequently (or how rarely) applied, Livingston concluded, capital punishment was at war with the feelings of the people, and thus had to be abolished.[22]

Benjamin Rush and Edward Livingston were among the most outspoken opponents of capital punishment in the early republic. But, as noted earlier, their efforts were not crowned by success. When Livingston died in New York in 1836, not a single state of the Union had abolished the death penalty. Nevertheless, the influence of both reformers remained powerful in the long run. In their spirit, Robert Rantoul, Jr., for example, maintained in 1836 in the legislative body of the state of Massachusetts that "the spectacle of capital punishments is barbarizing, and promotive of cruelty and a disregard of life." In the 1830s, the morally degrading effects of public punishments, and the either rude or empathetic behavior of the emotional spectator were widely accepted as a fact, at least in the northeastern states of the Union. But the political consequences differed from those envisioned by Rush, Livingston, and other reformers. In the end, their criticism, which was based on the figure of the emotional spectator, was of crucial importance for the reorganization of the execution procedure in the 1830s.[23]

Reorganizing the Execution Procedure

Although public executions in the new republic were heavily criticized as festivals of disorder or as promotions of moral decay, the death penalty itself was firmly established in the minds of most people and in the criminal justice systems of the states. Death was still considered an absolutely necessary ultimate punishment for the worst crimes, such as murder and high treason. Criminals of that type were seen as an essential danger for life, limb, and liberty of the affected individuals and of the society at large. Still, proponents of the death penalty shared the abolitionist skepticism concerning the publicity of the punishment procedures and their degenerating effects. Since the early 1820s, most critics did not consider the death penalty itself, but the scenery of a public execution disturbing. The reorganization of the execution ritual with a limited public role appeared to be the only possible solution of this dilemma. In the words of New England cleric Jonathan Going, "The object of public justice would be better secured, if executions took place in the jail yard."[24]

In the 1820s, the public as well as legislative bodies intensively debated numerous public executions and the respective behavior of the emotional crowd, as, for example, in the case of John Lechler's hanging on 25 October 1822 in Lancaster, Pennsylvania. According to contemporary reports, which may have been inflated, executions such as Lechler's drew crowds of between 20,000 and 40,000 people into the towns and to the execution places. Though the mayor of Lancaster had issued a proclamation that prohibited the sale of liquor and tried to regulate public life on execution day, there was extensive unrest, drunkenness, gambling, and a display of other vices on the day of Lechler's death. Hanging day was a festive occasion that brought work and routine to a stop, and twenty-eight people were arrested during and immediately after Lechler's execution. In the criminal justice discourse those disturbing effects were less and less related to the death penalty itself but to the circumstances of the execution and the behavior of the crowd.[25]

Consequently, authorities began to experiment with ways of reducing the size of hanging-day crowds, for instance through the prohibition of liquor, the transfer of the hanging to the early morning hours, or the quickening of the procedure. Since taking these measures did not really succeed in changing the execution frenzy, the State of New York enacted a law intended to cope with the problems caused by public executions. County sheriffs were given the power to conduct executions behind prison walls with only a small number of carefully chosen official witnesses, but not a single execution followed this option.

Finally, in 1834, Pennsylvania was the first state to enact legal provisions for obligatory "private" executions. In the Pennsylvania Congress, a large majority of 62:13 voted that the punishment of death "be inflicted … within the walls or yard of the jail." In the following year, the states of New York, New Jersey, and Massachusetts followed, and until 1845 all the states in the Northeast had barred public displays of capital punishment as their legislatures sought "to prevent the vicious assemblages and demoralizing tendencies of public executions."[26]

Now, instead of an unlimited crowd of men, women, and children, only twelve male citizens of irreproachable reputation were required to witness an execution. They acted as representatives of the people, and an official account of these witnesses substituted for the public performance and "its contaminating and counteracting effects," as a report for the Senate of New York announced.[27] Thus, in the 1830s and 1840s the execution procedure was organized according to the prevalent paradigms of social stratification. Different levels of emotionality were constructed according to the race, class, and gender of a person. Presumably, only educated, upper-class, white men were considered to be able to hold their emotions in check and to retain a certain dignity and exterior seriousness when faced with displays of ultimate punishment. For sure, the legislative assemblies and committees that debated and decided on the execution procedure consisted of male members of the higher classes of society. Consequently, they considered themselves and their kin of good character and irreproachable reputation, and, at least to a certain extent, of emotional stability. These men thought of themselves as those self-determined "republican machines" that had been designated since the late eighteenth century as the leading and reliable figures of the postrevolutionary society.[28]

The crowd of the old public executions had increasingly been juxtaposed to these rational and enlightened men—the people around the scaffold were perceived as forming a dangerously irrational and highly emotional mob, consisting of members from the lower classes. Demographic shifts, growing cities, and seemingly increasing vice contributed to a general fear of the impoverished masses in the 1820s and 1830s. Group hatreds, insecurity, and the conditions of city life joined to produce a tense and volatile atmosphere.[29] And according to the contemporary conceptualization, people from the lower ranks of society still followed man's "naturally given" tendency toward visible emotional arousal, and they presumably lacked the education and the moral constitution to cope with a public presentation of violence. Moreover, gathering in a mob and witnessing the performance on the scaffold seemed to invigorate the given tendency of the lower classes toward rude behavior, violent cruelty, and moral decay. Consequently, the maintenance of a stable republic seemed to specifically require the exclusion of the lower classes from the spectacle of punishment. Only educated and presumably rational citizens from the higher classes were considered to be able to emotionally and intellectually cope with the sentiments that were aroused by the execution of a fellow human being.[30]

Class was not the only category of emotional classification and of cultural and social stratification that shaped the organization of the punishment procedure. When the new execution laws in the northeastern states were passed, only men were permitted as observers of "indoor" executions. In the 1820s, the shock in reports of crowds at public executions had climaxed with the description of the presence of women at the scaffold: "And to crown the whole [bunch of people], *women*! Yes, gracious heaven! soft, delicate, tender-hearted females who would faint at the killing of a chicken, went fifteen miles to see a fellow creature put to death!"[31] Thus, the new conceptualization of hanging day followed culturally preferred notions of gender differences and female "delicacy." The reorganization of the execution procedure corresponded to the doctrine of separate male and female spheres. Supposedly softer and less rational than men, women had to be kept out of politics, generally, and away from the execution procedure, specifically. The exclusion of women from executions reproduced the concept of naturally given differences between men and women, and it was a necessary consequence of women's supposedly greater emotion and lack of self-control. Females were presumed to be fragile and had to be protected from the revolting scenes of hangings. Furthermore, because women were conceptualized as keepers of morality and virtue, their attendance at executions had to be avoided.[32]

Conclusion

Beginning in the later seventeenth century, medical research and philosophical inquiry formed an expanding discourse with the emotional spectator at center stage. This discourse exerted a strong influence on the reconceptualization of the death penalty and the execution procedure during the late eighteenth and early nineteenth centuries. The act of putting someone to death was transformed from a dramatic, supposedly awe-inspiring presentation of power in the form of publicly performed violence into a carefully controlled situation, which reproduced the paradigms of the new republican society. Therefore, the form of spectatorship had to be changed in the early nineteenth century. The public crowd had to be reduced to a few selected presumably emotionally stable and self-controlled men.[33]

In this process, the emotional spectator was interwoven with the stratifying concepts of class, gender, and race.[34] Thus, the contemporaries differentiated between particular types of emotional spectators, and ascribed to them different capacities for self-control and proper behavior. Still, the concept of emotional self-control and its transfer into the execution process did not work without ruptures. In real life, the engendered and separate spheres were not as rigid as in their conceptualization. Women were active in the public sphere, for example as reformers or abolitionists in the fight against slavery as well as against the death penalty. Some of them, like the Massachusetts writer Lydia Maria Child, not only disapproved of capital punishment as legalized murder and privatized executions as "edifying exhibition in the great school of public morals." Child also criticized the exclusion of women from executions as misunderstood form of male "gallantry" and as "unjudicious partiality."[35]

Moreover, from the very beginning, the concept of serious and emotionally restrained upper-class men who completed their civic duty as cool witnesses of an execution turned out to be extremely fragile and ambiguous. Only very rarely was an indoor execution performed as a highly controlled and bureaucratic procedure, and the number of witnesses hardly ever remained restricted to twelve. There were frequent reports of dozens, hundreds, and occasionally even thousands of men of considerable social standing thronging the jail yards to experience the act of an execution. In the state of New York, for example, besides the "twelve respectable citizens" permitted to witness executions, sheriffs were authorized to appoint such deputies they considered "expedient." In consequence there was a run on execution tickets that the sheriffs often sold at high prices for an indoor festival of punishment, and critical journals bemoaned these "culpable evasions of the law." Whereas the socially and financially privileged members of society had the option to buy tickets for an execution, the lower classes gathered around the prison, climbing on trees and rooftops to cast at least a distant gaze upon the scene of death.[36]

As a result, critics such as Francis Lieber, a professor of political economy with a law degree from Jena and future author of the Lieber Codes, rejected the term "private" executions and preferred to speak of the "indoor manner of executing criminals" that had been established in the 1830s in the northeastern part of the United States—for "to call them not public is wrong."[37] Obviously, the execution of a fellow human being was still a horrifying experience that also aroused interest and perhaps even pleasure among the so-called higher classes, too. But, according to historic discourse, this "American way of executions" exemplified progress in civilization. Not the least, this progress was related to the efforts to ban violence and emotions from the public sphere. Still, this transformation of the execution procedure and its removal to the confines of the prison resulted in a different form of violence considered permissible. Thomas Upham, a Congregationalist minister, professor of moral and mental philosophy in Maine, and opponent of capital punishment, was outraged by the hiding of state-inflicted violence. In his "Manual for Peace" (1836), he reminded his readers that openness and visibility were the fundamental principles of republican government, and that indoor executions had to be considered "a great anomaly":

> Our courts of justice must be open to the public; the deliberations of our legislatures must be public ... but when life is to be taken, when a human being is to be smitten down like an ox, when a soul is to be violently hurled into eternity, the most solemn occasion that can be witnessed on earth, then the public must be excluded. But the American public will not long submit to this. ... If the continuance of capital punishments depends on their being inflicted in private, it may be regarded as certain that they cannot long exist in this country.[38]

Thomas Upham was wrong. Eventually, it was this relocation and restructuring of the execution procedure that enabled the continued existence of the death penalty.

Notes

1. Eliphalet Adams, *A Sermon Preached on the Occasion of the EXECUTION of Katherine Garret* (New London, CT: T. Green, 1738), 25, quoted in Karen Halttunen, *Murder*

Most Foul: The Killer and the American Gothic Imagination (Cambridge, MA; Harvard University Press, 1998), 11.

2. In addition to Halttunen: Daniel A. Cohen, "In Defense of the Gallows: Justifications of Capital Punishment in New England Execution Sermons, 1674–1825," *American Quarterly* 40 (1988): 147–64; Daniel A. Cohen, *Pillars of Salt, Monuments of Grace: New England Crime Literature and the Origins of American Popular Culture, 1674–1860* (Oxford: Oxford University Press, 1993); see as well *Pillars of Salt: An Anthology of Early American Criminal Narratives,* ed. Daniel E. Williams (Madison, WI: Madison House, 1993).
3. Cotton Mather, *Warnings from the Dead* (Boston: Bartholomew Green, 1693), 73.
4. Michel Foucault, *Discipline and Punish: The Birth of the Prison* (New York: Vintage Books, 1977), 58.
5. See David Garland, *Punishment and Modern Society: A Study in Social Theory* (Oxford: Oxford University Press, 1991), 213–47; for an overview see Karl Shoemaker, "The Problem of Pain in Punishment: Historical Perspectives," in *Pain, Death, and the Law,* ed. Austin Sarat (Ann Arbor: University of Michigan Press, 2001), 15–41; Alan Hyde, *Bodies of Law* (Princeton, NJ: Princeton University Press, 1997), 187–201; Thomas W. Laqueur, "Bodies, Details, and the Humanitarian Narrative," in *The New Cultural History,* ed. Lynn Hunt (Berkeley: University of California Press, 1989), 176–204. For the history of capital punishment in the United States see Jürgen Martschukat, *Die Geschichte der Todesstrafe in den USA: Von der Kolonialzeit bis zur Gegenwart* (Munich: Beck, 2002), and Stuart Banner, *The Death Penalty: An American History* (Cambridge, MA: Harvard University Press, 2002).
6. Norbert Elias, *The Civilizing Process* (Oxford: B. Blackwell, 1982); Pieter Spierenburg, *The Spectacle of Suffering: Executions and the Evolution of Repression* (Cambridge: Cambridge University Press, 1984); for a discussion of Elias and Spierenburg see Garland, *Punishment and Modern Society,* 216–29; for an inspiring critique of the concept of the civilizing process see Gerd Schwerhoff, "Zivilisationsprozeß und Geschichtswissenschaft: Norbert Elias' Forschungsparadigma in historischer Sicht," *Historische Zeitschrift* 266, no. 3 (1998): 561–605.
7. Robert Johnson, *Death Work: A Study of the Modern Execution Process* (Pacific Grove, CA: Brooks/Cole Publishing Company, 1990), 5; see for example Austin Sarat, "Introduction: On Pain and Death as Facts of Legal Life," in *Pain, Death, and the Law,* 1–14.
8. On the historiography of emotions see especially Peter N. Stearns and Carol Z. Stearns, "Emotionology: Clarifying the History of Emotions and Emotional Standards," *American Historical Review* 90, no. 4 (1985): 813–36; Jan Lewis and Peter N. Stearns, "Introduction," in *An Emotional History of the United States,* ed. Peter N. Stearns and Jan Lewis (New York: New York University Press, 1998), 1–14; see in the same volume Kenneth J. Gergen, "History and Psychology: Three Weddings and a Future," 15–29; Barbara H. Rosenwein, "Worrying About Emotions in History," *American Historical Review* 107, no. 3 (2002): 821–45.
9. George S. Rousseau and Roy Porter, "Introduction: Toward a Natural History of Mind and Body," in *The Languages of Psyche: Mind and Body in Enlightenment Thought,* ed. George S. Rousseau (Berkeley: University of California Press, 1990), 3–44, and in the same volume Robert G. Frank, Jr., "Thomas Willis and His Circle: Brain and Mind in Seventeenth-Century Medicine," 107–46; George S. Rousseau, "Nerves, Spirits, and Fibres: Towards Defining the Origins of Sensibility," *The Blue Guitar* 2 (1976): 125–53; Roy Porter, *Die Kunst des Heilens: Eine medizinische Geschichte von der Antike bis heute,* 2nd ed. (Heidelberg: Spektrum Akademischer Verlag, 2000), 243–45.

10. Peter Gay, "The Enlightenment as Medicine and as Cure," in *The Age of the Enlightenment: Studies Presented to Theodore Besterman,* ed. W. H. Barber (Edinburgh: St. Andrews University Publications, 1967), 375–86; Sergio Moravia, "From 'Homme Machine' to 'Homme Sensible': Changing Eighteenth-Century Models of Man's Image," *Journal of the History of the Ideas* 39 (1978): 45–60; Porter, *Die Kunst des Heilens,* 250–53; John Locke, *An Essay Concerning Human Understanding,* ed. Roger Woolhouse (London: Penguin, 1997 [1690]), is considered *the* paradigmatic text in the Anglo-American context; see for Locke, medicine, and ethics Rousseau, "Nerves, Spirits, and Fibres."
11. Francis Hutcheson, "A System of Moral Philosophy (1755)," in *Four Early Works on Motivation,* ed. Paul McReynolds (Gainesville, FL: Scholar's Facsimile & Reprint, 1969), 131–32.
12. Adam Smith, *Theory of Moral Sentiments,* ed. D. D. Raphael and Alec L. Macfie (Indianapolis, IN: Liberty Classics, 1982 [1759]), 9.
13. On the so-called cult of sensibility, see among others Janet Todd, *Sensibility: An Introduction* (London: Methuen, 1986); Norman S. Fiering, "Irresistible Compassion: An Aspect of Eighteenth-Century Sympathy and Humanitarianism," *Journal of the History of Ideas* 37 (1976): 195–218; quotes from Thomas Jefferson's letter to Thomas Law, 13 June 1814.
14. Hector St. John de Crèvecoeur, *Letters From an American Farmer* (London: Dent & Sons and New York: Dutton & Co., 1951 [1782]), 172–73: While walking on a small path, "leading through a pleasant wood," the farmer's attention is caught by a bunch of birds fluttering around a cage in a tree: "Horrid to think and painful to repeat, I perceived a negro, suspended in the cage, and left there to expire! I shudder when I recollect that the birds had already picked out his eyes, his cheek bones were bare; his arms had been attacked in several places, and his body seemed covered with a multitude of wounds. … The blood slowly dropped, and tinged the ground beneath. No sooner were the birds flown, that swarms of insects covered the whole body of this unfortunate wretch, eager to feed on his mangled flesh and to drink his blood. I found myself suddenly arrested by the power of affright and terror; my nerves were convulsed; I trembled, I stood motionless, involuntary contemplating the fate of this negro, in all its dismal latitude."
15. On the ambivalence of violence and its perception see esp. Halttunen, *Murder Most Foul,* 33–49; for the quotes from the crime reports, such as *A Brief Narrative of the Life and Confession of Barnett Davenport* (Hartford, CT, 1780), see Karen Halttunen, "Humanitarianism and the Pornography of Pain in Anglo-American Culture," *American Historical Review* 100, no. 2 (1995): 303–34; Karen Halttunen, "Early American Murder Narratives: The Birth of Horror," in *The Power of Culture: Critical Essays in American History,* ed. Richard W. Fox and T. J. Jackson Lears (Chicago: University of Chicago, 1993), 67–101; Fiering, "Irresistable Compassion," 200.
16. See for example Thomas W. Laqueur, "Crowds, Carnival and the State in English Executions, 1604–1868," in *The First Modern Society: Essays in English History in Honour of Lawrence Stone,* ed. A. L. Beier, David Cannadine, and James M. Rosenheim (Cambridge: Cambridge University Press, 1989), 305–55; for a discussion of the various approaches see Jürgen Martschukat, "Die öffentliche Hinrichtung: Ein 'Theater des Schreckens'?" *Kriminologisches Journal* 27, no. 3 (1995): 186–208.
17. On early modern Europe see Jürgen Martschukat, *Inszeniertes Töten: Eine Geschichte der Todesstrafe vom 17. bis zum 19. Jahrhundert* (Cologne: Böhlau, 2000); Jürgen Martschukat, "Der 'Massstab für die geistige Bildungsstufe eines Volkes und die Moralität eines Zeitalters': Die Todesstrafe in Diskurs und Praxis im 18. und 19. Jahrhundert," *Historische Anthropologie* 9, no. 1 (2001): 1–26; Richard Evans, *Rituals of Retribution: Capital Punishment in Germany, 1600–1987* (Oxford: Oxford University Press, 1996);

V. A. C. Gatrell, *The Hanging Tree: Executions and the English People, 1770–1868* (Oxford: Oxford University Press, 1994); on the United States see Louis P. Masur, *Rites of Execution: Capital Punishment and the Transformation of American Culture, 1776–1865*, 2nd ed. (Oxford: Oxford University Press, 1991).

18. Cesare Beccaria, *Über Verbrechen und Strafen;* trans. and ed. Wilhelm Alff (Frankfurt am Main: Insel, 1966 [1764]), 112, 116 (§ 28); Marcello T. Maestro, *Cesare Beccaria and the Origins of Penal Reform* (Philadelphia: Temple University Press, 1973): 34–45, 125–43; Marcello T. Maestro, "A Pioneer for the Abolition of Capital Punishment: Cesare Beccaria," *Journal of the History of the Ideas* 34 (1973): 463–68; Masur, *Rites of Execution,* 50–54. On the overall reform movement against corporal punishment see Myra C. Glenn: *Campaigns against Corporal Punishment: Prisoners, Sailors, Women and Children in Antebellum America* (Albany: State University of New York Press, 1984).
19. Masur, *Rites of Execution,* 61–70, the letter to Adams from 21 July 1789 is quoted on page 64–65; Louis P. Masur, "The Revision of Criminal Law in Post-Revolutionary America," *Criminal Justice History* 8 (1987): 21–35; Michael Meranze, *Laboratories of Virtue: Punishment, Revolution, and Authority in Philadelphia, 1760–1835* (Chapel Hill: University of North Carolina Press, 1996), 87–127; Lisbeth Haakonssen, *Medicine and Morals in the Enlightenment: John Gregory, Thomas Percival and Benjamin Rush* (Amsterdam: Rodopi, 1997), 187–234; Benjamin Rush, *An Enquiry into the Effects of Public Punishments upon Criminals and upon Society* (Philadelphia: Joseph James, 1787); Benjamin Rush, *Considerations on the Injustice and Impolicy of Punishing Murder by Death* (Philadelphia: Mathew Carey, 1792); see for similar arguments William Bradford, *An Inquiry How Far the Punishment of Death Is Necessary in Pennsylvania with Notes and Illustrations* (Philadelphia: T. Dobson, 1793), and the attached statement by Caleb Lownes, *An Account of the Alteration and Present State of the Penal Laws of Pennsylvania;* on the meaning of self-control in the cultural and social realm of the early republic see C. Dallett Hemphill, "Class, Gender, and the Regulation of Emotional Expression in Revolutionary-Era Conduct Literature," in *An Emotional History of the United States,* ed. Stearns and Lewis, 38–51; on republicanism see Robert E. Shalhope, *The Roots of Democracy: American Thought and Culture, 1760–1800* (Boston: Twayne Publishers, 1990), 27–52.
20. A collection of essays and a helpful introduction is given by Philip E. Mackey, ed., *Voices Against Death: American Opposition to Capital Punishment, 1787–1975* (New York: Burt Franklin, 1976), here especially xviii–ixx; most of the contemporary arguments were summarized by Roland Diller, *Discourse on Capital Punishment* (New Holland, PA: New Holland Debating Society, 1825).
21. Philip E. Mackey, "Edward Livingston and the Origin of the Movement to Abolish Capital Punishment in America," *Louisiana History* 16 (1975): 145–66; Edward Livingston, *Remarks on the Expediency of Abolishing the Punishment of Death* (Philadelphia: J. Harding, 1831).
22. The quotes are from Edward Livingston, "Report Made to the Legislature of Louisiana, in March 1822," Livingston, *Remarks on the Expediency,* 5–20.
23. Robert Rantoul, Jr., "Has Society the Right to Take Away Life? (1836)," in *Voices Against Death,* ed. Mackey, 34–55.
24. Jonathan Going, *A Discourse Delivered at Worcester, 11 December 1825, the Sabbath after the Execution of Horace Carter* (Worcester, MA: W. Manning, 1825), 11, quoted in Masur, *Rites of Execution,* 96–97; see as well the *Report on the Expediency of Abolishing Public Executions* (Harrisburg, PA: Henry Welsh, 1833).
25. Negley K. Teeters, "Public Executions in Pennsylvania: 1682–1834 (1960)," in *Crime and Justice in American History: Historical Articles on the Origins and Evolution of Ameri-*

can Criminal Justice, ed. Eric H. Monkkonen, 2 vols. (Westport, CT: Meckler, 1991), 1:756–835; see for New York Michael Madow, “Forbidden Spectacle: Executions, the Public and the Press in Nineteenth-Century New York,” *Buffalo Law Review* 43, no. 2 (1995): 461–562, esp. 498–506.

26. On the state who refuses to take responsibility for the violence of the punishment see Foucault, *Discipline and Punish,* 9; Madow, “Executions, the Public and the Press,” 503–10; Teeters, “Public Executions in Pennsylvania: 1682–1834,” 787.
27. S. Rep. No. 79, NY 58th session 10 (1835), quoted after Madow, “Executions, the Public and the Press,” 508.
28. Hemphill, “Class, Gender, and the Regulation of Emotional Expression,” in *An Emotional History of the United States,* ed. Stearns and Lewis, 38–51; Michael Kimmel, *Manhood in America: A Cultural History* (New York: Free Press, 1996), 21, 45; Kimmel quotes “republican machines” from Benjamin Rush, “Address to the Ministers of the Gospel of Every Denomination in the United States Upon Subjects Interesting to Morals,” from 1788.
29. See for example Carl E. Prince, “The Great ‘Riot Year’: Jacksonian Democracy and Patterns of Violence in 1834,” *Journal of the Early Republic* 5, no. 1 (1985): 1–19; Michael Feldberg, *The Turbulent Era: Riot and Disorder in Jacksonian Democracy* (Oxford: Oxford University Press, 1980).
30. Masur, *Rites of Execution,* 93–116.
31. The essay from the magazine *Berkshire American* was reprinted on 2 December 1826 in *The Escritoir* (Albany, NY) and is quoted in Madow, *Rites of Execution,* 503.
32. The sharp historiographic distinction between public and private spheres and the supposedly corresponding gender stereotypes have been increasingly criticized in recent years. By referring to the concept of separate spheres, I do not doubt the multiple interactions of men and women in antebellum America. I understand the separate spheres concept as contemporary paradigm, and, moreover, in the case of the reorganization of the execution procedure, it showed its possibly powerful effects. For a discussion of the separate spheres concept see for example, Linda K. Kerber et al., “Beyond Roles, Beyond Spheres: Thinking About Gender in the Early Republic,” *William and Mary Quarterly* 46, no. 3 (1989): 565–81; Susan M. Reverby and Dorothy O. Helly, eds., *Gendered Domains: Rethinking Public and Private in Women's History* (Ithaca, NY: Cornell University Press, 1992); Barbary Hey, *Women's History und Poststrukturalismus: Zum Wandel der Frauen- und Geschlechtergeschichte in den USA* (Pfaffenweiler: Centaurus, 1995), 17–34; on the exclusion of women from executions see Masur, *Rites of Execution,* 112.
33. See for a similar approach Austin Sarat, “Killing Me Softly: Capital Punishment and the Technologies for Taking Life,” in *Courting Death: The Law of Mortality,* ed. Desmond Manderson (London: Pluto Press, 1999), 53–76; Foucault, *Discipline and Punish,* 48–49.
34. In my essay, I have not used race as analytical category, but African Americans did not partake as spectators of indoor executions.
35. Lydia Maria Child, “Letters from New York” (1845), reprinted in *Capital Punishment in the United States: A Documentary History,* ed. Bryan Vila and Cynthia Morris (Westport, CT: Greenwood Press, 1997), 58–62.
36. Teeters, “Public Executions in Pennsylvania: 1682–1834,” 788; Madow, “Executions, the Public and the Press,” 511–23.
37. *The Life and Letters of Francis Lieber,* ed. Thomas Sergeant Perry (Boston: James R. Osgood, 1882), 170, quoted after Masur, *Rites of Execution,* 111.
38. Thomas Upham, “The Manual of Peace (1836) ,” in *Capital Punishment in the United States,* ed. Vila and Morris, 50–51.

Bibliography

Banner, Stuart. *The Death Penalty: An American History.* Cambridge, MA: Harvard University Press, 2002.

Cohen, Daniel A. "In Defense of the Gallows: Justifications of Capital Punishment in New England Execution Sermons, 1674–1825." *American Quarterly* 40 (1988): 147–64.

———. *Pillars of Salt, Monuments of Grace: New England Crime Literature and the Origins of American Popular Culture, 1674–1860.* Oxford: Oxford University Press, 1993.

Elias, Norbert. *The Civilizing Process.* Oxford: B. Blackwell, 1982.

Evans, Richard. *Rituals of Retribution: Capital Punishment in Germany, 1600–1987.* Oxford: Oxford University Press, 1996.

Feldberg, Michael. *The Turbulent Era: Riot and Disorder in Jacksonian Democracy.* Oxford: Oxford University Press, 1980.

Fiering, Norman S. "Irresistible Compassion: An Aspect of Eighteenth-Century Sympathy and Humanitarianism." *Journal of the History of Ideas* 37 (1976): 195–218.

Foucault, Michel. *Discipline and Punish: The Birth of the Prison.* New York: Vintage Books, 1977.

Frank, Robert G., Jr. "Thomas Willis and His Circle: Brain and Mind in Seventeenth-Century Medicine." In *The Languages of Psyche: Mind and Body in Enlightenment Thought,* edited by George S. Rousseau, 107–46. Berkeley: University of California Press, 1990.

Garland, David. *Punishment and Modern Society: A Study in Social Theory.* Oxford: Oxford University Press, 1991.

Gatrell, V. A. C. *The Hanging Tree: Executions and the English People, 1770–1868.* Oxford: Oxford University Press, 1994.

Gay, Peter. "The Enlightenment as Medicine and as Cure." In *The Age of the Enlightenment: Studies Presented to Theodore Besterman,* edited by W. H. Barber, 375–86. Edinburgh: St. Andrews University Publications, 1967.

Gergen, Kenneth J. "History and Psychology: Three Weddings and a Future." In *An Emotional History of the United States,* edited by Peter N. Stearns and Jan Lewis, 15–29. New York: New York University Press, 1998.

Glenn, Myra C. *Campaigns against Corporal Punishment: Prisoners, Sailors, Women and Children in Antebellum America.* Albany: State University of New York Press, 1984.

Haakonssen, Lisbeth. *Medicine and Morals in the Enlightenment: John Gregory, Thomas Percival and Benjamin Rush.* Amsterdam: Rodopi, 1997.

Halttunen, Karen. "Early American Murder Narratives: The Birth of Horror." In *The Power of Culture: Critical Essays in American History,* edited by Richard W. Fox and T. J. Jackson Lears, 67–101. Chicago: University of Chicago, 1993.

———. "Humanitarianism and the Pornography of Pain in Anglo-American Culture." *American Historical Review* 100, no. 2 (1995): 303–34.

———. *Murder Most Foul: The Killer and the American Gothic Imagination.* Cambridge, MA: Harvard University Press, 1998.

Hemphill, C. Dallett. "Class, Gender, and the Regulation of Emotional Expression in Revolutionary-Era Conduct Literature." In *An Emotional History of the United States,* edited by Peter N. Stearns and Jan Lewis, 38–51. New York: New York University Press, 1998.

Hey, Barbary. *Women's History und Poststrukturalismus: Zum Wandel der Frauen- und Geschlechtergeschichte in den USA.* Pfaffenweiler: Centaurus, 1995.

Hyde, Alan. *Bodies of Law.* Princeton, NJ: Princeton University Press, 1997.

Johnson, Robert. *Death Work: A Study of the Modern Execution Process.* Pacific Grove, CA: Brooks/Cole Publishing Company, 1990.

Kerber, Linda K., Nancy Cott, Robert Gross, Lynn Hunt, Carroll Smith-Rosenberg, and Christine M. Stansell. "Beyond Roles, Beyond Spheres: Thinking About Gender in the Early Republic." *William and Mary Quarterly* 46, no. 3 (1989): 565–81.

Kimmel, Michael. *Manhood in America: A Cultural History.* New York: Free Press, 1996.

Laqueur, Thomas W. "Bodies, Details, and the Humanitarian Narrative." In *The New Cultural History,* edited by Lynn Hunt, 176–204. Berkeley: University of California Press, 1989.

———. "Crowds, Carnival and the State in English Executions, 1604–1868." In *The First Modern Society: Essays in English History in Honour of Lawrence Stone,* edited by A. L. Beier, David Cannadine, and James M. Rosenheim, 305–55. Cambridge: Cambridge University Press, 1989.

Lewis, Jan, and Peter N. Stearns. "Introduction." In *An Emotional History of the United States,* edited by Peter N. Stearns and Jan Lewis, 1–14. New York: New York University Press, 1998.

Mackey, Philip E. "Edward Livingston and the Origin of the Movement to Abolish Capital Punishment in America." *Louisiana History* 16 (1975): 145–66.

———., ed. *Voices Against Death: American Opposition to Capital Punishment, 1787–1975.* New York: Burt Franklin, 1976.

Madow, Michael. "Forbidden Spectacle: Executions, the Public and the Press in Nineteenth-Century New York." *Buffalo Law Review* 43, no. 2 (1995): 461–562.

Maestro, Marcello T. "A Pioneer for the Abolition of Capital Punishment: Cesare Beccaria." *Journal of the History of the Ideas* 34 (1973): 463–68.

———. *Cesare Beccaria and the Origins of Penal Reform.* Philadelphia: Temple University Press, 1973.

Martschukat, Jürgen. "Die öffentliche Hinrichtung: Ein 'Theater des Schreckens'?" *Kriminologisches Journal* 27, no. 3 (1995): 186–208.

———. *Inszeniertes Töten: Eine Geschichte der Todesstrafe vom 17. bis zum 19. Jahrhundert.* Cologne: Böhlau, 2000.

———. "Der 'Massstab für die geistige Bildungsstufe eines Volkes und die Moralität eines Zeitalters': Die Todesstrafe in Diskurs und Praxis im 18. und 19. Jahrhundert." *Historische Anthropologie* 9, no. 1 (2001): 1–26.

———. *Die Geschichte der Todesstrafe in den USA: Von der Kolonialzeit bis zur Gegenwart.* Munich: Beck, 2002.

Masur, Louis P. "The Revision of Criminal Law in Post-Revolutionary America." *Criminal Justice History* 8 (1987): 21–35.

———. *Rites of Execution: Capital Punishment and the Transformation of American Culture, 1776–1865,* 2nd ed. Oxford: Oxford University Press, 1991.

Meranze, Michael. *Laboratories of Virtue: Punishment, Revolution, and Authority in Philadelphia, 1760–1835.* Chapel Hill: University of North Carolina Press, 1996.

Moravia, Sergio. "From 'Homme Machine' to 'Homme Sensible': Changing Eighteenth-Century Models of Man's Image." *Journal of the History of the Ideas* 39 (1978): 45–60.

Perry, Thomas Sergeant, ed. *The Life and Letters of Francis Lieber.* Boston: James R. Osgood, 1882.

Porter, Roy. *Die Kunst des Heilens: Eine medizinische Geschichte von der Antike bis heute,* 2nd ed. Heidelberg: Spektrum Akademischer Verlag, 2000.

Prince, Carl E. "The Great 'Riot Year': Jacksonian Democracy and Patterns of Violence in 1834." *Journal of the Early Republic* 5, no. 1 (1985): 1–19.

Reverby, Susan M., and Dorothy O. Helly, eds. *Gendered Domains: Rethinking Public and Private in Women's History.* Ithaca, NY: Cornell University Press, 1992.

Rosenwein, Barbara H. "Worrying About Emotions in History." *American Historical Review* 107, no. 3 (2002): 821–45.

Rousseau, George S. "Nerves, Spirits, and Fibres: Towards Defining the Origins of Sensibility." *The Blue Guitar* 2 (1976): 125–53.

Rousseau, George S., and Roy Porter. "Introduction: Toward a Natural History of Mind and Body." In *The Languages of Psyche: Mind and Body in Enlightenment Thought,* edited by George S. Rousseau, 3–44. Berkeley: University of California Press, 1990.

Sarat, Austin. "Killing Me Softly: Capital Punishment and the Technologies for Taking Life." In *Courting Death: The Law of Mortality,* edited by Desmond Manderson, 53–76. London: Pluto Press, 1999.

———., ed. *Pain, Death, and the Law.* Ann Arbor: University of Michigan Press, 2001.

Schwerhoff, Gerd. "Zivilisationsprozeß und Geschichtswissenschaft: Norbert Elias' Forschungsparadigma in historischer Sicht." *Historische Zeitschrift* 266, no. 3 (1998): 561–605.

Shalhope, Robert E. *The Roots of Democracy: American Thought and Culture, 1760–1800.* Boston: Twayne Publishers, 1990.

Shoemaker, Karl. "The Problem of Pain in Punishment: Historical Perspectives." In *Pain, Death, and the Law,* edited by Austin Sarat, 15–41. Ann Arbor: University of Michigan Press, 2001.

Spierenburg, Pieter. *The Spectacle of Suffering: Executions and the Evolution of Repression.* Cambridge: Cambridge University Press, 1984.

Stearns, Peter N., and Carol Z. Stearns. "Emotionology: Clarifying the History of Emotions and Emotional Standards." *American Historical Review* 90, no. 4 (1985): 813–36.

Teeters, Negley K. "Public Executions in Pennsylvania: 1682–1834 (1960)." In *Crime and Justice in American History: Historical Articles on the Origins and Evolution of American Criminal Justice,* 2 vols., edited by Eric H. Monkkonen, 1:756–835. Westport, CT: Meckler, 1991.

Todd, Janet. *Sensibility: An Introduction.* London: Methuen, 1986.

Vila, Bryan, and Cynthia Morris, eds. *Capital Punishment in the United States: A Documentary History.* Westport, CT: Greenwood Press, 1997.

Williams, Daniel E., ed. *Pillars of Salt: An Anthology of Early American Criminal Narratives.* Madison, WI: Madison House, 1993.

Chapter 10

Emotions, American Society, and Discourses on Sexuality

Michael Hochgeschwender

> Whenever female orgasm and frigidity are discussed, a false distinction is made between the vaginal and the clitoral orgasm. Frigidity has generally been defined by men as the failure of women to have vaginal orgasms. Actually the vagina is not a highly sensitive area and it is not constructed to achieve orgasms. It is the clitoris which is the center of sexual sensitivity and which is the female equivalent of the penis.
>
> – Anne Koedt, "The Myth of the Vaginal Orgasm"

These were the opening lines of one of the most influential articles of the women's liberation movement of the late 1960s and early 1970s. Published in 1970, Anne Koedt's "The Myth of the Vaginal Orgasm" triggered a long and passionate debate[1] about one of the strongest emotions—orgasm, especially female orgasm,[2] a debate that encapsulated the broader social, cultural, and economic matrix of female sexuality. Henceforth, I will focus on two different aspects of this debate. On the one hand, I will show how Koedt's arguments immediately became an object of ongoing and heated discussions among feminists and subsequently a focal point of American discourses on sexuality ever since. On the other hand, my aim is to place the conflicts and attitudes of the late 1960s and early 1970s into a broader perspective and to shed some light on the underlying long-term social and sociosexual

---

Notes for this section begin on page 216.

developments shaping those discourses. This broader perspective is based on the assumption that economic processes, especially the different modes of production, are indeed causal agents for the shift of different discourses. Emotions and discourses on emotions are, therefore, results of processes of social and cultural construction based on socioeconomic frameworks. They do not stand for themselves, isolated from any given social situation. Thus, without the discoursive representation of an emotion and the social basis of this discourse, we do not really have anything like an emotion. Besides, I will focus shortly on religious discourses on sexuality, which are often neglected. Thus, I will deal with Roman Catholic sexual discourses because they provide us with the most coherent scheme among religiously inspired narratives on sexuality. This may serve as a rather sketchy hint at alternative models of the discoursive construction of sexualities and involved emotions. I will close by touching upon a number of methodological problems of discourse analysis in the field of long-range sociosexual developments.

The orgasm debate of the early 1970s did not start out of the blue.[3] After the events of the Freedom Summer in 1964, the student movement's female activists had grown increasingly angry about male domination and patriarchal patterns within the movement. Neither the heterodox Marxist, New Left ideological approach nor the everyday behavior of the overwhelmingly male leadership seemed to fit female needs and interests. Radicalism, at least in many women's eyes, had lost its dramatic appeal of being a revolutionary agent capable of reorganizing Western societies in a holistic manner. As long as New Left radicalism just prolonged traditional male domination, it lost its appeal for women, who were gradually becoming aware of their own identity. Problems beyond class struggle and social revolution, both at least in part shaped by predominantly male interests, increasingly moved into the center of their discussions. A genuinely female perspective had to include different issues based on female experiences and aims. Therefore, it was necessary to form new discourses independent of the existing, male-dominated discourses of the Students for a Democratic Society (SDS) politicos,[4] enabling women to search for intellectual and emotional autonomy and to overcome the shortcomings of Marxist traditionalism. The androcentric character of revolutionary rhetoric suggested that any genuinely female approach had to search for a transformed language and different agendas. The so-called private issues of female bodily experience and sexual identity were a relevant starting point for this process. It seemed obvious that these issues were of little significance within a male-dominated agenda.

At bottom, even the sexual revolution was not transforming things fast enough. During its first phase in the early 1960s, it showed little concern for authentic female interests. The newly won sexual liberty primarily served male purposes. Many women were convinced that they had lost the right to deny male libertarian fantasies and to insist upon their sexual independence. Therefore, the quest for a self-defined female sexual identity certainly constituted an issue of broader social relevance. The orgasm debate in effect was an emblem of the second women's liberation movement's battlecry: "The Personal is the Political."[5] The controversy about female sexual emotions not only questioned the traditional dominance of heterosexual, phallocentric, and penetrationist sexuality by accident in order to buttress women's search for their own sexual pleasure and satisfaction with scientific and theoretical appeal.[6] Moreover, it explicitly and substantially subjected the entire apparatus of patriarchal institutions centered around matrimony and monogamy to fundamental criticism. Both cultural and social conventions about sexuality and male-female relationships were freshly interpreted with the help of a coherent critical approach.[7]

Furthermore, the orgasm debate allowed the questioning of the dominance of heterosexuality as a sociocultural and sociosexual construct based on patriarchical sexual preferences. Thus it opened a window of opportunity for a new, specifically female definition of the intrinsic values of lesbianism. Interestingly, lesbianism was no longer interpreted as a primarily intimate habit, as something "personal," but rather as an act of revolutionary action and of sisterly solidarity, as something utterly "political." In particular, the orgasm debate provided radical feminism[8] with an up-to-date language for reformulating existing discourses. Feminist radicals, such as Shulamith Firestone and Kate Millett, enthusiastically praised Koedt's supposedly fresh insights.[9] The conflation of the personal and the political engendered a dialectic, the consequences of which were far reaching. As long as one could politicize the personal, the very opposite became possible as well. A personalization or a depoliticization of the political entered the realm of possibility. During the burnout phase of the 1970s, it indeed materialized. In the end, many veterans of the radical student movement fled from overpoliticization and the lack of a clear-cut private sphere into the depoliticized vagueness of New Age and the Hippie movement. Usually this was a problem of the male politicos who had led the SDS. As a relatively young wing of the movement, feminism managed to overcome the burdens of this inherent dialectic for a considerable period of time.

The attacks of radical feminism in the early 1970s were, however, part of a much broader movement that had already framed modernity since the 1830s and 1840s. It was centered around the question of how to define female sexuality in modern, liberal, and capitalist society—production-oriented with a focus on discipline and self-control, or consumerist including a certain sexual libertinism.[10] To be more precise: the problem was one of regulating discourses on female sexual identity and disciplining female social behavior toward a penetrationist account of a vaginally centered female sexuality. This was an important issue on the bourgeois agenda because it helped interpret female sexuality as calm, passionless, and virtuous. Thus the passions of human sexuality, female and male, could be tempered. Ultimately, they could be brought into compliance with the new necessities of a well-regulated mode of production enforced by the rising industrial and capitalist order.

According to this regulatory scheme, the heated emotions of passionate love had to be reinterpreted. Romantic love and sentimentalism were substitutes for the lust and pain of original emotions.[11] Central elements of these regulative discourses were based on notions of virtuous self-control, utility, order, and bourgeois efficiency. I am, thus, fully aware of the fact that a majority of modern neurobiological scientists and psychiatrists tend to conceptually distinguish between sex and orgasm on the one hand and emotions on the other hand. Therefore, the orgasm in itself would not be acknowledged as an emotion per se, while emotions would, nonetheless, be added to the corporeal and psychological functions of orgasm. This, however, seems to be the result of a naturalistic and reductionist point of view that artificially (or just methodologically) separates functions of the body and the soul. The orgasm, though, inherently involves psychophysical feelings of sexual lust and lust is, without any doubt, a strong emotion. Moreover, this reductionist view ignores the cultural construction and sociocultural representation of the female orgasm within the broader framework of specifically modern conceptions of emotions, such as for example love and lust.

The radical feminism of the early 1970s was then confronted with Freudianism, an elaborate, utterly inward, and the most individualist and coherent of these regulatory systems, perhaps the one most adapted to modern times. What is quite often overlooked, radical feminism had, moreover, the advantage of profiting from the results of a slowly but more and more visibly changing mode of production that helped to enhance the attraction of a renewal of sexual theories.[12] The rise of a culture of consumerism since the 1920s necessitated a change in attitudes toward sexuality and partnership. They lost their relevance as keystones of productionism. Sexuality also became an integral part of the new consumerist culture. Rather than restrict sexuality in order to provide the normative underpinnings for the efficiency of the process of production, consumerism was able to transform sexuality into a focal element of its own survival. This, paradoxically and quite unintentionally, implicated radical feminism and its criticism of the early modern perspectives on sexuality in the organic restructuring of the very societal system it sought to overcome. On the other hand, it is important to stress the fact that all these social developments may have been necessary conditions for the changes in sexual discourses and practice, but they were by no means sufficient causes. We will have to identify other relevant causal agents.

Sexuality in the Nineteenth Century

In order to understand this struggle over discursive hegemony between radical feminism and orthodox Freudianism, we have to move further back in time—into the early nineteenth century when the industrial revolution had its first breakthroughs, and more specifically, into the year 1823 when the female ovum was discovered. Before 1823, Europeans, with the possible exception of the Aristotelian school,[13] had believed that the clitorally stimulated, passionate female orgasm was an essential and materially efficient cause of reproduction.[14] The Roman Catholic Church had even penalized any attempt to suppress the female orgasm in order to prevent conception. This was part of an ongoing strategy to separate the sacramentalized marriage from the influences of bourgeois and industrial societies by stressing the *bonum proli* as a central element of the *fructus sacramenti*.[15] The whole ecclesiastical argumentation was still based on principles dating to Galenian and other ideas of later antiquity, which in turn formed part of a permanent conservative strategy of withdrawal from the effects of modernity.

While the Catholic Church focused on numerous progeny and only accidentally tolerated the sexual emotions of women, popular handbooks on sexuality stressed the necessity of lustful female emotions and the causal relationship with conception. Here, passions were a central but nonsubstantial element of intercourse, basically justified by their efficiency in producing children.[16] Nonetheless, the nonsubstantial character of female orgasm was regarded more positively than in the tradition of the church.

In opposition to the theological yet antimodern implications underlying the official ecclesiastical argumentation,[17] the secular handbooks first and foremost wanted to stabilize a worldly society. Both the secular and the theological approach to female sexuality were male dominated, but they were conceived within the restrictions of an agrarian mode of production that was based on a certain superficial cooperation between the sexes. Nevertheless, with the discovery of the female ovum, things changed rapidly, at least in theory. The new caste of professionalized physicians[18] had experimentally proven that even chloroformed women lacking any sign of obvious passion were able to become pregnant. Consequently, the centuries-old mutual consent–mutual pleasure discourse that had previously shaped theory and practice of dealing with sexual emotions was rapidly torn asunder. The very lack of function of female orgasm in a utilitarian society made its quest utterly irrelevant.[19] Thus more than two thousand years of male and female experience were denied their validity by a single set of empirical data interpreted in a new framework based on the notion of practical efficiency and the belief in bourgeois rationality. Physicians, gynecologists, and later even a reluctant clergy started to think within the terms of the newly invented tradition of female passionlessness and the absolute supremacy of a vaginal-penetrationist sexuality. This whole concept fit neatly into the broader development of liberal market economies and self-disciplined bourgeois societies. Opposing experiences were therefore interpreted as symptoms of a psychopathological disease of predominantly female persons depraved of the ingenuity of their sex.[20]

The mutual pleasure discourse subsequently became more and more obscure during the 1850s to the 1870s, but it survived beneath the surface of a strict Victorian morality at least as a factual lifestyle,[21] though not as an effective discursive rival of the new and hegemonic sexual code. From the 1860s onward, Victorian and Progressive middle-class reformers aggressively demanded obedience to the penetrationist theory. This was part of their broader search for social order within a rapidly developing and changing world.[22] Disciplining sexuality seemed like a necessary element of structuring the unknown mobility of urbane, secular, and industrial Western societies. Nonsentimentalized emotions were interpreted as dangers to progress and order.[23] Interestingly enough, even female reformers sometimes ardently defended the new sexual ideology because it helped them shape their own ideas about women as the better part of mankind.[24]

However, the strictness of the utilitarian discourse on the singular validity of vaginal penetrationism had unexpected consequences. Before the 1830s female hysteria had been treated by midwives and gynecologists with clitorally stimulated orgasms.[25] In the following decades this procedure became implausible, because it was deemed both unscientific and immoral. This was the result of a facile ethical conclusion drawn from scientific premises, a classical naturalistic fallacy. But science not only failed as an adequate basis for ethics, it also failed in the search for other methods of effectively fighting hysteria. Starting in the 1850s, a widespread pandemia of female hysteria irritated contemporaries.[26] Everybody knew that the symptoms of the disease called "hysteria" were produced by depraved sexuality, but modern ideology allowed for no practical solutions based on this knowledge. As gynecologists proved unable to treat women conventionally, they risked losing their acceptance as scientists. Therefore, they recommended the most drastic solution: clitoridectomy and "female castration."[27] By removing the clitoris or the ovaries they were able to control seemingly inappropriate forms of female arousal and to reinstall proper emotional control and a lack of passion. But even this most radical operation did not prevent hysteria from becoming an integral part of everyday life, especially among modern middle-class women.

Approximately between 1895 and 1900 the hysteria pandemia coincided with another frightening and disorderly type of conduct: the negation of Victorian-Progressive[28] morality by working-class immigrants and the rising, consumerist leisure class. The middle-class nuclear family, a once-secure haven of morale, was weakened by the use of contraceptive methods, by abortion, and by increasing numbers of divorces, a general pattern that intensified during World War I. The movie industry, an early stronghold of consumerist reevaluation of moral and emotional standards, propagated a more relaxed and promiscuous lifestyle, and the automobile provided young people with a helpful means for pre- and extramarital sexual relationships far beyond Victorian-Progressivist moral rules and regulations.[29] Even in small-town America, lower-class juries were no longer willing to follow the established authority of their middle-class judges in order to automatically punish statutory rape or other offenses against Victorian sexual codes.[30] Obviously, the cultural hegemony of the Victorian-Progressivist middle classes and the basic acceptance of this hegemony by lower-class people was undermined. The first two decades of the twentieth century were marked by a rapid decline of early modern standards of disciplined emotions and sexual conduct. This process was intertwined with the parallel rise of consumerist attitudes and the decline of a productionist world-view based on the assumptions of Fordism and Taylorism.

Two further points merit our attention: First, industrial productionism lost the overwhelming appeal it had had during the early Industrial Revolution. However, some of its specific necessities, such as the continuingly obliging character of self-control and self-discipline, survived and were superficially combined with the relaxed emotional protocols of consumerism.[31] Second, no matter how disturbing to the middle classes, the developments between 1900 and the 1920s were still based on an androcentric and penetrationist attitude toward sexuality. Moreover, the middle classes, fearing the advent of Bolshevik revolution and the quantitative rise of the working classes, tried to regain their cultural hegemony and reestablish a well-ordered society.[32] They viewed the impact of modernization on the traditional family (a rising number of divorces, nonmarital sexual relationships, new female lifestyles, and decreasing reproductive rates) as a moral decline.[33] Perhaps even more important was the effect of the Great Depression, which abruptly terminated the 1920s belief in consumerism[34] and individual libertarianism. It took American society about thirty years to regain its former confidence. Sudden change and an undercurrent of conservatism together engendered a stable discourse of orderliness.

Freudian Dogmas

All this provided the basis for an even more modern way of regulating human reproduction, safeguarding male dominance, and integrating sexual emotions into a framework of overall self-control, but without denying individualist hopes for sexual and emotional liberation. Between 1905 and 1933 Sigmund Freud and the orthodox-loyalist Freudian faction of psychoanalysts (Marie Bonaparte, Kurt Abraham, and Helene Deutsch) reforged the classical Victorian-Progressive narrative.[35] In so doing Freud and the Freudians lifted the bourgeois taboo on sexually explicit language. Consequently, sexuality turned into a central and legitimate subject matter of public and scientific debates. This suggested to many that Freudianism in its core was a liberating theory or—depending on one's point of view—an attack against traditional values. However, as far as the enforcement of sexual protocols was concerned, the Freudian solution of the problem of emotional self-control basically remained within the limits of conservatism. To a certain extent, it was even stricter than the familiar Victorian-Progressive mode of control. Freudian theory was based on the internal assent and individual participation of those concerned. As a result, Freudianism was not an external social control that guaranteed the self-disciplining of people, as they themselves became the main agents of their own adaptation to society. Individual liberation and individual self-control were fused into a single, indivisible process. This voluntary participation of individuals was made possible by the emphatic and deliberate insistence on the scientific and modern nature of Freudianism. At least according to the standards of the nineteenth century, Freudianism emerged as a sort of super-Progressivism, elaborate in its theory and practice, based on several sets of premises, and equally theoretically inspiring and practically sound.[36]

Freud and his disciples skillfully introduced elements of more traditional approaches into their own fresh insights. Positivism and evolutionary, environmentalist Social Darwinism shaped Freudianism's understanding of empirical analyses and scientific approaches.[37] Especially the three-step program of staged or sequential developmentalism that underlay Freud's entire theory of civilizing behavior and maturing sexuality was based on presumptions established by Auguste Comte, Herbert Spencer, and Charles Darwin.[38] These elements were combined with insights from the contemporary sexual sciences, such as, for instance, the writings of Richard von Krafft-Ebing and Havelock Ellis.[39] At least in the beginning, though, Freudianism lacked the specific indeterminacies that always guaranteed the scientific survival of Darwinism. Therefore, it had to be based on a certain dogmatism in order to establish itself as a science. Only later on, in the 1960s, did Freudianism become an undetermined world view.

Since the sciences of the late nineteenth and early twentieth centuries were based on developmentalism, female sexual identity was constructed around distinct developmental periods. Puberty was of outmost importance in forming female gender roles, at least according to Freud and his disciples.[40] In the vein of contemporary reductionism, Freud interpreted the female clitoris and the male penis in an organic analogy as homologous organs.[41] Based on empirical observation, he also concluded that prepubertal girls stimulated themselves sexually predominantly with help of the clitoris.

These two interpretations were combined with his theoretical insights. One of Freud's most prominent dogmatic beliefs was the concept of preadolescent bisexuality.[42] Freud defined clitoral orgasm as preadolescent, i.e., immature orgasm. By introducing developmentalism he and, even more importantly, Marie Bonaparte, were later able to buttress the theory that a mature woman had to experience vaginal orgasms in order to be mature, for only vaginal orgasms were mature orgasms. The development from clitoral to vaginal orgasms was not interpreted as a moral development from bad to good, but as a process from immature to mature, as a matter of emotional self-control. Clitoral orgasms, therefore, were childish and semi-male, symbols of a stalled development to the naturally or socially gendered self. According to Freud, the mature, vaginal sexuality, however, was the result of male penetration. While Freud, in marked contradiction to Victorian-Progressive discourse, did not believe in the myth of a lack of female passion, he nevertheless favored a combination of androcentric, penetrationist attitudes and the necessity of libidinal sublimation as an instrument of social discipline. This was quite important, because Freudianism actively shaped female gender expectations in a dramatically conservative way. Since women obviously lacked the civilizing effects of castration fear, they were less able to assimilate the fruits of an enlightened civilization and its culture. The dominance of men emerged as a byproduct of natural processes, while the necessities of sublimation and emotional self-control were of greater importance for women. The control of female passion was unavoidable in order to strengthen the progress and development of civilization. As a logical consequence, clitoral stimulation, whether in heterosexual or homosexual intercourse, was de facto outlawed. The misogynist character of this theory is hard to overlook.[43] In fact, the liberating elements of Freudianism seem more accidental against this substantial background of conformism. Freudian feminism has been struggling with these implications to this very day.[44] Even the standard pro-Freudian arguments, stressing the ingenious coherence and liberating effects of Freudianism, may not outweigh the overall impression of psychoanalysis as an integral part of a conservative backlash.[45]

None of Freud's basic assumptions were the result of sound empirical study—neither the clitoris-penis homology, nor the mature-immature scheme or the connection between castration fear, libidinal sublimation, and predisposition for or against civilization. While the clitoris-penis analogy was simply based on the common error grounded on a prima facie conclusion, which confused phenotypical analogy and functional homology,[46] the mature-immature scheme rested on implicit moral judgments from the Victorian era and on the deep belief in differing but uniform stages of the development of the individual and the species. The last two basic assumptions, castration fear and sublimation, were typical Freudian dogmas. But the integration of all factors into a coherent framework and the results of further research based on Freudian theory seemed fruitful and promising. At the very least, Freudianism provided the discussions about sexuality and emotional self-control in modern industrial societies with a purportedly scientific and useful basis that was much more complex than any competing account.

It would, nonetheless, be utterly wrong to assert the discursive hegemony of orthodox Freudianism in the United States after it had appeared in the early 1910s.[47] Quite the opposite was true. On the one hand, the results of World War I led to a more repressive mode of control. But this was not predominantly caused by Freudian theories. Yet the Victorian-Progressivist tradition of externalized legal regulation was still alive—as manifest, for example, when the movie industry was disciplined by the combined efforts of Progressivist reformers and Roman Catholic conservatives in 1923 and 1934. On the other hand, the spreading of orthodox Freudianism was severely hindered by the rise of cultural relativism, as propagated by cultural anthropology[48] at several American universities. Together, cultural relativism and cultural anthropology were able to transform Freudianism into a specifically American form of Neo-Freudianism that emphasized the cultural and social construction of identities.

Neo-Freudianism ardently opposed the naturalistic outlook of substantialist Freudian orthodoxy. Karen Horney was instrumental in this transformation. Hence, her "excommunication" by Freud and his disciples was not so dissimilar from the fate of Carl Gustav Jung, Wilhelm Reich, or Alfred Adler some years earlier.[49] A special case was Lou Andreas Salomé, whose sexual life opposed Freud's teachings in practice, even if she remained within the theoretical limits of her master.[50] Freudian orthodoxy increasingly developed into a church-like community with strictly enforced rules. Only after Freud's death in 1938 and the subsequent renaissance of Freudianism was orthodoxy able to regain lost ground. During the 1940s and 1950s, the theories of the Freudian school became inescapable for anybody who showed an interest in psychology, psychoanalysis, and questions of sexual behavior.[51] Even opponents had to take into account Freudian influences that reached as far as popular detective novels as well as Hollywood movies or textbooks on sexuality, childrearing, and marital problems.

Freudianism and Twentieth-Century Alternatives

Orthodox Freudianism may not have been the leading scientific approach, but it had effectively gained control of public discourses. Certainly, the dogmatic structure of Freudianism made its overall performance quite persuasive. However, it was never as dominant as the standard narrative of both Freudianism and radical feminism tend to make us believe. During the 1940s and 1950s, several other discourses rivaled for hegemony. One can name at least the following five different opinions.[52]

Orthodox Freudianism Stressing a Vaginally Centered Sexuality and Vaginal Orgasms

In the eyes of the Freudians, only male penetration caused a mature female sexuality. Thus any alternate form of sexual pleasure was interpreted as psychological disease. To be sure, Freud himself never openly propagated the doctrine of clitoral orgasm, but when his loyal disciple Marie Bonaparte introduced it into the discussions of the inner circle of Freudianism in 1932, Freud was still alive. In view of the Freudian school's authoritarian internal structure, it was therefore highly improbable that this was done without the agreement of her master. By reproducing the technicist approach of early nineteenth-century gynecologists, Bonaparte even went so far as to demand a transfer of the clitoris nearer to the vagina in order to combine the mature vaginal orgasm with the more intense yet immature pleasure of the clitoral orgasm. Modern surgical techniques provided the means to correct nature and to adapt human experiences to the conclusions of theory. Nevertheless, Bonaparte's position was the most radical one and never became the opinion of the school. But it dramatically symbolized the technicism and dogmaticism of the Freudians.[53]

Neo-Freudianism[54] with Its Emphasis on Cultural Relativism

Neo-Freudianism was based on the premises of a vaginally centered ideology, but without serious concern for the whole problem. In spite of cultural anthropology's findings, Neo-Freudians shared many of orthodoxy's fundamental assumptions. They merely tried to evade the substantialist naturalism and dogmaticism of Freudian theory,[55] but this was because their general interest concentrated on different problems, such as the cultural and social construction of the self or the social background of sexuality. The works of Margaret Mead on the seemingly liberal sexuality of Polynesian islanders were significant for this approach. Female sexuality was regularly interpreted within the conventional parameters of penetration, castration fear, and the mature-immature dichotomy. The Neo-Freudians were less technicist, less authoritarian, and less dogmatic than their Freudian rivals, without, however, managing to fundamentally question the premises of the orthodox view.

The Revolutionary, Antibourgeois, and Heterodox Marxist Approach

Wilhelm Reich,[56] while successfully adopting the premodern esteem for orgasms (male and female), was not really interested in the question of a hierarchy of orgasms. Reich considered vaginal stimulation the regular way of reaching an orgasm. But he never excluded the possibility of clitoral orgasms. Orgasm in itself was an aim and, on top of that, a means of revolution. The emotional power of orgasms, according to Reich, was an element of overcoming the prudery of bourgeois class society. This correlation between the bourgeois control of sexual arousal and the stability of conventional middle-class societies was a central element of Reich's criticism. Thus he put forth an argument that, later on among radical feminists, led to the qualification of the personal as the political and to the acceptance of revolutionary consequences. Reich's problem, however, was his idiosyncratic personality. The number of his disciples was extremely limited. Furthermore, the Marxism of Reich was counterproductive to the spreading of his sexual theories, and not only in the United States did anticommunists during the Cold War era denounce every attempt to promote Marxist analytic tools.[57] It was Marxism itself that was unable to comprehend the revolutionary impetus of Reich's thoughts. As long as Marxists, even anti-Stalinist ones, preferred to think along the lines of class struggle, the role of gender and sexuality was usually underestimated.[58] The analysis of the modes of production and of emotional control was never combined in a coherent theory. It was only a logical result of this structural dilemma that Michel Foucault, when he started focusing on sexual power relations, bitterly denounced Marxist approaches.[59] This in turn led to a one-sided standpoint, which excluded the intrinsic relationship between modes of production and sexual power relations. The richness of the fundamental insights of Reich was thus never put to use. Only during the 1960s did some members of the student protest movement think along the lines of the Reichian narrative, but they remained a minority.[60]

Mutual Consent–Mutual Pleasure Discourse

Some elements of the traditional, premodern mutual consent–mutual pleasure discourse had survived within the Judeo-Christian tradition, especially among Roman Catholic moral theology, whose impact shaped the sexual lives of millions of persons all over the world. This part of the story is usually forgotten, but Catholic traditionalism was nonetheless an influential element in shaping discourses even within modern industrial societies. It therefore was an integral part of the dialectics of modernity. However, traditionalism had two main problems that over the decades minimized its impact on discursive developments. On the one hand, only a shrinking number of adults in the United States and Europe accepted the rigid moral codes of the Catholic Church (and some Protestant denominations). After the encyclical *Humanae Vitae* of Pope Paul VI in 1968,[61] this number declined further. On the other hand, traditional religious discourse lacked an interest in the purely technical question of how to reach an orgasm. Sometimes the pleasures of orgasm in itself were denounced as sinful without regard for the way in which they were produced. Yet it was not emotions that were denounced by ecclesiastical authorities. Their teaching was not necessarily part of the ongoing attempt to control the emotions of producers and consumers. It was a much older tradition that tried to safeguard the stability of the church against sexual arousal, not against emotion in general. This predominantly Augustinian heritage made the church a rather weak but nonetheless existing rival for discursive hegemony. Interestingly, religious discourse was the only one that existed beyond the actual developments of the modes of production, because it was grounded in earlier rural traditions. This also intensified the problem of how the tenets of tradition could be communicated to secularized masses in an industrial society.

The Business of Sex Doctors

But the mutual consent–mutual pleasure discourse found its revival in a more modernized incarnation. Among the so-called sex doctors and in marital guides, some elements of preindustrial thought were reinterpreted.[62] In the end, it was this discourse that in combination with Reichian insights provided the basis for radical feminism and the orgasm debate of the 1970s.[63] This discourse ultimately ended the predominance of orthodox Freudianism because it served two different yet intertwined purposes.

First, the renewed mutual consent–mutual pleasure discourse was able to provide an enormous amount of empirical ammunition for its position. Therefore, it fit into the dominant picture of scientific research. It was even able to introduce cultural relativism into its own narrative. This allowed the discourse of the sex doctors to establish itself as a sound alternative to Freudianism. Second, mutual pleasure was an adequate position in a society that during the 1950s found its way back to consumerism.[64] By "scientifically proving" the acceptability of mutual pleasure in whatever way, sexuality could be transformed from a dangerous emotion that might potentially undermine the utilitarian productive efforts of a modern society into an element of consumption. The rising sex business became, more or less unintentionally, an integral part of modern consumer societies.[65] The dangers of sexuality were turned into a market of fun and leisure and thereby diminished in their critical function. Now, finally, politically irrelevant sexual fun overwhelmed passionate emotionality, but only after a period of intense politicization. The synthesis of this dialectic of transformation evolved during the 1970s.

This development had its roots in the 1920s, when sex doctors like Van der Velde emphasized the idea that female orgasm ought to be an integral part of a pleasing sexual act.[66] It was empiricist scientists such as Alfred C. Kinsey, William H. Masters, and Virginia Johnson Masters who continued to undermine the Freudian position by constructing a new narrative of orgasm that stressed a single point: there was but one orgasm.[67] During the 1950s a majority of orthodox Freudians already had to deal with the effects of their own therapeutic and personal sexual experiences. They had to acknowledge that about 90 percent of all female orgasms were clitorally stimulated. Gradually practical experience overwhelmed theory. But still, Freudians rejected women's search for sexual relief. They told them that their wishes were nothing but neurotic. When Masters and Johnson were able to prove the unity of orgasm and the central role of clitoral stimulation in this unified orgasm, Freudianism had to withdraw because ultimately Freudians and the sex doctors shared the same scientific beliefs in empiricism. Consequently, in 1960 and 1967 the Freudian loyalists Helene Deutsch and Mary Jane Sherfy, and even Marie Bonaparte, officially renounced the Freudian dogma,[68] years before radical feminists politicized the new insights. With the unintentional help of radical feminism, the results of the doctors' discourse became even more popular than before. Nonetheless, some changes were less dramatic. The doctors and radical feminists still shared some common features. The focus of both was on mere techniques. This was a legacy of the 1950s and 1960s modernist emphasis on technology and scientifically planned progress. Only in the burnout phase of the 1970s did the mutual consent–mutual pleasure discourse develop its emotional impact.[69]

This temporal integration of a de-emotionalized, pleasuring sexuality into the liberal-capitalist consumer society of the 1970s and 1980s requires an explanation, considering the failure of the same project in the 1920s. Perhaps the reevaluation of female passion and female sexuality was only possible because the consumer society of the 1970s was much more stable than that of the 1920s. Even the economic crisis of 1973 did not affect the overall process. Again, we can speculate that this stability was made possible by a long-term change in the modes of production from the Second Industrial Revolution to the so-called information society with its consumerist implications. Fully developed consumerism, though, depended heavily on the results of former productionism. Only because the majority of people in the Western world had deeply internalized the strict discipline that nineteenth- and early twentieth-century industrial production had imposed upon them (emotional self-control, accepting time regulations, school education), the often involuntary liberalization of emotional codes became bearable. Hence a less powerful mode of internal and external discipline seemed in order.

Another factor was of utmost importance: Thanks to the newly invented contraceptive methods of the 1960s, birth-control pills, it became possible to effectively separate sexuality from reproduction.[70] Therefore the utilitarian lack of efficiency that had reduced the importance and function of female orgasms in the nineteenth century could be overcome. The modes of reproduction were no longer the focus of sexuality. Within the broader context of consumerism, female joy of sex had regained a function and the vaginal-penetrationist standpoint had lost its utility, since it was unable to guarantee mutual satisfaction. Penetration even lost its significance for reproduction. Any new hierarchy of orgasms—male-penetrationist, female-penetrationist, and female-nonpenetrationist—lost its purpose, as long as sexual emotion formed part of an overall consumerist attitude. However, the penetrationist attitude still dominated male discourses on female sexuality. It was believed to be the "real thing."[71]

This essay raises some methodological issues about the usefulness of Foucault's discourse analysis.[72] With regard to social constructionism, Wendy Hollway recently posed the question of how the social construction of identity works within a system of pluralistic discourses.[73] This question can be reframed: How is it possible to explain the hegemonic shift between rivaling discourses? What are the principles and agents of these shifts? It is theoretically unsatisfactory to artificially unify different and contradictory discourses into a single superdiscourse with several smaller subdiscourses. This would only postpone the problem. One could argue within a Foucaultian framework[74] that the search for the underlying principles of discursive shifts may in fact be the search for a cause, something that modern and postmodern epistemology rule out. However, discourse analysis and genealogy want to describe discursive shifts. Otherwise they would present a rather static world view. Therefore, on a basic level, one needs at least noncausal principles of change, because a mere description of change logically needs to be informed by the knowledge that there is a change. Yet this knowledge depends on the knowledge of the underlying principles. But there is no reasonable way that would allow us to distinguish between noncausal principles and causes in a strict fashion.[75]

I propose to try to solve this methodological and logical problem by generally reintroducing causal principles into discourse analysis. Moreover, this can be done specifically in a twofold manner: First, with regard to our specific problem, it seems to be necessary to combine discursive analysis with elements of a structural, socioeconomic analysis of modes of production that may serve as general principles of change,[76] a *causa remota*. Second, it is also necessary to reintroduce the experiences of individual, free-willed actors, that serve as agents of specific change. Only personal agents can make a choice between rivaling discourses and can explain specific singular changes in form of a *causa proxima*. This combination of a text-oriented yet non-Foucaultian discourse analysis; a modified, structural interpretation, whether Marxist or not; and a history of individual agents and their specific experiences[77] might become a fruitful concept for further research in the field of gender studies. In particular, the history of emotions and the history of experiences, as long as they include individual agents, enable a more synthetic interpretation of discursive shifts and rivaling discourses.[78]

Notes

1. Sue Scott and Stevi Jackson, "Sexual Skirmishes and Feminist Factions: Seventy-Five Years of Debate on Women and Sexuality," in *Feminism and Sexuality: A Reader,* ed. Stevi Jackson and Sue Scott (New York: Columbia University Press, 1996), 12–13.
2. Male orgasm has as yet not been subject to intense research. Neither male nor feminist scholarship is overly interested in this issue. Cf. for example George L. Mosse, *The Image of Man: The Creation of Modern Masculinity* (New York: Oxford University Press, 1996), or Michael Kimmel, *Manhood in America: A Cultural History* (New York: Free Press, 1996).
3. Mary Jo Buhle, *Feminism and Its Discontents: A Century of Struggle with Psychoanalysis* (Cambridge, MA: Harvard University Press, 1998), 212–20.
4. Todd Gitlin, *The Sixties: Years of Hope, Days of Rage,* 3rd ed. (New York: Bantam Books, 1993), 108–9, 362–76.
5. Scott and Jackson, "Sexual Skirmishes," 1–6.
6. This attitude had had a precursor in the post–World War I "cult of the clitoris and sexual passion," cf. Angus McLaren, *Twentieth-Century Sexuality: A History* (Oxford: Blackwell, 1999), 9–22. This cult, however, was based on fear of a further decline of traditionalist meanings of sexuality. Penetrationism signifies an ideology that defines sexuality exclusively by the male penetration of the female vagina, an idea that can be traced back to both classical antiquity and early Christianity.
7. For a critique of a possible feminist essentialism see Andrea Dworkin, "Biological Superiority: The World's Most Dangerous and Deadly Idea," in Jackson and Scott, *Feminism and Sexuality,* 57–61; cf. further in Diane Richardson, "Constructing Lesbian Sexualities," in ibid., 276–86, and Jackson, "Social Construction," in ibid., 62–65. Cf. Jeffrey Weeks, *Sexuality* (London: Routledge, 1986), 11–31. For a critique of social constructionism see Richard Norton, *The Myth of the Modern Homosexual: Queer History and the Search for Cultural Unity* (London: Cassell, 1997), 6–32. Cf. moreover Arlene Stein, *Shameless: Sexual Dissidence in American Culture* (New York: New York University Press, 2006).
8. With regard to the internal distinctions of the women's liberation movement, I follow Rosemarie Tong, *Feminist Thought: A Comprehensive Introduction* (Boulder, CO: Westview, 1989), 71–138.
9. Buhle, *Feminism,* 218–33.

10. Cf. Alan Hunt, *Governing Morals: A Social History of Moral Regulation* (Cambridge: Cambridge University Press, 1999), 57–139.
11. Cf. in general Peter Gay, *The Bourgeois Experience: Victoria to Freud*, vol. 2: *The Tender Passion* (New York: Oxford University Press, 1982); see additionally Anthony Giddens, *The Transformation of Intimacy: Sexuality, Love, and Eroticism in Modern Societies* (Stanford, CA: Stanford University Press, 1992), 38–47.
12. Cf. William Leach, *True Love and Perfect Union: The Feminist Reform of Sex and Society* (New York: Basic Books, 1980).
13. Leah Otis-Court, *Lust und Liebe: Geschichte der Paarbeziehungen im Mittelalter* (Frankfurt am Main: Fischer, 2000), 103–6.
14. Sabine Zur Nieden, *Weibliche Ejakulation: Variationen zu einem uralten Streit der Geschlechter* (Stuttgart: Ferdinand Enke, 1994), 39–49; cf. as well Jack Larkin, *The Reshaping of Everyday Life, 1790–1840* (New York: HarperPerennial, 1988), 191–203; on the regulational aspects of early modern sexuality see Merril D. Smith, ed., *Sex and Sexuality in Early America* (New York: New York University Press, 1998), or Albert L. Hurtado, *Intimate Frontiers: Sex, Gender, and Culture in Old California* (Albuquerque: University of New Mexico Press, 1999).
15. Cf. for instance Heinrich Denzinger and Peter Hünermann, eds., *Enchiridion symbolorum, definitionum et declarationum de rebus fidei et morum,* 38th ed. (Freiburg im Breisgau: Herder, 1999), 765–66, 773–74, 809–10, 846–49, 990, 1007–21.
16. Carl N. Degler, *At Odds: Women and the Family in America from the Revolution to the Present* (Oxford: Oxford University Press, 1981), 251.
17. The original intention of the teaching of the church was the attempt to evade the radical asceticism of dualistic heresies and the libertarianism of parts of ancient pagan society. The church was interpreted as the *tertium gentis* based on a specific morale, that could include a moderate asceticism and sexual relationships among married couples, cf. Aline Rousselle, *Der Ursprung der Keuschheit* (Stuttgart: Kreuz Verlag, 1989), and Peter Brown, *The Body and the Society: Men, Women, and Sexual Renunciation in Early Christianity* (New York: Columbia University Press, 1988).
18. Cf. James H. Cassidy, *Medicine in America: A Short History* (Baltimore: Johns Hopkins University Press, 1991), 67–95; G. J. Barker-Benfield, *The Horrors of the Half-Known Life: Male Attitudes toward Women and Sexuality in Nineteenth-Century America,* 2nd ed. (New York: Routledge, 2000), 82–90; Degler, *At Odds*, 254–57.
19. Zur Nieden, *Weibliche Ejakulation*, 38. Cf. Michael Foucault, *Sexualität und Wahrheit,* vol. 1: *Der Wille zum Wissen* (Frankfurt am Main: Suhrkamp, 1998).
20. Primarily intense erotic companionships between women served as a residual zone of a specific female sexuality, cf. Sheila Jeffreys, "Women's Friendships and Lesbianism," in Jackson and Scott, *Feminism and Sexuality,* 46–53.The other opposition against the Victorian-Progressivist interpretation of sexuality rose from working-class women, immigrants, undisciplined bourgeois *bohèmes,* and, in particular, from utopian "free-love" partisans, that combined traditional antinomism with anti-industrialist attitudes, cf. Ronald G. Walters, *American Reformers, 1815–1860* (New York: Hill and Wang, 1978), 39–75, 145–92; Steven Mintz, *Moralists and Modernizers: America's Pre-Civil War Reformers* (Baltimore: Johns Hopkins University Press, 1995), and Barbara Goldsmith, *Other Powers: The Age of Suffrage, Spiritualism, and the Scandalous Victoria Woodhull* (New York: Alfred A. Knopf, 1998).
21. Thomas J. Schlereth, *Victorian America: Transformations in Everyday Life, 1876–1915* (New York: HarperCollins, 1991), 245; Degler, *At Odds,* 260–70.
22. John Whiteclay Chambers, *The Tyranny of Change: America in the Progressive Era, 1890–1920,* 2nd ed. (New York: St. Martin's Press, 1992), 1–172.

23. Cf. in general Daniel E. Sutherland, *The Expansion of Everyday Life, 1860–1876* (Fayetteville: University of Arkansas Press, 1989), 111–17. For a more positive evaluation of the heritage of Progressivism see Ellis W. Hawley, *The Great War and the Search for a Modern Order: A History of the American People and Their Institutions, 1917–1933*, 2nd ed. (New York: St. Martin's Press, 1992), 11–12; Stanley Coben, *Rebellion against Victorianism: The Impetus for Cultural Change in 1920s America* (New York: Oxford University Press, 1991), 3–35. See Giddens, *Transformation*, 18–34; Barker-Benfield, *Horrors*, 182–83, 203. The most vivid example of the regulatory power of Victorian-Progressivism is certainly Anthony Comstock, cf. Jesse F. Battan, "The Word Made Flesh: Language, Authority, and Sexual Desire in Late Nineteenth-Century America," in *Journal of the History of Sexuality* 3 (1992): 223–44.
24. Cobden, *Rebellion*, 91–111; Alun Munslow, *Discourse and Culture: The Creation of America, 1870–1920* (London: Routledge, 1992), 89–109.
25. Rachel P. Maines, *The Technology of Orgasm: 'Hysteria', the Vibrator, and Women's Sexual Satisfaction* (Baltimore: Johns Hopkins University Press, 1998), 1–2. Problematically, Maines tends to homogenize the causal structures of this change with the help of a single Foucaultian power discourse stressing the link between power and penetration, ibid., 3–7.
26. Giddens, *Transformation*, 21–22; Maines, *Technology*, 21–47.
27. Barker-Benfield, *Horrors*, 24–32, 125–26.
28. Sharon R. Ullman, *Sex Seen: The Emergence of Modern Sexuality in America* (Berkeley: University of California Press, 1997), 4–5.
29. Molly Haskell, *From Reverence to Rape: The Treatment of Women in the Movies*, 2nd ed. (Chicago: University of Chicago Press, 1987), 42–152.
30. Françoise Thébaud, ed., *Geschichte der Frauen: 20. Jahrhundert* (Frankfurt am Main: Büchergilde Gutenberg, 1995), 96–99; Ullman, *Sex Seen*, 18–44.
31. Cf. for example William Leach, *Land of Desire: Merchants, Power, and the Rise of a New American Culture* (New York: Vintage Books, 1993); Schlereth, *Victorian America*, 140–67; Michael Kammen, *American Cultures, American Tastes: Social Change in the 20th Century* (New York: Basic Books, 1999), 47–70, 162–241.
32. Thébaud, *Frauen*, 55–96, and Mark Mazower, *Der dunkle Kontinent: Europa im 20. Jahrhundert* (Berlin: Alexander Fest, 2000), 140–42.
33. Ullman, *Sex Seen*, 72–100; Buhle, *Feminism*, 91–92.
34. Cf. David M. Kennedy, *Freedom from Fear: The American People in Depression and War, 1929–1945* (New York: Oxford University Press, 1999), 122–23, 354–58; Harvey Green, *The Uncertainty of Everyday Life, 1915–1945* (Fayetteville: University of Arkansas Press, 1992), 128–35; Gerald D. Nash, *The Crucial Era: The Great Depression and World War II, 1929–1945*, 2nd ed. (New York: St. Martin's Press, 1992), 10–25; more specifically Buhle, *Feminism*, 121.
35. Jackson, "Social Construction," 65–68; Maines, *Technology*, 42–47, 52–65. Maines explicitly distinguishes the development in the Freud-dominated United States from that of France, where clinical psychology survived the Freudian attack.
36. Buhle, *Feminism*, 1–4. For a more positive account of the impact of Freudian psychoanalysis as a liberating ideology of the modern era cf. Eli Zaretsky, *Freuds Jahrhundert. Die Geschichte der Psychoanalyse* (Wien: Paul Zsolnay Verlag, 2006), 65–96. Zaretsky, however, evades the issue of the female orgasm.
37. Cf. Carl N. Degler, *In Search of Human Nature: The Decline and Revival of Darwinism in American Thought* (New York: Oxford University Press, 1991), 105–10, Buhle, *Feminism*, 4–11, 29–35.
38. For instance Mike Hawkins, *Social Darwinism in European and American Thought, 1860–1945: Nature as Model and Nature as Threat* (Cambridge: Cambridge University

Press, 1997), 21–38. Cf. further in Richard Hofstadter, *Social Darwinism in American Thought,* 4th ed. (Boston: Beacon Press, 1992), 31–66.

39. Ullman, *Sex Seen,* 49; Buhle, *Feminism,* 36–37.
40. Sigmund Freud, *Drei Abhandlungen zur Sexualtheorie und verwandte Schriften,* 3rd ed. (Frankfurt am Main: Fischer, 1965), 169–86; Nancy J. Chodorow, *Feminities, Masculinities, Sexualities: Freud and Beyond* (Lexington: University of Kentucky Press, 1994), 1–32.
41. Freud himself was much more interested in male than in female sexuality. Cf. Buhle, *Feminism,* 30–31.
42. Ibid., 31–35.
43. John Heidenry, *What Wild Ecstasy: The Rise and Fall of the Sexual Revolution* (New York: Simon & Schuster, 1997), 17; Luce Irigaray, "The Sex Which Is Not One," in Jackson and Scott, *Feminism and Sexuality,* 79–83; Koedt, "Vaginal Orgasm," in ibid., 112–13; Carolyn Heilbrun, *The Education of a Woman: The Life of Gloria Steinem* (New York: Dial Press, 1995), 406.
44. Tong, *Feminist Thought,* 139–72; Thébaud, *Frauen,* 298–300.
45. For an opposite viewpoint cf. Estelle Roith, *The Riddle of Freud: Jewish Influences on his Theory of Female Sexuality* (London: Tavistock Publications, 1987), 18–35.
46. Zur Nieden, *Weibliche Ejakulation,* 5, 24.
47. Gert Raeithel, *Geschichte der Nordamerikanischen Kultur,* vol. 2: *Vom Bürgerkrieg bis zum New Deal, 1860–1930* (Weinheim: Parkland, 1988), 556–58; Buhle, *Feminism,* 86–90 and 99–111.
48. Degler, *Search of Human Nature,* 113–38.
49. Edith Seiffert, *Was will das Weib? Zu Begehren und Lust bei Freud und Lacan* (Weinheim: Quadriga, 1987), 60.
50. Roith, *Riddle of Freud,* 40–49.
51. Buhle, *Feminism,* 123–64.
52. Cf. for example David Allyn, *Make Love, Not War: The Sexual Revolution, An Unfettered History* (New York: Little, Brown, 2000), and Beth Bailey, *Sex in the Heartland* (Cambridge, MA: Harvard University Press, 1999).
53. Cf. Giddens, *Transformations,* 124–32; a more positive view is presented by Seiffert, *Was will das Weib?* 16–56. With regard to a Lacanian reinterpretation of Freud cf. ibid., 96–120, and Jacqueline Rose: "Feminine Sexuality," in Jackson and Scott, *Feminism and Sexuality,* 74–78.
54. Gert Raeithel, *Geschichte der nordamerikanischen Kultur,* vol. 3: *Vom New Deal bis zur Gegenwart, 1930–1988* (Weinheim: Parkland, 1988), 245–48; Buhle, *Feminism,* 52–84.
55. Scott and Jackson, "Sexual Skirmishes," in Jackson and Scott, *Feminism and Sexuality,* 6–12; Ann Oakley, "Sexuality," in ibid., 35–39.
56. Wilhelm Reich, *Die sexuelle Revolution: Zur charakterlichen Selbststeuerung des Menschen,* 3rd ed. (Frankfurt am Main: Europäische Verlagsanstalt, 1969), and Wilhelm Reich, *Der Einbruch der sexuellen Zwangsmoral: Zur Geschichte der sexuellen Ökonomie,* 2nd ed. (Köln: Kiepenheuer & Witsch, 1995). Cf. Thébaud, *Frauen,* 263–65, 301–6.
57. Cf. Richard Gid Powers, *Not Without Honor: The History of American Anticommunism* (New Haven, CT: Yale University Press, 1998).
58. Cf. Tong, *Feminist Thought,* 61–70.
59. *Mikrophysik der Macht: Michel Foucault über Strafjustiz, Psychiatrie und Medizin* (Berlin: Merve Verlag, 1976), 105–13.
60. John Heidenry, *What Wild Exstasy: The Rise and Fall of the Sexual Revolution* (New York: Simon and Schuster, 1997), 171.

61. Denzinger and Hünermann, *Enchiridion,* 1348–52. With regard to the Catholic position on lust, arousal, and sexuality cf. Randall G. Colston, "Simon Blackburn and John Paul II on Lust and Chastity," in *The Thomist* 70, no. 1 (January 2006): 71–101.
62. Heidenry, *Exstasy,* 17–65; Zur Nieden, *Weibliche Ejakulation,* 74–89.
63. It may be possible, though, to interpret the so-called discovery of the G-spot by Gräfenberg in 1946 as an attempted penetrationist backlash. Cf. Zur Nieden, *Weibliche Ejakulation,* 47–56.
64. Cf. for example Joan Jacobs Brumberg, *The Body Project: An Intimate History of American Girls* (New York: Vintage Books, 1997), 208–9. A critical, but multifaceted review of the 1950s is presented by Joanne Meyerowitz, "Beyond the *Feminine Mystique*: A Reassessment of Post War Mass Culture, 1946–1958," in *Not June Cleaver: Women and Gender in Postwar America, 1945–1960,* ed. Joanne Meyerowitz (Philadelphia: Temple University Press, 1994), 292–62, and Donna Penn, "The Sexualized Women: The Lesbian, the Prostitute, and the Containment of Female Sexuality in Postwar America," in ibid., 358–81. Empirical data on female orgasms in consumerist society can be found in Malcolm Potts and Roger Short, *Ever since Adam and Eve: The Evolution of Human Society* (Cambridge: Cambridge University Press, 1999), 108.
65. On modern consumerism in the 1960s see David Steigerwald, *The Sixties and the End of Modern America* (New York: St. Martin's Press, 1995), 2, 8; James T. Patterson, *Grand Expectations: The United States, 1945–1974* (New York: Oxford University Press, 1996), 343–74, 784–89; William H. Chafe, *The Unfinished Journey: America Since World War II,* 4th ed., (New York: Oxford University Press, 1999), 117–22. Cf. also Dominique Puenzieux and Brigitte Ruckstuhl, *Medizin, Moral und Sexualität: Die Bekämpfung der Geschlechtskrankheiten Syphilis und Gonorrhöe in Zürich, 1870–1920* (Zürich: Chronos, 1994), 23–28.
66. Even before that, during the 1890s, some physicians started to base their accounts of sexuality on an empirical foundation, such as, for instance, Elisabeth Blackwell. The most famous empirical study was the Mosher Survey. Cf. Mary-Beth Norton and Ruth M. Alexander, eds., *Major Problems in American Women's History: Documents and Essays,* 2nd ed. (Lexington, MA: D. C. Heath, 1996), 222–28.
67. McLaren, *Sexuality,* 144–47, 176–78.
68. Mary Jane Sherfy, *The Nature and Evolution of Female Sexuality,* 3rd ed. (New York: Vintage Books, 1973), 14–29. By stressing the evolutionist, nonessentialist impact on the whole theory, Sherfy and Deutsch made the transformation (and survival) of Freudianism into a liberationist discourse possible.
69. Giddens, *Transformation,* 9–13.
70. Ibid., 83; Scott and Jackson, "Sexual Skirmishes", 3–6; McLaren, *Sexuality,* 167–76.
71. Maines, *Technology,* xiii–xiv.
72. Cf. for example Greg Ostrander, "Foucault's Disappearing Body," in *Body Invaders: Sexuality and Postmodern Condition,* ed. Arthur and Marieluise Kroker (London: Macmillan Education, 1988), 169–78. A useful introduction is Andrea D. Bührmann, "Geschlecht und Subjektivierung," in *Michel Foucault: Eine Einführung in sein Denken,* ed. Marcus S. Kleiner (Frankfurt am Main: Campus, 2001), 123–36.
73. Wendy Holloway, "Gender Difference and the Production of Subjectivity," in Jackson and Scott, eds., *Feminism and Sexuality,* 84–100; cf. Joseph Boone, *Libidinal Currents: Sexuality and the Shaping of Modernity* (Chicago: University of Chicago Press, 1998), 1–9.
74. For a critique of the Foucaultian standpoint see Giddens, *Transformation,* 181–82. Even more precise is James N. Davidson, *Kurtisanen und Meeresfrüchte: Die verzehrenden Leidenschaften im klassischen Athen* (Darmstadt: Wissenschaftliche Buchgesellschaft, 1999), 192–216, who points out the implausible character of Foucault's ahistorical argu-

mentation concerning the universal structure of penetrationist power relations under the circumstances of the Greek culture of the fourth century BC.

75. Foucault's concept of power is an example of a noncausal principle and the problems resulting from this approach. It is comparable with Schopenhauer's concept of the will. In both cases the connection between the fundamental concept and any discursive or phenomenal activity is less than obvious. Moreover, even the relation between Power and Will and acts (or discourses) of power and will is not precisely intelligible. Therefore, the two concepts tend to fade away into the thin air of metaphysics.
76. Cf. for example Munslow, *Discourse and Culture,* 1–67.
77. Cf. the rather elaborate account by Jackson, "Social Construction," 72; Giddens, *Transformation,* 1, 25–34; Jutta Nowosatko, "Erfahrung als Methode und als Gegenstand wissenschaftlicher Erkenntnis: Der Begriff der Erfahrung in der Soziologie," in *Die Erfahrung des Krieges: Erfahrungsgeschichtliche Perspektiven von der Französischen Revolution bis zum Zweiten Weltkrieg,* ed. Nikolaus Buschmann and Horst Carl (Paderborn: Schöningh, 2001), 27–50; Aribert Reimann, "Semantiken der Kriegserfahrung und historische Diskursanalyse: Britische Soldaten an der Westfront des Ersten Weltkrieges," in ibid., 173–94.
78. Heilbrun, *Education,* 374; Thébaud, *Frauen,* 575–76. A good example may be Ute Planert, "Der dreifache Körper des Volkes: Sexualität, Biopolitik und die Wissenschaft vom Leben," in *Geschichte und Gesellschaft* 26, no. 4 (2000): 539–76.

Bibliography

Allyn, David. *Make Love, Not War: The Sexual Revolution, An Unfettered History.* New York: Little, Brown, 2000.

Bailey, Beth. *Sex in the Heartland.* Cambridge, MA: Harvard University Press, 1999.

Barker-Benfield, G. J. *The Horrors of the Half-Known Life: Male Attitudes toward Women in Nineteenth-Century America.* 2nd ed. New York: Routledge, 2000.

Battan, Jesse F. "The Word Made Flesh: Language, Authority, and Sexual Desire in Late Nineteenth-Century America," in *Journal of the History of Sexuality* 3 (1992): 223–44.

Boone, Joseph. *Libidinal Currents: Sexuality and the Shaping of Modernity.* Chicago: University of Chicago Press, 1998.

Brown, Peter. *The Body and the Society: Men, Women, and Sexual Renunciation in Early Christianity.* New York: Columbia University Press, 1988.

Brumberg, Joan J. *The Body Project: An Intimate History of American Girls.* New York: Vintage Books, 1997.

Buhle, Mary Jo. *Feminism and Its Discontents: A Century of Struggle with Psychoanalysis.* Cambridge, MA: Harvard University Press, 1998.

Buschmann, Nikolaus and Horst Carl, eds. *Die Erfahrung des Krieges: Erfahrungsgeschichtliche Perspektiven von der Französischen Revolution bis zum Zweiten Weltkrieg.* Paderborn: Schöningh, 2001.

Cassidy, James H. *Medicine in America: A Short History.* Baltimore: Johns Hopkins University Press, 1991.

Chafe, William H. *The Unfinished Journey: America since World War II,* 4th ed. New York: Oxford University Press, 1999.

Chambers, John W. *The Tyranny of Change: America in the Progressive Era, 1890–1920,* 2nd ed. New York: St. Martin's Press, 1992.

Chodorow, Nancy J. *Femininities, Masculinities, and Sexualities: Freud and Beyond.* Lexington: University of Kentucky Press, 1994.

Coben, Stanley. *Rebellion against Victorianism: The Impetus for Cultural Change in 1920s America.* New York: Oxford University Press, 1991.

Colston, Randall G. "Simon Blackburn and John Paul II on Lust and Charity." *The Thomist* 70, no. 1 (January 2006): 71–101.

Davidson, James N. *Kurtisanen und Meeresfrüchte: Die verzehrenden Leidenschaften im klassischen Athen.* Darmstadt: Wissenschaftliche Buchgesellschaft, 1999.

Degler, Carl N. *At Odds: Women and the Family in America from the Revolution to the Present.* Oxford: Oxford University Press, 1981.

———. *In Search of Human Nature: The Decline and Revival of Darwinism in American Thought.* New York: Oxford University Press, 1991.

Denzinger, Heinrich, and Peter Hünermann, eds. *Enchiridion symbolorum, definitionum et declarationum de rebus fidei et morum,* 38th ed. Freiburg im Breisgau: Herder, 1999.

Dülmen, Richard van. *Kultur und Alltag in der Frühen Neuzeit.* 3 vols. Munich: Verlag C. H. Beck, 1999.

Foucault, Michel. *Mikrophysik der Macht: Michael Foucault über Strafjustiz, Psychiatrie und Medizin.* Berlin: Merve Verlag, 1976.

———. *Sexualität und Wahrheit.* 3 vols. Frankfurt am Main: Suhrkamp, 1998.

Freud, Siegmund. *Drei Abhandlungen zur Sexualtheorie und verwandte Schriften.* 3rd ed. Frankfurt am Main: Fischer, 1965.

Gay, Peter. *The Bourgeois Experience: Victoria to Freud,* 2 vols. New York: Oxford University Press, 1982.

Giddens, Anthony. *The Transformation of Intimacy: Sexuality, Love, and Eroticism in Modern Societies.* Stanford: Stanford University Press, 1992.

Gitlin, Todd. *The Sixties: Years of Hope, Days of Rage.* 3rd ed. New York: Bantam Books, 1993.

Goldsmith, Barbara. *Other Powers: The Age of Suffrage, Spiritualism, and the Scandalous Victoria Woodhull.* New York: Alfred A. Knopf, 1998.

Green, Harvey. *The Uncertainty of Everyday Life, 1915–1945.* Fayetteville: University of Arkansas Press, 1992.

Haskell, Molly. *From Reverence to Rape: The Treatment of Women in the Movies,* 2nd ed. Chicago: University of Chicago Press, 1987.

Hawkins, Mike. *Social Darwinism in European and American Thought, 1860–1945: Nature as Model and Nature as Threat.* Cambridge: Cambridge University Press, 1997.

Hawley, Ellis W. *The Great War and the Search for a Modern Order: A History of the American People and Their Institutions, 1917–1933,* 2nd ed. New York: St. Martin's Press, 1992.

Heidenry, John. *What Wild Exstasy: The Rise and Fall of the Sexual Revolution.* New York: Simon and Schuster, 1997.

Heilbrun, Carolyn. *The Education of a Woman: The Life of Gloria Steinem.* New York: Dial Press, 1995.

Hofstadter, Richard. *Social Darwinism in American Thought,* 4th ed. Boston: Beacon Press, 1992.

Hunt, Alan. *Governing Morals: A Social History of Moral Regulation.* Cambridge: Cambridge University Press, 1999.

Hurtado, Albert L. *Intimate Frontiers: Sex, Gender, and Culture in Old California.* Albuquerque: University of New Mexico Press, 1999.

Jackson, Stevi and Sue Scott, eds. *Feminism and Sexuality: A Reader.* New York, Columbia University Press, 1996.

Kammen, Michael. *American Cultures, American Tastes: Social Change in the 20th Century.* New York: Basic Books, 1999.

Kennedy, David M. *Freedom from Fear: The American People in Depression and War, 1929–1945.* New York: Oxford University Press, 1999.

Kimmel, Michael. *Manhood in America: A Cultural History.* New York: Free Press,1996.

Kleiner, Markus S., ed. *Michael Foucault: Eine Einführung in sein Denken.* Frankfurt am Main: Campus, 2001.

Koedt, Anne. "The Myth of the Vaginal Orgasm." In *Feminism and Sexuality: A Reader,* edited by Stevi Jackson and Sue Scott, New York: Columbia University Press, 1996.

Kroker, Arthur, and Marieluise Kroker, eds. *Body Invaders: Sexuality and Postmodern Condition.* London: Macmillan Education, 1988.

Larkin, Jack. *The Reshaping of Everyday Life, 1790–1840.* New York: HarperPerennial, 1988.

Leach, William. *True Love and Perfect Union: The Feminist Reform of Sex and Society.* New York: Basic Books, 1980.

———. *Land of Desire: Merchants, Power, and the Rise of a New American Culture.* New York: Vintage Books, 1993.

Lexikon der Psychologie, 3 vols. (1993).

McLaren, Angus. *Twentieth-Century Sexuality: A History.* Oxford: Blackwell, 1999.

Maines, Rachel P. *The Technology of Orgasm: 'Hysteria', the Vibrator, and Women's Sexual Satisfaction.* Baltimore: Johns Hopkins University Press, 1998.

Mazower, Mark. *Der dunkle Kontinent: Europa im 20. Jahrhundert.* Berlin: Alexander Fest, 2000.

Meyerowitz, Joanne, ed. *Not June Cleaver: Women and Gender in Postwar America, 1945–1960.* Philadelphia: Temple University Press, 1994.

Mintz, Steven. *Moralists and Modernizers: America's Pre-Civil War Reformers.* Baltimore: Johns Hopkins University Press, 1995.

Mosse, George L. *The Image of Man: The Creation of Modern Masculinity.* New York: Oxford University Press, 1996.

Munslow, Alun. *Discourse and Culture: The Creation of America, 1870–1920.* London: Routledge, 1992.

Nash, Gerald D. *The Crucial Era: The Great Depression and World War II, 1929–1945,* 2nd ed. New York: St. Martin's Press, 1992.

Norton, Mary-Beth, and Ruth M. Alexander, eds. *Major Problems in American Women's History,* 2nd ed. Lexington, MA: D. C. Heath, 1996.

Norton, Richard. *The Myth of the Modern Homosexual: Queer History and the Search for Cultural Unity.* London: Cassell, 1997.

Otis-Court, Leah. *Lust und Liebe: Geschichte der Paarbeziehungen im Mittelalter.* Frankfurt am Main: Fischer, 2000.

Patterson, James T. *Grand Expectations: The United States, 1945–1974.* New York: Oxford University Press, 1996.

Planert, Ute. "Der dreifache Körper des Volkes: Sexualität, Biopolitik und die Wissenschaft vom Leben." In *Geschichte und Gesellschaft* 26, no. 4 (2000); 539–76.

Potts, Malcolm, and Roger Short. *Ever since Adam and Eve: The Evolution of Human Society.* Cambridge: Cambridge University Press, 1999.

Powers, Richard G. *Not Without Honor: The History of American Anticommunism.* New Haven, CT: Yale University Press, 1998.

Puenzieux, Dominique, and Brigitte Ruckstuhl. *Medizin, Moral und Sexualität: Die Bekämpfung der Geschlechtskrankheiten Syphilis und Gonorrhöe in Zürich, 1870–1920.* Zürich: Chronos, 1994.

Raeithel, Gerd. *Geschichte der Nordamerikanischen Kultur.* 3 vols. Weinheim: Parkland, 1988.

Reich, Wilhelm. *Die sexuelle Revolution: Zur charakterlichen Selbststeuerung des Menschen.* 3rd ed. Frankfurt am Main: Europäische Verlagsanstalt, 1969.

———. *Der Einbruch der sexuellen Zwangsmoral: Zur Geschichte der sexuellen Ökonomie,* 2nd ed. Köln: Kiepenheuer & Witsch, 1995.

Roith, Estelle. *The Riddle of Freud: Jewish Influences on his Theory of Female Sexuality.* London: Tavistock Publications, 1987.

Rouselle, Aline. *Der Ursprung der Keuschheit.* Stuttgart: Kreuz Verlag, 1989.

Schlereth, Thomas J. *Victorian America: Transformations in Everyday Life, 1876–1915.* New York: HarperCollins, 1991.

Seiffert, Edith. *Was will das Weib? Zu Begehren und Lust bei Freud und Lacan.* Weinheim: Quadriga, 1987.

Sherfy, Mary J. *The Nature and Evolution of Female Sexuality,* 3rd ed. New York: Vintage Books, 1973.

Smith, Merril D., ed. *Sex and Sexuality in Early America.* New York: New York University Press, 1998.

Southerland, Daniel E. *The Expansion of Everyday Life, 1860–1876.* Fayetteville: University of Arkansas Press, 1989.

Steigerwald, David. *The Sixties and the End of Modern America.* New York: St. Martin's Press, 1995.

Stein, Arlene. *Shameless: Sexual Dissidence in American Culture.* New York: New York University Press, 2006.

Thébaud, Françoise, ed. *Geschichte der Frauen: 20. Jahrhundert.* Frankfurt am Main: Büchergilde Gutenberg, 1995.

Tong, Rosemarie. *Feminist Thought: A Comprehensive Introduction.* Boulder, CO: Westview, 1989.

Ullman, Sharon R. *Sex Seen: The Emergence of Modern Sexuality in America.* Berkeley: University of California Press, 1997.

Walters, Ronald G. *American Reformers, 1815–1860.* New York: Hill and Wang, 1978.

Weeks, Jeffrey. *Sexuality.* London: Routledge, 1986.

Zaretsky, Eli. *Freuds Jahrhundert: Die Geschichte der Psychoanalyse.* Wien: Paul Zsolnay Verlag, 2006.

Zur Nieden, Sabine. *Weibliche Ejakulation: Variationen zu einem uralten Streit der Geschlechter.* Stuttgart: Ferdinand Enke, 1994.

Chapter 11

DOES EVERY VOTE COUNT IN AMERICA?

Emotions, Elections, and the Quest for Black Political Empowerment

Britta Waldschmidt-Nelson

THE HISTORY OF emotions provides important keys to understanding human behavior and can be of great assistance in explaining wider political, social, and economic trends in American history.[1] This applies in particular to the history of African Americans, as racial conflicts in general and the black struggle for freedom and equality in particular repeatedly stirred public emotions in the United States to a degree hardly ever reached by other domestic issues. Thus, interracial relations have always been identified as an extremely emotionally charged aspect of American history, and in view of the new approaches to historical research proposed by the history of emotion, a closer examination of this phenomenon can offer significant additional insights into the close connection between emotions and politics. A broad and multifaceted cluster, such as the Civil Rights Movement or any other social protest movement, encompasses emotions on various levels and should therefore be analyzed from more than one perspective.

In dealing with the nature of emotions, a problem arises that has been addressed by psychologists, sociologists, and philosophers alike: is it actu-

Notes for this section begin on page 243.

ally possible to know anything at all about another person's emotions? The so-called internalist view would deny this, claiming one can only ever infer from one's own experience, which naturally has been formed and conditioned by one's particular cultural and social context. Thus, trying to put emotions into a historical perspective is further complicated as the constant change of these circumstances has to be taken into account. Psychologist Paul Ekman postulates more of an externalist approach. He has identified certain "basic emotions" including "happiness, surprise, fear, sadness, anger and disgust," which, as he argues, are common to all cultures as part of human nature and evolution.[2] Other scholars have been debating whether certain other emotions, such as jealousy and love, ought to be included or not. Nevertheless, Ekman's basic emotions are still central to psychological research in this field. For the historian this presents a promising opportunity, as the existence of a cross-cultural regularity might suggest that there also is a consistency throughout time. However, finding and assessing the authenticity of these emotions remains a problem, especially for historians, as they have to rely entirely on their sources of information of key emotional indicators like intonation, mood, or facial expression. The history of emotion, therefore, as historical research in general, is not so much concerned with *actually* identifying emotions for certain, but rather with analyzing the role they played in the greater social context.

Emotions, it may be argued, can be links within a causal chain. Intentionally evoked by rhetoric or unconsciously aroused by certain events and developments, they may occur as a reaction to previous and/or a motivation for ensuing actions. In the case of African American activists, for example, it was their frustration about the imposed political impotence coupled with their anger about racism and discrimination that moved them to speak out against the injustice they were experiencing. Positioning emotions thus in the causal network of historical argument is one way to grant them historical relevance, while even emotions historians have to admit that feelings rarely function as the sole reason for a particular course of events.

A related but slightly different approach deals with emotions or emotionality as general terms without specifying a particular sentiment. In these cases supposed emotionality observed as the attribute of a person or a social group can be instrumental in constructing a certain line of argument and reaching certain conclusions—for example, the long-standing prejudice that African Americans are prone to displaying more "primitive" emotions than whites, or the belief in a higher inclination to emotional reasoning that is generally assumed to be particular to women.

Apart from this approach—treating particular emotions, or emotionality in general, as elements instrumental to a historical argument—the question whether emotions themselves have a history, and if so, how it can be scrutinized has recently been posed as well. Thus Peter Stearns has developed the concept of "emotional style," which aims to combine the difficult interaction of emotional standards with the historical reality changing throughout time. He argues that adjustments within the legal system provide convincing proof of the normative nature of changes in the "emotional style" of a particular society.[3] Similarly, adhering to the mainstream emotional standard could be perceived as a way to inclusion. Martin Luther King Jr., for example, when speaking to larger public audiences was always very careful to distance his style of speaking from the emotionality usually associated with the Black Church in order to appeal to a white majority that generally disapproves of open, public displays of emotions.

This illustrates that the existence of minorities may also mean a varying emotional style within one society—a fact previous studies have not always taken into account.[4] This chapter will show that the black struggle for the right to vote also presented a confrontation of different emotional styles, and that these emotions can be regarded as instrumental and normative factors. Arguably, the multilayered efforts to gradually harmonize the emotional style of black communities—particularly black politicians—at least to some degree with those of the white majority of US society certainly have contributed to higher levels of racial reconciliation and integration in general and also to the success of the African American struggle for political empowerment.

"Primitive Emotions" versus "Rational Self-Restraint": The Role of Racial Stereotypes in the Struggle for Black Equality

The old but still powerful stereotype that black Americans are "more emotional" than whites tends to come to mind when thinking of African Americans and the topic of emotion. From the times of slavery until today, this stereotype has often been used, usually in a derogatory sense, since white society generally valued the rule of the intellect over one's emotional life as a sign of a person's maturity and strength. Thus describing black behavior as more primitive and more influenced by instinct (especially sexual instinct) and less by reason than white behavior has been a way to support the creed of white superiority. In fact, one of the arguments used by white racists to justify slavery and, later, racial segregation was that black behavior was so primitive, either childlike or animal-like ("black apes"), that black people needed to be guarded, ruled, and "civilized" by whites.[5] Even after the Civil War, Southern whites justified their brutal enforcement of social control with frequent references to the perceived emotional threat of black culture to Anglo-Saxon civilizational self-restraint. For example, the protection of white women's virtue from the supposedly insatiable sexual appetite of black males remained a powerful and leading motive for racist persecution and lynching until the 1960s.[6]

A similarly negative white disposition towards emotion and the ability of black self-restraint has overshadowed the African American struggle for political equality. While the more intense display of emotions and the expressiveness of black culture has often been admired and imitated by whites with regard to music, art, and literature, it was viewed as a handicap in the quest for social and political equality. It seemed incompatible with the particular "emotional style" that had been adopted in white politics. Consequently, most black civil rights activists worked hard to avoid any appearance of being "too emotional." One of the best examples for this strategy was developed by the most famous of all black civil rights leaders: Martin Luther King Jr.

The spirituality of the Black Church in which he was brought up (his father was the minister of Ebenezer Baptist Church in Atlanta, GA) had bestowed a deep faith in the love and justice of God as well as a feeling of self-worth ("somebodyness") upon King. This faith became King's primary source of strength as he dedicated his life to the black freedom struggle. However, while attending college, he became increasingly antagonistic toward the emotionalism of black churches. As he recalled later, he felt embarrassed by the open display of emotions during traditional black services and doubted that such behavior projected images of "intellectually respectable" religious faith. Not surprisingly, King refused to stay at Ebenezer (as his father had wished), obtained a PhD in theology from Boston University and became minister of Dexter Avenue Baptist Church in Montgomery, AL, whose members were mostly middle-class, highly educated, and "very respectable" blacks, who could appreciate his knowledge and the rhetorical brilliance of his sermons. King also encouraged his followers to avoid any identification with widespread contemporary stereotypes of lazy, loud, and messy blacks. During protest marches and demonstrations, black civil rights activists thus displayed serious and orderly behavior and strictly avoided any public display of emotions. Through shaping their manners, their language and rhetoric, even their clothing and hairstyles, they wanted to prove how intellectual, calm, and dignified black behavior could be—in short, to convey an image of African American people as respectable citizens in charge of their emotions, as required.[7]

At the same time, King masterfully combined the display of dignified behavior with the highly emotional appeal and rhetoric of the black sermon for his public speeches. In late August 1963, his most famous address, "I Have a Dream," deeply moved not only the 250,000 black and white people in the audience but millions who followed his speech on television and radio. It appealed to people's yearning for racial justice, brotherhood, and peace, and appealed to their responsibilities as Americans and as Christians. It strengthened black self-confidence and moved many whites to declare their solidarity with the black protest movement. Indirectly, this speech may even have helped to move Congress to pass the important Civil Rights Act of 1964. Among many contemporaries it created powerful emotions and a unique sense of hope and elation among civil rights activists.[8]

The black struggle against emotional stereotypes had a long history. The post–Civil War debate over the Fifteenth Amendment of the American Constitution, which was to grant African American males the right to vote, provided a particularly powerful earlier example.[9] Curiously enough, grave objections to this amendment not only came from white racist Southerners but also from women's rights activists.

A number of white women who had previously been major pillars of the abolitionist movement and strong advocates of black freedom and equality, such as Susan B. Anthony and Elizabeth Cady Stanton, now denounced the plan to grant black males the right to vote before women would obtain suffrage. Some black abolitionist veterans, such as Sojourner Truth, Charles Raymond, and Robert Purvis, agreed with them. Other black leaders, including Frederick Douglass and Frances Ellen Harper, as well as a number of white feminists like Lucy Stone and Julia Howe, were in favor of the Fifteenth Amendment, even though they all would have preferred it to include female suffrage, too.

The issue eventually resulted in the breakdown of the alliances between the feminist and abolitionist camps, and the American Equal Rights Association, cofounded by Anthony and Douglass after the Civil War to agitate for black and female suffrage, split into two different organizations in 1869.[10] The debate itself was characterized by highly emotional discussions. Frederick Douglass, for example, known as a very calm and collected speaker, made the following passionate plea to stress the greater urgency of black men to attain the vote: "When women, because they are women, are hunted down through the cities of New York and New Orleans; when they are dragged from their houses and hung upon lamp posts; when their children are torn from their arms, and their brains dashed upon the pavement; … then they will have an urgency to obtain the ballot equal to our own."[11]

And Susan B. Anthony sharply disagreed as the debate turned increasingly ugly. How deep the gulf between the former allies had become, and to what degree Anthony's friendship with and respect for Douglass as well as for the goals of the black freedom struggle had turned into hostility and racist condescension is evident in her bitter comment on the final passage of the amendment: "While the dominant party have with one hand lifted up two million black men and crowned them with the honor and dignity of citizenship, with the other they have dethroned fifteen million white women—their own mothers and sisters, their own wives and daughters—and cast them under the heel of the lowest orders of manhood."[12]

It was particularly painful to Anthony's former black friends to hear her characterizations of African Americans as inferior human beings unworthy of any right to vote. And Elizabeth Cady Stanton utilized traditional biases towards the supposedly uncontrollable lust and sexual appetite of black men to protest against their enfranchisement and implied that giving black men the right to vote was virtually a license for rape. This kind of tense, sometimes vitriolic disagreement between white woman's rights activists and the advocates of black civil rights would continue well into the mid-twentieth century, in some groups even until today.[13]

From Reconstruction to the 1960s: The Long, Uphill Battle for African American Civil and Voting Rights

After passage of the Fifteenth Amendment in 1870, African Americans quickly used this first chance at participation in the political decision-making process on the local, state, and national levels, and during the 1870s two black senators and a total of sixteen black representatives served in the US Congress. But many white Southerners remained emotionally and intellectually unable and unwilling to accept former slaves as social equals. Their fear of miscegenation, combined with their rage over the lost war, created a powerful cocktail of emotions that fostered their campaign to end this first period of African American political inclusion with the aim to confine blacks to "second-class citizenship" and especially to deprive them of their constitutionally guaranteed right to vote.

A complex system of so-called Black Codes or Jim Crow Laws was developed in the South—as ordinary state laws, sometimes even as part of a state's constitution. Next to segregating blacks from whites in all social aspects of public life and controlling blacks in the economic sector, one of the major goals of these laws was to exclude African Americans from politics.[14] As the white Southern senator Carter Glass put it: "The people of the original thirteen southern states curse and spit upon the Fifteenth Amendment—and have no intention of letting the Negro vote ... White supremacy is too precious a thing to surrender for the sake of a theoretical justice that would let a brutish African deem himself the equal of white men ... in Dixie."[15]

White racists soon managed to regain exclusive control over the political process in the South with the help of voter qualification requirements such as literacy tests, good conduct clauses or the infamous grandfather clause.

By stating that only those people whose grandfather had already voted could vote in a state, this clause was a very effective tool to disenfranchise African Americans without directly violating the Fifteenth Amendment.

In this process of exclusion, Southern whites complemented their legalistic approach with economic intimidation and a wide array of terror and violence. The Ku Klux Klan and other secret racist organizations such as the Knights of the White Camellia, the Red Shirts, or the White League enforced white supremacy with unrelenting cruelty and played a central role in the widespread practice of lynchings, of which more than 3,400 were officially recorded between 1890 and 1920 alone. The issue of black voting rights was not only a highly emotional one in theory; it was literally a matter of life and death for many African Americans.[16]

In consequence, black political representation declined sharply and the last black member of Congress, George H. White, lost his seat by the turn of the century accompanied by much sadness, frustration, and fear among African Americans faced with the end of their political representation. Only few dared to believe the prophecy White made during his emotional farewell address to Congress in January 1901: "This, Mr. Chairman, is perhaps the Negro's temporary farewell to the American Congress. But let me say, phoenix-like he will rise up some day and come again!"[17]

For almost half a century, black representation in Congress and black political participation in the South was virtually nonexistent.[18] And yet, African Americans continued their struggle for political rights, in particular the right to vote. Contemporary primary sources provide a thorough insight into the emotional force of determination, frustration, anger, and hope that enhanced this effort. In 1915, the National Association for the Advancement of Colored People (NAACP) scored its first significant victory[19]: the US Supreme Court outlawed the grandfather clauses in the constitutions of Oklahoma and Maryland. Five years later the Supreme Court declared the practice of all-white primaries in the state of Texas unconstitutional. And in 1957 (one year after the state of Alabama outlawed the NAACP), Congress finally passed the Civil Rights Act, which created the US Civil Rights Commission and authorized the Department of Justice to file suit against anyone who prevented people from registering to vote. Congress strengthened the power of the Civil Rights Commission in 1960 by mandating that local registration records be made available for investigation by the Justice Department. However, it soon became obvious that a federal county-by-county investigation process—such as allowed for in the acts—would be much too slow as an effective tool against black disenfranchisement in the South. Even the famous Civil Rights Act of 1964 could not solve this problem as it focused essentially on nonpolitical rights: it banned segregation and discrimination in all public places, federally funded programs, as well as in the general workplace; created the Equal Employment Opportunity Commission; and established a legal ground for affirmative action programs. Despite a record of success in the struggle for political participation and civil rights, African Americans in the South often remained excluded from voting by intimidation and a variety of educational tests or other requirements (e.g., "good conduct certificates"). The persistence of these barriers in the South called for additional legislative action. But President Johnson at that time refused to listen to King's advice, since he had other legislative priorities. Thus it took one more year of persistent advocacy until a new act to protect black voting rights was finally passed.[20]

"Questioning America": The Mississippi Freedom Summer and the Selma Campaign

Two pivotal initiatives in this struggle involved particularly high levels of emotions among the advocates as well as the opponents of black equality in the South. The first project, called "Freedom Summer," was organized by the Student Nonviolent Coordinating Committee (SNCC) together with Mississippi grassroots activists and was designed to educate blacks about their voting rights. With 42 percent African American citizens, Mississippi had a higher proportion of black people than any other state, while its black voter registration rate stagnated at only 6 percent, the lowest in the nation.

The Democratic Party, which had total control of the political system in Mississippi, barred African Americans from membership and thus from any form of participation in the political decision-making process. Civil rights activists challenged this rule and founded a new, interracial political body in the spring of 1964: the Mississippi Freedom Democratic Party (MFDP). Since the all-white election commission of Mississippi refused to recognize the MFDP as a party, thus excluding it from the regular election, the activists conducted a "freedom election" as part of their Freedom Summer campaign. The SNCC ran voter-education projects throughout the state, and all blacks who wanted to vote could participate in this election. Throughout the summer, the young freedom fighters were met with much hostility and violent resistance by white racists, which resulted in the death of nine black and two white civil rights activists. Over a hundred more were injured, their homes were bombed, black churches burned, and more than one thousand civil rights activists were imprisoned. But the "freedom election" continued and gained national fame as a delegation of MFDP members was chosen to represent Mississippi at the next National Democratic Party Convention.[21]

One of the most important leaders of the black Mississippi freedom struggle was the former sharecropper Fannie Lou Hamer. At age forty-two,

Hamer had experienced an awakening of her political conscience and joined the black freedom struggle when SNCC activists first came to Mississippi in 1962. She had lost her home and her job, and had been shot at and severely beaten as a consequence of her attempt to register to vote in Mississippi. Nevertheless, she continued her work for the movement and became vice chair of the MFDP in 1964. At the National Democratic Party Convention, which was held in August 1964 in Atlantic City, New Jersey, the MFDP delegates challenged the lily-white delegation of the so-called Regular Democrats and demanded to be seated. Their case was heard before the convention's credential committee and Hamer gave a moving account of the suffering that blacks had to endure if they tried to vote in Mississippi. Overwhelmed by her own emotions, Hamer broke into tears at the end of her testimony, calling out: "If the Freedom Democratic Party is not seated now, I question America. Is this the land of the free and the home of the brave? Where we have to sleep with our telephones off the hook because our lives be threatened daily, because we want to live as decent human beings in America?!"[22]

Her speech was broadcasted on national television and according to witnesses "electrified the nation," since "she brought the life and death reality of Mississippi into the homes of America." As a result of this speech, the credential committee received thousands of letters and phone calls by Americans who had heard Hamer on TV. Deeply moved, they all demanded the recognition of the MFDP delegation. Also, many newspapers wrote commentaries in the MFDP's favor. Such events evoking outrage, compassion, and even shame began to put the dominant "emotional style" of restraint into question. The *Philadelphia Independent*, for example, stated: "The Freedom Party has succeeded in putting their case before the entire convention and the world. If the seating battle is not resolved in their favor, Mississippi will still have been exposed as a vile place of gross corruption."[23]

In the end, after refusing the offer of two seats at large, the MFDP was not seated at the convention in 1964. However, the credentials committee of the Democratic Party did rule that in the future no racially segregated state delegation would ever be seated again. Since the Regular Democrats of Mississippi failed to integrate their party by the next Democratic Convention in Chicago in 1968, they lost their seats to the MFDP delegation, which was again led by Hamer. The power monopoly of white Democrats in Mississippi was finally broken, and Hamer received a standing ovation on the delegation floor when she took her seat. She was then elected as the first black female member of the Democratic National Committee, and the Democratic Party began to seriously examine its treatment of minorities. As Sherwin J. Markman, a prominent party member, recalled a decade later: "That examination, which flowed as a direct legacy from Fannie Lou Hamer, ultimately opened up the party—not only to Blacks, but to Chicanos, young people and women. All of these, who now take their party and franchise as their right, owe thanks to one determined and courageous black woman."[24]

The second important initiative in the struggle for black voting rights was the Selma Campaign of 1965, led by Martin Luther King Jr. and the Southern Christian Leadership Conference (SCLC).[25] After months of local demonstrations, which failed to end the exclusion of black voters in Alabama, King and other civil rights activists planned a big protest march from Selma to Montgomery, Alabama, to draw national attention to the problem. King was well aware of the fact that this kind of protest would probably lead to violent clashes with Selma's chief of police, Jim Clark, who was known for his racism and brutality. However, as he had done before (especially during his Birmingham Campaign of 1963), King chose to provoke conflict with the white power structure in the South, since he hoped that public emotion raised by such conflicts throughout America would work in favor of the civil rights movement.

As expected, Chief Clark and the governor of Alabama, George Wallace, tried to prevent the march by any means possible. This included a clash between white authorities and several hundred peaceful, nonarmed demonstrators, among them many women and children, who tried to march across Selma's Edmund Pettus Bridge on Sunday, 7 March 1965. The marchers were attacked and brutally beaten by white policemen and state troopers—some on horseback. The police used clubs and tear gas, and people were beaten to the ground and trampled upon as they were trying to run away from the troopers. Shouting, screaming, and crying filled the air. The violent scenes made some observers compare the situation in Selma to a civil war—and all of this happened right in front of television cameras.

Of course, the incident caused rage and frustration among many African Americans, and some questioned the wisdom of a strategy of nonviolent resistance. But once again King was able to control the emotions of his followers in Selma enough to keep them from fighting back.[26] Moreover, as he had hoped for, the pictures of this so-called Bloody Sunday caused protest and outrage not only all over the United States but also in many other countries. President Johnson was harshly criticized for his lack of action, and public support for a new law to protect black voting rights increased significantly.

Meanwhile, racist violence continued in Selma, resulting in the death of a number of demonstrators, among them James Reeb, a white Unitarian minister from Boston. On the day of Reeb's funeral, 15 March, President Johnson finally decided to take the initiative and announced in a televised speech before Congress his support for a strong new voting rights bill. Calling for support of the new legislation, he stressed the urgency of the civil rights cause to overcome racism and pledged to protect the black marchers in Alabama with federal troops. President Johnson closed his speech by quoting the words of one of the most popular civil rights songs: "I believe, we shall overcome."

According to witnesses, Martin Luther King Jr. was moved to tears when he heard the president say these words and finally take a stand to protect black voting rights. The march from Selma to Montgomery took place from 21 to 25 March and was a big success with over 25,000 attending the final demonstration. King's hope had come true: the planned conflict with the white power structure in Selma (confronting the emotions of racial pride, anger, and aggression of white racists), while maintaining an emotional balance among the members of the civil rights movement (maintaining the emotion of hope, courage, and self-confidence, while controlling fear, hate, and rage) had successfully focused the nation's—and to some extent the world's—attention on the brutal injustices against African Americans in the South.

The media, especially television, had communicated much of the emotionality of this struggle for racial justice to a national audience in an unprecedented fashion and with heretofore unknown intensity. The role of television as key factor of shaping public opinion was of particular importance in this context. Without the extensive TV coverage of racial injustice and white brutality on the one hand, and of the courage and suffering of black freedom fighters on the other hand, the civil rights movement would certainly not have been as successful as it was at that time. As a result, a growing majority of the American public felt empathy for the victims, sympathy for the black activists, contempt for white racists, and anger and shame about the state of the nation. With Johnson as well as a majority of the American public pushing for it, the new legislation was finally passed by Congress and signed into law on 6 August 1965.[27]

The Voting Rights Act of 1965: Beginning of a New Era

The Voting Rights Act of 1965 (VRA) immediately and effectively suspended all kind of tests and devices used to keep blacks from voting. The act also authorized inspections by the US Commission on Civil Rights in seven "covered" states of the South (those in which the disenfranchisement of African Americans had been the worst: Virginia, North Carolina, South Carolina, Georgia, Alabama, Mississippi, and Louisiana) to monitor voter registration and fair polling procedures. This guaranteed that all citizens who had been excluded before now had a chance to realize their constitutionally guaranteed right to vote. Thus, ninety-five years after its original passage, the Fifteenth Amendment was given validity again and was finally enforced with the full authority of the US government.

The significance of the VRA, which was renewed and extended in 1970, 1975, and 1982, can hardly be overestimated. Within a few years after its passage, black voter registration and black political representation increased rapidly all over the South: between 1965 and 1970 the number of eligible blacks who were registered to vote in the deep South more than doubled, and in some states the gains were even higher, as in Alabama, where black voter registration increased from 19 to 61 percent, or in Mississippi, which boasted an even more dramatic increase from 6 to 67 percent. The number of black elected officials (BEOs) in the South climbed from 72 in 1965 to 711 in 1970, and since then it has risen to over 5,000. Not only in the South, but all over the United States the number of BEOs has increased from a mere 300 in 1965 to about 9,000 today.

Since the 1960s, African American political inclusion has made significant gains. The number of black members of Congress increased from seven in 1965 to about forty at the turn of the twenty-first century. Today these black representatives, who founded the Congressional Black Caucus (CBC) in 1971 to coordinate their work, hold 8 percent of congressional seats and exercise a noticeable influence on the legislative decision-making process. Remarkably, they thus enjoy higher levels of political representation on Capitol Hill than other minorities or women—i.e., in the 109th Congress, African Americans, who constitute about 12.5 percent of the US population, hold 8 percent of the seats; with 13 percent of the population, Hispanic Americans hold less than 5 percent; Asian Americans (3 percent of the population) make up only 0.9 percent of the membership of congress; Native Americans (1 percent of the population) only 0.1 percent; and women, who constitute 51 percent of the US population, only hold 14.8 percent of seats on Capitol Hill.[28] Moreover, there has been significant progress on the state and local levels as African Americans have served as mayors of a number of America's major cities (such as New York; Washington, DC; Atlanta; Philadelphia; Chicago; or Los Angeles) and Douglas Wilder of Virginia was elected the first black governor in US history in 1989. Finally, the black vote has been an important factor for a number of white candidates in close elections. It not only provided the winning margin for President Carter's election in 1976 but was also essential to Bill Clinton's 1992 victory in the Democratic primaries.[29]

The Voting Rights Act enabled tremendous progress in the field of electoral politics for black Americans. And yet, African Americans are still underrepresented in the political system. For example, while making substantial progress compared to the time before 1965, the nine thousand BEOs are less than 2 percent of all elected officials. And since Reconstruction there have only been three African American senators (Edward Brooke, 1967–79; Carol Moseley-Braun, 1993–1999; and Barack Obama, 2004–2008). Among the many reasons for this underrepresentation, was and to some extent still is the continued racial prejudice that keeps some segments of the white majority from ever voting for a black candidate no matter how qualified he or she may be. In addition, the American electoral system with its majority and its multimember at-large elections constitutes a systemic disadvantage to minorities. Moreover, there have always been efforts by some white politicians to systematically dilute black voting power through the use of gerrymandering techniques, most of which were prohibited through the extension of the VRA of 1982. Thus, during the redistricting after the 1990 national census, eleven new black majority districts were created (ten of those in the South), which led to an impressive increase of the African American representation on the federal level after the 1992 election, when membership of the CBC rose from twenty-six to forty.[30]

"Voting for Change": Minorities, Women, and the 1992 Election

In addition to the creation of these new black majority districts, a number of other factors proved to be very helpful to minority and female candidates in that election. For example, the successful work of a number of political support groups for women was one of the main reasons for the great increase in the female membership of Congress in 1992 (from thirty-one to fifty-five).[31] Both African American and female candidates greatly benefited from the unusually high number of open seats in the election of 1992. For a long time, the so-called power of incumbency was a serious obstacle to new political candidates. Between 1892 and 1992 the reelection rate of incumbent members of Congress averaged about 92 percent, and since most of them were—and still are—white males, this obstacle has been particularly adverse to female and minority candidates. Therefore, such new candidates enjoy the greatest chances of success when they run for an open seat, i.e., in a district without an incumbent up for reelection.[32]

Redistricting had already created several open seats in 1992. Moreover, many incumbents decided not to run again that year because they were involved in one or both of two big scandals during the congressional sessions of 1991 and 1992: the so-called post-office scandal and the house-banking scandal. In both cases, some members of Congress had abused their congressional privileges to further their own private interests. And although the resulting financial damage to the taxpayers was comparatively limited, many voters were outraged about this abuse and lost trust in their political representation. The powerful emotional response to the scandals sufficed to prevent numerous representatives from seeking reelection. This growing anti-incumbent mood, which had been observed by the media since the beginning of the 1990s, was not only based on voter disgust about political scandals but also on anger about the huge deficit, discontent with federal politics in general, and a growing mistrust against all "Washington insiders." A large number of voters therefore wanted to give new candidates a chance. "Voting for Change" became the most frequently cited motto for the 1992 election.[33]

Contrary to white men, who had dominated Congress for so long, women and minority candidates were automatically perceived as "candidates of change." According to some political scientists, the collapse of the Soviet Union and the end of the Cold War presented a further advantage to female candidates, as the election campaign of 1992 was dominated by domestic rather than foreign policy issues. In this context it is important to note that along the lines of traditional gender stereotyping, women are often credited with more competence on so-called compassion issues (e.g., education, welfare, and health care) while men are credited with more competence in dealing with so-called force issues (e.g., law enforcement, military buildup, and war). Since the final decision of undecided voters is often based on an emotional bias, the prevalence of domestic over foreign policy issues in the 1992 election may actually have encouraged a significant number of voters to decide in favor of female candidates.[34] African American women—being female and generally perceived as "the ultimate outsiders" regarding the (corrupt) Washington political network—particularly benefited from this unique situation: their number in Congress rose from four to ten, among them the first black female senator in US History, Carol Moseley-Braun.[35]

In addition, the Anita Hill–Clarence Thomas affair created an emotional context highly conducive to the election of minority and female representatives.[36] In June of 1991, the only black member of the US Supreme Court, Thurgood Marshall, announced his resignation. Since Marshall had been a very liberal judge and a strong supporter of black civil rights and women's rights, the process of selecting a successor was followed closely by African Americans and feminists. President George Bush nominated the conservative black justice Clarence Thomas, whose confirmation by the US Senate appeared to be little more than a formality. But in October of 1991 the nomination was suddenly threatened by the testimony of law professor Anita Hill, who had worked for Thomas in the early 1980s and now accused him of sexual harassment during that time. Hill had decided to bring her case forward now, because she felt that a man of such grave character deficits should not become a member of the US Supreme Court. The hearings, which lasted for three days, were broadcast on national television and provoked a heated debate throughout the country.[37]

Public opinion was split regarding the trustworthiness of Hill and Thomas (who denied all charges) and the question whether Thomas should be confirmed as judge, while the final vote in the Senate produced a 52 to 48 majority in favor of Thomas's nomination. However, despite the hope of many conservatives, this vote did not bring an end to the controversy. On the contrary, the affair continued to influence public debate in the United States long after the confirmation was over, since it aroused deep, conflicting emotions not only in America but—due to extensive international media coverage—worldwide.[38]

The hearings, in which fourteen older white males questioned one young black woman, became infamous because of the aggressive, often chauvinistic fashion in which some of the members of the Senate Judiciary Committee tried to discredit Anita Hill and portray her as a paranoid and hysterical woman. This behavior, as well as the apparent lack of understanding among many senators regarding the seriousness of sexual harassment as a widespread problem in the workplace, infuriated feminists all over the country and a large segment of the public, which now felt it imperative to elect more women and minority representatives to a Congress so blatantly dominated by white men.[39]

The Hill-Thomas hearings served as a catalyst for change on three levels: First, they further contributed to the willingness of American voters to elect more women and minority candidates into political office in 1992. Second, they motivated a number of female politicians to run for national office now, who had been hesitant about taking this step before. Carol Moseley-Braun, for example, who at the time served as Recorder of Deeds in Cook County, Illinois, stressed that her anger about the course of these hearings, specifically the condescending and chauvinistic manner in which Illinois senator Alan Dixon interrogated Anita Hill, was the decisive factor in her decision to challenge Dixon.[40] The third effect of the hearings was that Political Action Committees (PAC's) for women saw a sharp increase in their membership and financial contributions. Membership in EMILY's List, for example, rose from three thousand to over twenty-four thousand between October 1991 and November 1992, and while the organization had less than $1 million to spend in 1990, it was able to contribute over $4 million for political training of female candidates and individual campaign support in 1992. Since all black women who ran for Congress that year were supported by EMILY's List, this factor certainly contributed to the success of their campaigns.[41] In addition to the creation of new black majority districts, the combination of several mainly emotion-based factors had a noticeable impact on the 1992 election and contributed significantly to the great increase of women and African Americans (especially black women) on Capitol Hill.[42]

Inclusion or Illusion? African American Access to Electoral Politics Today

From 1993 to 2004 the number of African Americans in Congress remained between thirty-nine and forty-one—with only minimal changes in CBC membership (since the turn of the century, all black representatives, except one who retired and was succeeded by his son, have been reelected). After the 2000 census, civil rights activists closely watched the new round of redistricting. While some hoped that it would further enhance the chances of black candidates to be elected in black majority districts, others feared that the numbers of these districts could actually be reduced, since there had been several legal challenges against them in the South.[43] The number of blacks in Congress remained stable, however, although the election of November 2000 still led to a highly emotional charge of political discrimination by the African American community and many civil rights organizations.

Through massive voter registration drives, the NAACP and other civil rights organizations had mobilized a record black turnout. Over 90 percent of all African Americans voted for the Democratic candidate, Al Gore, and thus contributed to his winning margin in the popular vote. Therefore, the black community was, of course, deeply disappointed that after the highly disputed election results in Florida, the intervention of a conservative Supreme Court eventually made the Republican candidate George W. Bush receive the majority of the Electoral College and thus gain the presidency.[44]

Many infuriated African Americans interpreted the election result as fraud and a clear indication of the exclusion of black voters in the state of Florida. Apparently, the governor of Florida, Jeb Bush (George W. Bush's brother), and his secretary of state, Katherine Harris, had ordered local election supervisors to purge sixty-four thousand voters from the registration lists because they had allegedly been convicted of a felony, which disqualifies anyone from voting in Florida. African Americans comprised 54 percent of the people on this "scrub list," the majority of them without a criminal record at all. But since most of them were completely surprised by the charges and unable to provide legal proof of their innocence at the polling stations, they were still excluded from voting. In addition, African Americans complained about intimidation on their way to polling stations (e.g., by police road blocks), inaccurate voter registration lists, and miscounts of ballots in black districts. Altogether, probably more than twenty thousand African Americans eligible to vote could not exercise this right in Florida—an imposing figure considering that Bush's margin of victory in that election was only 537 votes.[45]

Since African Americans had fought for the right to vote for such a long time, made so many sacrifices for it, and had—after the passage of the

Voting Rights Act and its extensions—finally begun to hope that they had a fair chance to participate in the political decision-making process, the election of November 2000 was a huge disappointment. Many outraged blacks regarded it as the worst setback of their voting rights in over thirty years. Just as in the 1960s, large protest marches ensued and civil rights leaders, including the Reverend Jesse Jackson, publicly voiced their protest against the election result. Even on inauguration day, in January 2001, there were demonstrations in Washington with people singing "Hail to the Thief!" And during the congressional session in which George W. Bush was officially declared winner of the presidential race, most members of the Congressional Black Caucus walked out in protest. At the same time, the NAACP filed suit against Florida's secretary of state, Katherine Harris, on the charge of systematic discrimination and exclusion of black voters.[46]

The lawsuit failed to produce sufficient evidence to achieve a conviction of Harris. But in June of 2001, the US Commission on Civil Rights, which had held extensive hearings in this matter, published its final report confirming that the Florida election included widespread voter disenfranchisement and that African Americans had been the principal victims of the system's inadequacies. While the commission also failed to find conclusive conspiratorial evidence, it still assigned much of the blame to Governor Jeb Bush and Secretary of State Harris. It called for further investigation by the Justice Department and recommended a fundamental reform of Florida's voting system. In response to the public outrage and charges of misuse of political office in support of his brother, Governor Bush had already signed an election reform act making some significant improvements of the election system in May 2001 (e.g., improving absentee voting, poll worker education, and maintenance of voter rolls). However, the commission demanded further action, since the issues of the disenfranchisement of former felons, the lack of accommodations for voters with disabilities, and a speedy appeal system for voters denied the right to vote on election day remained unresolved.[47]

Many civil rights activists and the Congressional Black Caucus at that time called for a new federal law that would mandate uniform standards for federal elections in all states. Most CBC members—such as Maxine Waters, who chaired the Democratic Caucus Special Committee on Election Reform, or John Conyers, who introduced the "Equal Protection of Voting Rights Act" in March of 2001—hoped that such a law would produce a more inclusive voting system nationwide and thus contribute to a noticeable further increase of black political representation.[48]

However, the congressional debate about election reform was put on hold by the tragic terrorist attack of 11 September 2001, when issues of national security outweighed all other concerns. It is remarkable to what extent the shock, grief, and fear triggered by the attack united Americans across all racial and ethnic lines in an almost unprecedented way. Many African Americans stated that they never felt as "American" and as included in the nationwide surge of patriotism as they did in the wake of 9/11. Hence this further stresses the unifying nature of a common emotional experience that is often also considered a key ingredient in patriotism. But while some observers enthusiastically regarded this change as the potential beginning of the end of the racial divide in America, critics pointed at the surge of attacks and discrimination against Muslim and Arab Americans, asserting that these "brown Americans" had simply replaced blacks as the focal point for racial aggression.[49]

It is difficult to assess whether race relations between white and black Americans are significantly different today to what they were before September 2001. Looking at recent publications by black scholars, public opinion polls, and the frequency of racial conflicts (e.g., charges of discrimination, race crimes, or white police brutality against African Americans), there seems to have been some progress, but certainly not enough to speak of a "closure of the racial divide." It is also rather unlikely that a new election reform law will be passed anytime soon, since this issue is still nowhere near the top of the national legislative agenda.[50]

However, although 89 percent of African Americans voted against George W. Bush in the 2004 election and were deeply disappointed by his landslide victory, there were also some welcome changes. For example, Bush appointed his former national security advisor, Condoleezza Rice, as the first black female secretary of state, and the number of African Americans elected to Congress rose from 39 to 43, among them the first black senator of the twenty-first century, Barack Obama. This new record high of African American representation on Capitol Hill was based not only on intense voter mobilization efforts by black organizations (which led to a 25 percent increase of the black voter turnout) but also on local election reforms and close public scrutiny against voter discrimination, triggered by the experience of November 2000 (while there was a slight change in individual members, the total number of CBC members remained at 43 after the 2006 election).

The election of Obama as the junior senator of Illinois already evoked many positive emotions in the black community and the so-called civil rights establishment. Since then Obama has gone on to stir hope and expectations for progressive social change not only among black but also white Americans, and even among people around the world. His two books—*Dreams from my Father* (1995) and *The Audacity of Hope* (2006)—were on the *New York Times* best-seller list for months, and the success of these very personal memoirs shows Obama's ability to connect with people of different racial heritage on a level that goes beyond mere political reasoning. He raised international attention for the first time through his stirring keynote address at the National Democratic Convention in July 2004. Calling out for national unity and the overcoming of racial division, while also demanding social justice and an end to all forms of discrimination, the son of a Kenyan-born father and a white mother from Kansas not only supports but personally embodies a "closure of the racial divide." Obama's serious and emotionally charged speech on race relations in America on 18 March 2008 also demonstrated this fact. His address—which is arguably one of the greatest pieces of public oratory on race since the 1960s—displays a deep level of understanding for both the frustration and bitterness of African Americans over past and present experiences of racism as well as the anger and resentment of those whites, especially white immigrants and their descendants, who have suffered from discrimination and poverty themselves and therefore have no tolerance for affirmative action. Indirectly addressing the continuous claims of some black nationalists that as a person of mixed racial heritage Obama isn't "black enough" to represent black interests, this speech was one of the factors that moved most African Americans to embrace the charismatic young senator as someone who is rooted in the black community, but not limited by it, and who is deeply committed to fighting racism as well as social injustice. Many African Americans as well as white liberals now see him as a new "beacon of hope" and even compare him to Martin Luther King Jr.

He has also been compared to John F. Kennedy, and following the example of that other charismatic young Democratic senator, Barack Obama not only decided to run for the US Presidency but, despite many odds, actually succeeded in obtaining the Democratic Party's nomination in the summer of 2008. When Barack Obama was elected president in November 2008, a black American attained the nation's highest office for the first time in American history,[51] and a record number of African Americans now hold seats in the US Congress—both of which facts can certainly be regarded as another step forward in the continuing quest for black political empowerment.

Notes

1. Cf. Peter Stearns, "Emotions History in the United States: Goals, Methods, and Promises" in this volume. I would like to thank my colleagues Charlotte Lerg and Jessica Gienow-Hecht for valuable hints and insights regarding the theory of Emotions History.

2. Paul Ekman, "Are There Basic Emotions?" *Psychological Review* 99, no. 3 (1992): 550–53.
3. Peter Stearns, "Emotional Change and Political Disengagement in the Twentieth-Century United States. A Case Study in Emotions History," *Innovation: The European Journal of Social Science Research* 10, no. 4 (Dec. 1997): 361–80.
4. Joel Pfister, "Book Review of Peter Stearns and Jan Lewis (Eds.): An Emotional History of the United States" (New York 1998), *Journal of the History of the Behavioral Sciences* 34, no. 4 (Fall 1998): 440–42.
5. For further analysis of the role of racial stereotypes in the debate about American slavery cf. Britta Waldschmidt-Nelson, "Von Affen, Waldmännern und Wechselbälgern: Koloniale Stereotypen bei Sealsfield und ihr kulturwissenschaftlicher Kontext," *Jahrbuch der Charles-Sealsfield-Gesellschaft*, ed. Günter Schnitzler und Waldemar Fromm (Freiburg im Breisgau: Rombach, 2004), 129–70.
6. Black female behavior was generally described as highly sexual and promiscuous ("Black Jezebel") to justify the sexual abuse of black women by white men. At the same time, black males who allegedly raped white women or "misbehaved" in a sexually suggestive way towards white women were punished brutally; cf. e.g., the conviction of the Scottsboro Boys (1931) or the murder of fourteen-year-old Emmett Till (1955). For studies on the culture of emotional constraint among white Anglo-Saxon Protestants on the one hand, and the roots of African American culture's emotional expressiveness on the other hand, cf. Ronald T. Takaki, *Iron Cages: Race and Culture in Nineteenth-Century America* (Seattle: University of Washington Press, 1988), and Peter Stearns, *Anger: The Struggle for Emotional Control in America's History* (Chicago: University of Chicago Press, 1986).
7. King described his efforts to avoid negative black stereotypes during his college years: "If I was a minute late to class, I was almost morbidly conscious of it. ... Rather than be thought of as always laughing, I'm afraid I was grimly serious for a time. I had a tendency to overdress, to keep my room spotless, my shoes perfectly shined and my clothes immaculately pressed." Cited in James H. Cone, *Martin & Malcolm & America: A Dream or a Nightmare* (Maryknoll, NY: Orbis, 1993). Also cf. ibid, 27–28; Britta Waldschmidt-Nelson, *Martin Luther King—Malcom X: Gegenspieler* (Frankfurt am Main: Fischer, 2001), 33–60, as well as William H. Chafe, *Civilities and Civil Rights: Greensboro, North Carolina, and the Black Struggle for Freedom* (New York: Oxford University Press, 1980).
8. For a further analysis of King's brilliant rhetoric, the significance of "I Have a Dream" and other famous King speeches, cf. e.g., Keith Miller, *Voice of Deliverance: The Language of Martin Luther King, Jr. and Its Sources* (Athens: University of Georgia Press, 1998), Peter Ling, *Martin Luther King, Jr.* (London: Routledge, 2002), and Frederick Sunnemark, *Ring Out Freedom! The Voice of Martin Luther King, Jr. and the Making of the Civil Rights Movement* (Bloomington: Indiana University Press, 2004).
9. The exact wording of the amendment was that the right of US citizens to vote should not be denied or abridged "on account of race, color, or previous condition of servitude." It was passed five years after the Civil War had ended slavery and two years after the Fourteenth Amendment had granted citizenship to all people, i.e., including blacks, who were born or naturalized in the US.
10. Cf. Paula Giddings, *When and Where I Enter: The Impact of Black Women on Race and Sex in America* (New York: Bantam Books, 1984), 64–74.
11. Cited in *The History of Woman Suffrage*, ed. Elizabeth Cady Stanton, Susan B. Anthony, and Mathilda Gage, 2 vols. (Rochester, NY, 1881), 2:382; reprinted in Giddings, *When and Where I Enter*, 67.

12. Cited in Rosalyn Terborg-Penn, "Afro-Americans in the Struggle for Woman Suffrage" (PhD diss., Howard University, 1977), 82; also cited in Giddings, *When and Where I Enter,* 66.
13. Stanton warned: "The Republican cry of 'Manhood Suffrage' creates an antagonism between black men and all women that will culminate in fearful outrages on womanhood, especially in the southern states." Cited in Terborg-Penn, "Afro-Americans in the Struggle for Woman Suffrage," 90; Giddings, *When and Where I Enter,* 66. For more information on the tension between gender and racial issues for African American women also cf. Peter Ling and Sharon Monteith, *Gender in the Civil Rights Movement* (New Brunswick, NJ: Rutgers University Press, 2004), as well as Gloria Joseph and Jill Lewis, *Common Differences: Conflicts in Black and White Feminist Perspective* (Boston: South End Press, 1986), and Britta Waldschmidt-Nelson, *From Protest to Politics: Black Women in the Civil Rights Movement and in the United States Congress* (Frankfurt: Campus, 1998).
14. James O. Horton and Lois E. Horton, *Hard Road to Freedom: The Story of African America* (New Brunswick, NJ: Rutgers University Press, 2001), 176–225; Vann Woodward, *The Strange Career of Jim Crow* (New York: Oxford University Press, 1974); and Eric Foner, *Reconstruction: America's Unfinished Revolution, 1863–1877* (New York: Harper and Row, 1988).
15. Cited in Mary F. Berry, "Voting Rights and Political Power in American History," in *Voting Rights in America,* ed. Joint Center for Political and Economic Studies (Washington, DC: JCPES, 1992), 62.
16. For more information on white terror against black politicians and the decline of black political power in the South after the end of Reconstruction, cf. the works cited above, as well as Eric Foner, *Nothing But Freedom: Emancipation and Its Legacy* (Baton Rouge: Louisiana State University Press, 1983).
17. Cited in Martina Hahn, "Zwei Jahrzehnte Congressional Black Caucus: Eine Repräsentanz zwischen Anspruch und Wirklichkeit" (MA thesis, University of Munich, 1991), 1. White was a former slave from North Carolina and the first legislator who introduced a bill to make lynching a federal crime.
18. There was no African American representative in Congress from 1901 until 1929, and only Illinois and New York elected a total of four blacks to Congress until 1955—Oscar De Priest (R-IL) 1929–33, Arthur W. Mitchell (D-IL) 1935–1943, William L. Dawson (D-IL) 1943–1970, and Adam Clayton Powell Jr. (D-NY) 1945–1967. The first Southern blacks elected to Congress since Reconstruction were Barbara Jordan (D-TX) and Andrew Young (D-GA) in 1973.
19. Founded in 1909, the NAACP remains until today the largest and most influential civil rights organization in the United States. For an excellent analysis of the organization's work, successes, and challenges with regard to voting rights cf. Manfred Berg, *The Ticket to Freedom: The NAACP and the Struggle for Black Political Integration* (Gainesville: University of Florida Press, 2005).
20. In the fall of 1964 Johnson was focusing on gaining congressional support for his "Great Society" initiative. Also FBI director Herbert Hoover at that time informed the president that King was a communist, a dangerous hypocrite, and that the SCLC was a subversive organization. For the souring of the once close relationship between Johnson and King, especially after King began to publicly criticize the war in Vietnam in 1967 cf. Ling, *King,* and Mark Stern, *Calculating Visions: Kennedy, Johnson, and Civil Rights—Perspectives on the Sixties* (New Brunswick, NJ: Rutgers University Press, 1992).
21. For more information on the SNCC and the civil rights struggle in Mississippi cf. e.g., Clayborne Carson, *In Struggle: SNCC and the Black Awakening of the 1960s* (Cambridge, MA: Harvard University Press, 1981); Kay Mills, *This Little Light of Mine: The*

Life of Fannie Lou Hamer (New York: Dutton, 1993); Charles Payne, *I've Got the Light of Freedom: The Organizing Tradition and the Mississippi Freedom Struggle* (Berkeley: University of California Press, 1995); and Waldschmidt-Nelson, *From Protest to Politics,* 50–98.

22. Cited in Juan Williams, *Eyes on the Prize: America's Civil Rights Years* (New York: Penguin, 1988), 241; also cf. Waldschmidt-Nelson, *From Protest to Politics,* 81–86.
23. Cf. *Philadelphia Independent,* 29 August 1964, 16; also cf. Waldschmidt-Nelson, *From Protest to Politics,* 82.
24. Cited in "Democrats: A Legacy From Fannie Lou Hamer," *Washington Post,* 20 March 1977, 23.
25. Founded in 1957, the SCLC was an umbrella organization for Christian civil rights groups in the South and played a leading role in the freedom struggle until the late 1960s. It still exists, but has lost influence since the death of King in 1968. Cf. David Garrow, *Bearing the Cross: Martin Luther King, Jr. and the Southern Christian Leadership Conference* (New York: Vintage, 1986).
26. Cf. ibid. and Howard Zinn, *SNCC: The New Abolitionists* (Boston: Beacon Press, 1964). The question of maintaining a strictly nonviolent approach to dealing with Southern racists was one of the issues that led to the split between the SCLC and SNCC. After so many of their staffers had been injured or killed during the Mississippi Freedom Summer, some SNCC workers began to carry guns for their own protection.
27. Cf. ibid., also cf. Chandler Davidson and Bernard Grofman, eds., *Quiet Revolution in the South: The Impact of the Voting Rights Act, 1965–1990* (Princeton, NJ: Princeton University Press, 1994).
28. With the exception of representatives Gary Franks (1991–1997) and J. C. Watts (1995–2003), all members of the CBC have been Democrats. For a more detailed analysis of the legislative work and voting behavior of African Americans in Congress, especially black women see Waldschmidt-Nelson, *From Protest to Politics,* and Katherine Tate, *Black Faces in the Mirror: African Americans and their Representatives in Congress* (Princeton, NJ: Princeton University Press, 2003).
29. Ibid., also cf. Joint Center for Political and Economic Studies (JCPES), *Black Elected Officials. A National Roster: 1971–2005,* 34 vols. (Washington, DC: JCPES Press, 1971–2005).
30. Cf. ibid, as well as Chandler Davidson, *Minority Vote Dilution* (Washington, DC: Howard University Press, 1984); Lani Guinier, *The Tyranny of the Majority: Fundamental Fairness in Representative Democracy* (New York: Free Press, 1994); C. Davison and G. Korbel, "At-Large Elections and Minority Group Representation," *Journal of Politics* 43 (1981): 982–1005; and F. Flake, "How to Undo a Century of Racism in Politics" *New York Times,* 11 July 1993, 18.
31. To counter the lack of party support and adequate financial resources, female political activists began to organize Political Action Committees (PACs) for women in the mid-1970s. The purpose of these PACs has been to build up networks, raise funds, and conduct training programs to promote the chances of success of female candidates. For the significance of women's PACs in the 1992 election cf. e.g., Susan Carroll and Wendy Strimling, *Women's Routes to Elective Office: A Comparison with Men's* (New Brunswick, NJ: Center for the American Woman and Politics, 1993), 61–82; Elizabeth Cook, Sue Thomas, and Clyde Wilcox, *The Year of the Woman: Myths and Realities* (Boulder, CO: Westview Press, 1994), 161–96.
32. The term *power of incumbency* stands for the advantage that an incumbent politician has in being able to use his or her popularity, legislative record, as well as the resources of his or her office for a reelection campaign. Cf. Cook, Thomas, and Wilcox, *Year of the Woman,* 9, 125.

33. Cf. B. Wolf, "Voter Anger Is Loud and Clear," *USA Today,* 18 March 1992, 8A; Cook, Thomas, and Wilcox, *Year of the Woman,* 133–35, 164.
34. The dominance of domestic policy issues was also one of the reasons why President George H. Bush, who had been celebrated as the glorious winner of the Gulf War in 1991, lost the election. In opinion polls in spring of 1992, 63% of all male and 73% of all female voters said that it would be beneficial for the general good of the United States to have more female members of Congress. Cf. Cook, Thomas, and Wilcox, *Year of the Woman,* 12–13, 123–37; R. Wolf, "Incumbents Face 'Triple Whammy' in November," *USA Today,* 19 March 1992, 5A; and D. Howlett, "For Some, a Great Notion: Parity," *USA Today,* 1 April 1992, 4A.
35. Waldschmidt-Nelson, *From Protest to Politics,* 162–63; also cf. the following statement by political analyst Ann Lewis: "Women are accurately seen as outsiders. They don't want politics-as-usual, because politics-as-usual leaves them out." Cited in L. Phillips and P. Edmonds, "Special Report: Women in Congress," *USA Today,* 1 April 1992, 1–5A.
36. Cf. Toni Morrison, ed., *Race-ing, Justice, En-gendering Power: Essays on Anita Hill, Clarence Thomas, and the Construction of Social Reality* (New York: Pantheon, 1992), M. Schwartz, "Female Candidates Break Record," *Washington Post,* May 25, 1992, A1+A18, and M. Feinsilber, "Anita Hill Apparently a Powerful Symbol," *Philadelphia Inquirer,* 28 April 1992, A12. For Hill's own account as well as sympathetic commentaries by Patricia Williams, Barbara Smith, and Eleanor Holmes Norton cf. "Capitol Hill's Worst Kept Secret: Sexual Harassment" in *Ms.*, January/February 1992, 32–45. For opposing views cf. G. Will, "Anita Hill's Tangled Web," *Newsweek,* 19 April 1993, 74; and David Brock, *The Real Anita Hill* (New York: Free Press, 1993).
37. Thomas had been director of the EEOC under Reagan, who then nominated him to the Circuit Court of Appeal in 1990. One reason for the relatively quick rise of Thomas under Republican presidents may have been the fact that there simply were not many highly qualified African American lawyers to be found in the Republican camp during the 1980s. Moreover, many white liberal senators held back criticism of Thomas since they were pleased that Bush had at least nominated a black candidate.
38. It is interesting to note that while a majority of African Americans asked in opinion polls supported Thomas, civil rights organizations such as the NAACP or the Rainbow Coalition opposed his nomination. The Hill-Thomas affair also led to a new debate on the issue of gender relations within the black community. Cf. bell hooks, Michele Wallace, Andrew Hacker, and Derrick Bell, "The Crisis of African American Gender Relations," *Transition* 5, no. 66 (1995): 91–175.
39. Cf. Barbara Ehrenreich's comment: "The visual that lingers [from the Hill-Thomas hearings] shows 14 white men confronting a species of human being that they would normally encounter only in the form of a hotel maid. Little clicks of raised consciousness could be heard throughout the land as women plotted to integrate the Senate Judiciary Committee." Barbara Ehrenreich, "What Do Women Have to Celebrate?" *Time,* 16 November 1992, 55.
40. Cf. Moseley-Braun's statement: "The angrier I got at the way the Senate was carrying on, the more I became convinced that it absolutely needed a healthy dose of democracy, that it wasn't enough to have millionaire white males over the age of 50 representing all the people in this country." Jill Nelson, "Carol Moseley Braun: Power Beneath Her Wings," *Essence* (1992): 57. For the effect of the Hill-Thomas hearings on the victories of black female candidates, especially Carol Moseley-Braun's, cf. A. Moore, "The Thomas-Hill Confrontation Is Showing Up in Primary Voting," *Philadelphia Inquirer,* 30 April 1992, A1; M. Schwartz, "Senate Upset Reflects Powerful Legacy of Thomas Hearings," *Washington Post,* 19 March 1992, A15; as well as interviews by the author with Senator

Moseley-Braun (19 May 1994) and her chief of staff, Mike Frazier (3 June 1993), cited in Waldschmidt-Nelson, *From Protest to Politics,* 170–72.

41. Cf. Candice Nelson's comment: "The Hill-Thomas hearings became a rallying point around which campaign contributions could be mobilized, enabling women's PACs to raise money in record numbers." Cook, Thomas, and Wilcox, *Year of the Woman,* 181. EMILY is an acronym for "Early Money Is Like Yeast (it makes the dough rise)" and it expresses the PAC's intention to help female candidates especially by supporting them in the early financing of their campaigns. EMILY's List was founded in 1985; it is the largest of over forty American women's PACs and it supports only Democratic candidates. The oldest women's PAC is the Women's Campaign Fund (WCF), which has existed since 1974 and is bipartisan, while the newest, the WISH-List (founded in March of 1992) supports only Republican, "pro-choice" candidates.
42. This led a number of journalists and scholars to call 1992 "The Year of the Woman" or "The Year of the Black Woman," cf. Waldschmidt-Nelson, *From Protest to Politics,* 159. While the percentage of all women in Congress rose from 5.8 to 10.2%, black female representation enjoyed the largest percentage increase in the 1992 election. In the 103rd Congress, 25% of all black members were women, while only 15.8% of Hispanic members, 14.3% of Asian, and 0% of Native American members were female.
43. In North Carolina, for example, white voters had gone to court claiming that the two newly created black majority districts discriminated against their rights. Until 1992, North Carolina had not sent a single black congressional representative since Reconstruction, for ninety-two years. Nevertheless, the conservative Supreme Court majority ruled in favor of these white plaintiffs in 1993 (*Shaw v. Reno*), arguing that the intentional creation of minority-majority districts was unconstitutional. Cf. David Bositis, "Redistricting 2001," *FOCUS: The Monthly Magazine of the Joint Center for Political and Economic Studies* (April 2001): 3–4.
44. Cf. Eddie N. Williams, "Fixing America's Voting System," *FOCUS* (January 2001): 2; Manning Marable, *Race Reform and Rebellion: The Second Reconstruction and Beyond in Black America, 1945–2006* (Jackson: University Press of Mississippi, 2007), 236–37.
45. The United States is the only democracy in the world where ex-felons are banned from voting (in thirteen states for life). This excludes about 13% of all black males from electoral participation. Cf. Mary K. Garber, "Prospects for Election Reform," *FOCUS* (March 2001): 5–8, and "US-Kongress bestätigt Bushs Wahlsieg," *Süddeutsche Zeitung,* 8 January 2001, 7.
46. Mary K. Garber, "NAACP Files Class-Action Suit," *FOCUS* (February 2001): Trendletter; Ellis Cose, "Getting Ready for the Fire This Time," *Newsweek,* 22 January 2001, 23.
47. Cf. Mary K. Garber, "Prospects for Election Reform," and "U.S. Civil Rights Commission Investigates Florida Voting Irregularities," *FOCUS* (February 2001): Trendletter; Marc Mauer, "Polls Closed to Many Black Men," *FOCUS* (May 2001): 7–8, Quintin J. Simmons, "Report Finds Racial Disparities in Florida Election," *FOCUS* (June 2001): Trendletter.
48. Edward Walsh, "Agreement Reached on Election Reform Bill," *Washington Post,* 15 November 2001, A16; Maxine Waters, "Restoring the Faith of Voters," *FOCUS* (February 2001): 7.
49. Cf. e.g., Eddie N. Williams, "Standing Against Racism in the Wake of Terror," *FOCUS* (September 2001): 2; David Bositis, "The Political Landscape, Then and Now," *FOCUS* (October 2001): 6–8.
50. Cf. Toya Wang, *African Americans, Voting Machines, and Spoiled Ballots: A Challenge to Election Reform* (New York: The Century Foundation, 2004); Henry Louis Gates Jr.,

America Behind the Color Line: Dialogue with African Americans (New York: Warner Books, 2004); Marvin D. Free, *Racial Issues in Criminal Justice: The Case of African Americans* (Westport, CT: Praeger, 2003); Abby L. Ferber, *Home-Grown Hate: Gender and Organized Racism* (New York: Routledge, 2004); and Marable, *Race, Reform, and Rebellion,* 238–56.

51. Joe Davidson, "Black Vote Strong: Black Caucus Grows," FOCUS (November–December 2004), 6–8; Marable, *Race, Reform, and Rebellion,* 239–56; Barack Obama, *Dreams from My Father: A Story of Race and Inheritance* (New York: Times Books, 2004); Barack Obama, *The Audacity of Hope* (New York: Crown, 2006); Lisa Rogak, ed., *Barack Obama in His Own Words* (New York: Carroll and Graf, 2007); and David Mendel, *Obama: From Promise to Power* (New York: Amistad, 2007).

The View from the Other Side: Emotions and Psychology

Chapter 12

The Fortunes of Emotion in the Science of Psychology and in the History of Emotions

Horst U. K. Gundlach

Psychology at present has no single and coherent answer to the general question, "What are emotions?" Psychologists offer many different answers, and some of these answers contradict one another. This is, of course, an unsatisfactory state of affairs, and is a sign that none of the answers so far given is unrestrictedly acceptable, that the question concerns a particularly complicated matter, and that the conceptual and research procedures psychology has at its disposal are not yet adequate.

Many answers psychologists offer seem to be dependent on the means and methods of research available in their times. A look at the research methods adopted in the last 150 years may help to place some of the answers in their appropriate context and explain their specific time- and method-bound contours. Emotion research in psychology looks like an unfinished journey in which general technological progress is used to generate forever-new research methods that in their turn modify the conceptualization of the matter in question.

Notes for this section begin on page 267.

Historical Summary of Psychological Research on Emotions

Research on emotion was for a long time concerned with immediate subjective experiences[1] or the cogitations about and the reminiscences of such experiences, transposed into words and sentences, and thereby relying on the concepts of a naive psychology of the particular society in which these words and sentences were employed. The subjective character either of the immediate experiences or of the verbal account meant to describe them generated a fundamental epistemological problem in that an intersubjective examination of their accuracy and veracity was evidently difficult or impossible to achieve. It became obvious that one had to try to find intersubjective or objective parameters complementing the reported subjective experiences.

For want of other methods, research in the nineteenth and most of the twentieth century has concentrated on surface or peripheral concomitants of emotions. Actors, and not only actors, had always known that facial expressions signal emotions, whether actual ones or staged ones. Theodor Piderit[2] tried to establish a scientific system of mimicry and physiognomics in their association to emotions, and Charles Darwin[3] famously observed the expression of emotion in man and animals, especially in their facial mimicry, but also in their posture and in autonomic nervous reactions like blushing and hair raising.

Physiologists and psychologists tried to illuminate the matter by investigating the physical alterations produced by the autonomic nervous system with the help of the research instruments available to those novelties of the nineteenth century, the physiological and psychological laboratories. The kymograph was used for recording changes in pulse or heart rate, blood pressure, and breathing; the plethysmograph for volume variations caused by blood circulation fluctuations in the forearm or in the penis; and the myograph for low-level muscular activity. The polygraph for investigating the galvanic skin reflex (the changes in electrical conductivity of the skin generated by the products of the sweat glands) joined the laboratory arsenal and later, misnamed as a "lie detector," found wide application also outside the laboratory.

Wilhelm Wundt (1832–1920) launched this new, instrument-aided branch of experimental psychological study, and his disciples, like the Copenhagen psychologist Alfred Lehmann[4] and the Cornell psychologist Edward Bradford Titchener,[5] followed his example. They knew that the state of emotion research was rudimentary: "The unsettled state of psychology of the affective processes is something of a scandal to experimental psychology" and concluded, "Corresponding to the dearth of settled facts, we have a hypertrophy of theory and a large controversial literature."[6] One hundred years later, we certainly have more settled facts, but a hypertrophy of theory and controversial literature remain.

The twentieth century enriched the research arsenal. In the 1920s, various methods for constructing attitude scales were invented, and attitudes were usually defined as consisting of a *cognitive* and an *affective* component. The affective component as measured by attitude scales is very likely not purely affective, but intensely filtered and modulated by cognitive processes like thoughts, values, or convictions. Improvements in photography, the new techniques of motion pictures, and the audio and video recording tapes allowed precise recordings of facial, postural, and vocal expression and opened the way to detailed studies Piderit and Darwin would have loved to have known. The use of low-voltage electrical currents led to electrocardiography and electroencephalography, which were also adopted by emotion research.

But all the objective methods mentioned so far concern merely peripheral or surface phenomena of the total process. What was going on in the center—that is, in the central nervous system, and particularly in the brain—while emotions take place was left in the darkest dark. Panksepp likens all the peripheral phenomena researched in the last 150 years to the "ghostly tracks in the bubble chamber detectors of particle physics,"[7] as they give only vague, approximate intimations of the underlying hormonal and neural dynamics in the brain substrates, especially in the emotional circuits in subcortical areas.

In the second half of the twentieth century, various steps in the direction of an objective exploration of this mysterious central interior were taken. Hormonal chemistry of the endocrine system, neurochemistry, and brain psychopharmacology were discovered and slowly used in the research of emotions. Behavioral and experiential consequences of brain injury and of brain surgery were explored. Chemical treatment and electrical stimulation of the brain (ESB) were introduced. It also became accepted that some questions could be tackled by using animal models. The maturation of evolutionary psychology led to fruitful research hypotheses.

The latest methods of noninvasive brain exploration, like computerized tomography (CT), MRI (magnetic resonance imaging), fMRI (functional magnetic resonance imaging), PET (positron emission tomography), SPET (single-photon emission tomography), and others, have opened new pathways to get to the core of the emotional process.

The Vague Consensus on Emotion in Psychology Textbooks

Although there is still no straightforward unanimity among psychologists on the question, "What are emotions?" there seems to exist a vague consensus in psychology textbooks as to what to look for if one talks about emotions. This consensus may be sketched in the following way.

Emotions are comprehensive processes/states[8] of varying intensity in an individual that follow certain *elicitors* (or stimuli or triggers), involving processes in organs controlled by the autonomic nervous system (*ANS*), expressing themselves in facial, vocal, and other movements (*expressions*), accompanied by so-called subjective *experiences* (or feelings) as well as by *cognitions,* and leading to specific impulsive *behavioral (conative) tendencies* that prepare for certain *behaviors* or actions.

For example, when I happen to perceive my sweetheart (the elicitor, obviously an acquired one), my heart rate, pulse, and breathing accelerate (thanks to the ANS); my voice gets sugary and produces gibberish, and my facial muscles may compose a foolish mien (the expression part); I feel lighthearted and cheerful (the subjective part, the immediate affective experience); a suitable thought gets shaped like "what a surprise she is here" (another subjective part, a propositional cognition); and I may sense the need to run in a straight line to the elicitor, irrespective of the risk of getting under a motorcar (the conative or behavioral tendency), maybe resulting in more or rather less clear-headed behavior.

So much for a superficial consensus displayed in most of the textbooks of psychology of the last twenty-odd years. What is lacking in this slightly outdated sketch is the most obvious, which also is, unfortunately, hidden and nearly unobservable—namely, endocrine processes and processes in various layers of the peripheral and central nervous system including the brain. Hardly anybody would want to deny that they play a central role in emotional processes, and that therefore they should be included in the consensus and in the sweetheart example. Eventually, as general psychology comes out of the eggshell of methodical behaviorism, they will be allowed to enter contemporary textbooks.

The Profusion of Disagreement on Emotion in Psychology

Emotions seem to be complex processes/states that are assemblages of various processes of the kind enumerated. One of the general problems surrounding emotions is which of these processes should be part of the aggregate concept of emotion. It will be easy to see that progress in research techniques is mirrored in the accumulation of these processes over the last 150 years and in some of the disagreements. No doubt, psychologists are still far from building a determinate general consensus. Quite the contrary. Disagreement on the question "What are emotions?" thrives, and it concerns all the points sketched in the above textbook consensus.

First, the elicitors. It seems that elicitors in the environment are not always required. Some psychologists would assert that they play an important role, but do not belong to the concept of emotions. In her absence, the mere thought of my sweetheart can engender the processes specified. Thoughts, whether memories or fantasies, are usually not considered belonging to the category of elicitors, unless one sees them as instances of spontaneous self-stimulation or assumes the inadvertent perception of stimuli associated with the elicitor. There might be spontaneously generated emotional processes/states, as direct stimulation (through chemicals or electrical currents or correspondingly located spontaneous tumors) of appropriate brain areas seems to demonstrate. There is, nevertheless, the widespread tendency to see elicitors as quasi-natural parts of the whole process, self-stimulation by thoughts as a later development possible in more complex brain structures, and chemical brain stimulation and ESB as an artificial and tumors as a pathological influence on the relevant neural structures.

Second, the results of the workings of the ANS seem to be generally accepted as part of the whole picture, unless, of course, one restricts emotions to the subjective portion, a position still maintained in some quarters. More space is usually given to the emotion-specificity of the outcome of autonomic nervous processes. The old thesis was that since we can distinguish between emotions, the accompanying peripheral processes must be distinguishable as well. However, it has proven difficult with the instruments of the nineteenth and early twentieth century to find decisive differences that correspond to distinct emotions. This opened the way for the famous thesis by Stanley Schachter and Jerome E. Singer that there is only one state of undifferentiated ANS arousal, the different emotions being products of different cognitive activity or interpretation, an influential thesis known as Cognitive Labeling Theory.[9] It is less popular today, but nonetheless a textbook matter. It is a product of the times when research methodology had to concentrate on the peripheral processes because there was hardly a method to get at the central processes, other than the attitude-measuring scales that rely, of course, on cognitions. As new methods of revealing central processes were introduced into emotion research, it became evident that peripheral processes are not relevant for emotional specificity of ANS processes, that cognitions were not the only realm of specificity, that nonsurface parts of the ANS do show emotion-specific reactions, and that emotions are associated with specific brain processes/states.

Third, expressive processes do not seem to be a necessary part of the picture. I may, for example, have acquired a habit of presenting a stoic, immutable, botoxed stiff-upper-lip countenance. Here the consensus, inspired by the work of Paul Ekman[10] and others who use the latest photographic, film, video, and audio equipment, goes in the direction of assuming that visually or auditorily perceptible expressive processes are typical of emotional processes in higher animals that live in social bands. As a general rule, they are more complex in those that, like *Homo sapiens* or *Canis lupus,* live in hierarchically structured bands than in others that live in herds, like *Equus caballus.* Little or no expressive movements are shown in species that live solitarily like *Ursus arctos.* In the case of *Homo sapiens,* the audible utterances may go from preverbal grunts or snorts related to ANS-controlled changes in breathing to paraverbal monosyllabics like "aah" or "ooh" to stereotyped, semantically charged articulations like scatological, sexual, or blasphemous curse words or phrases, whether crude or masked by euphemisms. Owing to Puritan coyness, this last component, though easy to observe and record, rarely makes it into American textbooks.

Fourth, even the subjective experience in the whole picture of emotion is controversial. Some would denounce all the other components as irrelevant, decreeing that emotions are nothing but those specific subjective experiences or mental occurrences, and that all the other components do not belong here. Joseph E. Ledoux, for example, defines emotions simply as "affectively charged, subjectively experienced states of awareness," and "conscious states."[11] Ken Gergen endorses the position that the psychology of emotion labors under what Whitehead called the *fallacy of misplaced concreteness* and that only the analysis of language games is adequate. His arguments rely on the controversial assumption that love, anger, guilt, etc. are mental predicates.[12] However, this conception of emotions as undilutedly subjective or mental has become rare in the psychology of the last 150 years. It was, of course, the dominant notion before emotion was dragged into the physiological and psychological laboratories.

Regarding the subjective experience, some would take the opposite view and declare it not at all a requisite part of the whole—since it does now and then happen, to my amazement, that other people observe from my facial expression, vocalizations, posture, or behavior that I am angry at something without my realizing that I actually am in this particular process/state. The question can also be formulated thus: are there unconscious or nonconscious emotions? If emotions are defined as "subjectively experienced states of awareness," then the answer can only be negative. But the case may not be that simple; just observe newborn babies or sleeping dogs. The impression that they go through emotional processes/states is hard to dismiss, but they do not seem to have awareness.

Fifth, the place of cognitions in emotional processes is often debated, as already touched on above. Some would object to the inclusion of cognitions as not altogether belonging to the realm of emotion, emotions being considered as precognitive functions of the mind or brain. Robert B. Zajonc, for example, states that "affect and cognition are separate and partially independent states."[13] The cognitive appraisal theory by Richard S. Lazarus, however, considers cognitions as an integrated feature of all emotional states[14] that determine the nature of the beginning emotional process and precede the subjective experience. The compromise here could be that although cognitions are as parts of emotions, they are such important stimulators and modifiers of these affective processes that they should not be left out of the whole picture. Another view of the role of cognitions is that they are necessary only in certain self-conscious evaluative emotions like pride or shame that cannot arise without certain cognitions, as developmental psychology has shown. But then, the question "What are cognitions?" is similarly fraught with dissent as is the question about emotion.

Sixth, the place of conations or behavioral tendencies and behaviors in emotions has been contested. Some would object to the inclusion of such unobservables as behavioral tendencies in any conception, unless they consist of minuscule muscular activity as registered by a myograph. Others would say that behavior cannot be part of emotion. But behavioristic philosophers like Gilbert Ryle would maintain that although the term *emotion* may have different meanings, it basically refers not to "occult inner states"[15] but to behavioral expression.

Seventh, the central neurohormonal processes were for a long time fairly invisible in the discussion of emotions, as nothing was known about them. But in recent decades and with the advent of suitable research techniques, they have become commonly accepted facets of the emotional processes, unless one subscribes to the experience-only view.

This has been an overview of the areas of disagreement regarding the typical components of the present-day textbook consensus on emotion. But dissent looms also in other aspects of our topic.

Further Points of Discord on Emotion

There is a general criticism of the vague consensus portrayed above: that it relies heavily on input and output aspects of the topic. Jaak Panksepp prefers an approach that defines emotions focusing on their adaptive, central integrative functions:

> Emotions are the psychoneural processes that are especially influential in controlling the vigor and patterning of actions in the dynamic flow of intense behavioral interchanges between animals, as well as with certain objects during circumstances that are especially important for survival. Each emotion has a characteristic "feeling tone" that is especially important in encoding the intrinsic values of these interactions, depending on whether they are likely to promote or hinder survival (in both the immediate personal and the longer-term repro-

> ductive sense). These affective functions are especially important in encoding new information, retrieving information on subsequent occasions, and perhaps also in allowing animals to generalize about new events rapidly and efficiently (i.e., allowing animals to jump to potentially adaptive "snap decisions"). The underlying neural systems may also compute levels of psychological homeostasis or equilibrium by evaluating an organism's adaptation or success in the environment.[16]

Functional definitions of emotions as outlined here are still rarely used in textbooks, but they might have a brilliant future.

Another bone of contention occasionally discussed but unresolved are the temporal confinements of an emotional process/state. The starting point is usually seen as the time of the appearance or perception of the elicitor or stimulus. But when does the ensuing process/state end and what are the manifestations of that ending? Proposals about the duration of emotions range from seconds to minutes to much longer time spans.

This is connected to the problem of whether it is worthwhile to distinguish between emotions and moods and temperaments, each involving a time span of a quite different magnitude. Whereas a temperament is usually accepted as nearly unchangeable and therefore different from an emotion, the distinction between a mood and an emotion is passionately debated.

In case a distinction between emotions and moods is accepted, their most obvious difference is identified as their duration. Emotions are seen as lasting from seconds to minutes, and moods from hours to days. An affective state that lasts for weeks and months, if it is not indicative of a definite temperament, might be so of an affective disorder. Paul Ekman[17] suggests that another difference between emotions and moods lies in their expressivity, emotions being coupled to expressive processes, whereas moods are not. But this does not appear to be an unmistakable criterion, since moods may manifest themselves in posture, mimic, or vocal pitch. Often noticed is the interactive relation between emotions and moods, as emotions are capable of changing moods, and moods liable to influence the quality and the intensity of an emotional reaction to an elicitor. This again may not supply a clear dividing line between the two. Other candidates like intentionality whose presence is supposedly required for emotions, but whose absence is supposedly required for moods, may also be inadequate.

Another field of disagreement concerns taxonomy. First, how to classify the various processes/states that are already correctly identified as emotions into subcategories such as anger or lust or joy? Should one proceed according to the phenomenal differences in immediate experience as has been customary for centuries, or according to differences in expression, or in brain processes, or should one adopt a classification based on reinforcement contingencies like Rolls[18]?

Second, which processes/states should be meaningfully gathered in the aggregate category[19] "emotion" and which ones should be excluded? Should, for example, startle be included or not? Or would it be better considered a reflex? Are emotions reflexes or not? Deliberations may be found in P. Ekman, W. V. Friesen, and R. C. Simons,[20] and R. C. Simons.[21] The fundamental question whether the taxon "emotion" makes any sense at all is rarely debated, but no satisfactory answer has been offered.

What about the affective feeling states connected with hunger, thirst, oxygen hunger, fatigue, excretion needs, or salt craving? They are usually treated under the headline of motivation, and not of emotion, since they all serve the homeostatical maintenance of the organism, *vulgo* bodily needs, and are not generated by external elicitors, but by processes/states within the organism. What about the affective feeling states connected to sexual activity in the widest sense? Should they be included in the bestiary of emotions, or would it better to let them go on squatting under the umbrella of motivation?

A further open question concerns the kind of entity that can have an emotion. Does it have to be necessarily an individual, or could it be also a group of individuals? Janice R. Kelly[22] affirms that the concept of a group emotion has a long history, but that unsurprisingly there is no common definition. Besides a group emotion, she also admits a group mood. Undeniably, these concepts are not nonsensical.

Why This Cacophony of Vague Consensus and Definite Dissent?

So far our sketch of major fields of disagreement among psychologists. It is far from being exhaustive. An outsider could very well despair about so much cacophony. But the emotional reaction of desperation ignores the fact that psychology is an empirical science that does not start with fixed and incorrigible definitions.

Psychology of emotions as psychology in general takes over everyday concepts, the concept of emotion in this case, with all its vagueness and imprecision. It is assumed that a more precise understanding of emotions will come primarily from studying single processes/states and individual taxons of such processes/states, not from ruminations over the essence or quintessence of the superior taxon emotion. And it is expected that in the long run this research will determine a better definition.

It would be an error to assume that empirical sciences accomplish only empirical research. As their history reveals, they distinguish themselves from other scientific enterprises in that they exhibit intricate feedback cycles between empirical findings and conceptual refinements. These refinements may be nonspectacular and cumulative or they may be drastic and radical, presenting instances of what has been called a scientific revolution.

The complex feedback sequences between empirical studies and conceptual amendment and adjustment may elude the outsider, as it often happens that a science retains older words even as the concepts they designate have been altered. Widely known examples from the science of mechanics are the words *force, work, energy,* and *power*—at a first glance everyday words, but they designate quite dissimilar concepts.

To clarify the constant interaction between empirical work and conceptualization, a short account using emotion as example might be helpful. It is necessary to make a threefold distinction, namely, between the word or the term *emotion,* the concept *emotion,* and the real thing/property/process/state *emotion,* and no doubt should ever be left as to which category is being dealt with.

The English word *emotion* is an artificial sign or symbol. Its designatum is the concept *emotion,* usually conceived as a collective or class concept. And it denotes a factual thing/property/process/state (whatever its ontological status), i.e., an emotion (or the set of emotions), its denotatum. The concept *emotion* refers to the factual thing/property/process/state, i.e., an emotion (or the set of emotions). The meaning (or intension) of a concept is typically explicated by propositions that connect it with other concepts.

We know the word *emotion* is used in modern English, approximately since David Hume, and similar words are used in other languages of European origin. We assume that this word designates a concept, and we assume that this concept has a factual reference class, namely, the emotions. Now in everyday language, the concepts that words designate are usually rather fuzzy—they wobble according to context and have no fixed boundaries. In different situations or by different people, the same word can be used to designate concepts that are not identical. Also, in everyday language, not much reflection is given to the question whether the things/properties/processes/states to which the concept is assumed to refer, or which a word is supposed to denote, can be grouped into a sensible set or class, in other words, form a natural (in the widest sense possible) kind.

In a science that deals with factual objects, this should be different. One has to ask what is the set of factual objects a concept is supposed to refer to. Does it make sense to use such a concept, and does the concept fit into the theory that is meant to represent the factual domain the actual object belongs to? No doubt the word *emotion* is used in the empirical science of psychology. Unfortunately, there is still a debate going on about the most proficient way to define the concept that the word should designate. Scientific concepts with empirical reference go through a process of evolution in which only those concepts should survive that serve best to grasp reality. Note that this is not a descriptive, but a prescriptive statement, as it is quite possible that, for example, ideological notions interfere with this evolution.

Empirical sciences start with provisional concepts and aim to move to better established ones, and "emotion" still belongs to the very provisional concepts in psychology. A multitude of voices inside psychology (and also outside) go on proposing refined definitions that to the outsider, and some insiders, sound cacophonous.

Looking back at the reported disagreements and keeping in mind the distinction between words and their denotata, and concepts and their referents, one will see that most disagreements mentioned so far concern the concept of emotion, not the referent emotion itself. They concern not so much factual matters but concepts that belong to a different level of discussion. Facts are mentioned in the debate in order to demonstrate that the concept an author proposes fits reality better than another concept, not to prove that older assumptions concerning factual matters have been proven wrong. The big battles about emotion, therefore, cannot be won by empirical studies alone, but empirical studies are liable to suggest which of various proposals for the definition of a concept is better suited to grasp the matter studied.

Take as the example the question whether emotions and moods are different processes. There is no yardstick available that allows you to measure reality and then come to an answer to this question. The question masquerades as a statement about facts, but is actually about concepts. Nonetheless, empirical studies will guide us in deciding whether it helps our understanding of the processes in question to form two different concepts "emotion" and "mood," and to allow or to prohibit propositions like "No mood is an emotion, and no emotion is a mood."

A debate about concepts is likely to results in a confusion of words. Since it is not customary to coin new words every time a new concept is suggested (see the above examples from mechanics), since it is inevitable that there be instances when we do not know exactly which concept an author means by a certain word. This state of affairs no doubt adds to the cacophonous impression of the occasional reader. Another nesting ground for misunderstandings is the fact that it is not always made clear if a discussion concerns a concept or the referent of that concept, and sporadically one must doubt if the author her/himself has a clear grasp of what she/he is talking about.

At any rate, the complex debate about the refinement of concepts is apt to produce an ever-growing cleavage between the concepts of everyday discourse and the concepts used inside the sciences. Recall the words *force* or *energy* in everyday language and in physics. Let us examine an example where such a gap is already discernible. In everyday discourse, *emotion* or words that designate subordinate concepts are often used to denote a disposition, not a process/state. For example, saying "I love x," or "I despise y," usually means: "If I encounter (actually or in deliberations) elicitors x, or y, the emotion of love, or of disdain, will spring up." Neither the lover of the Chinese cuisine nor the foreigner-despising xenophobe is in a permanent state of emotional arousal. Dispositions are generally excluded from the concept *emotion* used in psychological emotion research. Not so in everyday language, and neither is it so among historians of emotion. Such dispositions are studied in social psychology under the heading of attitude, and were also called sentiments in older days.

In short, the psychology of emotion is a field of study about which many more details are known today than in Titchener's times, but it still lingers in a fetal state as there is still vast dissent about the appropriate fundamental concepts. This is a problem for historians studying what they call the history of emotions. Psychology does not yet offer them a reliable conceptual toolbox, but rather the kind of hypertrophy Titchener laments, and so historians fall back on everyday language and its obscurities.

All the points made so far mostly concern the conceptual grip psychology wants to have on emotions. Psychologists assume that there are processes/states that naturally belong to an empirical science like psychology. Of course, this whole undertaking can be sabotaged by the opposite claim that the everyday concept of emotion that psychology has adopted is but a cultural artifact (or construct[23]) that has no distinct reference in a particular and definite kind of process/state, which is equivalent to a collective, society-specific or culture-specific hallucination or delusion or jest like Father Christmas, which may have the function or purpose of regulating social processes and stabilizing social power structures, and which can only be comprehended with this function. Psychologists in their majority are not of this conviction.

Some Unresolved Empirical Questions of Interest for the Historian of Emotion

Apart from the quandary of erecting a worthwhile concept of emotion and of its subordinate constituents, there are problems of an empirical nature with the processes/states themselves and about their causal connections. Here are some of the questions.

How do emotions interact? How does lust, for example, elicit shame or guilt? How do mixed emotions arise, and what would be an amalgam of emotions? How do emotions interact with perception, cognition (e.g., memory), motivation, conation, volition, behavior, and action? Are there really neurophysical and neurochemical markers that distinguish so-called basic emotions, whether it be the so-called seven deadly sins (Lust, Gluttony, Greed, Sloth, Wrath, Envy, and Pride), or the seven core emotional systems Panksepp identified (the four premammalian: FEAR, RAGE, SEEKING, and LUST, and the three mammalian: CARE, PANIC, PLAY)?[24]

There are questions of the plasticity of emotional reactions—in other words, of the role of learning in emotional reactions. Since all behavior in higher animals is a blend of innate and learned ingredients, what are the relevant learning processes, or what role is played by the different forms of learning like sensitization, habituation and dishabituation, classical conditioning, instrumental conditioning, or others? And what are the constraints on learning, in mice or in humans?

What about the trigger? Are there unconditional elicitors for specific emotions? How do conditional elicitors get installed? How similar is this to the classical conditioning of conditional reflexes? How plastic are autonomic nervous reactions? Is it for example possible to reduce through learning the amount of blood streaming to the face in the case of blushing in shame? How plastic is the expressive display, and to what degree can the learning of display rules modify facial expression? Presumably, a lot, as trained actors would certify.

This has been a short enumeration of some of the topics psychological research is involved with. Psychology has elucidated some details of these problems, but general statements cannot yet be deduced.

What Is the History of Emotions About?

The answer to the question of what the history of emotions is about appears self-evident: emotions, of course. But things are not that simple. Emotions are transitory, ephemeral processes/states, and past emotions have vanished, mostly without leaving any decipherable traces. We do not have any method to reconstruct the fury of a Cro-Magnon from the splintered bones of his enemies, or the grief of a disappointed rococo demoiselle from her tearful handkerchief. As emotions are very complex processes/states, it is unlikely that even in a laboratory enough material could be recorded to reconstruct the complete event together with the context in which it took place.

Although we have descriptions of emotions that the authors have experienced or observed in other beings, these cannot but be filtered through a perceptive apparatus too slow to register essential components of the process/state, processed by a cognitive apparatus already loaded with preconceptions, and tainted with what Peter Goldie[25] called postrationalizing. There is no sure way of backtracking from the written or printed record to the original processes/states. So the history of emotions can hardly be about the referents of the certainly vague but not totally indefinite concept *emotion* as used in present-day general psychology. And the appearance that the question is trivial must be deceptive.

It is not my intention to delimit the subject matter of the history of emotions. But allow me to cite some topics from the relevant literature in order to show their affinity to a branch of psychology rarely mentioned in the publications of historians. Among historians of emotions there is a discussion on the changing concepts of emotion and their subordinate taxa, which generally involves less the concepts used in science, but rather foremost the nebulous and fluctuating concepts used in everyday conversation. The discussion also deals with the word *emotion* and the metamorphoses or constancy of related words. At times, it is hard to discern whether the various claims are about words or concepts or factual matter.

There is an interest among historians as to how the conceptual framework fashioned by a society or a part of it is used to rank and evaluate—positively or negatively—the range of emotional events in humans and in animals. Their interest lies in the web of belief a society may weave to connect its worldview or parts of it to their traditional view of emotions, be it specific emotions or specific intensities of emotions. They are interested in the learning processes that connect neutral elicitors to an emotion, e.g., how a piece of cloth becomes a national flag with all the love and hate it might elicit. There is interest in how these learning processes occur, be it by accident or through planned indoctrination. These learning processes lead to emotional dispositions, i.e., a readiness to react emotionally in a certain way when the elicitor is perceived. And it is these dispositions that seem to attract more attention than the emotion process/state itself. Publications on love, anger, guilt, jealousy, hate, or joy usually concern dispositions, not emotions in the sense of general psychology.

There is an interest in the attitudes toward various emotions that flourish in various times and countries or societal segments, and also how these attitudes themselves have instigated emotional responses to the occurrence of emotions in oneself or in others. There is an interest in individual as well as in social cognitive reflections and deliberations about emotions, be it public preachings about deadly sins, or lust in the Oval Office, or lack of love of one's country. There is interest in the expressive part of emotions and in the societal display rules or norms and standards regulating the expression of emotions, in public or in private.

There are certainly many more topics that could be named here, but this short list may suffice to justify the following suspicion: that perhaps what historians of emotions scrutinize is in the end related to those dispositions psychologists call attitude, a very significant topic in social psychology. The textbooks of social psychology usually explain that there are three major conceptions of an attitude, a one-component, a two-component, and a three-component model. The first considers only the affect, the second comprises an affective and a cognitive, and the third an additional conative or behavioral component. Most textbooks add that today the second model is the most widely used and accepted.

Irrespective of these differences, I shall quote a number of past and current definitions of attitude from within social psychology with the purpose of showing how far what historians of emotions call emotion is comparable to what psychologists call attitude:

> An attitude is a mental and neural state of readiness, organized through experience, exerting a directive or dynamic influence upon the individual's response to all objects and situations with which it is related.[26]

> An enduring organization of motivational, emotional, perceptual, and cognitive processes with respect to some aspect of the individual's world.[27]

> A relatively enduring system of affective, evaluative reactions based upon and reflecting the evaluative concepts or beliefs which have been learned about the characteristics of a social object or class of social objects.[28]

> (a) A relatively enduring organization of beliefs, feelings and behavioural tendencies towards socially significant objects, groups, events or symbols. (b) A general feeling of evaluation—positive or negative—about some person, object or issue.[29]

I suspect that historians of emotions can find important aspects of their interest included in these descriptions. Granted, social psychologists often are content to look at the general affective value, either positive or negative, and do not always delve into the emotional specificity of that affect, but that does not mean that specific emotions are not treated. A casual perusal of any textbook of social psychology will assure one that they are.

For the time being I take the liberty to modestly propose that once the misunderstandings owing to different concepts being designated by homophone words are overcome, a cooperation between historians of emotions and psychologists could be much more fruitful in the realm of attitude research than in emotion research.

Notes

1. *Experience* here means the immediate, subjective, experiential part in the process of an emotion, not the experience that results from becoming aware of living through an affec-

tive process or from cogitating about it, which may then be articulated in letters, diaries, or other relatively permanent traces. Often the expression "emotional experience" is used ambiguously, which is bound to obscure the matter. For clarity it seems advisable to use different words or phrases for different things. Otherwise one might be tempted to deduce the immediate, subjective, experiential part in the process of an emotion from the products of an awareness of or cogitation about it. That would constitute a regression to an intellectualistic psychology, which the great experimentalist Wilhelm Wundt had criticized severely a long time ago. He also remarked that everyday or vulgar psychology was typically intellectualistic, and that any form of an intellectualistic psychology was unfit to deal with emotions, see W. Wundt, *Grundzüge der physiologischen Psychologie,* 6th ed., (Leipzig, 1911), 3:217.

2. Theodor Piderit, *Wissenschaftliches System der Mimik und Physiognomik* (Detmold: Klingenberg, 1867).
3. Charles Darwin, *The Expression of Emotion in Man and Animals* (London: Murray, 1872).
4. Alfred Lehmann, *Die Hauptgesetze des menschlichen Gefühlslebens. Eine experimentelle und analytische Untersuchung über die Natur und das Auftreten der Gefühlszustände nebst einem Beitrage zu deren Systematik,* (Leipzig: Reisland, 1892).
5. Edward Bradford Titchener, *Experimental Psychology: A Manual of Laboratory Practice,* 2 vols. (New York: Macmillan, 1901).
6. Titchener, *Experimental Psychology,* 149.
7. Jaak Panksepp, *Affective Neuroscience: The Foundations of Human and Animal Emotions* (New York: Oxford University Press, 1998), 9.
8. The expression "processes/states" may be clumsy, but it serves to take a neutral position in the debate whether it is sensible to distinguish emotions and moods, the latter usually seen as states, the former as processes. A state is, at any rate, a process with the change ratio of zero.
9. Stanley Schachter and Jerome E. Singer, "Cognitive, Social, and Physiological Determinants of Emotional State," *Psychological Review* 69 (1962): 379–99.
10. For example, Paul Ekman, *Emotions in the Human Face,* 2nd ed (Cambridge: Cambridge University Press, 1982).
11. Joseph E. Ledoux, "Emotional Processing, but Not Emotions, Can Occur Unconsciously," in *The Nature of Emotion. Fundamental Questions,* ed. Paul Ekman and Richard J. Davidson (New York: Oxford University Press, 1994), 291.
12. Kenneth J. Gergen, "History and Psychology: Three Weddings and a Future, " in *An Emotional History of the United States,* ed. Peter N. Stearns and Jan Lewis (New York: New York University Press, 1998), 23f.
13. Robert B. Zajonc, "On the Primacy of Affect," *American Psychologist* 39 (1984): 117.
14. Richard S. Lazarus, "Thoughts on the Relations between Emotion and Cognition," *American Psychologist* 37 (1982): 1021.
15. Gilbert Ryle, *The Concept of Mind* (London: Hutchison, 1949), 110.
16. Panksepp, *Affective Neuroscience,* 48.
17. Paul Ekman, "Moods, Emotions, and Traits," in *The Nature of Emotion: Fundamental Questions,* ed. Paul Ekman and Richard J. Davidson (New York: Oxfrod University Press, 1994), 56–58.
18. Edmund T. Rolls, *Emotion Explained* (Oxford: Oxford University Press, 2007).
19. Thomas Dixon, *From Passions to Emotions: The Creation of a Secular Psychological Category* (Cambridge: Cambridge University Press, 2003) provides a history of the creation of the fairly new category of emotion and the connected displacement of older categories like appetite, passion, affection, and sentiment.

20. Paul Ekman, Wallace V. Friesen, and Ronald C. Simons, "Is the Startle Reaction an Emotion?" *Journal of Personality and Social Psychology* 49 (1985): 1416–26.
21. Ronald C. Simons, *Boo! Culture, Experience, and the Startle Reflex* (New York: Oxford University Press, 1996).
22. Janice R. Kelly, "Mood and Emotions in Groups," in *Blackwell Handbook of Social Psychology: Group Processes,* ed. Michael A. Hogg and R. Scott Tinsdale (Malden, MA: Blackwell, 2001), 164–81.
23. Occasionally, one comes across the remark "emotion is a construct" (or "construction"). Although constructionists find phrases like "x is a construct" easily comprehensible, others have a hard time trying to make sense of it. It seems likely that the phrase is a faddish shorthand for: The word "x" designates a concept "x," and is supposed to denote actual processes/states. In some cases, the sense is therefore the trivial proposition: "x" is a concept. Trivial, because every concept is something like a construction, that is, a human-made invention. In other cases, it seems to mean: "x" refers to a hypothetical entity whose reality is not (yet) conclusively proven. In yet other cases, it seems to mean: "x" does not denote, and "x" does not refer, to anything real. Such statements are usually proffered ex cathedra. Granted, in cases like the phrase "Father Christmas," only infants would demand solid proof. In the cases of the word *emotion* and the concept *emotion,* however, this seems to be a question not simply for the armchair, but for the empirical sciences, and since the word *emotion* designates a host of different concepts, it is desirable to first clarify which concept is under examination.
24. Jaak Panksepp, "The Neuroevolutionary and Neuroaffective Psychobiology of the Prosocial Brain," in *Oxford Handbook of Evolutionary Psychology,* ed. Robin I. M. Dunbar and Louise. Barrett (Oxford: Oxford University Press, 2007), 145–62. He capitalizes the words to indicate that they designate new, distinctly defined concepts that are related to, but not identical with the ordinary concepts everyday language users assume are their designata.
25. Peter Goldie, *The Emotions: A Philosophical Exploration.* (Oxford: Clarendon Press, 2000).
26. Gordon W. Allport, "Attitudes," in *A Handbook of Social Psychology,* ed. Carl Murchison (Worcester, MA: Clark University Press, 1935), 810.
27. David Krech and Richard S. Crutchfield, *Theory and Problems of Social Psychology.* (New York: McGraw-Hill, 1948), 152.
28. Marvin E. Shaw and Jack M. Wright, *Scales for the Measurement of Attitudes* (New York: McGraw-Hill, 1967), 10.
29. Michael A. Hogg and Graham M. Vaughan, *Social Psychology,* 4th ed. (Harlow, UK: Pearson Prentice Hall, 2005), 150.

Bibliography

Allport, Gordon W. "Attitudes." In *A Handbook of Social Psychology,* edited by Carl Murchison, 798–844. Worcester, MA: Clark University Press, 1935.

Darwin, Charles. *The Expression of Emotion in Man and Animals.* London: Murray, 1872.

Dixon, Thomas. *From Passions to Emotions: The Creation of a Secular Psychological Category.* Cambridge: Cambridge University Press, 2003.

Ekman, Paul. *Emotions in the Human Face,* 2nd ed (Cambridge: Cambridge University Press, 1982).

———. "Moods, Emotions, and Traits." In *The Nature of Emotion: Fundamental Questions,* edited by Paul Ekman and Richard J. Davidson, 56–58. New York: Oxford University Press, 1994.

Ekman, Paul, Wallace V. Friesen, and Ronald C. Simons. "Is the Startle Reaction an Emotion?" *Journal of Personality and Social Psychology* 49 (1985): 1416–26.

Gergen, Kenneth. "History and Psychology: Three Weddings and a Future." In *An Emotional History of the United States,* edited by Peter N. Stearns and Jan Lewis, 15–29. New York, 1998.

Goldie, Peter *The Emotions: A Philosophical Exploration.* Oxford: Clarendon Press, 2000.

Hogg, Michael A., and Graham M. Vaughan. *Social Psychology,* 4th ed. Harlow, UK: Pearson Prentice Hall, 2005.

Kelly, Janice R. "Mood and Emotions in Groups." In *Blackwell Handbook of Social Psychology: Group Processes,* edited by Michael A. Hogg and R. Scott Tinsdale, 164–81. Malden, MA: Blackwell, 2001.

Krech, David and Richard S. Crutchfield, *Theory and Problems of Social Psychology.* New York: McGraw-Hill, 1948.

Lazarus, Richard S. "Thoughts on the Relations between Emotion and Cognition." *American Psychologist* 37 (1982): 1019–24.

Ledoux, Joseph E. "Emotional Processing, but Not Emotions, Can Occur Unconsciously." In *The Nature of Emotion: Fundamental Questions,* edited by Paul Ekman and Richrad J. Davidson, 291–92. New York: Oxfrod University Press, 1994.

Lehmann, Alfred. *Die Hauptgesetze des menschlichen Gefühlslebens: Eine experimentelle und analytische Untersuchung über die Natur und das Auftreten der Gefühlszustände nebst einem Beitrage zu deren Systematik.* Leipzig, Reisland, 1892.

Panksepp, Jaak. *Affective Neuroscience: The Foundations of Human and Animal Emotions.* New York: Oxford University Press, 1998.

———. "The Neuroevolutionary and Neuroaffective Psychobiology of the Prosocial Brain." In *Oxford Handbook of Evolutionary Psychology,* edited by Robin I. M. Dunbar and Louise Barrett, 145–62. Oxford, 2007.

Piderit, Theodor. *Wissenschaftliches System der Mimik und Physiognomik.* Detmold: Klingenberg, 1867.

Rolls, Edmund T. *Emotion Explained.* Oxford: Oxford University Press, 2007.

Ryle, Gilbert. *The Concept of Mind.* London: Hutchinson, 1949.

Schachter, Stanley, and Jerome E. Singer. "Cognitive, Social, and Physiological Determinants of Emotional State." *Psychological Review* 69 (1962): 379–99.

Shaw, Marvin E., and Jack M. Wright, *Scales for the Measurement of Attitudes.* New York: McGraw-Hill, 1967.

Simons. Ronald C. *Boo! Culture, Experience, and the Startle Reflex.* New York: Oxford University Press, 1996.

Titchener, Edward Bradford. *Experimental Psychology: A Manual of Laboratory Practice,* 2 vols. New York: Macmillan, 1901.

Wundt, Wilhelm *Grundzüge der physiologischen Psychologie,* 5th ed., 3 vols. Leipzig: Wilhelm Engelmann, 1902–1903.

———. *Grundzüge der physiologischen Psychologie,* 6th ed., 3rd. vol. Leipzig: Wilhelm Engelmann, 1911.

Zajonc, Robert B. "On the Primacy of Affect," *American Psychologist* 39 (1984): 117–23.

Index

B